Highways Act 1980

CHAPTER 66

ARRANGEMENT OF SECTIONS

A

PART IV

MAINTENANCE OF HIGHWAYS

Highways maintainable at public expense

A 3

PART VI

CONSTRUCTION OF BRIDGES OVER AND TUNNELS UNDER NAVIGABLE WATERS AND DIVERSION ETC. OF WATERCOURSES

Construction of bridges over and tunnels under navigable waters

Diversion etc. of watercourses

Interpretation

PART VII

PROVISION OF SPECIAL FACILITIES FOR HIGHWAYS

Part VIII

Stopping Up and Diversion of Highways and Stopping Up of Means of Access to Highways

Stopping up and diversion of highways

Stopping up of means of access to highways

Part IX

Lawful and Unlawful Interference with Highways and Streets

Protection of public rights

Damage to highways, streets etc.

A 4

Obstruction of highways and streets

Danger or annoyance to users of highways and streets

Precautions to be taken in doing certain works in or near streets or highways

Part X

New Streets

New street byelaws

Passing of plans deposited under byelaws

Requirements and prohibitions as to new streets

PART XI

MAKING UP OF PRIVATE STREETS

Introductory

The private street works code

PART XII

ACQUISITION, VESTING AND TRANSFER OF LAND ETC.

Introductory

Acquisition of land generally

PART XIV

MISCELLANEOUS AND SUPPLEMENTARY PROVISIONS

*Miscellaneous powers etc. of highway authorities
and local authorities*

ELIZABETH II

Highways Act 1980

1980 CHAPTER 66

An Act to consolidate the Highways Acts 1959 to 1971 and related enactments, with amendments to give effect to recommendations of the Law Commission.
[13th November 1980]

BE IT ENACTED by the Queen's most Excellent Majesty, by and with the advice and consent of the Lords Spiritual and Temporal, and Commons, in this present Parliament assembled, and by the authority of the same, as follows:—

PART 1

HIGHWAY AUTHORITIES AND AGREEMENTS BETWEEN AUTHORITIES

Highway authorities

1.—(1) The Minister is the highway authority for—

(*a*) any highway which is a trunk road;

(*b*) any highway as respects which an order made by him under any enactment expressly provides that he is to be the highway authority for it but does not direct that the highway is to be a trunk road;

(*c*) any highway (not falling within paragraph (*a*) above) transferred to him by an order under section 14 or 18 below;

(*d*) any other highway being a highway constructed by him, except where by virtue of section 2, 4(3) or 5(2) below or by virtue of some other enactment a local highway authority are the highway authority for it or where by means of an order made under section 14 or 18 below the highway is transferred to a local highway authority.

Highway authorities: general provision.

(2) Outside Greater London the council of a county are the highway authority for all highways in the county, whether or not maintainable at the public expense, which are not highways for which under subsection (1) above the Minister is the highway authority.

(3) The Greater London Council are the highway authority for all metropolitan roads; and the council of a London borough or the Common Council are the highway authority for all highways in the borough or, as the case may be, in the City, whether or not maintainable at the public expense, which are not for the time being metropolitan roads or highways for which under subsection (1) above the Minister is the highway authority.

(4) Subsection (2) above is subject, as respects any highway outside Greater London for which the Minister is not the highway authority under subsection (1) above, to any provision of this Act, or of any order made under this or any other Act, by virtue of which a council other than the council of the county in which the highway is situated are the highway authority therefor.

Highway authority for road which ceases to be a trunk road.

2. Where an order made under section 10 below directs that a trunk road shall cease to be a trunk road, then, as from the date specified in that behalf in the order, the following authority, that is to say—

    (*a*) where the road is situated outside Greater London, the council of the county, and

    (*b*) where the road is situated in a London borough, the Greater London Council or the council of the borough, according as the road is or is not designated by the order as a metropolitan road,

shall become the highway authority for the road.

Highway authority for approaches to and parts of certain bridges.

3.—(1) Where a bridge carries a highway for which the Minister is not the highway authority and part of the bridge is situated in one county and part in another the highway authority for the highway carried by the bridge and the approaches thereto is such one of the councils of those counties as may be agreed between them before such a day as the Minister may by order made by statutory instrument appoint or, in default of such agreement, as may be determined by the Minister.

(2) Where the Minister has made a determination under subsection (1) above the determination—

    (*a*) may be varied at the request of the council of either of the counties concerned; and (*b*) shall be varied to give effect to any request made jointly to the Minister by those councils;

and any such variation shall take effect on the 1st April falling not less than 3 months, and not more than 15 months, after the date on which the determination is varied.

(3) Where a bridge carries a highway for which the Minister is not the highway authority and subsection (1) above does not apply, but some part of one or more of the approaches to the bridge lies in a county different from the bridge itself, the highway authority for the whole of that approach or those approaches is the council of the county in which the bridge is situated.

(4) For the purposes of this section, the approaches to a bridge consist of so much of the highway or highways on either side of the bridge as is situated within 100 yards of either end of the bridge.

Agreements between authorities

4.—(1) The Minister and a local highway authority may enter into an agreement for providing, in relation to a highway specified in the agreement, being a highway that crosses or enters the route of a trunk road or is or will be otherwise affected by the construction or improvement of a trunk road, that any functions specified in the agreement, being functions of improvement exercisable as respects that highway by the local highway authority, shall be exercisable by the Minister on such terms and subject to such conditions (if any) as may be so specified.

Agreement for exercise by Minister of certain functions of local highway authority as respects highway affected by construction, etc. of trunk road.

(2) Where under an agreement made under this section any function of a local highway authority is exercisable by the Minister, then, for the purpose of exercising that function the Minister shall have the same powers under this Act (including highway land acquisition powers) as the local highway authority have for that purpose, and in exercising that function and those powers he shall have the like rights and be subject to the like liabilities as that authority.

(3) Where for purposes connected with any function exercisable by him under an agreement made under this section the Minister proposes to construct a new highway, every council (other than the council of a district) in whose area the proposed highway is situated shall be a party to the agreement and the agreement shall provide for a local highway authority specified in the agreement to become the highway authority for the highway on its completion.

(4) An agreement under this section made between the Minister and any other highway authority may provide for the payment of contributions—

(a) by the Minister to that other authority in respect of any additional liabilities imposed on that other authority in consequence of the provisions of the agreement;

(b) to the Minister by that other authority in respect of liabilities so imposed on the Minister, being liabilities which would otherwise have fallen to be discharged by that other authority;

and may also provide for the determination by arbitration of disputes as to the payment of such contributions.

(5) Any local highway authority who are a party to an agreement made under this section may contribute towards any expenses incurred by the Minister in executing any works to which the agreement relates.

Agreement for local highway authority to maintain and improve certain highways constructed or to be constructed by Minister.

5.—(1) The local highway authority may by agreement with the Minister undertake the maintenance and improvement of a highway in their area, being a highway (other than a trunk road) which the Minister proposes to construct or has, whether before or after the commencement of this Act, constructed.

(2) Where an agreement is made under this section the council who are a party to the agreement shall, on such date as may be provided by the agreement, become the highway authority for the highway to which the agreement relates.

Delegation etc. of functions with respect to trunk roads.

6.—(1) The Minister may by agreement with a county council, the Greater London Council, or a London borough council delegate to that council all or any of his functions (including functions under a local or private Act) with respect to the maintenance and improvement of, and other dealing with, any trunk road or any land which does not form part of a trunk road but which has been acquired by him in connection with a trunk road under section 239(2) or (4) or section 246 below; but he shall not delegate functions to a council under this subsection with respect to a trunk road or land outside their area, except with the consent of the council of the county or London borough in which the road or land is situated.

(2) A council shall, in the exercise of any functions delegated to them under subsection (1) above, act as agents for the Minister and in accordance with such conditions as he may

attach to the delegation, and among such conditions there shall
be included the following—

    (a) that the works to be executed and the expenditure to be incurred by the council in the discharge of the delegated functions shall be subject to the approval of the Minister;

    (b) that the council shall comply with any requirement of the Minister as to the manner in which any such works are to be carried out, and with any directions of the Minister as to the terms of contracts to be entered into for the purposes of the discharge of the delegated functions; and

    (c) that any such works shall be completed to the satisfaction of the Minister.

(3) If at any time the Minister is satisfied that a trunk road or land with respect to which functions are delegated under subsection (1) above is not in proper repair and condition, he may give notice to the council requiring them to place it in proper repair and condition within such time as may be specified in the notice, and if the notice is not complied with the Minister may do anything that seems to him necessary to place the road or land in proper repair and condition.

(4) A delegation to a council under subsection (1) above may be determined by notice given by the Minister to the council during the first 9 months of any calendar year, or the functions so delegated may be relinquished by a notice given by the council to the Minister during any such period; and the notice shall take effect as from 1st April in the calendar year following that in which it is given.

(5) The Minister may enter into an agreement with a county council, the Greater London Council or a London borough council—

    (a) for the construction of a trunk road, or

    (b) for the carrying out by them of any work of improvement of, or other dealing with, any trunk road or any such land as is mentioned in subsection (1) above;

and subsection (2) above applies to the discharge of the functions of a council under any such agreement and to the conditions to be included in any such agreement as it applies to the discharge of functions delegated under subsection (1) above to any such council and to the conditions to be attached to any such delegation.

(6) Where—

    (a) any functions have been delegated by the Minister to a county council under subsection (1) above, or (*b*) the Minister has entered into an agreement with a county council under subsection (5) above,

the county council may, with the consent of the Minister, enter into arrangements with a district council for the carrying out by the district council, in accordance with the arrangements, of such of the delegated functions or, as the case may be, of the functions to which the agreement relates as may be specified in the arrangements ; but no such arrangements shall provide for a district council to carry out any functions with respect to a trunk road or land outside their district except with the consent of the council of the district in which the road or land is situated.

(7) Plant or materials belonging to a council by whom functions fall to be exercised by virtue of a delegation, or agreement or arrangements under this section may be used by them for the purposes of those functions subject to the terms of the delegation, or agreement or arrangements.

(8) Nothing in this section limits the power of the Minister to enter into and carry into effect agreements with any person for any purpose connected with the construction, improvement or maintenance of, or other dealing with, a trunk road or otherwise connected with his functions relating to trunk roads under this or any other Act ; but no such agreement shall provide for the delegation of powers or duties of the Minister except in accordance with the provisions of this section.

Delegation etc. of functions with respect to metropolitan roads.

7.—(1) The Greater London Council may agree with any London borough council or the Common Council for the delegation to the borough council or Common Council of any of the functions of the Greater London Council with respect to the maintenance and improvement of, and other dealing with—

(*a*) the whole or any part of so much of any metropolitan road as lies within the borough or, as the case may be, the City ;

(*b*) any land which does not form part of a metropolitan road but has been acquired by the Greater London Council in connection with such a road under section 239 (4) or section 246 below.

1967 c. 76.

(2) For the avoidance of doubt it is hereby declared that the functions of the Greater London Council which may be delegated under subsection (1) above include the functions of that Council under section 12 of the Road Traffic Regulation Act 1967 (temporary prohibition or restriction of traffic on roads) with respect to any metropolitan road in the case of which that Council have so delegated their functions with respect to the maintenance of that road.

(3) A London borough council or the Common Council shall, in the discharge of any functions delegated under subsection (1) above, act as agents for the Greater London Council; and it shall be a condition of the delegation—

    (*a*) that the works to be executed and the expenditure to be incurred by the borough council or the Common Council in the discharge of the delegated functions shall be subject to the approval of the Greater London Council;

    (*b*) that the borough council or the Common Council shall comply with any requirement of the Greater London Council as to the manner in which, and the persons by whom, any works are to be carried out, and with any general directions of the Greater London Council as to the terms of contracts to be entered into for the purposes of the discharge of the delegated functions; and

    (*c*) that any such works shall be completed to the satisfaction of the Greater London Council.

(4) If at any time the Greater London Council are satisfied on the report of some officer of the Council or other person appointed by them for the purpose that a road or land with respect to which functions are delegated by them under subsection (1) above is not in proper repair or condition, they may give notice to the borough council or Common Council requiring them to place it in proper repair or condition and if the notice is not complied with within a reasonable time may themselves do anything which seems to them necessary to place it in proper repair or condition.

(5) A delegation to a London borough council or the Common Council under subsection (1) above may be determined by notice given to that council by the Greater London Council during the first 9 months of any calendar year, or the functions so delegated may be relinquished by notice given by the borough council or the Common Council to the Greater London Council within any such period; and the notice shall take effect as from 1st April in the calendar year following that in which it is given.

(6) The Greater London Council may enter into an agreement with the council of a London borough or the Common Council—

    (*a*) for the construction of a metropolitan road in the borough or, as the case may be, in the City, or

    (*b*) for the carrying out by the borough council or the Common Council of any particular work of improvement of, or other dealing with, any such road or part thereof or any such land as is mentioned in subsection (1) above;

PART I and subsections (3) and (4) above shall apply to the discharge of the functions of the borough council or Common Council under any such agreement, and to the conditions to be included in the agreement, as they apply to the discharge of functions delegated under subsection (1) above and to the conditions to be attached to any such delegation.

(7) The council of a London borough or the Common Council shall, if so required by the Greater London Council, undertake the maintenance of any metropolitan road within the borough or, as the case may be, within the City in consideration of such payments by the Greater London Council as may from time to time be agreed between them or, in default of such agreement, as may be determined by the Minister of Transport; and while that requirement remains in force the borough council or the Common Council shall have the like powers and be subject to the like duties and liabilities with respect to the maintenance of that road as if they were the highway authority therefor.

(8) Plant or materials belonging to a council by whom functions fall to be exercised by virtue of a delegation, agreement or requirement under this section may be used by them for the purposes of the exercise of those functions, subject to the terms of any delegation or any agreement between that council and the Greater London Council.

(9) Nothing in this section limits the power of the Greater London Council to enter into and carry into effect agreements with any person for any purpose connected with the construction, improvement or maintenance of, or other dealing with, a metropolitan road or otherwise connected with any functions of that Council relating to metropolitan roads; but no such agreement shall provide for the delegation of any powers or duties of the Greater London Council except in accordance with the provisions of this section.

Agreements between local highway authorities for doing of certain works.

8.—(1) Subject to the provisions of this section, local highway authorities may enter into agreements with each other for or in relation to the construction, reconstruction, alteration, improvement or maintenance of a highway for which any party to the agreement are the highway authority.

(2) An agreement under this section may provide, in relation to a highway specified in the agreement, being a highway for which one of the parties to the agreement are the highway authority, that any functions specified in the agreement, being functions exercisable as respects that highway by the highway authority therefor, shall be exercisable by some other party to the agreement on such terms and subject to such conditions (if any) as may be so specified.

(3) Where under an agreement made under this section any function of the highway authority for a highway is exercisable by another highway authority, then, for the purpose of exercising that function that other highway authority shall have the same powers under this Act (including highway land acquisition powers) as the highway authority for the highway have for that purpose, and in exercising that function and those powers they shall have the like rights and be subject to the like liabilities as that authority.

(4) The council of a county may not enter into an agreement under this section with the council of another county unless the counties adjoin each other.

(5) Expenses incurred in pursuance of an agreement made under this section shall be borne by the parties to the agreement in such proportions as may be determined by the agreement.

9.—(1) A council may enter into an agreement with the Minister for placing at his disposal for the purposes of his functions relating to highways, on such terms as may be provided by the agreement, the services of persons employed by the council and any premises, equipment and other facilities under the control of the council. *Seconding of staff etc.*

(2) For superannuation purposes service rendered by a person whose services are placed at the disposal of the Minister in pursuance of this section is service rendered to the council by whom that person is employed.

PART II
TRUNK ROADS, CLASSIFIED ROADS, METROPOLITAN ROADS, SPECIAL ROADS

Trunk roads

10.—(1) Subject to the provisions of this section, all such highways and proposed highways as immediately before the commencement of this Act were trunk roads within the meaning of the Highways Act 1959 continue to be, and to be known as, trunk roads. *General provision as to trunk roads.* *1959 c. 25.*

(2) The Minister shall keep under review the national system of routes for through traffic in England and Wales, and if he is satisfied after taking into consideration the requirements of local and national planning, including the requirements of agriculture, that it is expedient for the purpose of extending, improving or reorganising that system either—

   (*a*) that any highway, or any highway proposed to be constructed by the Minister, should become a trunk road,
     or

(*b*) that any trunk road should cease to be a trunk road,

he may by order direct that that highway or proposed highway shall become, or, as the case may be, that that road shall cease to be, a trunk road as from such date as may be specified in that behalf in the order.

(3) The power of the Minister under this section to direct that a highway or proposed highway shall become a trunk road shall include power to direct that a highway or proposed highway which he considers suitable for the purpose of relieving a main carriageway of the trunk road from local traffic shall become part of the trunk road, whether or not the highway or proposed highway is separated from the remainder of the road by intervening land.

(4) Without prejudice to the powers of the Minister under this Act—

    (*a*) to improve trunk roads by the construction of cycle tracks and footways for use in connection therewith, or

    (*b*) to provide such tracks or ways as part of any trunk road which he is authorised to construct,

the power under this section to direct that a highway proposed to be constructed by the Minister shall become a trunk road may be exercised in relation to any cycle track or footpath proposed to be constructed by the Minister on land separated by intervening land from the trunk road in connection with which it is to be used.

(5) Parts I and III of Schedule 1 to this Act have effect as to the making of an order under this section ; and Schedule 2 to this Act has effect as to the validity and date of operation of any such order.

(6) If objection to an order proposed to be made under this section is duly made in accordance with Part I of Schedule 1 to this Act by a council who are responsible for the maintenance of a highway to which the order relates, or who will become so responsible by virtue of the order, and is not withdrawn, the order shall be subject to special parliamentary procedure.

(7) If an order under this section directing that a highway proposed to be constructed by the Minister shall become a trunk road is revoked or varied by a subsequent order made at any time before the date on which the highway is opened for the purposes of through traffic, the revoking or varying order shall not be deemed for the purposes of section 2 above to be an order directing that a trunk road shall cease to be a trunk road.

(8) In addition to the case where a trunk road ceases to be a trunk road by virtue of an order made under this section, a trunk road shall cease to be a trunk road if the road is transferred from the Minister to some other highway authority to become part of a special road provided by that authority.

(9) No highway which is within the City shall be, or become, a trunk road, and without prejudice to the generality of the foregoing provision, none of the following bridges, that is to say, Blackfriars Bridge, London Bridge, Southwark Bridge and Tower Bridge, and no highway carried by any of those bridges, shall be, or become, a trunk road.

11.—(1) As from the date when a highway becomes a trunk road, any functions of construction, maintenance or improvement exercisable as respects that highway by a council under a local or private Act are to be deemed to have become exercisable by the Minister alone and while the highway remains a trunk road they shall continue to be so exercisable.

Local and private Act functions with respect to trunk roads.

(2) Where the Minister is satisfied that there has been conferred on a council by a local or private Act a function substantially similar to one conferred by a provision of this Act specified in Schedule 3 to this Act, he may, after consultation with the council, by order direct that, in relation to a trunk road, the function conferred by the local or private Act is to be exercisable in accordance with the following conditions:

> (a) where the provision of the local or private Act is similar to a provision of this Act specified in Part I of the said Schedule 3, that it is to be exercisable by the Minister only;
>
> (b) where the provision of the local or private Act is similar to a provision of this Act specified in Part II of the said Schedule, that, in so far as it is exercisable by a council, it is to be exercisable by that council (and, if the road is situated in Greater London, also by the Greater London Council), as well as by the Minister;
>
> (c) where the provision of the local or private Act is similar to a provision of this Act specified in Part III of the said Schedule, that, in so far as it is exercisable by a council, it is to be exercisable by that council with the consent of the Minister (and, if the road is situated in Greater London, also by the Greater London Council with such consent), as well as by the Minister.

(3) Where the Minister makes an order under this section in relation to a function conferred by a provision of a local or private Act, and the provision of this Act by which a function substantially similar to the first-mentioned function is conferred is, in relation to a trunk road, subject to any modification, the provision of the local or private Act shall, in relation to a trunk road, be subject to a similar modification, and the Minister may by the same order specify the modification to which the provision of the local or private Act is accordingly to be subject.

Classified roads

General provision as to principal and classified roads.

1966 c. 42.

1974 c. 7.

12.—(1) Subject to subsection (3) below, all such highways or proposed highways as immediately before the commencement of this Act—

(a) were principal roads for the purposes of any enactment or instrument which refers to roads or highways classified by the Minister as principal roads, either by virtue of having been so classified under section 27(2) of the Local Government Act 1966 (which is replaced by subsection (3) below), or by virtue of being treated as such in accordance with section 40(1) of the Local Government Act 1974,

(b) were (whether or not they also fall within paragraph (a) above) classified roads for the purposes of any enactment or instrument which refers to roads classified by the Minister (but does not specifically refer to their classification as principal roads), either by virtue of having been so classified under section 27(2) of the said Act of 1966, or by virtue of being treated as such in accordance with section 40(1) of the said Act of 1974, or

(c) were classified roads for the purposes of any enactment or instrument by virtue of being treated as such in accordance with section 27(4) of the said Act of 1966,

continue to be, and to be known as, principal roads or, as the case may be, classified roads (or both principal roads and classified roads of a category other than principal roads, in the case of highways falling within both paragraph (a) and paragraph (b) above) for the purposes specified in subsection (2) below.

(2) So far as a highway that continues to be a principal or classified road in accordance with subsection (1) above was, immediately before the commencement of this Act, a classified road for the purposes of any enactment repealed and replaced by this Act, it is a classified road for the purposes of the corresponding provision of this Act; and so far as any such

highway was immediately before the commencement of this Act a principal or classified road for the purposes of any other enactment, or any instrument, it so continues for the purposes of that enactment or instrument.

(3) The Minister may for the purposes of—

(a) any provision of this Act which refers to classified roads, or

(b) any other enactment or any instrument (whether passed or made before or after the passing of this Act) which refers to highways classified by the Minister,

classify highways or proposed highways, being highways or proposed highways for which local highway authorities are the highway authorities, in such manner as he may from time to time determine after consultation with the highway authorities concerned.

(4) References in any provision hereafter contained in this Act to classified roads are references to—

(a) any highway or proposed highway that for the time being is a classified road for the purposes of that provision by virtue of subsections (1) and (2) above ;

(b) any highway or proposed highway that for the time being is classified under subsection (3) above for the purposes of that provision, or for the purposes of enactments that include that provision ; and

(c) any highway or proposed highway that for the time being is classified under subsection (3) above as a principal road for the purposes of any enactment or instrument which refers to roads or highways classified by the Minister as principal roads.

13.—(1) The Minister may by order assign some other description to the highways which for the time being are principal roads for the purposes of any enactment or instrument (whether by virtue of section 12(1) and (2) above, or by virtue of having been so classified under section 12(3) above, or otherwise). Power to change designation of principal roads.

(2) If an order is made under subsection (1) above, then, except in so far as the order otherwise provides, any reference to a principal road in any enactment or instrument passed or made before the order is made (including an enactment in this Act) is to be construed as a reference to a highway of the description specified in the order.

(3) Nothing in subsection (1) above affects the power of the Minister under section 12(3) above to classify highways or proposed highways in such manner as he may determine after consultation with the highway authority concerned.

B

*Powers as respects roads that cross or join
trunk roads or classified roads*

Powers as
respects roads
that cross or
join trunk or
classified
roads.

14.—(1) Provision may be made by an order under this section in relation to a trunk road or a classified road, not being, in either case, a special road, for any of the following purposes : —

(a) for authorising the highway authority for the road—

(i) to stop up, divert, improve, raise, lower or otherwise alter a highway that crosses or enters the route of the road or is or will be otherwise affected by the construction or improvement of the road ;

(ii) to construct a new highway for purposes concerned with any such alteration as aforesaid or for any other purpose connected with the road or its construction, and to close after such period as may be specified in the order any new highway so constructed for temporary purposes ;

(b) for transferring to such other highway authority as may be specified in the order, as from such date as may be so specified, a highway constructed by the highway authority in pursuance of the order or any previous order made under this section ;

(c) for any other purpose incidental to the purposes aforesaid ;

and references in this section, with respect to an order made thereunder, to " the road " and " the highway authority " are references to, respectively, the trunk road or, as the case may be, classified road to which the order relates and the highway authority for that road.

(2) The provision that may be made pursuant to subsection (1)(c) above in an order under this section that provides for the stopping up or diversion of a highway, includes provision for the preservation of any rights—

(a) of statutory undertakers in respect of any apparatus of theirs which immediately before the date of the order is under, in, on, over, along or across the highway to be stopped up or diverted ; or

(b) of any sewerage authority in respect of any sewers or sewage disposal work of theirs which immediately before that date are under, in, on, over, along or across that highway.

(3) An order under this section—

(a) in relation to a trunk road shall be made by the Minister, and

(b) in relation to a classified road shall be made by the highway authority and confirmed by the Minister.

(4) Parts I and III of Schedule 1 to this Act have effect as to the making of an order under this section; and Schedule 2 to this Act has effect as to the validity and date of operation of any such order.

(5) Subject to subsection (4) above, an order under this section relating to a trunk road may come into operation on the same day as the order under section 10 above relating to that road.

(6) No order under this section authorising the stopping up of a highway shall be made or confirmed by the Minister unless he is satisfied that another reasonably convenient route is available or will be provided before the highway is stopped up.

(7) An order under this section may provide for the payment of contributions—

    (a) by the highway authority to any other highway authority in respect of any additional liabilities imposed on that other authority in consequence of the order or of any previous order made under this section;

    (b) to the highway authority by any other highway authority in respect of any liabilities so imposed on the first-mentioned authority that would otherwise have fallen to be discharged by that other authority;

and may also provide for the determination by arbitration of disputes as to the payment of such contributions.

Metropolitan roads

15.—(1) Subject to the provisions of this Act, all such highways and proposed highways as immediately before the commencement of this Act were metropolitan roads within the meaning of subsection (1) of section 29 of the Transport (London) Act 1969 (which subsection is replaced by subsection (2)(b) and (c) below) continue to be, and to be known as, metropolitan roads.

General provision as to metropolitan roads.

1969 c. 35.

(2) References in any provision of this Act and in any other enactment to metropolitan roads are to be construed as references to—

    (a) any highway or proposed highway that is for the time being a metropolitan road by virtue of subsection (1) above;

    (b) any highway or proposed highway in Greater London that is for the time being classified under section 12(3) above as a principal road for the purposes of any enactment or instrument which refers to roads or highways classified by the Minister of Transport as principal roads; and

PART II

(c) any other highway or proposed highway in Greater London that is for the time being designated as a metropolitan road by an order under section 10 above directing that the highway shall cease to be a trunk road.

(3) A certificate by or on behalf of the Minister of Transport that any highway or proposed highway in Greater London is, or is not, for the time being classified as provided by subsection (2)(*b*) above, or within subsection (2)(*a*) above by virtue of a corresponding classification under section 27(2) of the Local

1966 c. 42.

Government Act 1966, shall be evidence of the fact stated and any such certificate may describe the highway or proposed highway in question by reference to a map.

(4) The Greater London Council shall prepare and maintain a list of, and a map showing, the highways and proposed highways which are for the time being metropolitan roads and shall deposit a copy of that list and of that map with each of the London borough councils and the Common Council; and the Greater London Council and each of those other authorities shall make that list and map or, as the case may be, the copies thereof so deposited with them, available for inspection by the public at all reasonable hours.

(5) The provisions of subsections (2) to (4) above are to be deemed for the purposes of section 84 of the London Govern-

1963 c. 33.

ment Act 1963 (which relates to the making of supplementary and transitional provision by order) to be included in that Act.

Special roads

General provision as to special roads.

16.—(1) Subject to the provisions of this Act, all such highways or proposed highways as immediately before the commencement of this Act were special roads, as being highways or proposed highways provided, or to be provided, in pursuance of a scheme made, or having effect as if made, under section 11

1959 c. 25.

of the Highways Act 1959 (which section is replaced by subsections (3) to (10) below), continue to be, and to be known as, special roads.

(2) Roads that continue to be special roads by virtue of subsection (1) above continue, subject to the provisions of this Act, to be special roads for the use of traffic of the classes for the use of which they were special roads immediately before the commencement of this Act.

(3) A highway authority may be authorised by means of a scheme under this section to provide, along a route prescribed by the scheme, a special road for the use of traffic of any class prescribed thereby.

(4) Subject to subsection (10) below, a highway authority authorised by means of a scheme under this section, or any such scheme as is referred to in subsection (1) above, to provide a special road is in this Act referred to in relation to that road as the special road authority.

(5) A special road authorised by a scheme under this section may be provided—

(a) by means of the construction by the special road authority of a new highway along the route prescribed by the scheme or any part thereof;

(b) by means of the appropriation under subsequent provisions in that behalf of this Part of this Act of a highway comprised in that route for which the special road authority are the highway authority;

(c) by means of the transfer to the special road authority under subsequent provisions in that behalf of this Part of this Act of a highway comprised in that route for which they are not the highway authority.

(6) A scheme under this section authorising the provision of a special road shall—

(a) in the case of a road to be provided by the Minister, be made by the Minister; and

(b) in the case of a road to be provided by a local highway authority, be made by that authority and confirmed by the Minister.

(7) Parts II and III of Schedule 1 to this Act have effect as to the making of a scheme under this section; and Schedule 2 to this Act has effect as to the validity and date of operation of any such scheme.

(8) Before making or confirming a scheme under this section, the Minister shall give due consideration to the requirements of local and national planning, including the requirements of agriculture.

(9) If objection to a scheme under this section is duly made in accordance with Part II of the said Schedule 1 by the highway authority for a highway comprised in the route of the special road authorised by the scheme, and is not withdrawn, the scheme shall be subject to special parliamentary procedure.

(10) A scheme under this section may be submitted to the Minister jointly by any two or more local highway authorities, and any such scheme may determine which of those authorities shall be the special road authority for the special road or any part thereof, and may provide—

(a) for the performance by that authority, in relation to the road or that part thereof, of any of the highway functions of any other authority who are party to the application, and

    (*b*) for the making of contributions by that other authority to the special road authority in respect of expenditure incurred in the performance of those functions ;

and in relation to a special road provided or to be provided in pursuance of such a scheme, or any part of such a road, references in this Act to a special road authority are references to the highway authority who are by virtue of that scheme the special road authority for that road or part.

Classification of traffic for purposes of special roads.

17.—(1) Different classes of traffic may be prescribed by a scheme under section 16 above in relation to different parts of the special road to which the scheme relates.

(2) The classes of traffic prescribed by any such scheme shall be prescribed by reference to the classes set out in Schedule 4 to this Act.

(3) The Minister of Transport may by order amend the said Schedule 4 by varying the composition of any class of traffic specified therein or adding a further class of traffic to those so specified, and references in schemes under the said section 16 made (whether by the Minister of Transport or a local highway authority) before the date on which the order comes into operation to any class of traffic to which the order relates are to be construed as references to that class as varied by the order or, if the order so provides, as including references to an additional class created thereby, as the case may be.

Supplementary orders relating to special roads.

18.—(1) Provision in relation to a special road may be made by an order under this section for any of the following purposes:—

    (*a*) for appropriating as, or as part of, the special road, as from such date as may be specified in the order, a highway which is comprised in the route prescribed by the scheme authorising the special road and which is a highway for which the special road authority are the highway authority ;

    (*b*) for transferring to the special road authority, as from such date as may be specified in the order, a highway which is comprised in the route prescribed by the scheme authorising the special road and which is a highway for which they are not the highway authority ;

    (*c*) for authorising the special road authority—

        (i) to stop up, divert, improve, raise, lower or otherwise alter a highway that crosses or enters the route of the special road or is or will be otherwise affected by the construction or improvement of the special road ;

    (ii) to construct a new highway for purposes connected with any such alteration as aforesaid or for any other purpose connected with the special road or its construction, and to close after such period as may be specified in the order any new highway so constructed for temporary purposes ;

(d) for transferring to such highway authority as may be specified in the order, as from such date as may be so specified, a highway constructed by the special road authority in pursuance of the order or any previous order made under this section ;

(e) for authorising or requiring the special road authority to exercise, either concurrently with or to the exclusion of any local authority, any functions which, apart from the order, would be exercisable by that local authority in relation to the special road other than functions of that authority as local planning authority ;

(f) for any other purpose incidental to the purposes aforesaid or otherwise incidental to the construction or maintenance of, or other dealing with, the special road.

(2) The provision that may be made pursuant to subsection (1)(f) above in an order under this section that provides for the stopping up or diversion of a highway, includes provision for the preservation of any rights—

(a) of statutory undertakers in respect of any apparatus of theirs which immediately before the date of the order is under, in, on, over, along or across the highway to be stopped up or diverted ; or

(b) of any sewerage authority in respect of any sewers or sewage disposal works of theirs which immediately before that date are under, in, on, over, along or across that highway.

(3) An order under this section making provision in connection with a special road shall—

(a) in the case of a special road provided or to be provided by the Minister be made by the Minister ; and

(b) in the case of a special road provided or to be provided by a local highway authority, be made by that authority and confirmed by the Minister.

(4) Parts I and III of Schedule 1 to this Act have effect as to the making of an order under this section; and Schedule 2 to this Act has effect as to the validity and date of operation of any such order.

(5) Subject to subsection (4) above, an order under this section may come into operation on the same day as the scheme authorising the special road to which it relates.

(6) No order providing for the appropriation by or transfer to a special road authority of a highway comprised in the route prescribed by the scheme authorising the special road shall be made or confirmed by the Minister under this section unless either—

(a) he is satisfied that another reasonably convenient route is available for traffic other than traffic of the class authorised by the scheme, or will be provided before the date on which the appropriation or transfer takes effect, or

(b) he is satisfied that no such other route is reasonably required for any such other traffic;

and no order authorising the stopping up of a highway shall be made or confirmed by the Minister under this section unless he is satisfied that another reasonably convenient route is available or will be provided before the highway is stopped up.

(7) An order under this section may provide for the payment of contributions—

(a) by a special road authority to any other highway authority in respect of any additional liabilities imposed on that other authority in consequence of the provisions of the order or of any previous order made under this section,

(b) to a special road authority by any other authority in respect of any liabilities so imposed on the special road authority that would otherwise have fallen to be discharged by the other authority,

and may also provide for the determination by arbitration of disputes as to the payment of such contributions.

(8) In this section "local authority" means the Greater London Council, the Common Council and the council of a county, district, London borough, parish or community, and includes the parish meeting of a rural parish not having a separate parish council.

19.—(1) A special road to be provided by the Minister in pursuance of a scheme under section 16 above shall, except so far as it is provided by means of the appropriation or transfer of a highway, become a trunk road on such date as may be specified in the scheme.

(2) A highway (not being a trunk road) which, by means of an order under section 18 above, is appropriated as, or as part of, a special road to be provided by the Minister, and a highway which, by means of such an order, is transferred to the Minister, shall become a trunk road on the date on which it is so appropriated or is so transferred, as the case may be.

PART II

Certain special roads and other highways to become trunk roads.

20.—(1) Subject to the provisions of this section, the powers conferred on statutory undertakers by or under any enactment to lay down or erect any apparatus under, in, over, along or across any land shall not be exercisable in relation to any land comprised in the route of a special road except with the consent of the special road authority.

(2) The consent of a special road authority shall not be required under this section for the laying down or erection by statutory undertakers of any apparatus by way of renewal of any apparatus for the time being belonging to or used by them for the purpose of their undertaking.

(3) A consent of a special road authority under this section may be given subject to conditions, but those conditions shall not include a condition requiring any payment to be made by the undertakers to the special road authority in respect of the exercise of the powers to the exercise of which the consent is given.

(4) Where any apparatus in respect of which the consent of a special road authority is required under this section is to be laid down or erected along a line crossing the route of the special road but not running along that route, that authority—

(a) shall not withhold their consent under this section unless there are special reasons for doing so ; and

(b) may, if they give their consent subject to conditions, make contributions to the statutory undertakers in respect of any expenses incurred by them in complying therewith.

(5) Any dispute between a special road authority and any statutory undertakers in respect of—

(a) the withholding of the consent of that authority in respect of apparatus to be laid down or erected as mentioned in subsection (4) above, or

(b) the imposition of any condition on the grant of such consent, or

(c) the making of any contributions under subsection (4)(b) above,

shall be determined by arbitration ; and where the Minister is the special road authority the arbitrator shall be a single arbitrator appointed, in default of agreement between the parties concerned, by the President of the Institution of Civil Engineers.

(6) Where the consent of a special road authority is required under this section in respect of apparatus to be laid down or erected otherwise than as mentioned in subsection (4) above, and the special road authority are a local highway authority, then—

(a) if the apparatus is to be laid under a carriageway, the authority shall not give their consent except with the approval of the Minister ;

(b) if the consent of the authority is refused (otherwise than in consequence of the withholding of the Minister's approval under paragraph (a) above) or is granted subject to conditions (other than conditions approved by the Minister under that paragraph) the statutory undertakers may appeal to the Minister, and he may make such order as he thinks fit.

(7) The provisions of this section, so far as applicable, apply in relation to the sewers and sewage disposal works of any sewerage authority as they apply in relation to the apparatus of statutory undertakers.

(8) The provisions of this section shall have effect in addition to and not in substitution for the provisions of sections 156 and 159 below and of any other enactment restricting or regulating the powers of any statutory undertakers to break up or open streets or enter upon land for the purpose of laying down or erecting apparatus.

(9) For the purposes of this section the Post Office are to be deemed to be statutory undertakers.

Ancillary matters with respect to orders under section 14 or 18 and schemes under section 16

Extinguishment of rights of statutory undertakers as to apparatus etc. in connection with orders under section 14 or 18 and schemes under section 16.
1971 c. 78.

21.—(1) Without prejudice to section 20 above, sections 230 to 232 of the Town and Country Planning Act 1971, (power to extinguish rights of statutory undertakers and power of statutory undertakers to remove or re-site apparatus) apply in relation to any land specified in subsection (2) below as they apply in relation to land acquired by a Minister, a local authority or statutory undertakers under Part VI of that Act, or under any other enactment, or appropriated by a local authority for planning purposes ; and all such other provisions of that Act as apply for the purposes of those provisions (including sections

237(2) and (3), 238 and 240, which provide for the payment of compensation, and sections 233 to 236, which contain provisions consequential on the extinguishment of any rights under section 230) shall have effect accordingly.

(2) The land referred to in subsection (1) above is—

(a) land acquired or appropriated by a special road authority for the purposes of carrying out any works in pursuance of a scheme under section 16 above or an order under section 18 above ;

(b) land forming the site of any part of a highway which is appropriated by or transferred to a special road authority by means of an order under section 18 above ;

(c) land over which there subsists or has subsisted a highway the stopping up or diversion of which is or was authorised by an order under section 14 or 18 above.

(3) The provisions of the said Act of 1971 referred to in subsection (1) above have effect, as applied for the purposes of this section—

(a) in relation to any such land as is referred to in subsection (2)(a) or (b) above, subject to the modifications set out in Part I of Schedule 5 to this Act, and

(b) in relation to any such land as is referred to in sub-section (2)(c) above, subject to the modifications set out in Part II of that Schedule.

(4) Where any apparatus of public utility undertakers is removed in pursuance of a notice or order given or made under section 230 or 232 of the said Act of 1971, as applied for the purposes of this section in relation to any such land as is specified in paragraph (a) or (b) of subsection (2) above, any person who is the owner or occupier of premises to which a supply was given from that apparatus shall be entitled to recover from the special road authority compensation in respect of expenditure reasonably incurred by him, in consequence of the removal, for the purpose of effecting a connection between the premises and any other apparatus from which a supply is given.

(5) In this section " owner ", in relation to any premises, means a person, other than a mortgagee not in possession, who is for the time being entitled to dispose of the fee simple in the premises, whether in possession or in reversion, and includes also

PART II

a person holding or entitled to the rents and profits of the premises under a lease the unexpired term of which exceeds three years.

Application of section 21 to sewers and sewage disposal works of sewerage authorities.

22.—(1) Section 21(1) to (3) above, and the provisions of the Town and Country Planning Act 1971 applied by section 21(1) above apply, so far as applicable, in relation to the sewers and sewage disposal works of any sewerage authority as they apply in relation to the apparatus of statutory undertakers.

(2) In the provisions of the said Act of 1971, as applied for the purposes of this section, references to the appropriate Minister are to be construed—

> (*a*) in relation to matters arising in England, as references to the Secretary of State for the Environment ; and

> (*b*) in relation to matters arising in Wales, as references to the Secretary of State for Wales.

1971 c. 78.

(3) Where a public sewer is removed in pursuance of a notice or order given or made under section 230 or 232 of the Town and Country Planning Act 1971, as applied for the purposes of this section in relation to any such land as is specified in paragraph (*a*) or (*b*) of section 21(2) above, any person who is the owner or occupier of premises the drains of which communicated with that sewer, or the owner of a private sewer which communicated with that sewer, is entitled to recover from the special road authority compensation in respect of expenditure reasonably incurred by him, in consequence of the removal, for the purpose of making his drain or sewer communicate with any other public sewer or with a private sewage disposal plant.

(4) In this section " owner " has the same meaning as in section 21 above.

Compensation in respect of certain works executed in pursuance of orders under section 14 or 18.

23. Where, in pursuance of an order under section 14 or 18 above, the Minister, a special road authority or a local highway authority, as the case may be, execute in, or with respect to, a highway works which the highway authority for that highway have power to execute under Part V of this Act, the Minister, the special road authority or the local highway authority, as the case may be, shall be subject to the like liability to pay compensation to a person who sustains damage by reason of the execution of those works as would be the highway authority for that highway had those works been executed by that authority under the said Part V.

PART III

CREATION OF HIGHWAYS

24.—(1) The Minister may, with the approval of the Treasury, construct new highways; but where he proposes to construct a new highway other than— Construction of new highways and provision of road-ferries.

    (*a*) a trunk road,

    (*b*) a special road,

    (*c*) a highway the construction of which is authorised by an order relating to a trunk road under section 14 above or an order under section 18 above, or

    (*d*) a highway to be constructed for purposes connected with any function exercisable by him under an agreement made under section 4 above,

he shall give notice of his proposals to, and consider any representations by, every council through whose area the highway will pass.

(2) A local highway authority may construct new highways; but—

    (*a*) where a new highway to be constructed by such an authority will communicate with a highway for which the Minister is the highway authority; or

    (*b*) where a new highway to be constructed by a London borough council or the Common Council will communicate with a metropolitan road,

the communication shall not be made unless the manner in which it is to be made has been approved by the Minister (in a case falling within paragraph (*a*) above) or the Greater London Council (in a case falling within paragraph (*b*) above), as the case may be.

(3) The power of the Greater London Council to construct new highways under subsection (2) above shall be exercisable by them for the purpose of constructing a new highway communicating with a metropolitan road notwithstanding that the new highway will not itself be such a road; but before exercising that power that Council shall give notice of their proposals for the construction of the new highway to, and consider any representations by, the council who will be the highway authority for the new highway.

(4) The Minister or a local highway authority may provide and maintain new road-ferries.

Creation of
footpath or
bridleway by
agreement.

25.—(1) A local authority may enter into an agreement with any person having the necessary power in that behalf for the dedication by that person of a footpath or bridleway over land in their area.

An agreement under this section is referred to in this Act as a " public path creation agreement ".

(2) For the purposes of this section " local authority "—

1971 c. 78.

> (*a*) in relation to land outside Greater London means a county council, a district council or a joint planning board within the meaning of the Town and Country Planning Act 1971, being a board for an area which comprises any part of a National Park ; and

> (*b*) in relation to land in Greater London means the Greater London Council, a London borough council or the Common Council.

(3) Before entering into an agreement under this section a local authority shall consult any other local authority or authorities in whose area the land concerned is situated.

(4) An agreement under this section shall be on such terms as to payment or otherwise as may be specified in the agreement and may, if it is so agreed, provide for the dedication of the footpath or bridleway subject to limitations or conditions affecting the public right of way over it.

(5) Where a public path creation agreement has been made it shall be the duty of the local authority who are a party to it to take all necessary steps for securing that the footpath or bridleway is dedicated in accordance with it.

Compulsory
powers for
creation of
footpaths and
bridleways.

26.—(1) Where it appears to a local authority that there is need for a footpath or bridleway over land in their area and they are satisfied that, having regard to—

> (*a*) the extent to which the path or way would add to the convenience or enjoyment of a substantial section of the public, or to the convenience of persons resident in the area, and

> (*b*) the effect which the creation of the path or way would have on the rights of persons interested in the land,

account being taken of the provisions as to compensation contained in section 28 below,

it is expedient that the path or way should be created, the authority may by order made by them and submitted to and confirmed by the Secretary of State, or confirmed by them as an unopposed order, create a footpath or bridleway over the land.

An order under this section is referred to in this Act as a " public path creation order " ; and for the purposes of this section " local authority " has the same meaning as in section 25 above.

(2) Where it appears to the Secretary of State in a particular case that there is need for a footpath or bridleway as mentioned in subsection (1) above, and he is satisfied as mentioned in that subsection, he may, after consultation with each body which is a local authority for the purposes of this section in relation to the land concerned, make a public path creation order creating the footpath or bridleway.

(3) A local authority shall, before exercising any power under this section, consult any other local authority or authorities in whose area the land concerned is situated.

(4) A right of way created by a public path creation order may be either unconditional or subject to such limitations or conditions as may be specified in the order.

(5) A public path creation order shall be in such form as may be prescribed by regulations made by the Secretary of State, and shall contain a map, on such scale as may be so prescribed, defining the land over which a footpath or bridleway is thereby created.

(6) Schedule 6 to this Act shall have effect as to the making, confirmation, validity and date of operation of public path creation orders.

27.—(1) On the dedication of a footpath or bridleway in pursuance of a public path creation agreement, or on the coming into operation of a public path creation order, being— *Making up of new footpaths and bridleways.*

    (a) an agreement or order made by a local authority who are not the highway authority for the path in question, or

PART III

(*b*) an order made by the Secretary of State under section 26(2) above in relation to which he directs that this subsection shall apply,

the highway authority shall survey the path or way and shall certify what work (if any) appears to them to be necessary to bring it into a fit condition for use by the public as a footpath or bridleway, as the case may be, and shall serve a copy of the certificate on the local authority mentioned in paragraph (*a*) above or, where paragraph (*b*) applies, on such local authority as the Secretary of State may direct.

(2) It shall be the duty of the highway authority to carry out any works specified in a certificate under subsection (1) above, and where the authority have carried out the work they may recover from the authority on whom a copy of the certificate was served any expenses reasonably incurred by them in carrying out that work, including any expenses so incurred in the discharge of any liability for compensation in respect of the carrying out thereof.

(3) Notwithstanding anything in the preceding provisions of this section, where an agreement or order is made as mentioned in subsection (1)(*a*) above, the local authority making the agreement or order may—

(*a*) with the consent of the highway authority carry out (in place of the highway authority) the duties imposed by that subsection on the highway authority ; and

(*b*) carry out any works which, apart from this subsection, it would be the duty of the highway authority to carry out under subsection (2) above.

(4) Where the Secretary of State makes a public path creation order under section 26(2) above, he may direct that subsection (5) below shall apply.

(5) Where the Secretary of State gives such a direction—

(*a*) the local authority who, on the coming into force of the order, became the highway authority for the path or way in question shall survey the path or way and shall certify what work (if any) appears to them to be necessary to bring it into a fit condition for use by the public as a footpath or bridleway, as the case may be, and shall furnish the Secretary of State with a copy of the certificate ;

(b) if the Secretary of State is not satisfied with a certificate made under the foregoing paragraph, he shall either cause a local inquiry to be held or shall give to the local authority an opportunity of being heard by a person appointed by him for the purpose and, after considering the report of the person appointed to hold the inquiry or the person so appointed as aforesaid, shall make such order either confirming or varying the certificate as he may think fit ; and

(c) subject to the provisions of the last foregoing paragraphs, it shall be the duty of the highway authority to carry out the work specified in a certificate made by them under paragraph (a) above.

(6) In this section " local authority " means any council or any such joint planning board as is mentioned in section 25(2)(a) above.

28.—(1) Subject to the following provisions of this section, if, on a claim made in accordance with this section, it is shown that the value of an interest of a person in land is depreciated, or that a person has suffered damage by being disturbed in his enjoyment of land, in consequence of the coming into operation of a public path creation order, the authority by whom the order was made shall pay to that person compensation equal to the amount of the depreciation or damage.

Compensation for loss caused by public path creation order.

(2) A claim for compensation under this section shall be made within such time and in such manner as may be prescribed by regulations made by the Secretary of State, and shall be made to the authority by whom the order was made.

(3) For the purposes of the application of this section to an order made by the Secretary of State under section 26(2) above, references in this section to the authority by whom the order was made are to be construed as references to such one of the authorities referred to in that subsection as may be nominated by the Secretary of State for the purposes of this subsection.

(4) Nothing in this section confers on any person, in respect of a footpath or bridleway created by a public path creation order, a right to compensation for depreciation of the value of an interest in the land, or for disturbance in his enjoyment of land, not being in either case land over which the path or way was created or land held therewith, unless the creation of the

PART III   path or way would have been actionable at his suit if it had
               been effected otherwise than in the exercise of statutory powers.

               (5) In this section " interest ", in relation to land, includes any
               estate in land and any right over land, whether the right is
               exercisable by virtue of the ownership of an interest in land or
               by virtue of a licence or agreement, and in particular includes
               sporting rights.

Protection for   **29.** In the exercise of their functions under this Part of this
agriculture   Act relating to the making of public path creation agreements
and forestry. and public path creation orders it shall be the duty of councils
               and joint planning boards to have due regard to the needs of
               agriculture and forestry.

Dedication   **30.**—(1) The council of a parish or community may enter
of highway by into an agreement with any person having the necessary power
agreement   in that behalf for the dedication by that person of a highway
with parish or over land in the parish or community or an adjoining parish
community   or community in any case where such a dedication would in
council.   the opinion of the council be beneficial to the inhabitants of
               the parish or community or any part thereof.

               (2) Where the council of a parish or community have entered
               into an agreement under subsection (1) above for the dedication
               of a highway they may carry out any works (including works
               of maintenance or improvement) incidental to or consequential
               on the making of the agreement or contribute towards the
               expense of carrying out such works, and may agree or combine
               with the council of any other parish or community to carry out
               such works or to make such a contribution.

Dedication of   **31.**—(1) Where a way over any land, other than a way of
way as highway such a character that use of it by the public could not give rise
presumed   at common law to any presumption of dedication, has been
after public   actually enjoyed by the public as of right and without interrup-
use for 20   tion for a full period of 20 years, the way is to be deemed to
years.   have been dedicated as a highway unless there is sufficient
               evidence that there was no intention during that period to
               dedicate it.

               (2) The period of 20 years referred to in subsection (1) above
               is to be calculated retrospectively from the date when the right
               of the public to use the way is brought into question, whether
               by a notice such as is mentioned in subsection (3) below or
               otherwise.

(3) Where the owner of the land over which any such way as aforesaid passes—

(*a*) has erected in such manner as to be visible to persons using the way a notice inconsistent with the dedication of the way as a highway, and

(*b*) has maintained the notice after the 1st January 1934, or any later date on which it was erected,

the notice, in the absence of proof of a contrary intention, is sufficient evidence to negative the intention to dedicate the way as a highway.

(4) In the case of land in the possession of a tenant for a term of years, or from year to year, any person for the time being entitled in reversion to the land shall, notwithstanding the existence of the tenancy, have the right to place and maintain such a notice as is mentioned in subsection (3) above, so, however, that no injury is done thereby to the business or occupation of the tenant.

(5) Where a notice erected as mentioned in subsection (3) above is subsequently torn down or defaced, a notice given by the owner of the land to the appropriate council that the way is not dedicated as a highway is, in the absence of proof of a contrary intention, sufficient evidence to negative the intention of the owner of the land to dedicate the way as a highway.

(6) An owner of land may at any time deposit with the appropriate council—

(*a*) a map of the land on a scale of not less than 6 inches to 1 mile, and

(*b*) a statement indicating what ways (if any) over the land he admits to have been dedicated as highways;

and, in any case in which such a deposit has been made, statutory declarations made by that owner or by his successors in title and lodged by him or them with the appropriate council at any time—

(i) within six years from the date of the deposit, or

(ii) within six years from the date on which any previous declaration was last lodged under this section,

to the effect that no additional way (other than any specifically indicated in the declaration) over the land delineated on the said map has been dedicated as a highway since the date of the deposit, or since the date of the lodgment of such previous declaration, as the case may be, are, in the absence of proof of a contrary intention, sufficient evidence to negative the intention of the owner or his successors in title to dedicate any such additional way as a highway.

(7) For the purposes of the foregoing provisions of this section " owner ", in relation to any land, means a person who is for the time being entitled to dispose of the fee simple in the land ; and for the purposes of subsections (5) and (6) above " the appropriate council " means the council of the county or London borough in which the way (in the case of subsection (5)) or the land (in the case of subsection (6)) is situated or, where the way or land is situated in the City, the Common Council.

(8) Nothing in this section affects any incapacity of a corporation or other body or person in possession of land for public or statutory purposes to dedicate a way over that land as a highway if the existence of a highway would be incompatible with those purposes.

(9) Nothing in this section operates to prevent the dedication of a way as a highway being presumed on proof of user for any less period than 20 years, or being presumed or proved in any circumstances in which it might have been presumed or proved immediately before the commencement of this Act.

1949 c. 97.

(10) Nothing in this section or section 32 below affects subsection (4) of section 32 of the National Parks and Access to the Countryside Act 1949 (which provides that a map and statement prepared under that section are conclusive evidence as to the existence of the highways shown on the map and as to certain particulars contained in the statement), or of that subsection as applied by section 34(1) of that Act.

(11) For the purposes of this section " land " includes land covered with water.

Evidence of dedication of way as highway.

32. A court or other tribunal, before determining whether a way has or has not been dedicated as a highway, or the date on which such dedication, if any, took place, shall take into consideration any map, plan or history of the locality or other relevant document which is tendered in evidence, and shall give such weight thereto as the court or tribunal considers justified by the circumstances, including the antiquity of the tendered document, the status of the person by whom and the purpose for which it was made or compiled, and the custody in which it has been kept and from which it is produced.

Protection of rights of reversioners.

33. The person entitled to the remainder or reversion immediately expectant upon the determination of a tenancy for life, or pour autre vie, in land shall have the like remedies by action for trespass or an injunction to prevent the acquisition by the public of a right of way over that land as if he were in possession thereof.

34. Without prejudice to the foregoing provisions of this Part of this Act, a street which is not a highway and land to which section 232 below applies may become a highway by virtue of a declaration made by a county council, a London borough council or the Common Council in accordance with the provisions in that behalf contained in Part XI of this Act.

PART III
Conversion of
private street
into highway.

35.—(1) An agreement under this section may be entered into—

Creation of
walkways by
agreement.

(a) by a local highway authority, after consultation with the council of any district in which the land concerned is situated;

(b) by a district council, either alone or jointly with the local highway authority, after consultation with the local highway authority.

(2) An agreement under this section is an agreement with any person having an interest in any land on which a building is, or is proposed to be, situated, being a person who by virtue of that interest has the necessary power in that behalf,—

(a) for the provision of ways over, through or under parts of the building, or the building when constructed, as the case may be, or parts of any structure attached, or to be attached, to the building; and

(b) for the dedication by that person of those ways as footpaths subject to such limitations and conditions, if any, affecting the public right of way thereover as may be specified in the agreement and to any rights reserved by the agreement to that person and any person deriving title to the land under him.

A footpath created in pursuance of an agreement under this section is referred to below as a " walkway ".

(3) An agreement under this section may make provision for—

(a) the maintenance, cleansing and drainage of any walkway to which the agreement relates;

(b) the lighting of such walkway and of that part of the building or structure which will be over or above it;

(c) the provision and maintenance of support for such walkway;

(d) entitling the authority entering into the agreement or, where the agreement is entered into jointly by a district council and a local highway authority, either of those authorities to enter on any building or structure in which such walkway will be situated and to execute any works necessary to secure the performance of any obligation which any person is for the time being liable to perform by virtue of the agreement or of subsection (4) below ;

(e) the making of payments by the authority entering into the agreement or, where the agreement is entered into jointly by a district council and a local highway authority, either of those authorities to any person having an interest in the land or building affected by the agreement ;

(f) the termination, in such manner and subject to such conditions as may be specified in the agreement, of the right of the public to use such walkway ;

(g) any incidental and consequential matters.

(4) Any covenant (whether positive or restrictive) contained in an agreement under this section and entered into by a person having an interest in any land affected by the agreement shall be binding upon persons deriving title to the land under the covenantor to the same extent as it is binding upon the covenantor notwithstanding that it would not have been binding upon those persons apart from the provisions of this subsection, and shall be enforceable against those persons by the local highway authority.

(5) A covenant contained in an agreement under this section and entered into by a person having an interest in any land affected by the agreement is a local land charge.

(6) Where an agreement has been entered into under this section the appropriate authority may make byelaws regulating—

(a) the conduct of persons using any walkway to which the agreement relates ;

(b) the times at which any such walkway may be closed to the public ;

(c) the placing or retention of anything (including any structure or projection) in, on or over any such walkway.

(7) For the purposes of subsection (6) above, " the appropriate authority " means—

(a) where the agreement was entered into by a local highway authority, that authority ;

(b) where the agreement was entered into by a district council alone, that council ;

(c) where the agreement was entered into by a district council jointly with the local highway authority, the local highway authority ;

but in cases falling within paragraph (*c*) above the local highway authority shall before making any byelaw consult the district council, and in exercising his power of confirmation the Minister shall have regard to any dispute between the local highway authority and the district council.

(8) Not less than 2 months before an authority propose to make byelaws under subsection (6) above they shall display in a conspicuous position on or adjacent to the walkway in question notice of their intention to make such byelaws.

(9) A notice under subsection (8) above shall specify the place where a copy of the proposed byelaws may be inspected and the period, which shall not be less than 6 weeks from the date on which the notice was first displayed as aforesaid, within which representations may be made to the authority, and the authority shall consider any representations made to them within that period.

(10) The Minister of the Crown having power by virtue of section 236 of the Local Government Act 1972 to confirm 1972 c. 70. byelaws made under subsection (6) above may confirm them with or without modifications; and if he proposes to confirm them with modifications he may, before confirming them, direct the authority by whom they were made to give notice of the proposed modifications to such persons and in such manner as may be specified in the direction.

(11) Subject to subsection (12) below, the Minister, after consulting such representative organisations as he thinks fit, may make regulations—

    (*a*) for preventing any enactment or instrument relating to highways or to things done on or in connection with highways from applying to walkways which have been, or are to be, created in pursuance of agreements under this section or to things done on or in connection with such walkways;

    (*b*) for amending, modifying or adapting any such enactment or instrument in its application to such walkways;

    (*c*) without prejudice to the generality of paragraphs (*a*) and (*b*) above, for excluding, restricting or regulating the rights of statutory undertakers, sewerage authorities and the Post Office to place and maintain apparatus in, under, over, along or across such walkways;

    (*d*) without prejudice as aforesaid, for defining the circumstances and manner in which such walkways may be closed periodically or temporarily or stopped up and for prescribing the procedure to be followed before such a walkway is stopped up.

PART III

(12) Regulations under this section shall not exclude the rights of statutory undertakers, sewerage authorities or the Post Office to place and maintain apparatus in, under, along or across any part of a walkway, being a part which is not supported by any structure.

(13) Without prejudice to subsection (11) above, regulations under this section may make different provisions for different classes of walkways and may include such incidental, supplemental and consequential provisions (and, in particular, provisions relating to walkways provided in pursuance of agreements made before the coming into operation of the regulations) as appear to the Minister to be expedient for the purposes of the regulations.

(14) Nothing in this section is to be taken as affecting any other provision of this Act, or any other enactment, by virtue of which highways may be created.

PART IV

MAINTENANCE OF HIGHWAYS

Highways maintainable at public expense

Highways
maintainable
at public
expense.
1959 c. 25.

36.—(1) All such highways as immediately before the commencement of this Act were highways maintainable at the public expense for the purposes of the Highways Act 1959 continue to be so maintainable (subject to this section and to any order of a magistrates' court under section 47 below) for the purposes of this Act.

(2) Without prejudice to any other enactment (whether contained in this Act or not) whereby a highway may become for the purposes of this Act a highway maintainable at the public expense, and subject to this section and section 232(7) below, and to any order of a magistrates' court under section 47 below, the following highways (not falling within subsection (1) above) shall for the purposes of this Act be highways maintainable at the public expense:—

(a) a highway constructed by a highway authority, otherwise than on behalf of some other person who is not a highway authority;

1957 c. 56.

(b) a highway constructed by a council within their own area under Part V of the Housing Act 1957, other than one in respect of which the local highway authority are satisfied that it has not been properly constructed, and a highway constructed by a council outside their own area under the said Part V, being, in the latter case, a highway the liability to maintain which is, by virtue

of the said Part V, vested in the council who are the
local highway authority for the area in which the highway is situated;

(*c*) a highway that is a trunk road or a special road; and

(*d*) a highway, being a footpath or bridleway, created in
consequence of a public path creation order or a public
path diversion order or in consequence of an order
made by the Minister of Transport or the Secretary
of State under section 209 of the Town and Country 1971 c. **78.**
Planning Act 1971 or by a competent authority under
section 210 of that Act, or dedicated in pursuance
of a public path creation agreement.

(3) Paragraph (*c*) of subsection (2) above is not to be construed as referring to a part of a trunk road or special road consisting of a bridge or other part which a person is liable to
maintain under a charter or special enactment, or by reason of
tenure, enclosure or prescription.

(4) Subject to subsection (5) below, where there occurs any
event on the occurrence of which, under any rule of law relating
to the duty of maintaining a highway by reason of tenure, enclosure or prescription, a highway would, but for the enactment
which abrogated the former rule of law under which a duty
of maintaining highways fell on the inhabitants at large (section
38(1) of the Highways Act 1959) or any other enactment, 1959 c. **25.**
become, or cease to be, maintainable by the inhabitants at
large of any area, the highway shall become, or cease to be,
a highway which for the purposes of this Act is a highway
maintainable at the public expense.

(5) A highway shall not by virtue of subsection (4) above
become a highway which for the purposes of this Act is a highway maintainable at the public expense unless either—

(*a*) it was a highway before 31st August 1835; or

(*b*) it became a highway after that date and has at some
time been maintainable by the inhabitants at large of
any area or a highway maintainable at the public
expense;

and a highway shall not by virtue of that subsection cease to be
a highway maintainable at the public expense if it is a highway
which under any rule of law would become a highway maintainable by reason of enclosure but is prevented from becoming
such a highway by section 51 below.

(6) The council of every county and London borough and the
Common Council shall cause to be made, and shall keep

PART IV corrected up to date, a list of the streets within their area which are highways maintainable at the public expense.

(7) Every list made under subsection (6) above shall be kept deposited at the offices of the council by whom it was made and may be inspected by any person free of charge at all reasonable hours and in the case of a list made by the council of a county, the county council shall supply to the council of each district in the county an up to date list of the streets within the area of the district that are highways maintainable at the public expense, and the list so supplied shall be kept deposited at the office of the district council and may be inspected by any person free of charge at all reasonable hours.

Methods whereby highways may become maintainable at public expense

Provisions
whereby
highway
created by
dedication
may become
maintainable
at public
expense.

37.—(1) A person who proposes to dedicate a way as a highway and who desires that the proposed highway shall become maintainable at the public expense by virtue of this section shall give notice of the proposal, not less than 3 months before the date of the proposed dedication, to the council who would, if the way were a highway, be the highway authority therefor, describing the location and width of the proposed highway and the nature of the proposed dedication.

(2) If the council consider that the proposed highway will not be of sufficient utility to the public to justify its being maintained at the public expense, they may make a complaint to a magistrates' court for an order to that effect.

(3) If the council certify that the way has been dedicated in accordance with the terms of the notice and has been made up in a satisfactory manner, and if—

(a) the person by whom the way was dedicated or his successor keeps it in repair for a period of 12 months from the date of the council's certificate, and

(b) the way has been used as a highway during that period,

then, unless an order has been made in relation to the highway under subsection (2) above, the highway shall, at the expiration of the period specified in paragraph (a) above, become for the purposes of this Act a highway maintainable at the public expense.

(4) If the council, on being requested by the person by whom the way was dedicated or his successor to issue a certificate under subsection (3) above, refuse to issue the certificate, that person may appeal to a magistrates' court against the refusal, and the court, if satisfied that the certificate ought to have been issued, may make an order to the effect that subsection (3) above shall apply as if the certificate had been issued on a date specified in the order.

(5) Where a certificate has been issued by a council under subsection (3) above, or an order has been made under subsection (4) above, the certificate or a copy of the order, as the case may be, shall be deposited with the proper officer of the council and may be inspected by any person free of charge at all reasonable hours.

38.—(1) Subject to subsection (2) below, where any person is liable under a special enactment or by reason of tenure, enclosure or prescription to maintain a highway, the Minister, in the case of a trunk road, or a local highway authority, in any other case, may agree with that person to undertake the maintenance of that highway; and where an agreement is made under this subsection the highway to which the agreement relates shall, on such date as may be specified in the agreement, become for the purposes of this Act a highway maintainable at the public expense and the liability of that person to maintain the highway shall be extinguished.

Power of highway authorities to adopt by agreement.

(2) A local highway authority shall not have power to make an agreement under subsection (1) above with respect to a highway with respect to which they or any other highway authority have power to make an agreement under Part V or Part XII of this Act.

(3) Subject to the following provisions of this section, a local highway authority may agree with any person to undertake the maintenance of—

(a) a private carriage or occupation road which that person is willing, and has the necessary power, to dedicate as a highway; or

(b) a way which is to be constructed by that person, or by a highway authority on his behalf, and which he proposes to dedicate as a highway;

and where an agreement is made under this subsection the road or way to which the agreement relates shall, on such date as may be specified in the agreement, become for the purposes of this Act a highway maintainable at the public expense.

(4) Without prejudice to the provisions of subsection (3) above and subject to the following provisions of this section,

PART IV a local highway authority may, by agreement with railway, canal or tramway undertakers, undertake to maintain as part of a highway maintainable at the public expense a bridge or viaduct which carries the railway, canal or tramway of the undertakers over such a highway or which is intended to carry such a railway, canal or tramway over such a highway and is to be constructed by those undertakers or by the highway authority on their behalf.

(5) Where—

(*a*) any such highway as is referred to in paragraph (*b*) of subsection (3) above is intended to become a metropolitan road, or

(*b*) any such bridge or viaduct as is referred to in subsection (4) above crosses or will cross a metropolitan road,

the powers conferred by subsections (3) and (4) above shall, as respects that highway, bridge or viaduct, be exercisable by the Greater London Council and not by any other local highway authority.

(6) An agreement under this section may contain such provisions as to the dedication as a highway of any road or way to which the agreement relates, the bearing of the expenses of the construction, maintenance or improvement of any highway, road, bridge or viaduct to which the agreement relates and other relevant matters as the authority making the agreement think fit.

Adoption of certain highways in livestock rearing areas.
1955 c. 20.
(4 & 5 Eliz. 2.)

39. Where under section 1 of the Agriculture (Improvement of Roads) Act 1955 (proposals for effecting improvements in certain roads situated in, or affording access to, livestock rearing areas), a county council submit proposals to the Minister of Agriculture, Fisheries and Food for effecting an improvement to which that Act applies in respect of a highway that is not a highway maintainable at the public expense, and that Minister approves those proposals, then, without prejudice to any other enactment (whether contained in this Act or not) whereby the highway may become such a highway, the council submitting the proposals shall have power, by notice exhibited on or near the highway, to declare it to be for the purposes of this Act a highway maintainable at the public expense, and thereupon—

(*a*) the highway shall become such a highway, and

(*b*) if, apart from this section, any person would be liable to maintain the highway under a special enactment or by reason of tenure, enclosure or prescription, that liability shall be extinguished.

40. The foregoing provisions of this Part of this Act are without prejudice to the power or, as the case may be, the duty of the council of a county or London borough, or the Common Council, to adopt private streets as highways maintainable at the public expense under Part XI of this Act.

PART IV
Adoption of private streets.

Maintenance of highways maintainable at public expense

41.—(1) The authority who are for the time being the highway authority for a highway maintainable at the public expense are under a duty, subject to subsections (2) and (4) below, to maintain the highway.

Duty to maintain highways maintainable at public expense.

(2) An order made by the Minister under section 10 above directing that a highway proposed to be constructed by him shall become a trunk road may, as regards—

(a) a highway to which this subsection applies which becomes a trunk road by virtue of the order, or

(b) a part of a highway to which this subsection applies, being a part which crosses the route of the highway to be so constructed,

contain such a direction as is specified in subsection (4) below.

(3) Subsection (2) above applies to—

(a) any highway maintainable at the public expense by a local highway authority, and

(b) any highway other than a highway falling within paragraph (a) above or a highway maintainable under a special enactment or by reason of tenure, enclosure or prescription.

(4) The direction referred to in subsection (2) above is—

(a) in a case where the highway or part of a highway falls within subsection (3)(a) above, a direction that, notwithstanding subsection (1) above, it shall be maintained by the highway authority for that highway until such date, not being later than the date on which the new route is opened for the purposes of through traffic, as may be specified in a notice given by the Minister to that authority ; and

(b) in a case where the highway or part of a highway falls within subsection (3)(b) above, a direction that, notwithstanding subsection (1) above, the Minister is to be under no duty to maintain it until such date as aforesaid.

(5) Where an order under section 10 above contains a direction made in pursuance of subsections (2) to (4) above, then, until the date specified in the notice given by the Minister pursuant

PART IV
to the direction, in accordance with subsection (4) above, the powers of a highway authority under sections 97, 98, 270 and 301 below as respects the highway to which the direction relates are exercisable by the highway authority to whom the notice is required to be given, as well as by the Minister.

Power of district councils to maintain certain highways.

42.—(1) Subject to Part I of Schedule 7 to this Act, the council of a district may undertake the maintenance of any eligible highway in the district which is a highway maintainable at the public expense.

(2) For the purposes of subsection (1) above the following are eligible highways:—

(*a*) footpaths,

(*b*) bridleways, and

(*c*) roads (referred to in Schedule 7 to this Act as " urban roads ") which are neither trunk roads nor classified roads and which—

1967 c. 76.

(i) are restricted roads for the purposes of section 71 of the Road Traffic Regulation Act 1967 (30 m.p.h. speed limit), or

(ii) are subject to an order under section 74 of that Act imposing a special limit not exceeding 40 m.p.h., or

(iii) are otherwise streets in an urban area.

(3) The county council who are the highway authority for a highway which is for the time being maintained by a district council by virtue of this section shall reimburse to the district council any expenses incurred by them in carrying out on the highway works of maintenance necessary to secure that the duty to maintain the highway is performed, and Part II of Schedule 7 to this Act shall have effect for this purpose.

Power of parish and community councils to maintain footpaths and bridleways.

43.—(1) The council of a parish or community may undertake the maintenance of any footpath or bridleway within the parish or community which is, in either case, a highway maintainable at the public expense; but nothing in this subsection affects the duty of any highway authority or other person to maintain any such footpath or bridleway.

(2) The highway authority for any footpath or bridleway which a parish or community council have power to maintain under subsection (1) above, and a district council for the time being maintaining any such footpath or bridleway by virtue of section 42 above, may undertake to defray the whole or part

of any expenditure incurred by the parish or community council
in maintaining the footpath or bridleway.

(3) The power of a parish or community council under subsection (1) above is subject to the restrictions for the time being imposed by any enactment on their expenditure, but for the purposes of any enactment imposing such a restriction their expenditure is to be deemed not to include any expenditure falling to be defrayed by a highway authority or district council by virtue of subsection (2) above.

44. Where any person is liable under a special enactment or by reason of tenure, enclosure or prescription to maintain a highway, he may enter into an agreement with the highway authority for that highway for the maintenance by him of any highway maintainable at the public expense by the highway authority; but nothing in this section affects the duty of a highway authority to maintain a highway as respects which any such agreement is made.

Person liable to maintain highway may agree to maintain publicly maintainable highway.

45.—(1) For the purpose of repairing highways maintainable at the public expense by them, a highway authority may exercise such powers with respect to the getting of materials as are mentioned in this section.

Power to get materials for repair of publicly maintainable highways.

(2) Subject to subsection (3) below, the authority may search for, dig, get and carry away gravel, sand, stone and other materials in and from any waste or common land (including the bed of any river or brook flowing through such land).

(3) The authority—

(*a*) shall not in the exercise of their powers under subsection (2) above divert or interrupt the course of any river or brook, or dig or get materials out of any river or brook within 50 yards above or below a bridge, dam or weir;

(*b*) shall not in the exercise of those powers remove such quantity of stones or other materials from any sea beach as to cause damage by inundation or increased danger of encroachment by the sea; and

(*c*) shall not exercise those powers in any land forming part of a common to which section 20 of the Commons Act 1876 applies, except in accordance with that section.

1876 c. 56.

(4) Subject to subsection (5) below, the authority may gather and carry away stones lying upon any land in the county or London borough within which the stones are to be used.

(5) The authority—

> (*a*) shall not exercise the powers conferred by subsection (4) above in a garden, yard, avenue to a house, lawn, park, paddock or inclosed plantation, or in an inclosed wood not exceeding 100 acres in extent;
>
> (*b*) shall not in the case of any other inclosed land exercise those powers unless either they have obtained the consent of the owner and of the occupier of that land, or a magistrates' court has made an order authorising them to exercise those powers in the case of that land; and
>
> (*c*) shall not in the exercise of those powers remove such quantity of stones or other materials from any sea beach as to cause damage by inundation or increased danger of encroachment by the sea.

(6) If the authority cannot get sufficient materials by the exercise of their powers under the foregoing provisions of this section, a magistrates' court may make an order authorising them to search for, dig, get and carry away materials in and from any inclosed land in the county or London borough within which the materials are to be used, other than any such land as is mentioned in subsection (5)(*a*) above.

(7) For the purpose of repairing a bridge maintainable at the public expense and so much of a highway so maintainable as is carried by the bridge or forms the approaches to the bridge up to 100 yards from each end of the bridge, the authority may take and carry away the rubbish or refuse stones from any quarry in the county within which the materials are to be used or, if the materials are to be used in Greater London, from any quarry in Greater London.

(8) Subject to subsection (9) below, for the purpose of repairing or reconstructing a bridge maintainable at the public expense, the authority may be authorised by an order of a magistrates' court to quarry stone from any quarry in the county in which the bridge is or, if the bridge is in Greater London, from any quarry in Greater London.

(9) No order shall be made under subsection (8) above in relation to a quarry which has not been worked at any time during the 3 years immediately preceding the date on which a complaint for such an order is made; and no stone shall be taken from a quarry situated in a garden, yard, avenue to a house, lawn, paddock or inclosed plantation, or in land on which ornamental timber trees are growing, except with the consent of the owner of the quarry.

(10) An authority who exercise any of the powers conferred by this section shall pay compensation to persons interested in any land for any damage done thereto by the carriage of the materials obtained by the authority and also, in cases falling within subsection (6) or subsection (8) above, for the value of those materials.

(11) At least one month before making a complaint to a magistrates' court for an order under subsection (5) or subsection (6) above the authority shall give notice of their intention to make such a complaint to the owner, and to the occupier, of the land from which they propose to get materials.

(12) In relation to highways in respect of which a district council's powers of maintenance under section 42 above are exercisable, references in this section and section 46 below to a highway authority include references to the district council; and for the purposes of this section—

" inclosed land " includes any land in the exclusive occupation of one or more persons for agricultural purposes, though not separated by a fence or otherwise from adjoining land of another person, or from a highway ; and

" London borough " includes the City of London.

46.—(1) Where an excavation is made by a highway authority in the exercise of powers conferred by section 45 above, the authority shall—

Supplemental provisions with respect to the getting of materials under section 45.

(a) while work is in progress, and thereafter so long as the excavation remains open, keep the excavation sufficiently fenced to prevent accidents to persons or animals,

(b) if no materials are found therein, fill up the excavation within 3 days from the date on which the excavation was made,

(c) if materials are found, then within 14 days from the date on which sufficient materials have been obtained, fill up the excavation or slope it down and fence it off, if the owner or occupier of the land in question so requires, and thereafter keep it so fenced, and

(d) when filling up an excavation, make good and level the ground and cover it with the turf or clod dug therefrom.

C

PART IV

(2) An authority who fail to comply with any of the provisions of subsection (1) above are guilty of an offence and liable to a fine not exceeding £25.

(3) If in the exercise of powers conferred by section 45 above materials are dug so as to damage or endanger a highway, occupation road, ford, dam, mine, building, works or apparatus, the authority are guilty of an offence and, without prejudice to any civil proceedings which may be available against them, liable to a fine not exceeding £25.

(4) A person who, without the consent of the highway authority,—

    (*a*) takes away any materials purchased, gotten or gathered by them for the repair of highways, or

    (*b*) takes away any materials from a quarry or excavation opened by the authority before their workmen have ceased working thereat for 6 weeks,

is guilty of an offence and liable to a fine not exceeding £25 ; but in the case of a quarry or excavation in private grounds, nothing in this subsection prevents the owner or occupier from getting materials therefrom for his own private use and not for sale.

Power of magistrates' court to declare unnecessary highway to be not maintainable at public expense.

47.—(1) Where a highway authority are of opinion that a highway maintainable at the public expense by them is unnecessary for public use and therefore ought not to be maintained at the public expense, they may, subject to subsections (2) to (4) below, apply to a magistrates' court for an order declaring that the highway shall cease to be so maintained.

(2) No application shall be made under this section for an order relating to a trunk road, special road, metropolitan road, footpath or bridleway.

(3) Where a county council, as highway authority, propose to make an application under this section for an order relating to any highway, they shall give notice of the proposal to the council of the district in which the highway is situated, and the application shall not be made if, within 2 months from the date of service of the notice by the county council, notice is given to the county council by the district council that the district council have refused to consent to the making of the application.

(4) If a highway authority propose to make an application under this section for an order relating to a highway situated

in a parish or a community they shall give notice of the proposal—

(a) to the council of the parish or community, or

(b) in the case of a parish not having a separate parish council, to the chairman of the parish meeting,

and the application shall not be made if, within 2 months from the date of service of the notice by the highway authority, notice is given to the highway authority by the council of the parish or community or the chairman of the parish meeting, as the case may be, that the council or meeting have refused to consent to the making of the application.

(5) Where an application is made to a magistrates' court under this section, 2 or more justices of the peace acting for the petty sessions area for which the court acts shall together view the highway to which the application relates, and no further proceedings shall be taken on the application unless they are of opinion, after viewing the highway, that there was ground for making the application.

(6) The clerk to the justices who view a highway in accordance with the provisions of subsection (5) above shall, as soon as practicable after the view, notify the highway authority by whom an application under this section relating to the highway was made of the decision of the justices and, if the justices decide that there was ground for making the application, of the time, not being less than 6 weeks from the date of the notice, and place, at which the application is to be heard by a magistrates' court.

(7) A magistrates' court shall not hear an application under this section unless it is satisfied that the highway authority making the application have—

(a) not less than one month before the date on which the application is to be heard by the court, given notice to the owners and the occupiers of all lands adjoining the highway to which the application relates of the making of the application, and the purpose of it, and of the time and place at which the application is to be heard by the court, and

(b) given public notice in the terms and manner required by subsection (8) below.

(8) A highway authority making an application under this section shall publish, once at least in each of the 4 weeks immediately preceding the week in which the application is to be

PART IV   heard, in a local newspaper circulating in the area in which the highway to which the application relates is situated, a notice—

(a) stating that an application has been made to a magistrates' court under this section and the purpose of the application,

(b) describing the highway, and

(c) specifying the time and place at which the application is to be heard,

and shall cause a copy of the notice to be fixed, at least 14 days before the date on which the application is to be heard by the court, to the principal doors of every church and chapel in the parish or community in which the highway is situated, or in some conspicuous position near the highway.

(9) On the hearing of an application for an order under this section, a magistrates' court shall hear any person who objects to the order being made and may either dismiss the application or make an order declaring that the highway to which the application relates shall cease to be maintained at the public expense.

(10) Where an order is made under this section the highway to which the order relates shall cease to be a highway maintainable at the public expense.

(11) The highway authority on whose application an order is made under this section shall give notice of the making of the order to any public utility undertakers having apparatus under, in, upon, over, along or across the highway to which the order relates.

Power of
magistrates'
court to order
a highway
to be again
maintainable
at public
expense.
48.—(1) Subject to subsection (2) below, if it appears to a magistrates' court that, in consequence of any change of circumstances since the time at which an order was made under section 47 above, the highway to which the order relates has again become of public use and ought to be maintained at the public expense, the court may by order direct that the highway shall again become for the purposes of this Act a highway maintainable at the public expense.

(2) An order under this section shall not be made except on the application of a person interested in the maintenance of the highway to which the application relates, and on proof that not less than 1 month before making the application he gave notice to the highway authority for the highway of his intention to make an application under this section.

Maintenance of privately maintainable highways   **PART IV**

49. Where a person is liable to maintain the approaches to a bridge by reason of the fact that he is liable to maintain the bridge by reason of tenure or prescription, his liability to maintain the approaches extends to 100 yards from each end of the bridge.

Maintenance of approaches to certain privately maintainable bridges.

50.—(1) Where apart from section 41 above a person would under a special enactment or by reason of tenure, enclosure or prescription be under an obligation to maintain a footpath or bridleway, the operation of section 41(1) does not release him from the obligation.

Maintenance of privately maintainable footpaths and bridleways.

(2) The council of a district, parish or community may undertake by virtue of this subsection the maintenance of any footpath or bridleway within the district, parish or community (other than a footpath or bridleway the maintenance of which they have power to undertake under section 42 or, as the case may be, section 43 above) whether or not any other person is under a duty to maintain the footpath or bridleway; but nothing in this subsection affects the duty of any other person to maintain any such footpath or bridleway.

(3) The power of a district council under subsection (2) above is subject to Part I of Schedule 7 to this Act; and the power of a parish or community council under that subsection is subject to the restrictions for the time being imposed by any enactment on their expenditure.

51.—(1) If a person across whose land there is a highway maintainable at the public expense erects a fence between the highway and the adjoining land, and the fence is erected with the consent of the highway authority for the highway, he does not thereby become liable to maintain the highway by reason of enclosure.

No liability to maintain by reason of enclosure if highway fenced with consent of highway authority.

(2) Nothing in subsection (1) above is to be construed as imposing on any person a liability to maintain a highway by reason of enclosure.

52.—(1) A person liable to maintain a highway by reason of tenure, enclosure or prescription has, for the purpose of repairing it, the like powers with respect to the getting of materials as are conferred on a highway authority by section 45(2) to (6) above for the purpose of repairing highways maintainable at the public expense by them.

Power to get materials for repair of privately maintainable highways.

C 3

(2) A person on whom powers are conferred by this section is, with respect to the exercise of those powers, subject to the like duties and liabilities under section 45(10) and (11) above and under section 46(1) to (3) above as are a highway authority with respect to the exercise of the powers conferred on them by section 45.

Power of magistrates' court to extinguish liability to maintain privately maintainable highway.

53.—(1) Where a person is liable by reason of tenure, enclosure or prescription to maintain a highway, a magistrates' court may, on a complaint made either by that person or by the highway authority for the highway, make an order that the liability of that person to maintain the highway shall be extinguished, and on the extinguishment of that liability the highway, if it is not then a highway maintainable at the public expense, shall become for the purposes of this Act a highway maintainable at the public expense.

(2) Where a complaint is made to a magistrates' court under this section by a person liable as aforesaid to maintain a highway—

(a) the highway authority for the highway have a right to be heard by the court at the hearing of the complaint, and

(b) the court shall not make an order on the complaint unless it is satisfied that not less than 21 days before the date on which the complaint is heard by the court the complainant gave notice to the highway authority for the highway of the making of the complaint and of the time and place at which it was to be heard by the court.

(3) Where by virtue of an order under this section the liability of a person to maintain a highway is extinguished, that person is liable to pay to the highway authority for the highway such sum as may be agreed between him and that authority or, in default of agreement, as may be determined by arbitration to represent the value to him of the extinguishment of his liability.

(4) A sum payable by any person under subsection (3) above shall, at his option, be paid—

(a) as a lump sum, or

(b) by annual payments of such amount, and continuing for such number of years, as may be agreed between him and the highway authority or, in default of agreement, as may be determined by arbitration.

(5) Any matter which by virtue of subsection (3) or (4) above is to be determined by arbitration shall be determined by a single

arbitrator appointed, in default of agreement between the parties concerned, by the Minister.

(6) Nothing in this section affects any exemption from rating under any enactment as continued by section 117 of the General Rate Act 1967.

1967 c. 9.

54.—(1) Where a highway which a person is liable to maintain under a special enactment or by reason of tenure, enclosure or prescription is diverted in accordance with an order made under section 116 below, then—

Extinguishment of liability to maintain privately maintainable highway diverted by order of magistrates' court.

(*a*) the substituted highway becomes for the purposes of this Act a highway maintainable at the public expense, and

(*b*) the person liable as aforesaid to maintain the highway so diverted is liable to pay to the highway authority for the substituted highway such sum as may be agreed between him and that authority or, in default of agreement, as may be determined by arbitration to represent the value to him of the extinguishment of his liability.

(2) A sum payable by any person under subsection (1) above shall, at his option, be paid—

(*a*) as a lump sum, or

(*b*) by annual payments of such amount, and continuing for such number of years, as may be agreed between him and the highway authority or, in default of agreement, as may be determined by arbitration.

(3) Any matter which by virtue of subsection (1) or (2) above is to be determined by arbitration shall be determined by a single arbitrator appointed, in default of agreement between the parties concerned, by the Minister.

55.—(1) Where a highway comprising a bridge becomes a trunk road, and the bridge is transferred to the Minister under this Act, then, if immediately before the transfer the bridge was not a highway maintainable at the public expense, any liability of the owners of the bridge for the maintenance or improvement of it or of the highway carried by it is thereupon extinguished.

Extinguishment of liability to maintain or improve bridges comprised in trunk roads and special roads.

(2) Where the liability of the owners of a bridge is extinguished under subsection (1) above, the owners shall pay to the Minister such sum as may be agreed between them and the Minister or, in default of agreement, as may be determined by arbitration to represent the value to the owners of the extinguishment of their liability.

(3) Any sum payable by the owners of a bridge under sub-section (2) above shall, in so far as it exceeds any sum payable by the Minister to the owners under this Act, be paid, at the option of the owners—

(*a*) as a lump sum, or

(*b*) by annual instalments of such amount, and continuing for such number of years, as may be agreed between the owners and the Minister or, in default of agreement, as may be determined by arbitration, or

(*c*) by perpetual annual payments of such amount as may be so agreed or determined.

(4) The foregoing provisions of this section apply where a highway comprising a bridge is included in the route prescribed by a scheme under section 16 above authorising the provision of a special road by a local highway authority and the bridge is transferred to the special road authority, as they apply where such a highway becomes a trunk road and the bridge is transferred to the Minister; and accordingly those provisions have effect as if the references therein to a trunk road and to the Minister included references to a special road and to the special road authority.

(5) In this section—

" bridge " includes so much of the approaches thereto as supports or protects the surface of the trunk road or special road;

" owners ", in relation to a bridge, means the persons who, immediately before the transfer of the bridge to the Minister or the special road authority, were responsible for the maintenance of it, and includes any persons who, in pursuance of any agreement with the persons so responsible, were then discharging that responsibility on their behalf.

Enforcement of liability for maintenance

Proceedings for an order to repair highway.

56.—(1) A person (" the complainant ") who alleges that a way or bridge—

(*a*) is a highway maintainable at the public expense or a highway which a person is liable to maintain under a special enactment or by reason of tenure, enclosure or prescription, and

(*b*) is out of repair,

may serve a notice on the highway authority or other person alleged to be liable to maintain the way or bridge (" the respondent ") requiring the respondent to state whether he admits that the way or bridge is a highway and that he is liable to maintain it.

(2) If, within 1 month from the date of service on him of a notice under subsection (1) above, the respondent does not serve on the complainant a notice admitting both that the way or bridge in question is a highway and that the respondent is liable to maintain it, the complainant may apply to the Crown Court for an order requiring the respondent, if the court finds that the way or bridge is a highway which the respondent is liable to maintain and is out of repair, to put it in proper repair within such reasonable period as may be specified in the order.

(3) The complainant for an order under subsection (2) above shall give notice in writing of the application to the appropriate officer of the Crown Court and the notice shall specify—

(a) the situation of the way or bridge to which the application relates,

(b) the name of the respondent,

(c) the part of the way or bridge which is alleged to be out of repair, and

(d) the nature of the alleged disrepair ;

and the complainant shall serve a copy of the notice on the respondent.

(4) If, within 1 month from the date of service on him of a notice under subsection (1) above, the respondent serves on the complainant a notice admitting both that the way or bridge in question is a highway and that the respondent is liable to maintain it, the complainant may, within 6 months from the date of service on him of that notice, apply to a magistrates' court for an order requiring the respondent, if the court finds that the highway is out of repair, to put it in proper repair within such reasonable period as may be specified in the order.

(5) A court in determining under this section whether a highway is out of repair shall not be required to view the highway unless it thinks fit, and any such view may be made by any 2 or more of the members of the court.

(6) If at the expiration of the period specified in an order made under subsection (2) or (4) above a magistrates' court is satisfied that the highway to which the order relates has not been put in proper repair, then, unless the court thinks fit to extend the period, it shall by order authorise the complainant (if he has not the necessary power in that behalf) to carry out such works as may be necessary to put the highway in proper repair.

(7) Any expenses which a complainant reasonably incurs in carrying out works authorised by an order under subsection (6)

PART IV above are recoverable from the respondent summarily as a civil debt.

(8) Where any expenses recoverable under subsection (7) above are recovered from the respondent, then, if the respondent would have been entitled to recover from some other person the whole or part of the expenses of repairing the highway in question if he had repaired it himself, he is entitled to recover from that other person the whole or the like part, as the case may be, of the expenses recovered from him.

(9) Where an application is made under this section for an order requiring the respondent to put in proper repair a footpath or bridleway which, in either case, is a highway maintainable at the public expense and some other person is liable to maintain the footpath or bridleway under a special enactment or by reason of tenure, enclosure or prescription, that other person has a right to be heard by the court which hears the application, but only on the question whether the footpath or bridleway is in proper repair.

Default powers of highway authorities in respect of non-repair of privately maintainable highways.
57.—(1) Where a person is liable under a special enactment or by reason of tenure, enclosure or prescription to maintain a footpath or bridleway which, in either case, is a highway maintainable at the public expense, and the highway authority for the highway repair it in the performance of their duty to maintain it, they may, subject to subsection (3) below, recover the necessary expenses of doing so from that person in any court of competent jurisdiction.

(2) Where a person is liable as aforesaid to maintain a highway other than such a footpath or bridleway as is referred to in subsection (1) above the highway authority for the highway may, if in their opinion the highway is not in proper repair, repair it and, subject to subsection (3) below, recover the necessary expenses of doing so from that person in any court of competent jurisdiction.

(3) The right of recovery conferred by the foregoing provisions of this section is not exercisable—

(a) in a case where a highway authority repair a footpath or bridleway in obedience to an order of a court made under section 56 above, unless not less than 21 days before the date on which the application was heard by the court the authority gave notice to the person liable to maintain the path or way of the making of an application with respect to it and of the time and place at which the application was to be heard by the court (so however that there is no obligation to give notice to him under this paragraph if he was the person on whose application the order of the court was made);

(b) in any other case, unless the highway authority, before repairing the highway, have given notice to the person liable to maintain it that the highway is not in proper repair, specifying a reasonable time within which he may repair it, and he has failed to repair it within that time.

(4) Where a highway authority exercise a right of recovery from any person under the foregoing provisions of this section, then, if that person would have been entitled to recover from some other person the whole or part of the expenses of repairing the highway if he had repaired it himself, he is entitled to recover from that other person the whole or the like part, as the case may be, of the expenses recovered from him by the highway authority.

58.—(1) In an action against a highway authority in respect of damage resulting from their failure to maintain a highway maintainable at the public expense it is a defence (without prejudice to any other defence or the application of the law relating to contributory negligence) to prove that the authority had taken such care as in all the circumstances was reasonably required to secure that the part of the highway to which the action relates was not dangerous for traffic.

Special defence in action against a highway authority for damages for non-repair of highway.

(2) For the purposes of a defence under subsection (1) above, the court shall in particular have regard to the following matters:—

(a) the character of the highway, and the traffic which was reasonably to be expected to use it;

(b) the standard of maintenance appropriate for a highway of that character and used by such traffic;

(c) the state of repair in which a reasonable person would have expected to find the highway;

(d) whether the highway authority knew, or could reasonably have been expected to know, that the condition of the part of the highway to which the action relates was likely to cause danger to users of the highway;

(e) where the highway authority could not reasonably have been expected to repair that part of the highway before the cause of action arose, what warning notices of its condition had been displayed;

PART IV   but for the purposes of such a defence it is not relevant
to prove that the highway authority had arranged for a competent
person to carry out or supervise the maintenance of the part of
the highway to which the action relates unless it is also proved
that the authority had given him proper instructions with regard
to the maintenance of the highway and that he had carried out
the instructions.

(3) This section binds the Crown.

(4) This section does not apply to damage resulting from
breaking or opening or tunnelling or boring under a street by
way of code-regulated works, being damage resulting from an
event which occurred—

1950 c. 39.
(a) before the completion of the reinstatement or making
good of the relevant part of the street in pursuance of
the obligation imposed on the undertakers by section
7(2) of the Public Utilities Street Works Act 1950 ; or

(b) where the relevant part of the street is the subject of an
election under Schedule 3 to that Act (which, with
minor exceptions, limits the obligation of undertakers
to the execution of interim restoration), during the
period mentioned in paragraph 3(a) of that Schedule ;

and expressions used in this subsection and that Act have the
same meanings as in that Act.

Recovery by highway authorities etc. of certain expenses incurred
in maintaining highways

Recovery of
expenses due to
extraordinary
traffic.
59.—(1) Subject to subsection (3) below, where it appears to
the highway authority for a highway maintainable at the public
expense, by a certificate of their proper officer, that having
regard to the average expense of maintaining the highway or
other similar highways in the neighbourhood extraordinary
expenses have been or will be incurred by the authority in
maintaining the highway by reason of the damage caused by
excessive weight passing along the highway, or other extraordinary traffic thereon, the highway authority may recover
from any person (" the operator ") by or in consequence of
whose order the traffic has been conducted the excess expenses.

(2) In subsection (1) above " the excess expenses " means such
expenses as may be proved to the satisfaction of the court having
cognizance of the case to have been or to be likely to be incurred
by the highway authority by reason of the damage arising from
the extraordinary traffic ; and for the purposes of that subsection
the expenses incurred by a highway authority in maintaining a
highway are (without prejudice to the application of this
section to a by-pass provided under this Act for use in connection

with a cattle-grid) to be taken to include expenses incurred by them in maintaining a cattle-grid provided for the highway under this Act.

(3) If before traffic which may cause such damage commences the operator admits liability in respect of such traffic, then—

> (*a*) the operator and the highway authority may agree for the payment by the operator to the highway authority of a sum by way of a composition of such liability, or
>
> (*b*) either party may require that the sum to be so paid shall be determined by arbitration ;

and where a sum has been so agreed or determined the operator is liable to pay that sum to the highway authority and is not liable to proceedings for the recovery of the excess expenses under subsection (1) above.

(4) Any sums recoverable under this section are recoverable in the High Court or, if the claim does not exceed £500, in the county court in the district in which the highway or any part of it is situated.

(5) Proceedings for the recovery of any sums under this section shall be commenced within 12 months from the time at which the damage has been done or, where the damage is the consequence of any particular building contract or work extending over a long period, not later than 6 months from the date of completion of the contract or work.

(6) In the application of this section to highways for which the Minister is the highway authority the words " by a certificate of their proper officer " in subsection (1) are to be omitted.

60.—(1) Where by reason of undertakers' works (other than works for purposes of a railway undertaking or a tramway undertaking) the use of a highway is restricted or prohibited under section 12 of the Road Traffic Regulation Act 1967, or under any other enactment, and the traffic restricted or prohibited uses as an alternative route a highway of a lower classification, the person executing the works shall pay to the highway authority (if the latter highway is a highway maintainable at the public expense) or to the street managers (if it is not) an amount equal to any cost reasonably incurred by the authority or managers of— *Liability of certain persons for cost of use of alternative route where highway closed by reason of their works.* *1967 c. 76.*

> (*a*) strengthening the latter highway, in so far as the strengthening is done with a view to, and is necessary for, the use of it by the traffic in question ; or
>
> (*b*) making good any damage to the latter highway occurring in consequence of the use of it by the traffic in question.

(2) The reference in subsection (1) above to works for purposes of a railway undertaking or a tramway undertaking includes a reference to works executed primarily for those purposes but for other purposes also.

(3) For the purposes of subsection (1) above the order of classification of highways, from higher to lower, is to be taken to be the following, that is to say, trunk roads, classified roads and highways that are neither trunk roads nor classified roads.

(4) If, in relation to a claim for a payment under subsection (1) above, any question arises—

(*a*) whether the cost in respect of which the claim is made was in fact incurred,

(*b*) whether such cost was incurred in such circumstances or in respect of such works, as are mentioned in subsection (1) above,

(*c*) as to the amount of such cost, or

(*d*) whether such cost was reasonably incurred,

the question is to be determined by a single arbitrator appointed, in default of agreement between the parties concerned, by the President of the Institution of Civil Engineers.

(5) In this section " railway ", " street managers ", " tramway " and " undertakers' works " have the same meanings respectively as in the Public Utilities Street Works Act 1950.

1950 c. 39.

Regulations supplementing maintenance powers
of district councils

Regulations supplementing maintenance powers of district councils.   **61.** The Minister may by regulations empower district councils, in relation to highways in respect of which their powers of maintenance under sections 42 and 50 above are exercisable, to exercise subject to such terms and conditions as may be specified in the regulations such additional powers as appear to him—

(*a*) to be appropriate to supplement powers of maintenance ; and

(*b*) to correspond to powers exercisable in relation to highways by highway authorities ;

and accordingly in those sections, in Schedule 7 to this Act and in any other enactment referring to the powers of district councils under those sections, the expressions " maintenance " and " maintain " where used with respect to the powers of

district councils under those sections, are to be construed as PART IV
including the carrying out of operations in the exercise of powers
conferred on district councils by regulations under this section.

PART V

IMPROVEMENT OF HIGHWAYS

General power of improvement

62.—(1) The provisions of this Part of this Act have effect General
for the purpose of empowering or requiring highway authorities power of
and other persons to improve highways. improvement.

(2) Without prejudice to the powers of improvement
specifically conferred on highway authorities by the following
provisions of this Part of this Act, any such authority may,
subject to subsection (3) below, carry out, in relation to a
highway maintainable at the public expense by them, any work
(including the provision of equipment) for the improvement of
the highway.

(3) Notwithstanding subsection (2) above, but without prejudice to any enactment not contained in this Part of this Act,
work of any of the following descriptions shall be carried out
only under the powers specifically conferred by the following
provisions of this Part of this Act, and not under this section—

    (a) the division of carriageways, provision of roundabouts
        and variation of the relative widths of carriageways and
        footways ;

    (b) the construction of cycle tracks ;

    (c) the provision of subways, refuges, pillars, walls, barriers,
        rails, fences or posts for the use or protection of persons
        using a highway ;

    (d) the construction and reconstruction of bridges and
        alteration of level of highways ;

    (e) the planting of trees, shrubs and other vegetation and
        laying out of grass verges ;

    (f) the provision, maintenance, alteration, improvement or
        other dealing with cattle-grids, by-passes, gates and
        other works for use in connection with cattle-grids ;

    (g) the execution of works for the purpose of draining a
        highway or of otherwise preventing surface water from
        flowing on to it ;

    (h) the provision of barriers or other works for the pur-
        pose of affording to a highway protection against
        hazards of nature.

(4) A highway authority may alter or remove any works executed by them under this section.

(5) In relation to any highway in Greater London maintainable at the public expense which is neither a trunk road nor a metropolitan road, subsections (2) to (4) above have effect for the purposes of, and of the provision of equipment for, the erection, maintenance, alteration or removal of traffic signs which are light signals for controlling the movement of vehicular traffic or of pedestrians (but for those purposes only) as if that highway were maintainable by the Greater London Council and not by the London borough council concerned or, as the case may be, by the Common Council.

Relief of main carriageway of trunk road from local traffic

Relief of main carriageway of trunk road from local traffic.
63. Without prejudice to section 10(3) above, the Minister may construct as part of a trunk road a highway for the purpose of relieving a main carriageway of the trunk road from local traffic ; but this section does not authorise the construction of a highway which is separated from the remainder of the trunk road by intervening land.

Dual carriageways, roundabouts and cycle tracks

Dual carriageways and roundabouts.
64.—(1) Where a highway maintainable at the public expense consists of or comprises a made-up carriageway, the highway authority liable to maintain it may construct and maintain works in that carriageway—

(a) along any length of the highway, for separating a part of the carriageway which is to be used by traffic moving in one direction from a part of the carriageway which is to be used (whether at all times or at particular times only) by traffic moving in the other direction ;

(b) at crossroads or other junctions, for regulating the movement of traffic.

(2) The powers conferred by subsection (1) above include power, in relation to any such works as are referred to in that subsection—

(a) to light them,

(b) to pave, grass or otherwise cover them or any part of them,

(c) to erect pillars, walls, rails or fences on, around or across them or any part of them, and

(d) to plant on them trees, shrubs and other vegetation either for ornament or in the interests of safety.

(3) A highway authority may alter or remove any works constructed by them under this section.

(4) As respects a metropolitan road, the powers of a highway authority under this section may be exercised, with the consent of the Greater London Council, by the council of the London borough in which the road is situated or, in the case of a road situated in the City, by the Common Council.

(5) Where there are carried out in exercise of the powers under subsections (1) to (4) above works in relation to which, apart from this subsection, the provisions of Part II of the Public Utilities Street Works Act 1950 (which regulate the relations between an authority carrying out road alterations and undertakers whose apparatus is affected by them) would not apply, those provisions shall apply in relation to the works as if the works were of a kind mentioned in section 21(1)(*a*) of that Act and, where the works are carried out under subsection (4) above, as if they were carried out by the Greater London Council.

1950 c. 39.

65.—(1) Without prejudice to section 24 above, a highway authority may, in or by the side of a highway maintainable at the public expense by them which consists of or comprises a made-up carriageway, construct a cycle track as part of the highway; and they may light any cycle track constructed by them under this section.

Cycle tracks.

(2) A highway authority may alter or remove a cycle track constructed by them under this section.

Safety provisions

66.—(1) It is the duty of a highway authority to provide in or by the side of a highway maintainable at the public expense by them which consists of or comprises a made-up carriageway, a proper and sufficient footway as part of the highway in any case where they consider the provision of a footway as necessary or desirable for the safety or accommodation of pedestrians; and they may light any footway provided by them under this subsection.

Footways and guard-rails etc. for publicly maintainable highways.

(2) A highway authority may provide and maintain in a highway maintainable at the public expense by them which consists of or comprises a carriageway, such raised paving, pillars, walls, rails or fences as they think necessary for the purpose of safeguarding persons using the highway.

(3) A highway authority may provide and maintain in a highway maintainable at the public expense by them which consists of a footpath, such barriers, rails or fences as they think necessary for the purpose of safeguarding persons using the highway.

(4) The powers conferred by the foregoing provisions of this section to provide any works include power to alter or remove them.

(5) The power conferred by subsection (3) above, and the power to alter or remove any works provided under that subsection, shall not be exercised so as to obstruct any private access to any premises or interfere with the carrying out of agricultural operations.

(6) The powers of a highway authority under subsections (2) and (3) above may, with the consent of the Minister, be exercised by the council of a county in relation to any part within the county but outside Greater London of a highway for which the Minister is the highway authority.

(7) The powers of a highway authority under subsections (2) and (3) above may, with the consent of the highway authority, be exercised by the council of a London borough or, as the case may require, by the Common Council in relation to any part within the borough, or the City, of a highway for which the council, or the Common Council, are not the highway authority.

(8) A highway authority or council shall pay compensation to any person who sustains damage by reason of the execution by them of works under subsection (2) or (3) above.

Guard-rails etc. in private streets.

67.—(1) Subject to the provisions of this section, in any street which is not a highway maintainable at the public expense and which consists of or comprises a carriageway a local authority may provide and maintain such pillars, rails or fences as they think necessary for the purpose of safeguarding persons using the street.

(2) The power under subsection (1) above to provide any works includes power to alter or remove them.

(3) Schedule 8 to this Act (consents before carrying out work in streets) applies to the powers conferred on local authorities by this section.

(4) A local authority shall pay compensation to any person who sustains damage by reason of the execution by them of works under this section.

(5) In this section " local authority " means any of the following, namely, the council of a district or London borough, the Greater London Council, the Common Council and the Council of the Isles of Scilly.

68.—(1) A highway authority may, in relation to a highway maintainable at the public expense by them which consists of or comprises a made-up carriageway, construct and maintain works in that carriageway for providing places of refuge for the protection of pedestrians crossing the carriageway.

(2) Subsections (2) to (5) of section 64 above apply in relation to works mentioned in subsection (1) above as they apply in relation to works mentioned in subsection (1) of that section.

69.—(1) For the purpose of protecting from danger traffic along a highway which consists of or comprises a made-up carriageway, or of making the crossing of it less dangerous to pedestrians, the highway authority for the highway may construct, light and maintain subways under the highway for the use of pedestrians, and may alter, remove or close temporarily any such subway.

(2) With respect to highways in Greater London, the powers of a highway authority under subsection (1) above may be exercised with that authority's consent—

(a) in the case of a highway for which the Minister is the highway authority, by the council of a London borough or the Common Council, as respects any parts of the highway in that council's area ; and

(b) in the case of a metropolitan road, by the council of a London borough or the Common Council, as respects any part of the highway in that borough or, as the case may be, in the City.

(3) Subsection (1) above has effect in relation to a road which consists of or comprises a made-up carriageway and to which the public have access, but which is not a highway, as if it were a highway and as if the council of the district or London borough in which the road is situated were the highway authority for it or, in the case of a road situated in the City, as if the Common Council were the highway authority for it.

70.—(1) Without prejudice to any other powers of theirs to construct or reconstruct bridges, the highway authority for any highway may, for the purpose of protecting traffic along the highway from danger, or of making the crossing of it less dangerous to, or easier for, pedestrians, construct, light and maintain a bridge over the highway for the use of pedestrians, and may alter, remove or close temporarily any such bridge.

(2) A bridge constructed under this section may form part of a bridge constructed for the use of vehicles or of a bridge providing a way from premises on one side of a highway to

premises on the other or a means of access from a highway to any premises.

(3) The supports of, and approaches to, a bridge constructed under this section may be situated—

(*a*) in the highway over which the bridge is to be constructed ; or

(*b*) subject to subsection (4) below, in any other highway that crosses or enters the route of the first-mentioned highway.

(4) The supports of, or approaches to, a bridge to be constructed under this section shall not be constructed in such a highway as is mentioned in subsection (3)(*b*) above unless the highway authority by whom the bridge is to be constructed are the highway authority for that highway or the highway authority for it have given their consent.

(5) Where any bridge proposed to be constructed under this section by a highway authority will provide or improve an access to a highway from any street vested in some other highway authority or any other premises, the highway authority may enter into agreements with that other authority or any person having an interest in those premises—

(*a*) for the making by the other party to the agreement of contributions towards the expenses to be incurred by the highway authority in constructing, lighting and maintaining the bridge ;

(*b*) with respect to the use of the bridge and its maintenance.

(6) A highway authority shall pay compensation to any person who sustains damage by reason of the execution by them under this section of works in or over a highway.

Margins for horses and livestock.

71.—(1) It is the duty of a highway authority to provide in or by the side of a highway maintainable at the public expense by them which consists of or comprises a made-up carriageway adequate grass or other margins as part of the highway in any case where they consider the provision of margins necessary or desirable for the safety or accommodation of ridden horses and driven livestock ; and a highway authority may light a margin provided by them under this section.

(2) A highway authority may alter or remove a margin provided by them under this section.

Widths

72.—(1) A highway authority may widen any highway for Widening
which they are the highway authority and may for that purpose of highways.
agree with a person having power in that behalf for the dedication of adjoining land as part of a highway.

(2) A council or joint planning board have the like power
to enter into a public path creation agreement under section 25
above, or to make a public path creation order under section 26
above, for the purpose of securing the widening of an existing
footpath or bridleway as they have for the purpose of securing
the creation of a footpath or bridleway, and references in those
sections to the dedication or creation of a footpath or bridleway
are to be construed accordingly.

(3) The council of a parish or community have the like power
to enter into an agreement under section 30 above for the
purpose of securing the widening of an existing highway in the
parish or community or an adjoining parish or community as
they have for the purpose of securing the dedication of a highway, and references in that section to the dedication of a highway are to be construed accordingly.

73.—(1) Where in the opinion of a highway authority—   Power to
  (*a*) a street which is a highway maintainable at the public prescribe
        expense by them is narrow or inconvenient, or without line for
        any sufficiently regular boundary line, or   widening
  (*b*) it is necessary or desirable that such a street should be street.
        widened,
the authority may prescribe in relation to either one side or both
sides of the street, or at or within a distance of 15 yards from
any corner of the street, a line to which the street is to be
widened (in this section referred to as an " improvement line ").

(2) Where an improvement line prescribed under this section
in relation to any street is in force, then, subject to subsections
(3) and (4) below, no new building shall be erected, and no
permanent excavation below the level of the street shall be made,
nearer to the centre line of the street than the improvement line,
except with the consent of the authority who prescribed the line,
and the authority may give a consent for such period and subject
to such conditions as they may deem expedient.

(3) The prohibition imposed by subsection (2) above does not
affect any right of statutory undertakers to make an excavation
for the purpose of laying, altering, maintaining or renewing any
main, pipe, electric line, cable, duct or other work or apparatus.

(4) Where an authority prescribe an improvement line under
this section, a person aggrieved by the decision to prescribe the

PART V line or by the refusal of consent under subsection (2) above or by the period for which the consent is given or any conditions attached to it may appeal to the Crown Court.

(5) A condition imposed in connection with the giving of a consent under subsection (2) above is binding on the successor in title to every owner, and on every lessee and every occupier, of any land to which it relates.

(6) If a person contravenes the provisions of this section, or any condition imposed in connection with the giving of a consent under it, he is, without prejudice to any other proceedings which may be available against him, guilty of an offence and liable to a fine not exceeding £25 ; and if the offence is continued after conviction he is guilty of a further offence and liable to a fine not exceeding £2 for each day on which the offence is so continued.

(7) Where in the opinion of a highway authority an improvement line prescribed by them under this section, or any part of such a line, is no longer necessary or desirable and should be revoked, they may revoke the line or that part of it.

(8) Schedule 9 to this Act has effect in relation to the prescription of an improvement line under this section and to the revocation of such a line or any part of it.

(9) Any person whose property is injuriously affected by the prescribing of an improvement line under this section is, subject to the following provisions thereof, entitled to recover from the authority who prescribed the line compensation for the injury sustained.

(10) A person is not entitled to compensation on account of any building erected, contract made, or other thing done, after the date on which a plan showing the improvement line was deposited in accordance with the provisions of paragraph 5 of Schedule 9 to this Act, except as regards work done for the purpose of finishing a building the erection of which had begun before that date, or of carrying out a contract made before that date.

(11) Nothing in this section applies to or affects, without the consent of the undertakers concerned—

   (a) any property occupied or used by railway undertakers for the purposes of a railway comprised in the railway undertaking ; or

   (b) any property belonging to any of the following undertakers and used by them for the following purposes respectively, that is to say, by canal undertakers for those of a canal comprised in the canal undertaking, by inland navigation undertakers for those of a navigation comprised in the inland navigation undertaking, by dock undertakers for those of a dock comprised in the dock undertaking, or by harbour undertakers for those of a harbour comprised in the harbour undertaking ; or

(c) any land used by gas undertakers for the manufacture or storage of gas, by electricity undertakers for the generation of electricity or by water undertakers as a pumping station or reservoir for water.

A consent required by this subsection shall not be unreasonably withheld, and any question whether the withholding of such a consent is unreasonable shall, except where the street in question is one for which the Minister is the highway authority, be determined by the Secretary of State.

(12) In relation to any prohibition or restriction on the use of land or buildings imposed by the Minister by the prescription of an improvement line under this section or by virtue of any condition imposed by him in connection with the giving of a consent under subsection (2) above, section 1(1)(c) of the Local Land Charges Act 1975 shall have effect as if the references to 1975 c. 76. the date of the commencement of that Act were omitted.

(13) In this section " building " includes any erection however, and with whatever material, it is constructed and any part of a building, and " new building " includes any addition to an existing building.

74.—(1) Subject to the provisions of this section, a highway Power to authority may prescribe, in relation to either one side or both prescribe a building line. sides of a highway maintainable at the public expense for which they are the highway authority, a frontage line for building (in this section referred to as a " building line ").

(2) Where a building line prescribed under this section in relation to any highway is in force, no new building, other than a boundary wall or fence, shall be erected, and no permanent excavation below the level of the highway shall be made, nearer to the centre line of the highway than the building line, except with the consent of the authority who prescribed the line ; and the authority may give a consent for such period and subject to such conditions as they deem expedient.

(3) The prohibition imposed by subsection (2) above does not affect any right of light railway, tramway, electricity, gas or

water undertakers to make an excavation for the purpose of laying, altering, maintaining or renewing any main, pipe, electric line, duct or other apparatus.

(4) A condition imposed in connection with the giving of a consent under subsection (2) above is binding on the successor in title to every owner, and on every lessee and every occupier, of any land to which it relates.

(5) If a person contravenes the provisions of this section, or any condition imposed in connection with the giving of a consent under it, he is, without prejudice to any other proceedings which may be available against him, guilty of an offence and liable to a fine not exceeding £25 ; and if the offence is continued after conviction, he is guilty of a further offence and liable to a fine not exceeding £2 for each day on which the offence is so continued.

(6) Where in the opinion of a highway authority a building line prescribed by them under this section, or any part of such a line, is no longer necessary or desirable and should be revoked, they may revoke the line or that part of it.

(7) Schedule 9 to this Act has effect in relation to the prescription of a building line under this section and to the revocation of such line or any part of it.

(8) Any person whose property is injuriously affected by the prescribing of a building line under this section is entitled, subject to subsection (9) below, to recover from the authority who prescribed the line compensation for the injury sustained.

(9) A person is not entitled to compensation under subsection (8) above—

(a) unless he made a claim within 6 months from the date on which the building line was prescribed or, if the claimant is a person to whom a notice of the prescribing of the line was required to be given by paragraph 8 of Schedule 9 to this Act, within 6 months from the date on which such a notice was given to him ; or

(b) on account of anything done by him after the date on which a notice of the proposal to prescribe the line was served on him, except so far as it was done for the purpose of finishing a building the erection of which had begun before that date, or of carrying out a contract made before that date.

(10) Any two or more authorities on whom powers are conferred by this section may by agreement exercise those powers jointly, and the agreement may provide for the apportionment of any expenses incurred under it.

(11) Nothing in this section applies to or affects, without the consent of the undertakers concerned—

> (*a*) any land belonging to any of the following undertakers, and held by them for the following purposes respectively, that is to say, by railway undertakers for those of a railway comprised in the railway undertaking, by canal undertakers for those of a canal comprised in the canal undertaking, by inland navigation undertakers for those of a navigation comprised in the inland navigation undertaking, by dock undertakers for those of a dock comprised in the dock undertaking, or by harbour undertakers for those of a harbour comprised in the harbour undertaking ; or

> (*b*) any land used by gas undertakers for the manufacture or storage of gas, by electricity undertakers for the generation of electricity or by water undertakers as a pumping station or reservoir for water.

A consent required by this subsection shall not be unreasonably withheld, and any question whether the withholding of such a consent is unreasonable shall, except where the highway in question is one for which the Minister is the highway authority, be determined by the Minister.

(12) In relation to any prohibition or restriction on the use of land or buildings imposed by the Minister by the prescription of a building line under this section or by virtue of any condition imposed by him in connection with the giving of a consent under subsection (2) above, section 1(1)(c) of the Local Land Charges Act 1975 has effect as if the reference to the date 1975 c. 76. of the commencement of that Act were omitted.

(13) In this section—

> " building " and " new building " have the same meaning respectively as in section 73 above ; and

> " light railway undertakers " means persons authorised by any enactment to carry on a light railway undertaking.

75.—(1) Where a highway maintainable at the public expense comprises both a footway or footways and a carriageway, the highway authority may vary the relative widths of the carriageway and of any footway.

(2) Where any part of a highway is carried by a bridge over a railway, canal, inland navigation, dock or harbour or forms the approaches to such a bridge, the powers conferred by this section shall not be exercised in relation to that part without the consent of the railway, canal, inland navigation, dock or harbour undertakers concerned.

(3) A consent required by subsection (2) above shall not be unreasonably withheld, and any question whether the withholding of such consent is unreasonable shall be determined by the Minister.

Levels

Levelling
of highways.
76. A highway authority may execute works for levelling a highway maintainable at the public expense by them.

Alteration
of levels.
77.—(1) Without prejudice to section 76 above, a highway authority may raise or lower or otherwise alter, as they think fit, the level of a highway maintainable at the public expense by them.

(2) A highway authority shall pay compensation to any person who sustains damage by reason of the execution by them of works under this section.

Corners

Cutting off
of corners.
78. A highway authority may execute works for cutting off the corners of a highway maintainable at the public expense by them.

Prevention of
obstruction
to view at
corners.
79.—(1) Where, in the case of a highway maintainable at the public expense, the highway authority for the highway deem it necessary for the prevention of danger arising from obstruction to the view of persons using the highway to impose restrictions with respect to any land at or near any corner or bend in the highway or any junction of the highway with a road to which the public has access, the authority may, subject to the provisions of this section, serve a notice, together with a plan showing the land to which the notice relates,—

(a) on the owner or occupier of the land, directing him to alter any wall (other than a wall forming part of the structure of a permanent edifice), fence, hoarding, paling, tree, shrub or other vegetation on the land so as to cause it to conform with any requirements specified in the notice; or

(b) on every owner, lessee and occupier of the land, restraining them either absolutely or subject to such conditions as may be specified in the notice from causing or permitting any building, wall, fence, hoarding, paling, tree, shrub or other vegetation to be erected or planted on the land.

(2) A notice under subsection (1) above may at any time be withdrawn by the authority by whom it was given.

(3) A notice restraining the erection of any building on land shall not be served by a highway authority except with the consent of the council of the district in which the land is situated or if the land is situated in a London borough or the City and the highway authority concerned is the Greater London Council or the Minister, with the consent of the council of that London borough or the Common Council, as the case may require.

(4) A copy of a notice under subsection (1)(*a*) above shall be served on the owner or on the occupier of any land according as the notice was served on the occupier or on the owner of it.

(5) A notice under subsection (1)(*b*) above does not prevent any owner, lessee or occupier of any land from executing or permitting the reconstruction or repair, in such manner as not to create any new obstruction to the view of persons using the adjacent highways, of any building which was on the land before the service of the notice.

(6) A restriction imposed by a notice under subsection (1) above comes into force on the service of the notice and, while in force, is binding on the successor in title to every owner, and on every lessee and every occupier, of the land to which it relates.

(7) A person on whom a notice has been served under subsection (1) above may, within 14 days from the date of the receipt of the notice by him, give notice to the authority by whom the notice was given objecting to any requirement specified in it, or to any restriction imposed by it, and stating reasons for his objections.

(8) Where notice is given under subsection (7) above the question whether the notice under subsection (1) above is to be withdrawn as respects any requirement or restriction objected to shall be determined, if the parties so agree, by a single arbitrator appointed by them and, in default of agreement, shall be determined by a county court, and in determining a question under this subsection the arbitrator or court shall have power to order that the requirement or restriction objected to shall have effect subject to such modifications, if any, as the arbitrator or court may direct.

(9) A person on whom a notice is served under subsection (1) above may, notwithstanding anything in any conveyance, or in

PART V

any lease or other agreement, do all such things as may be necessary for complying with the requirements of the notice.

(10) Subject to the provisions of this section, if a person on whom a notice is served under subsection (1) above contravenes the provisions of the notice, he is, without prejudice to any other proceedings which may be available against him, guilty of an offence and liable to a fine not exceeding £25 ; and if the offence is continued after conviction, he is guilty of a further offence and liable to a fine not exceeding £2 for each day on which the offence is so continued.

(11) Any person sustaining loss in direct consequence of any requirement of a notice served under subsection (1) above, and any person who proves that his property is injuriously affected by restrictions imposed by a notice served under that subsection, is entitled, if he makes a claim within 6 months from the date of service of the notice, to recover from the authority by whom the notice was served compensation for the injury sustained.

(12) A person on whom a notice is served under subsection (1) above is entitled to recover from the authority by whom the notice was served any expenses reasonably incurred by him in carrying out any directions contained in the notice.

(13) If any question arises under subsection (12) above whether any expenses were reasonably incurred by any person as there provided, it shall be determined, if the parties so agree, by a single arbitrator appointed by them and, in default of agreement, shall be determined by a county court.

(14) Any two or more authorities on whom powers are conferred by this section may by agreement exercise those powers jointly, and the agreement may provide for the apportionment of any expenses incurred under it.

(15) Nothing in this section—

    (a) authorises the service by a local highway authority of a notice under this section with respect to any wall forming part of an ancient monument or other object of archaeological interest, except with the consent of the Secretary of State ; or

    (b) applies with respect to a wall belonging to any of the following undertakers, that is to say, railway undertakers, canal undertakers, inland navigation undertakers, dock undertakers, or harbour undertakers, where the wall forms part of or is necessary for the maintenance of a railway comprised in the railway undertaking, a canal comprised in the canal undertaking, a navigation comprised in the inland navigation undertaking, a dock comprised in the dock undertaking, or a harbour comprised in the harbour undertaking.

(16) In relation to any prohibition or restriction on the use of land or buildings imposed by the Minister by a notice served by him under this section, section 1(1)(c) of the Local Land Charges Act 1975 has effect as if the references to the date of the commencement of that Act were omitted.

PART V
1975 c. 76.

(17) In this section—

"building" includes any erection however, and with whatever material, it is constructed, and any part of a building;

"wall" includes any partition, with whatever material it is constructed, and any bank.

Fences and boundaries

80.—(1) Subject to the provisions of this section, a highway authority may erect and maintain fences or posts for the purpose of preventing access to—

Power to fence highways.

   (a) a highway maintainable at the public expense by them,

   (b) land on which in accordance with plans made or approved by the Minister they are for the time being constructing or intending to construct a highway shown in the plans which is to be a highway so maintainable, or

   (c) land on which in pursuance of a scheme under section 16 above, or of an order under section 14 or 18 above, they are for the time being constructing or intending to construct a highway.

(2) A highway authority may alter or remove a fence or post erected by them under this section.

(3) The powers conferred by this section shall not be exercised so as to—

   (a) interfere with a fence or gate required for the purpose of agriculture; or

   (b) obstruct a public right of way; or

   (c) obstruct any means of access for the construction, formation or laying out of which planning permission has been granted under Part III of the Town and Country Planning Act 1971 (or under any enactment replaced by the said Part III); or

1971 c. 78.

   (d) obstruct any means of access which was constructed, formed or laid out before 1st July 1948, unless it was constructed, formed or laid out in contravention of restrictions in force under section 1 or 2 of the Restriction of Ribbon Development Act 1935.

1935 c. 47.

PART V

(4) As respects—

(a) a highway that is a trunk road, and

(b) land on which the Minister is for the time being constructing or intending to construct a highway that is, or is to be, a trunk road, either in accordance with plans made by him in which the road is shown or in pursuance of a scheme under section 16 above,

the powers under this section may be exercised not only by the Minister but also, where the road or land is outside Greater London, by the council of the county in which it is situated, or where the road or land is in Greater London, by the Greater London Council and the council of the London borough in which it is situated.

Provision of highway boundary posts.

81. A highway authority may erect and maintain, in a highway for which they are the highway authority, posts or stones to mark the boundary of the highway and may alter or remove any post or stone erected by them under this section.

Cattle-grids

Provision of cattle-grids and by-passes.

82.—(1) Where, whether on the representations of owners or occupiers of agricultural land or otherwise, and after such consultation with any such owners and occupiers as the highway authority consider requisite, it appears to the highway authority for a highway which consists of or comprises a carriageway expedient so to do for controlling the passage of animals along the highway, the authority may, subject to the provisions of this section and sections 83 to 90 below, provide for the highway, and maintain, a cattle-grid in the highway or partly in the highway and partly in adjoining land.

(2) Where a highway authority provide a cattle-grid under this Act they shall also provide, either by means of a gate or other works on the highway or by means of a by-pass, or partly by one of those means and partly by the other, and maintain, facilities for the passage under proper control of animals and all other traffic that is unable to pass over the cattle-grid and is entitled by law to go along the highway.

(3) Save as provided by subsection (4) below, the powers conferred by the foregoing provisions of this section do not include power to place any part of a cattle-grid in land not forming part of the highway and not belonging to the highway authority, or to provide a by-pass on land not belonging to the highway authority, except in so far as is authorised by any such agreement as is provided for by section 87 below.

(4) Where after complying with the provisions of Schedule 10 to this Act the highway authority determine, as respects any common or waste land not forming part of the highway but

adjoining the highway or adjacent thereto, that it is expedient so to do, the authority may place any part of a cattle-grid in, or provide a by-pass on, any of that land notwithstanding that it does not form part of the highway and does not belong to the authority.

(5) Without prejudice to subsection (3) above, a highway authority shall not provide a by-pass along any part of a highway unless, after complying with the provisions of Schedule 10 to this Act, the authority determine that it is expedient so to do.

(6) In this Act—

" cattle-grid " means a device designed to prevent the passage of animals, or animals of any particular description, but to allow the passage of all or some other traffic, and includes any fence or other works necessary for securing the efficient operation of the said device ; and

" by-pass ", in relation to a cattle-grid provided for a highway, means a way, over land not comprised within the limits of the highway, for the traffic for which the by-pass is provided, with a public right of way thereover—

(a) for that traffic, or

(b) if any part of the by-pass is provided along an existing highway, for that traffic and for any other traffic entitled to use the highway before the by-pass was provided,

subject in either case to the limitation that there may be placed on the way any such gate or other works as may be necessary for the proper control of all or any of such traffic and the efficient operation of the cattle-grid for use in connection with which the by-pass is provided ;

and references in this Act to the provision or maintenance of a by-pass include references to the provision or maintenance of any such gate or other works.

(7) Subject to subsection (8) below, a highway authority may alter or improve—

(a) a cattle-grid or by-pass provided under this Act for a highway for which they are the highway authority ;

(b) any works provided for use in connection with such a cattle-grid or provided for the purposes of such a by-pass.

(8) A highway authority shall not carry out any alteration or improvement under subsection (7) above whereby traffic of a description which before the alteration or improvement could lawfully have gone along the highway (either by passing over the

PART V

cattle-grid or by going through a gate or along a by-pass provided under subsection (2) above) will be prevented from so going along the highway.

Removal of
cattle-grids
and dis-
continuance
of by-passes.

83.—(1) Where it appears to a highway authority, after such consultation with such owners and such occupiers of agricultural land as the highway authority consider requisite, that a cattle-grid provided under this Act for a highway for which they are the highway authority is no longer required, the authority may remove the cattle-grid and any gate or other works on the highway which have been provided for use in connection with it, making good the site thereof.

(2) Where a by-pass has been provided for use in connection with a cattle-grid and the highway authority remove the cattle-grid they may direct that the by-pass is to be discontinued, and where they give such a direction they may remove all or any of the works provided for the purposes of the by-pass.

(3) If a direction under subsection (2) above so provides, then as from such date as may be specified in the direction the public right of way over the by-pass shall be extinguished.

(4) Where a by-pass or any part of one has been provided along an existing highway, then—

   (a) notwithstanding subsection (3) above, a direction under subsection (2) above shall not extinguish any right of way which existed before the by-pass was provided ;

   (b) if the cattle-grid for use in connection with which the by-pass was provided is removed, as soon as may be thereafter the highway authority shall (whether or not they direct that the by-pass is to be discontinued, but without prejudice to their power to remove works under subsection (2) above if they do so direct) remove so much of the works provided for the purpose of the by-pass as obstructs the exercise of any right of way existing before the by-pass was provided.

Maintenance
of cattle-grids
and by-passes.

84.—(1) A cattle-grid provided under this Act for a highway, a gate or other works on a highway provided for use in connection with such a cattle-grid, and any works provided for the purposes of a by-pass provided under this Act, are maintainable by the highway authority for the highway.

(2) A by-pass provided under this Act shall, unless and until the highway authority give a direction discontinuing the by-pass, in all cases be a highway which for the purposes of this Act is a highway maintainable at the public expense for which that authority are the highway authority.

85.—(1) Where a highway maintainable at the public expense is intersected, joined or continued by a highway for which the highway authority are an authority other than the highway authority for the first-mentioned highway, the following provi- sions have effect.

(2) The highway authority for the first mentioned highway (" the first authority ") and the other authority (" the second authority ") may enter into an agreement as to the exercise by the second authority of that authority's powers under sections 82 and 83 above in relation to the highway for which they are the highway authority; and any such agreement may provide for the first authority to defray the whole or any part of the expenses incurred by the second authority in consequence of the agreement.

(3) The second authority shall not unreasonably refuse to enter into an agreement under this section; and if any question arises as to the terms (including terms as to payments) to be included in such an agreement, or whether the refusal of that authority to enter into such an agreement is unreasonable, the question shall be determined by arbitration.

86.—(1) Where—

    (*a*) any person has the right to install a gate or gates in a highway, and

    (*b*) a highway authority providing or proposing to provide a cattle-grid in the highway under section 82 above determine, after complying with the provisions of Schedule 10 to this Act, that the purpose for which the above-mentioned right is exercisable will be adequately achieved by the provision of the cattle-grid,

the right is not exercisable, so long as the cattle-grid is provided, except with the approval of the highway authority, and the highway authority may require that a gate or gates installed in the exercise of the right before the provision of the cattle-grid shall be removed or may themselves remove any such gate or gates.

(2) The highway authority shall on demand repay any expenses reasonably incurred in removing a gate in compliance with a requirement under this section.

(3) Where in pursuance of subsection (1) above a gate has been removed (whether by, or in compliance with a requirement of, the highway authority) and the highway authority subsequently remove the cattle-grid, then, if within 12 months from the date of the removal of the cattle-grid a person reinstalls a gate in the exercise of a right the exercise of which was suspended while the cattle-grid was provided, the highway

PART V   authority shall on demand repay the expenses reasonably incurred in reinstalling the gate.

(4) No objection shall be made or proceedings brought in respect of the purported exercise by a highway authority of their powers under subsection (1) above as respects a gate or gates on the ground that no right to install the gate or gates existed ; but the purported exercise by the authority of their powers under that subsection shall not affect the question whether any such right existed, or prejudice the powers of the highway authority or any other person under any enactment (including an enact-ment in this Act) or rule of law to protect public rights of way or to prevent or remove obstructions.

Agreements for use of land for cattle-grids or by-passes.

87.—(1) A highway authority may, for the purpose of provid-ing, altering or improving a cattle-grid or by-pass under the powers conferred by this Part of this Act, enter into an agree-ment under this section with persons interested in any land for the use of the land for that purpose ; and (without prejudice to the provision of other matters in the agreement) there shall be exercisable by the highway authority and the public such rights over the land as may be specified in the agreement.

(2) An agreement under this section may contain provisions for payment to persons who are parties to it in consideration of the use of the land or otherwise in respect of their entering into the agreement.

(3) The provisions of an agreement under this section bind the interest of any person who is a party to the agreement notwith-standing any devolution of that interest, and also bind any interest of any person which is thereafter created (whether imme-diately or not) out of that interest ; but save as aforesaid an agreement under this section shall not operate so as to prejudice the rights of a person not a party to it or confer upon any other person any right against him.

(4) A tenant for life may enter into an agreement under this section relating to the settled land or any part of it either for consideration or gratuitously, and—

1925 c. 18.   (a) this subsection is to be construed as one with the Settled Land Act 1925 ;

1925 c. 20.   (b) that Act and section 28 of the Law of Property Act 1925 (which confers the powers of a tenant for life on trustees for sale), apply as if the power conferred by this subsection had been conferred by that Act ; and

(c) for the purposes of section 72 of the Settled Land Act 1925 (disposition by a tenant for life) and of any other relevant statutory provision, entering into an agreement under this section is to be treated as a disposition.   PART V

(5) A university or college to which the Universities and College Estates Act 1925 applies may enter into an agreement under this section relating to any land belonging to it either for consideration or gratuitously, and that Act applies as if the power conferred by this subsection had been conferred by that Act.   1925 c. 24.

(6) Where land is glebe land or other land belonging to an ecclesiastical benefice, the incumbent of the benefice and, where land is part of the endowment of any other ecclesiastical corporation, the ecclesiastical corporation, may with the consent of the Church Commissioners enter into an agreement under this section relating to the land either for consideration or gratuitously, and the Ecclesiastical Leasing Acts apply as if the power conferred by this subsection had been conferred by those Acts, except that the consent of the patron of an ecclesiastical benefice is not requisite.

(7) An agreement under this section is a local land charge.

88.—(1) A highway authority may enter into an agreement with a person at whose instance a cattle-grid has been or is to be provided by them under this Act, or any other person willing to make a contribution towards expenses of the authority under this Act in connection with a cattle-grid, for the making by that person of such a contribution (whether by a single payment or by periodical payments) of such amount as may be specified in the agreement and either towards all such expenditure of the authority or towards such description of such expenditure as may be so specified.   Contributions towards expenditure of highway authorities.

(2) An agreement under this section may contain such incidental and consequential provisions as appear to the parties to it expedient for the purposes of the agreement, and in particular such an agreement providing for a contribution towards the cost of installing a cattle-grid may provide for repayment of the contribution, to such extent as may be specified in the agreement, in the event of the cattle-grid being removed.

(3) In determining whether or not to provide a cattle-grid, a highway authority shall be entitled to have regard to the extent to which persons who in the opinion of the authority will derive special benefit from the provision of the cattle-grid are willing to enter into agreements under this section.

D 2

PART V
Delegation
to certain
authorities
of functions
of Minister.

89.—(1) Subsections (1) to (4) of section 6 above apply, as respects trunk roads, to the functions of the Minister under the foregoing provisions of this Part of this Act relating to cattle-grids, and to his functions under Schedule 10 to this Act in so far as they are conferred on him as highway authority.

(2) Plant or materials belonging to a council to whom functions are delegated under this section may be used by them for the purposes of those functions, subject to the terms of the delegation.

Protection
of bridges
and railways.

90.—(1) A highway authority shall not, in the exercise of functions relating to cattle-grids conferred by this Part of this Act, carry out any work in—

(*a*) so much of a highway as is carried by a bridge maintainable by a person other than the highway authority or so much of a highway as is comprised within the immediate approaches to such a bridge,

(*b*) so much of a highway passing under such a bridge as is within 10 feet of any part of the bridge or of the foundations of the bridge, or

(*c*) so much (if any) of a highway passing above a tunnel provided for the purpose of a railway undertaking of railway undertakers as is within 10 feet of any part of the tunnel,

except with the consent of the person liable to maintain the bridge or of the railway undertakers, as the case may be.

(2) Where consent under this section is withheld the highway authority may refer the matter to the Minister and if, after affording to the highway authority and to the said person, or to the railway undertakers, as the case may be, an opportunity of being heard by a person appointed by the Minister for the purpose, and considering his report, the Minister so directs, the work may be carried out notwithstanding that the consent has been withheld but subject to compliance with any conditions which the Minister may impose.

Construction, reconstruction, improvement etc. of bridges

Construction
of bridge
to carry
existing
highway
maintainable
at public
expense.

91. A highway authority may construct a bridge to carry a highway maintainable at the public expense but the Minister shall not construct such a bridge without the approval of the Treasury.

92. Without prejudice to any other powers they have under this Part of this Act, a highway authority may reconstruct a bridge which is a highway maintainable at the public expense by them, either on the same site or on a new site within 200 yards of the old one.

93.—(1) If the owners of a bridge to which this section applies or a local highway authority entitled by virtue of section 95 below to exercise with respect to such a bridge the powers conferred by this section consider—

(*a*) that the bridge is or may be, by reason of its construction, position, or state of repair, dangerous or unsuitable for the requirements of road traffic as then existing or the expected development thereof, or

(*b*) that the responsibility for the maintenance and improvement of the highway carried by the bridge or of the approaches to it should for any reason be transferred from the owners to a highway authority,

the owners or the authority may apply to the Minister for an order to provide for the reconstruction, improvement or maintenance of the bridge, or of the highway carried by the bridge, or of the approaches to the bridge.

(2) Where an application is made to the Minister under subsection (1) above, he may, subject to the provisions of this section, make an order under this section, but before making such an order he shall consult the owners of the bridge and every local highway authority entitled to exercise with respect to it the powers conferred by this section, and if either the owners or any such local highway authority request him so to do shall hold an inquiry.

(3) Subject to the provisions of this section, the Minister may by an order made under this section—

(*a*) require the execution, either by the owners or by a highway authority, of such works of reconstruction or improvement as may be specified in the order;

(*b*) determine and direct by whom the bridge, the highway carried by the bridge and the approaches to the bridge are to be maintained;

(*c*) provide for the transfer to and vesting in a highway authority of the property in the bridge, or the highway carried by the bridge, or the approaches to the bridge, and of all or any rights and obligations attaching to the bridge, or to such highway or approaches;

(*d*) in the case of a swing bridge, determine and direct by whom and in what manner it is to be operated ;

(*e*) modify, so far as he considers necessary for giving effect to the order, any statutory provisions applicable to the bridge other than the provisions of a public general Act ;

(*f*) make such incidental, consequential and supplementary provisions, including provisions authorising the owners of the bridge or a highway authority to construct works which are necessary to enable them to comply with a requirement or direction contained in the order, as may appear to him to be necessary or proper for the purposes of the order.

(4) Subject to the provisions of this section, the Minister may, on his own initiative and without any application under subsection (1) above, make an order under this section with respect to a trunk road bridge if, on such grounds as are referred to in subsection (1) above, it seems to him fit and proper so to do ; but, before making such an order, he shall consult the owners of the bridge (unless after diligent inquiry their names and addresses cannot be ascertained), and, if the owners request him so to do, shall hold an inquiry.

(5) In relation to an order made under this section with respect to a trunk road bridge, subsection (3)(*c*) above has effect with the substitution, for the reference to a highway authority, of a reference to the Minister.

(6) Subject to section 95(9) below, this section applies to any bridge (other than a highway maintainable at the public expense) which carries a highway consisting of or comprising a carriageway over a railway, over a canal, river, creek, watercourse, marsh or other place where water flows or is collected or over a ravine or other depression, other than a bridge to which a right to levy tolls is attached.

(7) Schedule 11 to this Act has effect in relation to the making and carrying out of orders under this section.

Powers of highway authorities and bridge owners to enter into agreements.

94.—(1) A highway authority may agree with the owners of a bridge to which this section applies and with respect to which the highway authority are entitled by virtue of section 95 below to exercise the powers conferred by this section—

(*a*) for the payment by the highway authority of contributions towards the cost of the reconstruction, improvement or maintenance of the bridge, or of the highway carried by the bridge, or of the approaches to the bridge ;

(*b*) for the transfer to the highway authority, on such terms as may be agreed, of the responsibility for the improvement and maintenance of the highway carried by the bridge, or of the approaches to it ;

(*c*) for the transfer to the highway authority, on such terms as may be agreed, of the property in the bridge, the highway carried by the bridge, and the approaches to the bridge, and of all or any rights and obligations attaching to the bridge, or to such highway or approaches ;

and the owners of the bridge may enter into and carry into effect any such agreement, notwithstanding that the bridge was constructed under statutory powers.

(2) Subject to section 95(9) below, this section applies to any bridge (other than a highway maintainable at the public expense) which carries a highway over a railway or highway, over a canal, river, creek, watercourse, marsh or other place where water flows or is collected or over a ravine or other depression.

(3) Where an agreement made under this section provides for the transfer to the highway authority of rights or obligations attaching to a bridge, then as from the date of the transfer the highway authority may exercise the rights transferred and shall, to the exclusion of the owners, be subject to the obligations transferred.

95.—(1) Subject to subsection (2) below, the powers conferred by sections 93 and 94 above on a highway authority or a local highway authority are exercisable— *Supplemental provisions as to orders and agreements under sections 93 and 94.*

(*a*) in the case of a bridge outside Greater London, by the council of the county in which the bridge is situated ;

(*b*) in the case of a bridge in Greater London the highway over which is a metropolitan road or partly a metropolitan road, by the Greater London Council ;

(*c*) in the case of any other bridge in Greater London, by the council of the borough in which it is situated, or, if it is in the City, by the Common Council.

(2) In the case of a trunk road bridge, the powers conferred on a highway authority by section 94 above are exercisable by the Minister ; and neither those powers nor the powers conferred on a local highway authority by section 93 above are exercisable with respect to such a bridge by a local highway authority.

(3) Where a bridge other than a trunk road bridge is situated partly in one area and partly in another, the powers conferred by sections 93 and 94 above on a highway authority or a local highway authority are exercisable by the council who, by virtue of section 3 above, are the highway authority for the whole of the bridge or, if there is no such highway authority, by any council who could have exercised those powers if their area had included the whole of the bridge.

(4) For the purposes of the foregoing provisions of this section, the highway carried by a bridge, and the approaches to the bridge, are to be deemed to be part of the bridge.

(5) Where—

> (*a*) a bridge crossing a railway is owned by railway under-takers and the railway is leased to other such under-takers, or
>
> (*b*) a bridge crossing a canal is owned by canal undertakers and the canal is leased to other such undertakers,

references in sections 93 and 94 above and in this section to the owners of the bridge, railway or canal include references to those other undertakers.

(6) Nothing in sections 93 and 94 above or in this section or in any order made under section 93 above, authorises the stop-page of traffic on a canal without the consent of the canal owners, and a highway authority carrying out works authorised by any of the said sections, or by any such order, with respect to a bridge crossing a canal shall take such steps as may be necessary to prevent, so far as practicable, interference with traffic on the canal.

(7) The consent of the owners of a canal to the temporary stoppage of traffic on it pursuant to subsection (6) above shall not be unreasonably withheld, and any question whether the withholding of such a consent is unreasonable shall be deter-mined by the Minister.

(8) In sections 93 and 94 above and in this section—

> " approaches " in relation to a bridge, means approaches for the maintenance of which the owners of the bridge are responsible and which connect the bridge to the highway maintainable at the public expense ;
>
> " trunk road bridge " means a bridge the highway over which is a trunk road or partly a trunk road ;
>
> " canal " includes inland navigation ;

and for the purposes of the said sections the towing path of a canal is to be deemed to form part of the canal.

(9) Sections 93 and 94 above and this section do not apply to any bridge which crosses the Manchester Ship Canal and is owned by the Manchester Ship Canal Company.

Miscellaneous improvements

96.—(1) Subject to the provisions of this section, a highway authority may, in a highway maintainable at the public expense by them, plant trees and shrubs and lay out grass verges, and may erect and maintain guards or fences and otherwise do anything expedient for the maintenance or protection of trees, shrubs and grass verges planted or laid out, whether or not by them, in such a highway.

Powers of highway and local authorities to plant trees, lay out grass verges, etc.

(2) A highway authority may alter or remove any grass verge laid out, whether or not by them, in a highway maintainable at the public expense by them and any guard, fence or other thing provided, whether or not by them, for the maintenance or protection of any tree, shrub or verge in such a highway.

(3) Subject to the following provisions of this section, a highway authority may exercise the like powers as are conferred by subsections (1) and (2) above on any land acquired in exercise of powers conferred on them by section 239(2) to (4) below, notwithstanding that the land does not form part of a highway.

(4) A local authority, if they are not the highway authority for a highway maintainable at the public expense in their area, may, with the consent of the highway authority, exercise with respect to that highway any of the powers conferred by subsections (1) and (2) above on the highway authority.

(5) Subject to the restrictions for the time being imposed by any enactment on their expenditure, the council of a parish or community may, with the consent of the highway authority for a highway maintainable at the public expense in the parish or community, exercise with respect to that highway any of the powers conferred by subsections (1) and (2) above on the highway authority.

(6) No tree, shrub, grass verge, guard or fence shall be planted, laid out or erected under this section, or, if planted, laid out or erected under this section, allowed to remain, in such a situation as to hinder the reasonable use of the highway by any person entitled to use it, or so as to be a nuisance or injurious to the owner or occupier of premises adjacent to the highway.

(7) If damage is caused to the property of any person by anything done in exercise of the powers conferred by this section, that person is entitled, subject to subsection (8) below, to

recover compensation for it from the authority or parish or community council by whom the powers were exercised.

(8) A person is not entitled to compensation under subsection (7) above if his negligence caused the damage; and if his negligence contributed to the damage the compensation under that subsection shall be reduced accordingly.

(9) Any two or more highway authorities on whom powers are conferred by this section may by agreement exercise those powers jointly, and the agreement may provide for the apportionment of any expenses incurred under it.

(10) References in this section to trees or shrubs are to be construed as including references to plants of any description.

Lighting of highways.

97.—(1) The Minister and every local highway authority may provide lighting for the purposes of any highway or proposed highway for which they are or will be the highway authority, and may for that purpose—

    (*a*) contract with any persons for the supply of gas, electricity or other means of lighting; and

    (*b*) construct and maintain such lamps, posts and other works as they consider necessary.

(2) A highway authority may alter or remove any works constructed by them under this section or vested in them under Part III of the Local Government Act 1966 or section 270 below.

1966 c. 42.

(3) A highway authority shall pay compensation to any person who sustains damage by reason of the execution of works under this section.

1961 c. 64.

(4) Section 45 of the Public Health Act 1961 (attachment of street lamps to buildings) and section 81 of that Act (summary recovery of damages for negligence) apply to a highway authority who are not a council of a kind therein mentioned as they apply to such a council.

Delegation of lighting functions of highway authority.

98.—(1) A highway authority may agree with a lighting authority for the delegation to the lighting authority of any of the functions of the highway authority with respect to the lighting of any highway or part of a highway within the area of the lighting authority.

(2) A lighting authority shall, in the discharge of any functions delegated to them under subsection (1) above, act as agents

for the highway authority; and it shall be a condition of the delegation—

(a) that the works to be executed or expenditure to be incurred by the lighting authority in the discharge of the delegated functions are to be subject to the approval of the highway authority;

(b) that the lighting authority are to comply with any requirement of the highway authority as to the manner in which any such works are to be carried out, and with any directions of the highway authority as to the terms of contracts to be entered into for the purposes of the discharge of the delegated functions; and

(c) that any such works are to be completed to the satisfaction of the highway authority.

(3) If at any time the highway authority are satisfied that a lighting system in respect of which the functions of that authority are delegated under this section is not in proper repair or condition, they may give notice to the lighting authority requiring them to place it in proper repair or condition, and if the notice is not complied with within a reasonable time may themselves do anything which seems to them necessary to place the system in proper repair or condition.

(4) A highway authority may agree with a lighting authority for the carrying out by the lighting authority of any works in connection with a lighting system provided or to be provided by the highway authority within the area of the lighting authority; and subsections (2) and (3) above apply to the conditions to be included in and to the discharge of functions pursuant to any such agreement, as they apply to the conditions to be attached to a delegation of functions under subsection (1) above and the discharge of functions so delegated.

(5) A delegation to a lighting authority under this section may be determined by notice given to that authority by the highway authority during the first 9 months of any calendar year, and functions delegated to a lighting authority under this section may be relinquished by notice given by that authority to the highway authority during any such period; and any such notice shall take effect as from 1st April in the calendar year following that in which it is given.

99. A highway authority may, in relation to a highway maintainable at the public expense by them, execute works for the conversion of the highway into a metalled highway.

Metalling of highways.

100.—(1) The highway authority for a highway may, for the purpose of draining it or of otherwise preventing surface water from flowing on to it, do all or any of the following:—

> (*a*) construct or lay, in the highway or in land adjoining or lying near to the highway, such drains as they consider necessary ;
>
> (*b*) erect barriers in the highway or in such land as aforesaid to divert surface water into or through any existing drain;
>
> (*c*) scour, cleanse and keep open all drains situated in the highway or in such land as aforesaid.

(2) Where under subsection (1) above a drain is constructed or laid, or barriers are erected, for the purpose of draining surface water from a highway or, as the case may be, diverting it into an existing drain, the water may be discharged into or through that drain and into any inland waters, whether natural or artificial, or any tidal waters.

(3) A highway authority shall pay compensation to the owner or occupier of any land who suffers damage by reason of the exercise by the authority of any power under subsection (1) or (2) above.

(4) If a person, without the consent of the highway authority, alters, obstructs or interferes with a drain or barrier which has been constructed, laid or erected by the authority in exercise of their powers under subsection (1) above, or which is under their control, then—

> (*a*) the authority may carry out any work of repair or reinstatement necessitated by his action and may recover from him the expenses reasonably incurred by them in so doing, and
>
> (*b*) without prejudice to their right to exercise that power, he is guilty of an offence and liable to a fine not exceeding three times the amount of those expenses.

(5) Without prejudice to their powers under the foregoing provisions of this section, a highway authority may, for the purpose of the drainage of a highway or proposed highway for which they are or, as the case may be, will be the highway authority, exercise any powers exercisable by a water authority under the Public Health Act 1936 for the purposes of the drainage of highways within the area of that authority.

(6) Where the highway authority are a county council they shall, before exercising any powers under the Public Health Act 1936 by virtue of subsection (5) above, give notice of their intention to do so to the district council, and the water authority, within whose area the powers are proposed to be exercised.

(7) A person who is liable to maintain a highway by reason of tenure, enclosure or prescription shall, for the purpose of draining it, have the like powers as are conferred on a highway authority by subsections (1) and (2) above for that purpose, and subsections (3) and (4) above shall have effect in relation to a highway so maintainable as if references therein to a highway authority and to subsection (1) or (2) above included references to the person liable to maintain that highway and to this subsection respectively.

(8) This section is without prejudice to any enactment the purpose of which is to protect water against pollution.

(9) In this section—

" drain " includes a ditch, gutter, watercourse, soak-away, bridge, culvert, tunnel and pipe ; and

" owner ", in relation to any land, means a person, other than a mortgagee not in possession, who is for the time being entitled to dispose of the fee simple in the land, whether in possession or in reversion, and includes also a person holding or entitled to the rents and profits of the land under a lease the unexpired term of which exceeds 3 years.

101.—(1) If it appears to the highway authority for any highway that a ditch on land adjoining or lying near to the highway constitutes a danger to users of the highway, the authority may— Power to fill in roadside ditches etc.

(a) if they consider the ditch unnecessary for drainage purposes and any occupier of the land known to the authority agrees in writing that it is unnecessary for those purposes, fill it in ; or

(b) place in the ditch, or in land adjoining or lying near to it, such pipes as they consider necessary in substitution for the ditch, and thereafter fill it in.

(2) A highway authority shall pay compensation to the owner or occupier of any land who suffers damage by reason of the exercise by the authority of any power under subsection (1) above.

(3) If a person, without the consent of the highway authority, opens up or keeps open any ditch which has been filled in under subsection (1) above (except as may be reasonably necessary for the purpose of doing work on any pipes placed in the ditch), then—

(a) the authority may carry out any work of repair or reinstatement necessitated by his action and may recover from him the expenses reasonably incurred by them in so doing; and

(*b*) without prejudice to their right to exercise that power, he is guilty of an offence and liable to a fine not exceeding three times the amount of those expenses.

1936 c. 49   (4) Nothing in section 263 of the Public Health Act 1936 (which prohibits the culverting of watercourses in certain districts without the approval of the local authority) applies to anything done under subsection (1) above.

(5) A highway authority shall not exercise their powers under subsection (1) above in such a manner as to be likely to cause damage to or affect the drainage of any land or works used for the purposes of a railway or canal undertaking, except—

(*a*) after giving not less than 14 days' notice to the undertakers of the manner in which it is proposed to exercise those powers; and

(*b*) in accordance with any reasonable requirements of the undertakers of which notice is given to the authority within 14 days from the date of service of the authority's notice;

and any question whether any such requirement is reasonable shall, in default of agreement, be determined by the Minister.

(6) In this section, " ditch " includes a watercourse and any part of a ditch or watercourse, and " pipes " including culverts, tunnels and other works.

Provision of works for protecting highways against hazards of nature.   **102.**—(1) The highway authority for a highway maintainable at the public expense may provide and maintain such barriers or other works as they consider necessary for the purpose of affording to the highway protection against snow, flood, landslide or other hazards of nature; and those works may be provided on the highway or on land which, or rights over which, has or have been acquired by the highway authority in the exercise of highway land acquisition powers for that purpose.

(2) The powers conferred by subsection (1) above to provide any works shall include power to alter or remove them.

(3) A highway authority shall pay compensation to any person who suffers damage by reason of the execution by them under this section of any works on a highway.

Provision of posts to indicate depth of flood water.   **103.**—(1) It shall be the duty of a highway authority to provide, in connection with any highway for which they are the highway authority and which is subject to flooding to any considerable depth, graduated posts or stones in any case where they consider the provision thereof necessary or desirable for the purpose of indicating the depth of water covering the highway.

(2) A highway authority may alter or remove any post or stone provided by them under this section.

104. A highway authority may, in relation to a highway maintainable at the public expense by them, treat the highway for mitigating the nuisance of dust.

Mitigating nuisance of dust.

105. A highway authority may improve any road-ferry provided by them under this Act.

Power to improve road-ferries.

PART VI

CONSTRUCTION OF BRIDGES OVER AND TUNNELS UNDER NAVIGABLE WATERS AND DIVERSION ETC. OF WATERCOURSES

Construction of bridges over and tunnels under navigable waters

106.—(1) Provision may be made by an order made by the Minister under this subsection or under section 10 above (orders for trunk roads) for the construction of a bridge over or a tunnel under any specified navigable waters as part of a trunk road.

Orders and schemes providing for construction of bridges over or tunnels under navigable waters.

(2) Provision may be made by a scheme under section 16 above (schemes for special roads) for the construction of a bridge over or a tunnel under specified navigable waters as part of a special road.

(3) Provision may be made by a scheme made by a local highway authority under this subsection, and confirmed by the Minister, for the construction of a bridge over or a tunnel under specified navigable waters as part of a highway or proposed highway which is or is to be a highway (other than a special road) maintainable at the public expense by the authority.

(4) Provision may be made by an order under section 14 above (roads that cross or join trunk or classified roads) or section 18 above (supplementary orders relating to special roads)—

    (*a*) for the construction of a bridge over or tunnel under specified navigable waters as part of a highway which is to be altered or constructed in pursuance of the order ;

    (*b*) where the order authorises the highway authority by whom it is made to provide a new means of access to any premises from a highway, for the access to be provided by means of a bridge over specified navigable waters and for the construction of the bridge.

(5) Parts I and III of Schedule 1 to this Act have effect as to the making of an order under subsection (1) above, Parts II and III of that Schedule have effect as to the making of a scheme under subsection (3) above and Schedule 2 to this Act has effect as to the validity and date of operation of any such order or scheme.

(6) A scheme under subsection (3) above may be submitted to the Minister jointly by any two or more local highway authorities, and any such scheme may determine which of those authorities is to be the highway authority for the bridge or tunnel or any part of it, and may provide—

    (a) for the performance by that authority, in relation to the bridge or tunnel or that part of it, of any of the highway functions of any other authority who are party to the application, and

    (b) for the making of contributions by that other authority to the highway authority in respect of expenditure incurred in the performance of those functions.

(7) References in this section, in relation to any order or scheme, to specified navigable waters are references to such navigable waters (whether the sea, a river or other waters) as may be specified in the order or scheme.

(8) References in the following provisions of this Part of this Act to an order or scheme which provides for the construction of a bridge over or a tunnel under navigable waters are references to any order or scheme made under or by virtue of subsection (1), (2), (3) or (4) above.

Provisions supplementary to section 106.

107.—(1) Before making or confirming an order or scheme which provides for the construction of a bridge over or a tunnel under navigable waters, the Minister shall take into consideration the reasonable requirements of navigation over the waters affected by the order or scheme.

(2) An order or scheme which provides for the construction of such a bridge shall include such plans and specifications as may be necessary to indicate the position and dimensions of the proposed bridge including its spans, headways and waterways, and in the case of a swing bridge shall contain such provisions as the Minister considers expedient for regulating its operation.

(3) An order or scheme which provides for the construction of such a tunnel shall include such plans and specifications as may be necessary to indicate the position and dimensions of the

proposed tunnel, including its depth below the bed of the
navigable waters.

(4) If objection to an order or scheme proposed to be made
or, as the case may be, to an order or scheme made and proposed
to be confirmed, is duly made in accordance with Schedule 1
to this Act by any navigation authority or water authority on
whom notice is required to be served under paragraph 3 or,
as the case may be, paragraph 11 of that Schedule, on the
ground that the bridge or tunnel is likely to obstruct or impede
the performance of their functions under any enactment, or to
interfere with the reasonable requirements of navigation over
the waters affected by the order or scheme, as the case may be,
and the objection is not withdrawn, the order or scheme, as the
case may be, shall be subject to special parliamentary procedure.

Diversion etc. of watercourses

108.—(1) An order made under this subsection may authorise
a highway authority to divert such part of any navigable watercourse as may be specified in the order if, in the opinion of the
authority, the diversion of that part is necessary or desirable
in connection with— Power to divert navigable watercourses.

  (*a*) the construction, improvement or alteration of a
      highway;

  (*b*) the provision of a new means of access to any premises
      from a highway; or

  (*c*) the provision of a maintenance compound or, if that
      authority are a special road authority, of a service area.

(2) An order under subsection (1) above shall—

  (*a*) if the authority proposing to divert the watercourse is
      the Minister, be made by him; and

  (*b*) if that authority are a local highway authority, be made
      by that authority and confirmed by the Minister.

(3) Parts I and III of Schedule 1 to this Act have effect as to
the making of any order under subsection (1) above, and
Schedule 2 to this Act has effect as to the validity and date of
operation of any such order.

(4) An order or scheme which provides for the construction of
a bridge over or a tunnel under any navigable waters may
authorise the highway authority by whom the bridge or tunnel
is to be constructed to divert such part of any navigable watercourse as may be specified in the order or scheme if, in the
opinion of that authority, the diversion of that part is necessary
or desirable for purposes connected with the bridge or tunnel,
or its construction.

(5) An order under section 14 or 18 above may authorise the highway authority by whom the order is made to divert such part of any navigable watercourse as may be specified in the order if, in the opinion of that authority, the diversion of that part is necessary or desirable in connection with—

> (*a*) the construction or improvement of the trunk road, special road or classified road, as the case may be, to which the order relates ;
>
> (*b*) the construction or alteration of any other highway to which the order relates ;
>
> (*c*) the provision in pursuance of the order of a new means of access to any premises ; or
>
> (*d*) the provision of a maintenance compound in connection with the trunk road, special road or classified road, as the case may be, to which the order relates or, in the case of an order under section 18, the provision of a service area.

(6) Where by virtue of an order under subsection (1) above or an order or scheme falling within subsection (4) or (5) above a highway authority are authorised to divert any part of a navigable watercourse they may also divert any towing path or other way adjacent to that part.

Provisions supplementary to section 108.   **109.**—(1) Where a navigable watercourse is to be diverted in pursuance of an order under section 108(1) above or of any order or scheme falling within section 108(4) or (5) above, any new length of watercourse provided in pursuance of the order or scheme shall be such as will or, but for any bridge or tunnel constructed over or under it in pursuance of any order or scheme falling within section 108(4), would be navigable in a reasonably convenient manner by vessels of a kind which immediately before the date of the coming into operation of the order or scheme were accustomed to use that part of the watercourse which is to be replaced by the new length.

(2) Where works for the diversion of a watercourse are carried out by a highway authority in accordance with any such order or scheme and any person suffers damage in consequence thereof by the depreciation of any interest in any land to which he is entitled or by reason of the fact that his right of access to a watercourse is extinguished or interfered with then, unless the works are carried out on land, or in the exercise of rights, acquired compulsorily in the exercise of highway land acquisition powers, that person is entitled to recover from the highway authority compensation under this subsection in respect of that damage.

110.—(1) Subject to the provisions of this section, a highway authority may divert any part of a watercourse, other than a navigable watercourse, or carry out any other works on any part of a watercourse, including a navigable watercourse, if, in the opinion of that authority, the carrying out of the works is necessary or desirable in connection with— PART VI
Power to
divert
non-navigable
watercourses
and to carry
out other
works on any
watercourse.

   (*a*) the construction, improvement or alteration of a highway;

   (*b*) the provision of a new means of access to any premises from a highway; or

   (*c*) the provision of a maintenance compound, a trunk road picnic area, a lorry area or a service area.

(2) This section does not apply to any works which a highway authority are authorised to carry out by virtue of an order or scheme which has been made or confirmed in accordance with Schedule 1 to this Act.

(3) Before carrying out any works under this section, the highway authority shall consult every council in whose area the works are to be carried out.

(4) Where works are carried out by a highway authority under this section and any person suffers damage in consequence thereof by the depreciation of any interest in any land to which he is entitled or by reason of the fact that his right of access to a watercourse is extinguished or interfered with, then, unless the works are carried out on land, or in the exercise of rights, acquired compulsorily in the exercise of highway land acquisition powers, that person is entitled to recover from the highway authority compensation under this subsection in respect of the damage.

(5) Subject to subsection (7) below, a highway authority who propose to carry out any works under this section shall serve on the owner and the occupier of the land affected a notice stating their intention to carry out those works and describing them and informing him that he may within 28 days after service of the notice on him by notice to the authority object to the proposed works.

(6) If within that period the owner or occupier of the land affected objects to the proposed works and the objection is not withdrawn, then—

   (*a*) if the objection is to works proposed to be carried out by the Minister, he shall consider the objection before carrying them out; and

   (*b*) if the objection is to works proposed to be carried out by a local highway authority, they shall not carry them

PART VI

out without the consent of the Minister who may grant such consent either unconditionally or subject to such terms and conditions as he thinks just.

(7) Subsections (5) and (6) above do not have effect in relation to works that are to be carried out—

(a) on land that has been acquired by the highway authority in question, either compulsorily or by agreement, in the exercise of highway land acquisition powers, for the purpose of carrying out those works, or

(b) in the exercise of rights so acquired by that authority for that purpose.

Interpretation

Interpretation of Part VI.

111.—(1) In this Part of this Act " navigable waters " and " navigable watercourse " means waters or a watercourse, as the case may be, over which a public right of navigation exists ; and any waterway comprised in the undertaking of the British Waterways Board which is for the time being specified in Part I or Part II of Schedule 12 to the Transport Act 1968 (commercial and cruising waterways) is to be deemed to be navigable waters and a navigable watercourse for the purposes of this Part of this Act.

1968 c. 73.

(2) References in this Part of this Act to an order or scheme which provides for the construction of a bridge over or a tunnel under navigable waters are to be construed in accordance with section 106(8) above.

PART VII

PROVISION OF SPECIAL FACILITIES FOR HIGHWAYS

Provision of picnic sites and public conveniences for users of trunk roads.

112.—(1) The Minister may provide on land adjoining, or in the vicinity of, a trunk road that is not a special road a picnic site for motorists and others likely to use the road with space for parking vehicles and a means of access to and from a highway.

An area of any such land as aforesaid in which there are, or are to be, provided such a picnic site, parking space and means of access as aforesaid is in this Act referred to as a " trunk road picnic area ".

(2) The Minister may erect buildings and execute works on a trunk road picnic area for the purpose of providing all or any of the following : —

(a) parking places for vehicles,

(*b*) a means of access to or from the area from or to a highway,

(*c*) public sanitary conveniences (including lavatories), and

(*d*) facilities for the provision and consumption of meals and refreshments,

and may equip buildings erected by him under this subsection with such furniture and apparatus as may be necessary for the purpose of providing such conveniences or facilities.

(3) The Minister may manage a trunk road picnic area, but may not provide meals or refreshments on such an area.

(4) The Minister may make arrangements with some other person, other than a council,—

(*a*) for such conveniences or facilities as are referred to in subsection (2) above to be provided by that other person, or

(*b*) for meals or refreshments to be provided on the trunk road picnic area by that other person ;

and the powers of the Minister under this subsection include power to lease the trunk road picnic area or any part of it to that other person.

(5) The Minister may provide public sanitary conveniences (including lavatories) in proper and convenient situations on or under land forming part of a trunk road that is not a special road, or adjoining, or in the vicinity of, such a road and may manage such conveniences.

(6) The Minister shall pay compensation to any person who sustains damage by reason of the execution by him under this section of any works on or under a trunk road.

(7) A council may contribute towards any expenses incurred by the Minister under this section.

(8) Nothing in section 88 of the Public Health Act 1936 (restriction on erection of public sanitary conveniences in, or accessible from, streets) affects the powers of the Minister under this section.

1936 c. 49.

113.—(1) The Minister may by agreement with a council delegate to the council all or any of his functions with respect to the management of a trunk road picnic area or with respect to the management of public sanitary conveniences provided by him under section 112(5) above.

Exercise by council of functions of Minister with respect to management or provision of picnic sites etc.

(2) Subsections (2) to (4) of section 6 above (discharge of functions delegated by Minister to council and termination of

delegation) apply in relation to functions delegated, and a delegation, to a council under subsection (1) above as they apply in relation to functions delegated, and a delegation, to a council under subsection (1) of that section.

(3) The Minister may enter into agreements with a council—

(a) for the provision by the council on a trunk road picnic area of a picnic site for motorists and others likely to use the road,

(b) for the doing by the council of anything which he has power to do on that area under section 112(2) or (3) above, or

(c) for the discharge by the council of all or any of his functions under section 112(5) above,

so, however, that subsections (2) and (3) of section 6 above apply to the discharge of the functions of a council under any such agreement and to the conditions to be included in any such agreement as they apply to the discharge of functions delegated under that section to a council and to the conditions to be attached to any such delegation.

(4) Plant or materials belonging to a council to whom functions are delegated under subsection (1) above or with whom an agreement is made under subsection (3) above may be used by them for the purposes of those functions or of that agreement, subject to the terms of the delegation or agreement.

(5) Where any functions of the Minister as respects a trunk road picnic area stand delegated to a council under subsection (1) above, or are functions of a council by virtue of an agreement under subsection (3) above, then, except in so far as any conditions attached to the delegation or included in the agreement, as the case may be, otherwise provide, that council—

(a) shall make available any relevant facilities and services for those who do not normally reside in the area of the council as freely as for those who do ;

(b) shall have power to make reasonable charges for any relevant facilities or services ;

(c) may arrange for any relevant facilities or services to be provided by some other person and, when they make such arrangements, may authorise that person to make reasonable charges for them ; and

(d) may arrange with some other person, other than another council, for the provision by that other person of meals or refreshments on the trunk road picnic area.

References in this subsection to relevant facilities and services are references to facilities and services provided by the council in exercise of powers exercisable by them by virtue of the dele- gation or agreement referred to in this subsection.

(6) Any power to provide buildings or other premises, or any services or facilities, or anything else, exercisable by a council by virtue of any such delegation or agreement as is referred to in subsection (5) above includes power to enter into agreements with some other person for the use, on such terms as may be agreed, of anything, or any facilities or services, provided by, or under the control of, that other person and, if it appears convenient, for the services of any staff employed in connection therewith.

(7) Where any functions of the Minister with respect to the management or provision of public sanitary conveniences stand delegated to a council under subsection (1) above, or are functions of a council by virtue of an agreement under subsection (3) above, the council may make byelaws as to the conduct of persons using or entering those conveniences.

114.—(1) Where the highway authority for a highway or proposed highway are or, as the case may be, will be a county council they may provide public sanitary conveniences (including lavatories) in proper and convenient situations on or under land adjoining, or in the vicinity of, the highway or proposed highway, and may manage such conveniences.

Provision of public conveniences by county council for users of roads for which they are the highway authority.

(2) Before providing any conveniences under subsection (1) above a county council shall give notice of their intention to do so to the council of the district in which the conveniences will be situated.

(3) A county council who provide conveniences under subsection (1) above may make byelaws as to the conduct of persons using or entering them.

(4) The powers in subsection (1) above are without prejudice to section 87 of the Public Health Act 1936 (provision of public conveniences by local authorities) and nothing in section 88 of that Act (restriction on erection of public sanitary conveniences in, or accessible from, streets) affects the powers of a county council under that subsection.

1936 c. 49.

115.—(1) A highway authority may provide on land adjoining, or in the vicinity of, a highway or proposed highway for which they are or, as the case may be, will be the highway authority

Provision of areas for parking heavy goods vehicles, etc.

an area, which may be used for all or any of the following purposes:

(a) the parking of heavy goods vehicles;

(b) the transfer of goods to or from any such vehicle from or to any other vehicle; and

(c) the temporary storage of goods which have been or are to be carried or hauled by heavy goods vehicles.

An area provided under this section is in this Act referred to as a " lorry area ".

(2) For the purpose of enabling a lorry area to be used as mentioned in subsection (1) above, the highway authority by whom the area is provided may erect buildings and execute works on the area for the purpose of providing all or any of the following:

(a) parking places for heavy goods vehicles and, if the lorry area is to be used for either or both of the purposes mentioned in subsection (1)(b) and (c) above, parking places for other vehicles which will be on the area in connection with that purpose or those purposes;

(b) a means of access to or from the area from or to a highway;

(c) facilities for the accommodation of persons who will be on the lorry area in connection with any purpose for which the area may be used in pursuance of subsection (1) above or with the provision on the area of any such facilities as are mentioned in this subsection;

(d) facilities for the provision of meals and refreshments for such persons as are mentioned in paragraph (c) above;

(e) facilities for handling and storing goods which have been or are to be carried or hauled by heavy goods vehicles;

(f) service station facilities for such vehicles and for other vehicles entitled to be on the lorry area;

(g) sanitary conveniences (including lavatories) for such persons as are mentioned in paragraph (c) above;

and may install or provide in buildings erected by them under this subsection or elswhere on the lorry area such equipment, furniture and apparatus as may be necessary for the purpose of providing such facilities or conveniences.

(3) A highway authority may make arrangements with some other person, other than a council, for anything which that authority have power to do under subsection (2) above to be done by that other person and may lease the lorry area or any part of it to that other person, but may not themselves operate any such facilities as are mentioned in paragraphs (*c*), (*d*), (*e*) and (*f*) of that subsection.

(4) Where a lorry area is provided by the Minister under this section he may enter into agreements with a council for the exercise by the council of all or any of his powers under subsection (2) above or of the powers conferred on him in his capacity as a highway authority by virtue of subsection (6) below.

(5) Subsections (2) and (3) of section 6 above (discharge of functions delegated by the Minister to a council) apply to the exercise of the powers of a council under any agreement made under subsection (4) above and to the conditions to be included in any such agreement as they apply to the discharge of functions delegated under that section to a council and to the conditions to be attached to any such delegation.

(6) Section 31 of the Road Traffic Regulation Act 1967 (power 1967 c. 76. to make orders as to use of certain parking places) applies in relation to a lorry area as it applies in relation to an off-street parking place provided under section 28 of that Act, as if for references to a local authority and such a parking place there were substituted references to a highway authority and a lorry area respectively; and sections 84A, 84B, 84C, 84D and 85 of that Act (provisions with respect to certain orders and offences, including orders and offences under the said section 31) have effect as if—

    (*a*) references therein to the said section 31 and a local authority included references to that section as applied by this subsection and a local highway authority respectively;

    (*b*) references in section 84D to a parking place included references to a lorry area; and

    (*c*) the reference in section 85(2) to the local authority for the parking place included a reference to the highway authority by whom the lorry area was provided.

(7) A council may contribute towards any expenses incurred by the Minister under this section.

(8) In this section—

" goods " includes goods or burden of any description ;

" heavy goods vehicle " means a motor vehicle constructed or adapted for use for the carriage or haulage of goods and having an unladen weight of 2 tons or more, or a trailer ;

1972 c. 20.

" motor vehicle " has the same meaning as in the Road Traffic Act 1972 ;

" trailer " means a vehicle constructed or adapted for use for the carriage of goods and drawn or intended to be drawn by a motor vehicle.

PART VIII

STOPPING UP AND DIVERSION OF HIGHWAYS AND STOPPING UP OF MEANS OF ACCESS TO HIGHWAYS

Stopping up and diversion of highways

Power of magistrates' court to authorise stopping up or diversion of highway.

116.—(1) Subject to the provisions of this section, if it appears to a magistrates' court, after a view, if the court thinks fit, by any two or more of the justices composing the court, that a highway (other than a trunk road or a special road) as respects which the appropriate authority have made an application under this section—

(a) is unnecessary, or

(b) can be diverted so as to make it nearer or more commodious to the public,

the court may by order authorise it to be stopped up or, as the case may be, to be so diverted.

(2) For the purposes of subsection (1) above, the appropriate authority are—

(a) in relation to a metropolitan road, the local authority for the area in which the road is situated acting with the consent of the Greater London Council ; and

(b) in relation to any other highway, the highway authority for the highway.

A consent required by this subsection shall not be unreasonably withheld.

(3) If an authority propose to make an application under this section for an order relating to any highway (other than a classified road) they shall give notice of the proposal to—

(a) the council of the district in which the highway is situated ; and

(b) if the highway is in England, the council of the parish (if any) in which the highway is situated or, if the parish does not have a separate parish council, to the chairman of the parish meeting ; and

(c) if the highway is in Wales, the council (if any) of the community in which the highway is situated ;

and the application shall not be made if within 2 months from the date of service of the notice by the authority notice is given to the authority by the district council or by the parish or community council or, as the case may be, by the chairman of the parish meeting that the council or meeting have refused to consent to the making of the application.

(4) An application under this section may be made, and an order under it may provide, for the stopping up or diversion of a highway for the purposes of all traffic, or subject to the reservation of a footpath or bridleway.

(5) An application or order under this section may include 2 or more highways which are connected with each other.

(6) A magistrates' court shall not make an order under this section unless it is satisfied that the applicant authority have given the notices required by Part I of Schedule 12 to this Act.

(7) On the hearing of an application under this section the applicant authority, any person to whom notice is required to be given under paragraph 1 of Schedule 12, any person who uses the highway and any other person who would be aggrieved by the making of the order applied for, have a right to be heard.

(8) An order under this section authorising the diversion of a highway—

(a) shall not be made unless the written consent of every person having a legal interest in the land over which the highway is to be diverted is produced to and deposited with the court ; and

(b) except in so far as the carrying out of the diversion may necessitate temporary interference with the highway, shall not authorise the stopping up of any part of the highway until the new part to be substituted for the part to be stopped up (including, where a diversion falls to be carried out under orders of 2 different courts, any necessary continuation of the new part in the area of the other court) has been completed to the satisfaction of 2 justices of the peace acting for the same petty sessions area as the court by which the order was made and a certificate to that effect signed by them has been transmitted to the clerk of the applicant authority.

(9) Every order under this section shall have annexed to it a plan signed by the chairman of the court and shall be transmitted by the clerk of the court to the proper officer of the applicant authority, together with any written consents produced to the court under subsection (8) above.

(10) Part II of Schedule 12 to this Act applies where, in pursuance of an order under this section, a highway is stopped up or diverted and, immediately before the order is made, there is under, in, upon, over, along or across the highway any apparatus belonging to or used by any statutory undertakers for the purpose of their undertaking.

Application for order under section 116 on behalf of another person.

117. A person who desires a highway to be stopped up or diverted but is not authorised to make an application for that purpose under section 116 above may request the highway authority or local authority who, by virtue of that section, are the appropriate authority in relation to the highway to make such an application ; and if the authority grant the request they may, as a condition of making the application, require him to make such provision for any costs to be incurred by them in connection with the matter as they deem reasonable.

Stopping up of footpaths and bridleways.

118.—(1) Where it appears to a council as respects a footpath or bridleway in their area (other than one which is a trunk road or a special road) that it is expedient that the path or way should be stopped up on the ground that it is not needed for public use, the council may by order made by them and submitted to and confirmed by the Secretary of State, or confirmed as an unopposed order, extinguish the public right of way over the path or way.

An order under this section is referred to in this Act as a " public path extinguishment order ".

(2) The Secretary of State shall not confirm a public path extinguishment order, and a council shall not confirm such an order as an unopposed order, unless he or, as the case may be, they are satisfied that it is expedient so to do having regard to the extent (if any) to which it appears to him or, as the case may be, them that the path or way would, apart from the order, be likely to be used by the public, and having regard to the effect which the extinguishment of the right of way would have as respects land served by the path or way, account being taken

of the provisions as to compensation contained in section 28 PART VIII
above as applied by section 121(2) below.

(3) A public path extinguishment order shall be in such form as may be prescribed by regulations made by the Secretary of State and shall contain a map, on such scale as may be so prescribed, defining the land over which the public right of way is thereby extinguished.

(4) Schedule 6 to this Act has effect as to the making, confirmation, validity and date of operation of public path extinguishment orders.

(5) Where, in accordance with regulations made under paragraph 3 of the said Schedule 6, proceedings preliminary to the confirmation of the public path extinguishment order are taken concurrently with proceedings preliminary to the confirmation of a public path creation order or public path diversion order made under section 119 below then, in considering—

    (*a*) under subsection (1) above whether the path or way to which the public path extinguishment order relates is needed for public use, or

    (*b*) under subsection (2) above to what extent (if any) that path or way would apart from the order be likely to be used by the public,

the council or the Secretary of State, as the case may be, may have regard to the extent to which the public path creation order or the public path diversion order would provide an alternative path or way.

(6) For the purposes of subsections (1) and (2) above, any temporary circumstances preventing or diminishing the use of a path or way by the public shall be disregarded.

(7) In this section and in sections 119 to 121 below " council " includes a joint planning board, within the meaning of the Town and Country Planning Act 1971, for an area which com- 1971 c. 78. prises any part of a National Park.

119.—(1) Where an owner, lessee or occupier of land crossed Diversion of by a footpath or bridleway (other than one which is a trunk road footpaths and or a special road) satisfies the council in whose area the land bridleways. is situated that for securing the efficient use of the land or of other land held with it or providing a shorter or more commodious path or way it is expedient that the line of the path or way across the land, or part of that line, should be diverted (whether on to other land of his or on to land of another owner, lessee or occupier), the council may, subject to subsection (2) below, by order made by them and submitted to and confirmed by the Secretary of State, or confirmed as an unopposed order,—

    (*a*) create, as from such date as may be specified in the order, any such new footpath or bridleway as appears to the council requisite for effecting the diversion, and (*b*) extinguish, as from such date as may be so specified in accordance with the provisions of subsection (3) below, the public right of way over so much of the path or way as appears to the council requisite as aforesaid.

An order under this section is referred to in this Act as a " public path diversion order ".

(2) A public path diversion order shall not alter a point of termination of the path or way—

(*a*) if that point is not on a highway, or

(*b*) (where it is on a highway) otherwise than to another point which is on the same highway, or a highway connected with it, and which is substantially as convenient to the public.

(3) Where it appears to the council that work requires to be done to provide necessary facilities for the convenient exercise of any such new public right of way as is mentioned in subsection (1)(*a*) above, the date specified under subsection (1)(*b*) above shall be later than the date specified under subsection (1)(*a*) by such time as appears to the council requisite for enabling the work to be carried out.

(4) A right of way created by a public path diversion order may be either unconditional or (whether or not the right of way extinguished by the order was subject to limitations or conditions of any description) subject to such limitations or conditions as may be specified in the order.

(5) Before determining to make a public path diversion order the council may require the owner, lessee or occupier on whose representations they are acting to enter into an agreement with them to defray, or to make such contribution as may be specified in the agreement towards,—

(*a*) any compensation which may become payable under section 28 above as applied by section 121(2) below, or

(*b*) where the council are the highway authority for the path or way in question, any expenses which they may incur in bringing the new site of the path or way into fit condition for use for the public, or

(*c*) where the council are not the highway authority, any expenses which may become recoverable from them by the highway authority under the provisions of section 27(2) above as applied by subsection (9) below.

(6) The Secretary of State shall not confirm a public path diversion order, and a council shall not confirm such an order as an unopposed order, unless he or, as the case may be, they are satisfied that the diversion to be effected by it is expedient

as mentioned in subsection (1) above, and further that the path or way will not be substantially less convenient to the public in consequence of the diversion and that it is expedient to confirm the order having regard to the effect which—

   (*a*) the diversion would have on public enjoyment of the path or way as a whole,

   (*b*) the coming into operation of the order would have as respects other land served by the existing public right of way, and

   (*c*) any new public right of way created by the order would have as respects the land over which the right is so created and any land held with it,

so, however, that for the purposes of paragraphs (*b*) and (*c*) above the Secretary of State or, as the case may be, the council shall take into account the provisions as to compensation referred to in subsection (5)(*a*) above.

(7) A public path diversion order shall be in such form as may be prescribed by regulations made by the Secretary of State and shall contain a map, on such scale as may be so prescribed,—

   (*a*) showing the existing site of so much of the line of the path or way as is to be diverted by the order and the new site to which it is to be diverted,

   (*b*) indicating whether a new right of way is created by the order over the whole of the new site or whether some part of it is already comprised in a footpath or bridleway, and

   (*c*) where some part of the new site is already so comprised, defining that part.

(8) Schedule 6 to this Act has effect as to the making, confirmation, validity and date of operation of public path diversion orders.

(9) Section 27 above (making up of new footpaths and bridleways) applies to a footpath or bridleway created by a public path diversion order with the substitution, for references to a public path creation order, of references to a public path diversion order and, for references to section 26(2) above, of references to section 120(3) below.

120.—(1) Where a footpath or bridleway lies partly within and partly outside the area of a council the powers conferred by sections 118 and 119 above on the council extend, subject to subsection (2) below, to the whole of the path or way as if it lay wholly within their area.

Exercise of powers of making public path extinguishment and diversion orders.

(2) The powers of making public path extinguishment orders and public path diversion orders conferred by sections 118 and 119 above are not exercisable by a council—

(a) with respect to any part of a footpath or bridleway which is within their area, without prior consultation with the other council in whose area that part of the footpath or bridleway is situated ;

(b) with respect to any part of a footpath or bridleway which is outside their area, without the consent of every council in whose area it is ; and

(c) with respect to any part of a footpath or bridleway in a National Park, without prior consultation with the Countryside Commission.

(3) Where it appears to the Secretary of State as respects a footpath or bridleway that it is expedient as mentioned in section 118(1) above that the path or way should be stopped up, or where an owner, lessee or occupier of land crossed by a footpath or bridleway satisfies the Secretary of State that a diversion of it is expedient as mentioned in section 119(1) above, then if—

(a) no council having power to do so have made and submitted to him a public path extinguishment order or a public path diversion order, as the case may be, and

(b) the Secretary of State is satisfied that, if such an order were made and submitted to him, he would have power to confirm the order in accordance with the provisions in that behalf of sections 118 and 119 above,

he may himself make the order after consultation with the appropriate authority.

(4) A council proposing to make a public path diversion order such that the authority who will be the highway authority for a part of the path or way after the diversion will be a different body from the authority who before the diversion are the highway authority for it shall, before making the order, notify the first mentioned authority.

(5) Where under subsection (3) above the Secretary of State decides to make a public path diversion order, he may require the owner, lessee or occupier on whose representations he is acting to enter into an agreement with such council as he may specify for the owner, lessee or occupier to defray, or to make such contribution as may be specified in the agreement towards any such compensation or expenses as are specified in paragraphs (a), (b) and (c) of section 119(5) above.

PART VIII
Supplementary
provisions as
to public path
extinguish-
ment and
diversion
orders.

121.—(1) A public path extinguishment order or a public path diversion order affecting in any way the area of more than one council may contain provisions requiring one of the councils to defray, or contribute towards, expenses incurred in consequence of the order by another of the councils ; and a public path diversion order diverting a part of the line of a path or way from a site in the area of one local highway authority to a site in the area of another may provide that the first mentioned authority are to continue to be the highway authority for that part of the path or way after the diversion.

(2) Section 28 above (compensation for loss caused by public path creation order) applies in relation to public path extinguishment orders and to public path diversion orders as it applies in relation to public path creation orders but as if the references in it to section 26(2) above were references to section 120(3) above.

(3) Section 29 above (protection for agriculture and forestry) applies in relation to the making of public path extinguishment orders and public path diversion orders as it applies in relation to the making of public path creation agreements and public path creation orders.

(4) The Secretary of State shall not make or confirm a public path extinguishment order or a public path diversion order, and a council shall not confirm such an order as an unopposed order, if the order extinguishes a right of way over land under, in, upon, over, along or across which there is any apparatus belonging to or used by any statutory undertakers for the purpose of their undertaking unless the undertakers have consented to the making or, as the case may be, confirmation of the order.

(5) A consent under subsection (4) above may be given subject to the condition that there are included in the order such provisions for the protection of the undertakers as they reasonably require, but a consent under that subsection shall not be unreasonably withheld, and any question whether the withholding of such a consent is unreasonable or whether any requirement is reasonable shall be determined by the appropriate Minister.

(6) In subsection (5) above the " appropriate Minister " means—

    (*a*) in relation to statutory undertakers carrying on an undertaking for the supply of electricity, gas, hydraulic power or water, the Secretary of State ; and

    (*b*) in relation to any other statutory undertakers, the Minister.

E

PART VIII
Power to make
temporary
diversion
where highway
about to be
repaired or
widened.

122.—(1) A highway authority who are about to repair or widen a highway, and a person who is about to repair or widen a highway maintainable by him by reason of tenure, enclosure or prescription, may, subject to the provisions of this section, construct on adjoining land a temporary highway for use while the work is in progress.

(2) Where any damage is sustained by the owner or occupier of any land in consequence of the construction of a highway on that land in exercise of a power conferred by this section the owner or occupier of the land may recover compensation in respect of that damage from the authority or other person by whom the highway was constructed.

(3) Nothing in this section authorises interference with land which is part of the site of a house, or is a garden, lawn, yard, court, park, paddock, plantation, planted walk or avenue to a house, or is inclosed land set apart for building or as a nursery for trees.

Saving and
interpretation.

123.—(1) The provisions of any enactment contained in the foregoing provisions of this Part of this Act do not prejudice any power conferred by any other enactment (whether contained in this Part of this Act or not) to stop up or divert a highway, and do not otherwise affect the operation of any enactment not contained in this Part of this Act relating to the extinguishment, suspension, diversion or variation of public rights of way.

1971 c. 78.

(2) Unless the context otherwise requires, expressions in the foregoing provisions of this Part of this Act, other than expressions to which meanings are assigned by sections 328 and 329 below, have the same meanings respectively as in the Town and Country Planning Act 1971.

Stopping up of means of access to highways

Stopping up
of private
access to
highways.

124.—(1) Subject to subsection (3) below, where the highway authority for a highway consider that a private means of access from the highway to any premises is likely to cause danger to, or to interfere unreasonably with, traffic on the highway, they may be authorised by an order made in accordance with this section to stop up the means of access.

(2) An order under this section shall be made by the highway authority for the highway in question and, if they are a local highway authority, shall be confirmed either by the Minister or, where subsection (5) below allows, by the highway authority themselves.

(3) No order under this section relating to an access to any premises shall be made by the Minister or, in the case of an

order made by a local highway authority, confirmed either by the Minister or by that authority unless the Minister or, as the case may be, the confirming authority is or are satisfied—

(a) that no access to the premises from the highway in question is reasonably required, or

(b) that another reasonably convenient means of access to the premises is available or will be provided by the Minister or, as the case may be, the local highway authority.

(4) Subject to subsection (5) below, the Minister may make regulations for prescribing the procedure to be followed in connection with the making and confirmation of orders under this section, and such regulations shall in particular make provision—

(a) for the publication in such manner as may be prescribed by the regulations of notice of the order proposed to be made or confirmed and for service on such persons as may be so prescribed of a copy of that notice and of such other documents, if any, as may be so prescribed ;

(b) as to the content of that notice ;

(c) for objections to the making of an order by the Minister received within such period as may be so prescribed and not withdrawn, to be considered by him ;

(d) for objections to the confirmation of an order made by a local highway authority to be considered by the Minister if any of the objections to the confirmation of the order received within such period as may be so prescribed and not withdrawn was made by an owner, lessee or occupier of any premises with a private means of access which the order would authorise the highway authority to stop up ;

(e) for objections to the confirmation of an order made by a local highway authority received within such period as may be so prescribed and not withdrawn to be considered by the local highway authority if there is no objection received within that period from an owner, lessee or occupier such as is mentioned in paragraph (d) above or if all such objections so received are withdrawn before the order is referred to the Minister for confirmation ;

(f) for the making of modifications in the order, whether in consequence of any objections or otherwise, before the order is made or confirmed.

E 2

(5) In the case of an order made by a local highway authority under this section—

 (*a*) if no objection to the confirmation of the order is received within the period prescribed by regulations under subsection (4) above ; or

 (*b*) if every such objection so received is withdrawn ; or

 (*c*) if every such objection so received from an owner, lessee or occupier of any premises with a private means of access which the order would authorise the highway authority to stop up is withdrawn,

the local highway authority may themselves confirm the order, with or without modifications.

(6) Before confirming an order with modifications the local highway authority, if they consider that the proposed modifications will make a substantial change in the order, shall inform every such owner, lessee or occupier as is mentioned in subsection (5)(*c*) above and every other person who appears to them to be likely to be affected by the modifications to the order—

 (*a*) of their intention to make the order ; and

 (*b*) of the form in which they propose to make it.

(7) The local highway authority shall give every such person as is mentioned in subsection (6) above an opportunity to make representations with regard to the order, and shall consider any representations with regard to it which any such person makes.

(8) Schedule 2 to this Act has effect as to the validity and date of operation of any order under this section.

Further powers to stop up private access to premises.
1971 c. 78.

125.—(1) Subject to subsection (2) below an order under section 14 or 18 above (orders for certain purposes connected with trunk, classified or special roads) and an order under section 211 of the Town and Country Planning Act 1971 (order by Minister to stop up or divert highway that crosses etc. a main highway) may authorise the appropriate authority—

 (*a*) to stop up any private means of access to premises adjoining or adjacent to land comprised in the route of the relevant road, or forming the site of any works authorised by the order or by any previous order made under the same enactment ;

 (*b*) to provide a new means of access to any such premises.

(2) For the purposes of subsection (1) above—

 (*a*) the appropriate authority in the case of an order under section 211 of the Town and Country Planning Act 1971 is the highway authority for the main highway, and in any other case is the authority by whom the order is made ; and

(*b*) the relevant road is the trunk road, classified road, PART VIII
special road or, as the case may be, main highway to
which the order relates.

(3) No order authorising the stopping up of a means of access
to premises shall be made or confirmed by the Minister by virtue
of subsection (1)(*a*) above unless he is satisfied—

   (*a*) that no access to the premises is reasonably required, or

   (*b*) that another reasonably convenient means of access to
the premises is available or will be provided in pursuance of an order made by virtue of subsection (1)(*b*)
above or otherwise.

(4) Section 215 of the Town and Country Planning Act
1971 (procedure for making certain orders) in its application
to an order under section 211 of that Act which by virtue of
subsection (1)(*a*) above authorises the stopping up of a private
means of access to premises has effect as if the persons on
whom the Minister is required by section 215(2) and (7) to serve
certain documents relating to the order included the owner and
the occupier of those premises.

In this subsection " owner " in relation to any premises, means
a person, other than a mortgagee not in possession, who is for
the time being entitled to dispose of the fee simple in the
premises, whether in possession or in reversion, and includes
also a person holding or entitled to the rents and profits of the
premises under a lease the unexpired term of which exceeds
3 years.

126.—(1) Where—

   (*a*) an order under section 124 above, or

   (*b*) an order, by virtue of section 125 above, under section 14 or 18 above or under section 211 of the Town
and Country Planning Act 1971,

authorises a highway authority to stop up a private means of
access to any premises, then, notwithstanding anything in section 80(3) above, that authority may stop up the access in any
way that seems to them appropriate, but not, if the order in question is under section 124 above, so as to obstruct any highway.

Provisions
supplementary
to sections
124 and 125
etc.

(2) Where a means of access to any premises—

   (*a*) is stopped up in pursuance of any such order as is
specified in subsection (1) above, or

   (*b*) is limited by virtue of any restrictions imposed on the
use (including the crossing) of a special road under
Part II of this Act, or by section 13 of the Road
Traffic Regulation Act 1967, or by regulations made
under that section,

1967 c. 76.

and any person suffers damage in consequence thereof by the depreciation of any interest in the premises to which he is entitled or by being disturbed in his enjoyment of the premises he is entitled to recover compensation in respect of that damage from the appropriate authority.

(3) The appropriate authority for the purpose of subsection (2) above in cases falling within paragraph (*a*) or that subsection is the highway authority authorised by the order to stop up the means of access and in cases falling within paragraph (*b*) of that subsection is the special road authority.

(4) Where any person is entitled to compensation in respect of any matter under subsection (2) above he is not entitled to recover compensation in respect of the same matter under any other enactment.

Stopping up private access to premises by agreement.

127. The highway authority for a highway may agree with the occupier of any premises and any other person having an interest in them that any private means of access to the premises from the highway shall be stopped up by that authority in any way which seems to them appropriate but not so as to obstruct any highway ; and an agreement under this section may make provision for the payment by the highway authority to the other party of compensation in respect of the damage (if any) suffered by him in consequence of the stopping up of the means of access.

Penalty for using access which has been stopped up.

128. Any person who uses an access which has been stopped up by virtue of section 124, 125 or 127 above other than a person exercising a public right of way is guilty of an offence and liable to a fine not exceeding £50.

Further provisions with respect to new means of access.

129.—(1) Without prejudice to their power to provide a new means of access to any premises when authorised to do so by an order made under any enactment, a highway authority—

(*a*) who by virtue of an order under section 124 above or an agreement under section 127 above have stopped up a means of access to any premises or propose to do so ; or

(*b*) who consider it necessary or expedient in connection with the construction, improvement or alteration of a highway to provide a new means of access to any premises,

may, subject to subsection (2) below, provide a new means of access to those premises from any highway or proposed highway.

(2) If a highway authority proposing to provide a new means of access under subsection (1) above are not the highway authority for the highway from which the access will be provided

or, as the case may be, will not become the highway authority for it on the completion of its construction, they shall not provide the access without the consent of the authority who are, or will become, the highway authority for that highway.

(3) Where a private means of access to any premises is proposed to be stopped up by virtue of section 124 or 125 above and another means of access to those premises from a highway is available or is to be provided, then, in determining for the purposes of section 124 or 125 whether that other means of access is or, as the case may be, will be reasonably convenient the Minister or, in the case of an order under section 124 which a local highway authority have power to confirm, that authority shall have regard—

    (a) to the need, if any, for a means of access from the highway to different places on those premises, and

    (b) to any roads, paths or other ways on those or other premises which are or will be capable of providing such a means.

(4) The provision of a new means of access to any premises from a highway under this section or under or by virtue of section 124, 125 or 127 above includes the provision of a road, path or other way on those or any other premises.

PART IX

LAWFUL AND UNLAWFUL INTERFERENCE WITH HIGHWAYS AND STREETS

Protection of public rights

130.—(1) It is the duty of the highway authority to assert and protect the rights of the public to the use and enjoyment of any highway for which they are the highway authority, including any roadside waste which forms part of it.

(2) Any council may assert and protect the rights of the public to the use and enjoyment of any highway in their area for which they are not the highway authority, including any roadside waste which forms part of it.

(3) Without prejudice to subsections (1) and (2) above, it is the duty of a council who are a highway authority to prevent, as far as possible, the stopping up or obstruction of—

    (a) the highways for which they are the highway authority, and

    (b) any highway for which they are not the highway authority, if, in their opinion, the stopping up or obstruction of that highway would be prejudicial to the interests of their area.

Protection of public rights.

E 4

(4) Without prejudice to the foregoing provisions of this section, it is the duty of a local highway authority to prevent any unlawful encroachment on any roadside waste comprised in a highway for which they are the highway authority.

1972 c. 70.
(5) Without prejudice to their powers under section 222 of the Local Government Act 1972, a council may, in the performance of their functions under the foregoing provisions of this section, institute legal proceedings in their own name, defend any legal proceedings and generally take such steps as they deem expedient.

(6) If the council of a parish or community or, in the case of a parish or community which does not have a separate parish or community council, the parish meeting or a community meeting, represent to a local highway authority—

> (a) that a highway as to which the local highway authority have the duty imposed by subsection (3) above has been unlawfully stopped up or obstructed, or

> (b) that an unlawful encroachment has taken place on a roadside waste comprised in a highway for which they are the highway authority,

it is the duty of the local highway authority, unless satisfied that the representations are incorrect, to take proper proceedings accordingly and they may do so in their own name.

(7) Proceedings or steps taken by a council in relation to an alleged right of way are not to be treated as unauthorised by reason only that the alleged right is found not to exist.

Damage to highways, streets etc.

Penalty for damaging highway etc.
131.—(1) If a person, without lawful authority or excuse—

> (a) makes a ditch or excavation in a highway which consists of or comprises a carriageway, or

> (b) removes any soil or turf from any part of a highway, except for the purpose of improving the highway and with the consent of the highway authority for the highway, or

> (c) deposits anything whatsoever on a highway so as to damage the highway, or

> (d) lights any fire, or discharges any firearm or firework, within 50 feet from the centre of a highway which consists of or comprises a carriageway, and in consequence thereof the highway is damaged,

he is guilty of an offence.

(2) If a person without lawful authority or excuse pulls down or obliterates a traffic sign placed on or over a highway, or a milestone or direction post (not being a traffic sign) so placed, he is guilty of an offence; but it is a defence in any proceedings under this subsection to show that the traffic sign, milestone or post was not lawfully so placed.

(3) A person guilty of an offence under this section is liable to a fine not exceeding £20 or, in the case of a second or subsequent conviction under this section, to a fine not exceeding £50.

132.—(1) A person who, without either the consent of the highway authority for the highway in question or an authorisation given by or under an enactment or a reasonable excuse, paints or otherwise inscribes or affixes any picture, letter, sign or other mark upon the surface of a highway or upon any tree, structure or works on or in a highway is guilty of an offence and liable to a fine not exceeding £100 or, in the case of a second or subsequent conviction under this subsection, to a fine not exceeding £200.

Unauthorised marks on highways.

(2) The highway authority for a highway may, without prejudice to their powers apart from this subsection and whether or not proceedings in respect of the matter have been taken in pursuance of subsection (1) above, remove any picture, letter, sign or other mark which has, without either the consent of the authority or an authorisation given by or under an enactment, been painted or otherwise inscribed or affixed upon the surface of the highway or upon any tree, structure or works on or in the highway.

133. If the footway of a street that is a highway maintainable at the public expense is damaged by or in consequence of any excavation or other work on land adjoining the street, the highway authority for the highway may make good the damage and recover the expenses reasonably incurred by them in so doing from the owner of the land in question or the person causing or responsible for the damage.

Damage to footways of streets by excavations.

134.—(1) Where a footpath or bridleway crosses agricultural land or land which is being brought into use for agriculture, then, if—

Ploughing of footpath or bridleway.

(a) it is proposed in accordance with the rules of good husbandry to plough the land, and

(b) it is convenient, in so ploughing the land, to plough the path or way together with the rest of the land, the public right of way shall be subject to the condition that the occupier shall have the right, subject to the following provisions of this section, to plough the path or way as well as the rest of the land.

(2) This section does not confer any right to plough so much of a footpath or bridleway as follows what are for the time being the headlands or sides of a field or enclosure.

(3) Before ploughing a footpath or bridleway in the exercise of the right conferred by this section the occupier shall give to the highway authority for the path or way not less than 7 days' notice of his intention to plough it.

(4) Subject to section 135 below, where a footpath or bridleway is ploughed in the exercise of the right conferred by this section the occupier of the land shall as soon as may be after the ploughing is completed and in any event—

(a) not later than 6 weeks from the date of giving notice of intention to plough under subsection (3) above, or

(b) if, in contravention of that subsection, no such notice was given, not later than 3 weeks from the time when the occupier began to plough the footpath or bridleway,

make good the surface of the path or way so as to make it reasonably convenient for the exercise of the public right of way.

(5) A person who fails to comply with subsection (3) or (4) above is guilty of an offence and liable—

(a) in the case of a failure to comply with subsection (3), to a fine not exceeding £10,

(b) in the case of a failure to comply with subsection (4), to a fine not exceeding £200 ;

and where a person is convicted of failing to comply with subsection (4) and the offence is continued after the conviction he is guilty of a further offence and liable to a fine not exceeding £1 for each day on which the offence is so continued.

(6) It is the duty of a highway authority to enforce the provisions of subsections (3) to (5) above as respects any footpath or bridleway for which they are the highway authority ; and subject to subsection (7) below no proceedings in respect of an offence under those provisions shall be brought except by the authority required by this subsection to enforce those provisions as respects the path or way in question.

(7) Proceedings in respect of an offence under subsection (4) above may be brought by the council of the parish or community in which the path or way in question is situated or by the council of the district within whose area the path or way is situated.

(8) Without prejudice to subsections (6) and (7) above, if a footpath or bridleway is ploughed and the occupier has no right to plough it, or if there is a failure to comply with subsection (4) above, a competent authority, after giving to the occupier not less than 14 days' notice of their intention, may take all necessary steps for making good the surface of the path or way so as to make it reasonably convenient for the exercise of the public right of way.

(9) A competent authority may recover from the occupier the amount of any expenses reasonably incurred by the authority in and in connection with the exercise of their powers under subsection (8) above.

(10) For the purposes of subsections (8) and (9) above the following are competent authorities—

(a) in the case of a footpath or bridleway which is for the time being maintained by a district council by virtue of section 42 or 50 above, that council and also the highway authority, and

(b) in the case of any other footpath or bridleway, the highway authority.

(11) Nothing in this section prejudices any limitation or condition having effect apart from this section.

135.—(1) If on the application of the occupier the highway authority are satisfied that it is expedient in the interests of good farming that the period of 6 or 3 weeks mentioned in section 134(4) above should be extended the highway authority may—

(a) order the temporary diversion of the path or way until such date as may be specified in the order, being a date not more than 3 months after the time when the occupier began to plough the footpath or bridleway, and

(b) by the order extend the period of 6 weeks or 3 weeks mentioned in section 134(4) so as to expire on that date.

(2) On the making of the order the highway authority shall forthwith cause a copy of it to be displayed in a prominent position at the ends of the diversion.

(3) In deciding whether to make an order under this section a highway authority shall take into account the interests of the users of the path or way.

PART IX

(4) An order under this section diverting a path or way—

(a) shall not affect the line of a path or way on land now occupied by the applicant,

(b) shall not divert any part of the path or way on to land not occupied by the applicant, unless written consent to the making of the order has been given by the occupier of that land, and by any other person whose consent is needed to obtain access to the land,

(c) may require as a condition of the taking effect of the order the provision of any necessary facilities for the convenient use of the diversion,

and the highway authority may enter into an agreement with the applicant for the provision of any such facilities by the highway authority at the expense of the applicant.

Damage to highway consequent on exclusion of sun and wind.

136.—(1) If a highway which consists of or comprises a carriageway is being damaged in consequence of the exclusion from it of the sun and wind by a hedge or tree (other than a tree planted for ornament or for shelter to a building, courtyard or hop ground), a magistrates' court may by order require the owner or occupier of the land on which the hedge or tree is growing, so to cut, prune or plash the hedge or prune or lop the tree as to remove the cause of damage.

(2) The power of a magistrates' court to make an order under subsection (1) above is exercisable on a complaint made by the highway authority for the highway, or, in the case of a highway maintainable by reason of tenure, enclosure or prescription, by the person liable to maintain the highway.

(3) If a person against whom an order under subsection (1) above is made fails to comply with it within 10 days from such date as may be specified in the order, he is guilty of an offence and liable to a fine not exceeding £25, and the highway authority or other person on whose complaint the order was made may carry out the work required by the order and may recover the expenses reasonably incurred by them or him in so doing from the person in default.

(4) No person shall be required by an order made under this section, nor is any person permitted by subsection (3) above, to cut or prune a hedge at any time between the last day of September and the first day of April.

Obstruction of highways and streets

Penalty for wilful obstruction.

137.—(1) If a person, without lawful authority or excuse, in any way wilfully obstructs the free passage along a highway he is guilty of an offence and liable to a fine not exceeding £50.

(2) A constable may arrest without warrant any person whom PART IX
he sees committing an offence against this section.

138. If a person, without lawful authority or excuse, erects a Penalty for
building or fence, or plants a hedge, in a highway which consists erecting
of or comprises a carriageway he is guilty of an offence and building,
liable to a fine not exceeding £50. etc., in
highway.

139.—(1) A builder's skip shall not be deposited on a high- Control of
way without the permission of the highway authority for the builders'
highway. skips.

(2) A permission under this section shall be a permission
for a person to whom it is granted to deposit, or cause to be
deposited, a skip on the highway specified in the permission, and
a highway authority may grant such permission either unconditionally or subject to such conditions as may be specified in
the permission including, in particular, conditions relating to—

(a) the siting of the skip;

(b) its dimensions;

(c) the manner in which it is to be coated with paint and
other material for the purpose of making it immediately visible to oncoming traffic;

(d) the care and disposal of its contents;

(e) the manner in which it is to be lighted or guarded;

(f) its removal at the end of the period of permission.

(3) If a builder's skip is deposited on a highway without a
permission granted under this section, the owner of the skip
is, subject to subsection (6) below, guilty of an offence and
liable to a fine not exceeding £100.

(4) Where a builder's skip has been deposited on a highway
in accordance with a permission granted under this section, the
owner of the skip shall secure—

(a) that the skip is properly lighted during the hours of
darkness;

(b) that the skip is clearly and indelibly marked with the
owner's name and with his telephone number or
address;

(c) that the skip is removed as soon as practicable after it has been filled ;

(d) that each of the conditions subject to which that permission was granted is complied with ;

and, if he fails to do so, he is, subject to subsection (6) below, guilty of an offence and liable to a fine not exceeding £100.

(5) Where the commission by any person of an offence under this section is due to the act or default of some other person, that other person is guilty of the offence, and a person may be charged with and convicted of the offence by virtue of this subsection whether or not proceedings are taken against the first-mentioned person.

(6) In any proceedings for an offence under this section it is a defence, subject to subsection (7) below, for the person charged to prove that the commission of the offence was due to the act or default of another person and that he took all reasonable precautions and exercised all due diligence to avoid the commission of such an offence by himself or any person under his control.

(7) A person charged with an offence under this section is not, without leave of the court, entitled to rely on the defence provided by subsection (6) above unless, within a period ending 7 clear days before the hearing, he has served on the prosecutor a notice in writing giving such information identifying or assisting in the identification of that other person as was then in his possession.

(8) Where any person is charged with an offence under any other enactment for failing to secure that a builder's skip which has been deposited on a highway in accordance with a permission granted under this section was properly lighted during the hours of darkness, it is a defence for the person charged to prove that the commission of the offence was due to the act or default of another person and that he took all reasonable precautions and exercised all due diligence to avoid the commission of such an offence by himself or any person under his control.

(9) Where a person is charged with obstructing, or interrupting any user of, a highway by depositing a builder's skip on it, it is a defence for the person charged to prove that the skip was deposited on it in accordance with a permission granted under this section and either—

(a) that each of the requirements of subsection (4) above had been complied with ; or (*b*) that the commission of any offence under that subsection was due to the act or default of another person and that he took all reasonable precautions and exercised all due diligence to avoid the commission of such an offence by himself or any person under his control.

(10) Nothing in this section is to be taken as authorising the creation of a nuisance or of a danger to users of a highway or as imposing on a highway authority by whom a permission has been granted under this section any liability for any injury, damage or loss resulting from the presence on a highway of the skip to which the permission relates.

(11) In this section and section 140 below—

" builder's skip " means a container designed to be carried on a road vehicle and to be placed on a highway or other land for the storage of builders' materials, or for the removal and disposal of builders' rubble, waste, household and other rubbish or earth ; and

" owner ", in relation to a builder's skip which is the subject of a hiring agreement, being an agreement for a hiring of not less than one month, or a hire purchase agreement, means the person in possession of the skip under that agreement.

140.—(1) The following provisions of this section have Removal of effect in relation to a builder's skip deposited on a highway builders' notwithstanding that it was deposited on it in accordance with skips. a permission granted under section 139 above.

(2) The highway authority for the highway or a constable in uniform may require the owner of the skip to remove or reposition it or cause it to be removed or repositioned.

(3) A person required to remove or reposition, or cause to be removed or repositioned, a skip under a requirement made by virtue of subsection (2) above shall comply with the requirement as soon as practicable, and if he fails to do so he is guilty of an offence and liable to a fine not exceeding £50.

(4) The highway authority for the highway or a constable in uniform may themselves remove or reposition the skip or cause it to be removed or repositioned.

(5) Where a skip is removed under subsection (4) above, the highway authority or, as the case may be, the chief officer of police shall, where practicable, notify the owner of its removal, but if the owner cannot be traced, or if after a reasonable

period of time after being so notified he has not recovered the skip, the highway authority or chief officer of police may dispose of the skip and its contents.

(6) Any expenses reasonably incurred by a highway authority or chief officer of police in the removal or repositioning of a skip under subsection (4) above or the disposal of a skip under subsection (5) above may be recovered from the owner of the skip in any court of competent jurisdiction or summarily as a civil debt.

(7) Any proceeds of the disposal of a skip under subsection (5) above shall be used in the first place to meet the expenses reasonably incurred in the removal and disposal of the skip and thereafter any surplus shall be given to the person entitled to it if he can be traced and if not may be retained by the highway authority or the chief officer of police, as the case may be; and any surplus so retained by a chief officer of police shall be paid into the police fund.

(8) References in this section to expenses incurred in the removal of a skip include references to expenses incurred in storing the skip until it is recovered by the owner or, as the case may be, disposed of.

(9) The owner of a skip is not guilty of an offence under section 139(4) above of failing to secure that a condition relating to the siting of the skip was complied with if the failure resulted from the repositioning of the skip under subsection (3) or (4) above.

Restriction on planting of trees etc. in or near carriageway.

141.—(1) Subject to sections 64 and 96 above and section 142 below, no tree or shrub shall be planted in a made-up carriageway, or within 15 feet from the centre of a made-up carriageway.

(2) If a tree or shrub is planted in contravention of this section the highway authority for the highway or, in the case of a highway maintainable by reason of tenure, enclosure or prescription, the person liable to maintain the highway, may by notice given either to the owner or to the occupier of the land in which the tree or shrub is planted require him to remove it within 21 days from the date of service of the notice.

(3) If a person fails to comply with a notice under subsection (2) above he is guilty of an offence and liable to a fine not exceeding £25 and if the offence is continued after conviction he is guilty of a further offence and liable to a fine not exceeding 50p for each day on which the offence is so continued.

142.—(1) The highway authority for a highway may by a licence granted under this section permit the occupier or the owner of any premises adjoining the highway to plant and maintain, or to retain and maintain, trees, shrubs, plants or grass in such part of the highway as may be specified in the licence.

(2) The highway authority may, as they think fit—

    (a) grant a licence under this section to the person who at the time of the grant is the occupier of such premises and insert in the licence provisions prohibiting assignment of the licence and providing for its duration; or

    (b) grant such a licence to the owner of such premises and his successors in title and insert in the licence provisions providing for the licence to be annexed to those premises and providing for its duration;

and references in this section to the licensee are references to the person who is for the time being entitled by virtue of such a licence to do anything permitted by it to be done.

(3) No fine, rent or other sum of money is payable in respect of such a licence except—

    (a) a reasonable sum in respect of legal or other expenses incurred in connection with the grant of the licence; and

    (b) an annual charge of a reasonable amount for administering the licence;

and any such sum is recoverable from the licensee.

(4) It shall be a condition of every licence granted by virtue of subsection (2)(b) above that within one month after any change in the ownership of the premises in question takes place the licensee is to inform the highway authority of it.

(5) A highway authority may attach to any such licence such conditions as they consider necessary to ensure the safety and convenience of passengers in the highway and to prevent traffic therein being delayed, to prevent any nuisance or annoyance being caused to the owners or occupiers of other premises adjoining the highway and to protect the apparatus of statutory undertakers, sewerage authorities and the Post Office.

(6) A highway authority may by notice served on the licensee withdraw a licence granted by them under this section—

    (a) on the expiration of such period as may be specified in the notice, being a period of not less than 7 days beginning with the date of service of the notice on the licensee, if any condition of the licence is contravened by the licensee;

(*b*) on the expiration of such period as may be so specified, being a period of not less than 3 months beginning with the said date, if the authority consider the withdrawal of the licence is necessary for the purpose of the exercise of their functions as a highway authority.

(7) Where a licence under this section expires or is withdrawn or surrendered, the highway authority by whom it was granted—

(*a*) may remove all or any of the trees, shrubs, plants or grass to which the licence relates and reinstate the highway and may recover the expenses reasonably incurred by them in so doing from the last licensee ; or

(*b*) if satisfied that the last licensee can, within such reasonable time as they may specify, remove such trees, shrubs, plants or grass or such of them as they may specify and reinstate the highway, may authorise him to do so at his own expense.

In this subsection " the last licensee " means the person who immediately before the expiration, withdrawal or surrender of the licence in question was the licensee or, if that person has died, his personal representatives.

(8) The licensee and the person who immediately before the expiration, withdrawal or surrender of a licence under this section was the licensee or, if that person has died, his personal representatives shall indemnify the highway authority against any claim in respect of injury, damage or loss arising out of—

(*a*) the planting or presence in a highway of trees, shrubs, plants or grass to which the licence relates, or

(*b*) the execution by any person of any works authorised by the licence or by the highway authority under subsection (7) above, or

(*c*) the execution by or on behalf of the highway authority of any works under subsection (7) above ;

but this subsection is not to be taken as requiring any person to indemnify the highway authority against any claim in respect of injury, damage or loss which is attributable to the negligence of that authority.

(9) If any person plants a tree or shrub in a highway otherwise than in pursuance of a licence granted under this section, the tree or shrub is to be deemed, for the purposes of section 141 above, to have been planted in contravention of that section.

(10) Where the land on which a highway is situated is owned by the highway authority for the highway, nothing in subsection (3) above is to be taken as affecting the rights of that

authority as the owner of that land to grant to any person, for such consideration as they think fit, the right to plant any thing in that land.

143.—(1) Where a structure has been erected or set up on a highway otherwise than under a provision of this Act or some other enactment, a competent authority may by notice require the person having control or possession of the structure to remove it within such time as may be specified in the notice.

For the purposes of this section the following are competent authorities—

(*a*) in the case of a highway which is for the time being maintained by a district council by virtue of section 42 or 50 above, that council and also the highway authority, and

(*b*) in the case of any other highway, the highway authority.

(2) If a structure in respect of which a notice is served under this section is not removed within the time specified in the notice, the competent authority serving the notice may, subject to subsection (3) below, remove the structure and recover the expenses reasonably incurred by them in so doing from the person having control or possession of the structure.

(3) The authority shall not exercise their power under subsection (2) above until the expiration of one month from the date of service of the notice.

(4) In this section " structure " includes any machine, pump, post or other object of such a nature as to be capable of causing obstruction, and a structure may be treated for the purposes of this section as having been erected or set up notwithstanding that it is on wheels.

144.—(1) Subject to subsection (2) below, a local authority may—

(*a*) erect flagpoles, pylons and other structures on any highway in their area for the purpose of displaying decorations ;

(*b*) make slots in such a highway for the purpose of erecting the structures ; and

(*c*) remove any structure erected or slot made by the authority in pursuance of paragraph (*a*) or (*b*) above ;

and any structures or slots which may be erected or made by virtue of this subsection are hereafter in this section referred to as " relevant works ".

(2) A local authority are not entitled to exercise the powers conferred on them by subsection (1) above in respect of a highway for which they are not the highway authority except with the consent in writing of the highway authority for the highway, and are not entitled to exercise those powers in respect of so much of a highway as—

    (*a*) is carried by a bridge which a body other than the local authority and the highway authority has a duty to maintain ; or

    (*b*) forms part of the approaches to such a bridge and is supported or protected by works or materials which a body other than the local authority and the highway authority has a duty to maintain,

except with the consent in writing of that body.

In this subsection " bridge " includes a structure which carries a highway superimposed over a cutting.

(3) A highway authority or other body may give their consent in pursuance of subsection (2) above on such terms as they think fit (including in particular, without prejudice to the generality of the preceding provisions of this subsection, terms providing for the highway authority or body to remove any of the relevant works and reinstate the highway and to recover the reasonable cost of doing so from the local authority to whom the consent was given).

(4) It is the duty of an authority by whom relevant works are erected or made by virtue of the preceding provisions of this section—

    (*a*) to ensure that the works are erected or made so as to obstruct the highway in question as little as is reasonably possible, so as not to obscure or conflict with traffic signs connected with the highway and so as to interfere as little as is reasonably possible with the enjoyment of premises adjacent to the highway and with, and with access to, any apparatus in or on the highway which belongs to or is used or maintained by statutory undertakers ; and

    (*b*) to ensure that while the works are retained they are properly maintained and, so far as it is necessary to light them to avoid danger to users of the highway, are properly lit ; and

    (*c*) if the authority are not the highway authority for the highway, to indemnify the highway authority against any payments falling to be made by the highway authority in consequence of the works.

(5) A person who without lawful authority interferes with or removes any relevant works is guilty of an offence and liable to a fine not exceeding £50 or, in the case of a second or subsequent conviction under this subsection, to a fine not exceeding £100.

(6) In this section—

"local authority" means any of the following, namely, the council of a county, district or London borough, the Greater London Council, the Common Council, the Council of the Isles of Scilly and a parish or community council; and

"statutory undertakers" means any of the following, namely, any body which is a statutory undertaker within the meaning provided by section 329(1) below, the Post Office, any public authority exercising functions by virtue of any provision of sections 14 and 15 of the Water Act 1973 (which relate to sewerage) and any person entitled to the benefit of a licence in respect of the highway in question under section 181 below.

1973 c. 37.

145.—(1) Where there is a gate of less than the minimum width across so much of a highway as consists of a carriageway, or across a highway that is a bridleway, the highway authority for the highway may by notice to the owner of the gate require him to enlarge the gate to that width or remove it.

Powers as to gates across highways.

In this subsection "the minimum width" means, in relation to a gate across so much of a highway as consists of a carriageway, 10 feet and, in relation to a gate across a bridleway, 5 feet, measured in either case between the posts of the gate.

(2) If a person on whom a notice under subsection (1) above is served fails to comply, within 21 days from the date of service of the notice on him, with a requirement of the notice, he is guilty of an offence and liable to a fine not exceeding 50p for each day during which the failure continues.

146.—(1) Any stile, gate or other similar structure across a footpath or bridleway shall be maintained by the owner of the land in a safe condition, and to the standard of repair required to prevent unreasonable interference with the rights of the persons using the footpath or bridleway.

Duty to maintain stiles etc. on footpaths and bridleways.

(2) If it appears to the appropriate authority that the duty imposed by subsection (1) above is not being complied with, they may, after giving to the owner and occupier not less than 14 days' notice of their intention, take all necessary steps for repairing and making good the stile, gate or other works.

For the purposes of this section the appropriate authority is—

(*a*) in the case of a footpath or bridleway which is for the time being maintained by a district council by virtue of section 42 or 50 above, that council, and

(*b*) in the case of any other footpath or bridleway, the highway authority.

(3) The appropriate authority may recover from the owner of the land the amount of any expenses reasonably incurred by the authority in and in connection with the exercise of their powers under subsection (2) above, or such part of those expenses as the authority think fit.

(4) The appropriate authority shall contribute not less than a quarter of any expenses shown to their satisfaction to have been reasonably incurred in compliance with subsection (1) above, and may make further contributions of such amount in each case as, having regard to all the circumstances, they consider reasonable.

(5) Subsection (1) above does not apply to any structure—

(*a*) if any conditions for the maintenance of the structure are for the time being in force under section 147 below, or

(*b*) if and so long as, under an agreement in writing with any other person, there is a liability to maintain the structure on the part of the appropriate authority or, where the appropriate authority are a district council, on the part of either the appropriate authority or the highway authority.

Power to authorise erection of stiles etc. on footpath or bridleway. **147.**—(1) The following provisions of this section apply where the owner, lessee or occupier of agricultural land, or of land which is being brought into use for agriculture, represents to a competent authority, as respects a footpath or bridleway that crosses the land, that for securing that the use, or any particular use, of the land for agriculture shall be efficiently carried on, it is expedient that stiles, gates or other works for preventing the ingress or egress of animals should be erected on the path or way.

For the purposes of this section the following are competent authorities—

(*a*) in the case of a footpath or bridleway which is for the time being maintained by a district council by virtue of section 42 or 50 above, that council and also the highway authority, and

(b) in the case of any other footpath or bridleway, the highway authority.

(2) Where such a representation is made the authority to whom it is made may, subject to such conditions as they may impose for maintenance and for enabling the right of way to be exercised without undue inconvenience to the public, authorise the erection of the stiles, gates or other works.

(3) Where an authorisation in respect of a footpath or bridleway is granted under this section the public right of way is to be deemed to be subject to a condition that the stiles, gates or works may be erected and maintained in accordance with the authorisation and so long as the conditions attached to it are complied with.

(4) For the purposes of section 143 above, any stile, gate or works erected in pursuance of an authorisation under this section is to be deemed to be erected under this section only if the provisions of the authorisation and any conditions attached to it are complied with.

(5) In this section references to agricultural land and to land being brought into use for agriculture include references to land used or, as the case may be, land being brought into use, for forestry.

(6) Nothing in this section prejudices any limitation or condition having effect apart from this section.

148. If, without lawful authority or excuse—

> *Penalty for depositing things or pitching booths etc. on highway.*

(a) a person deposits on a made-up carriageway any dung, compost or other material for dressing land, or any rubbish, or

(b) a person deposits on any highway that consists of or comprises a made-up carriageway any dung, compost or other material for dressing land, or any rubbish, within 15 feet from the centre of that carriageway, or

(c) a person deposits any thing whatsoever on a highway to the interruption of any user of the highway, or

(d) a hawker or other itinerant trader pitches a booth, stall or stand, or encamps, on a highway.

he is guilty of an offence and liable to a fine not exceeding £50.

149.—(1) If any thing is so deposited on a highway as to constitute a nuisance, the highway authority for the highway may by notice require the person who deposited it there to remove it forthwith and if he fails to comply with the notice the authority may make a complaint to a magistrates' court for a removal and disposal order under this section.

> *Removal of things so deposited on highways as to be a nuisance etc.*

(2) If the highway authority for any highway have reasonable grounds for considering—

> (*a*) that any thing unlawfully deposited on the highway constitutes a danger (including a danger caused by obstructing the view) to users of the highway, and

> (*b*) that the thing in question ought to be removed without the delay involved in giving notice or obtaining a removal and disposal order from a magistrates' court under this section,

the authority may remove the thing forthwith.

(3) The highway authority by whom a thing is removed in pursuance of subsection (2) above may either—

> (*a*) recover from the person by whom it was deposited on the highway, or from any person claiming to be entitled to it, any expenses reasonably incurred by the authority in removing it, or

> (*b*) make a complaint to a magistrates' court for a disposal order under this section.

(4) A magistrates' court may, on a complaint made under this section, make an order authorising the complainant authority—

> (*a*) either to remove the thing in question and dispose of it or, as the case may be, to dispose of the thing in question, and

> (*b*) after payment out of any proceeds arising from the disposal of the expenses incurred in the removal and disposal, to apply the balance, if any, of the proceeds to the maintenance of highways maintainable at the public expense by them.

(5) If the thing in question is not of sufficient value to defray the expenses of removing it, the complainant authority may recover from the person who deposited it on the highway the expenses, or the balance of the expenses, reasonably incurred by them in removing it.

(6) A magistrates' court composed of a single justice may hear a complaint under this section.

Duty to remove snow soil etc. from highway.   **150.**—(1) If an obstruction arises in a highway from accumulation of snow or from the falling down of banks on the side of the highway, or from any other cause, the highway authority shall remove the obstruction.

(2) If a highway authority fail to remove an obstruction which it is their duty under this section to remove, a magistrates' court may, on a complaint made by any person, by order require the authority to remove the obstruction within such period (not being less than 24 hours) from the making of the order as the court thinks reasonable, having regard to all the circumstances of the case.

(3) In considering whether to make an order under this section and, if so, what period to allow for the removal of the obstruction, the court shall in particular have regard to—

(a) the character of the highway to which the complaint relates, and the nature and amount of the traffic by which it is ordinarily used,

(b) the nature and extent of the obstruction, and

(c) the resources of manpower, vehicles and equipment for the time being available to the highway authority for work on highways and the extent to which those resources are being, or need to be, employed elsewhere by that authority on such work.

(4) Where they are under a duty to remove an obstruction under subsection (1) above, a highway authority may—

(a) take any reasonable steps (including the placing of lights, signs and fences on the highway) for warning users of the highway of the obstruction;

(b) sell any thing removed in carrying out the duty, unless the thing is claimed by its owner before the expiration of 7 days from the date of its removal;

(c) recover from the owner of the thing which caused or contributed to the obstruction, or where the thing has been sold under paragraph (b) above, from its previous owner, the expenses reasonably incurred as respects the obstruction in carrying out the duty and in exercising any powers conferred by this subsection, but so that no such expenses are recoverable from a person who proves that he took reasonable care to secure that the thing in question did not cause or contribute to the obstruction.

(5) Where a highway authority sell any thing in exercise of their powers under subsection (4) above, then—

(a) if any expenses are recoverable under that subsection by the authority from the previous owner of the thing, they may set off the expenses against the proceeds of sale (without prejudice to the recovery of any balance of the expenses from the previous owner) and shall pay over any balance of the proceeds to the previous owner ; and

  (b) if no expenses are so recoverable, they shall pay over the whole of the proceeds of sale to the previous owner.

(6) The foregoing provisions of this section apply to a person liable to maintain a highway by reason of tenure, enclosure or prescription as they apply to the highway authority for that highway, and references in those provisions to a highway authority are to be construed accordingly.

Prevention of soil etc. being washed on to street.

151.—(1) A competent authority may, by notice to the owner or occupier of any land adjoining a street which is a highway maintainable at the public expense, require him, within 28 days from the date of service of the notice, to execute such works as will prevent soil or refuse from that land from falling, or being washed or carried, on to the street or into any sewer or gully in it in such quantities as to obstruct the street or choke the sewer or gully.

For the purposes of this section the following are competent authorities—

  (a) in relation to a street outside Greater London, the highway authority for the street and also the council of the district in which the street is situated ; and

  (b) in relation to a street within Greater London, the council of the London borough in which the street is situated or, if it is situated in the City of London, the Common Council and also, if the street is a metropolitan road, the Greater London Council.

(2) A person aggrieved by a requirement under this section may appeal to a magistrates' court.

(3) Subject to any order made on appeal, if a person on whom a notice is served under this section fails to comply with it within the period specified in subsection (1) above, he is guilty of an offence and liable to a fine not exceeding £20 for a first offence and £50 for a second or subsequent offence ; and if the offence is continued after conviction, he is guilty of a further offence and liable to a fine not exceeding £1 for each day on which the offence is so continued.

Powers as to removal of projections from buildings.

152.—(1) A competent authority may by notice to the occupier of any building require him to remove or alter any porch, shed, projecting window, step, cellar, cellar door, cellar window, sign, signpost, sign iron, showboard, window shutter, wall, gate, fence or other obstruction or projection which has been erected or placed against or in front of the building and is an obstruction to safe or convenient passage along a street.

(2) A notice under subsection (1) above may, at the option of the authority, be served on the owner of the building instead of on the occupier or may be served on both the owner and the occupier.

(3) A person aggrieved by a requirement under subsection (1) above may appeal to a magistrates' court.

(4) Subject to any order made on appeal, if a person on whom a notice under subsection (1) above is served fails to comply, within 14 days from the date of service of the notice on him, with a requirement of the notice, he is guilty of an offence and liable to a fine not exceeding £25.

(5) Where an authority serve a notice under subsection (1) above on any person and he is guilty of an offence by reason of his failure to comply with a requirement of the notice within the time specified in subsection (4) above then, whether or not proceedings are taken against him in respect of the offence, the authority may remove the obstruction or projection to which the notice relates and may recover the expenses reasonably incurred by them in so doing from the owner or occupier of the building if, in either case, he is a person on whom the notice was served.

(6) In a case where a requirement under subsection (1) above is made in connection with an obstruction or projection not erected or placed by the occupier of the relevant building Schedule 13 to this Act applies in relation to any sum paid by the occupier in complying with a requirement under that subsection or, where the requirement is not complied with, in reimbursing the relevant authority for expenses reasonably incurred by them under subsection (5) above.

(7) Subsection (1) above does not apply in respect of any such obstruction or projection as is there mentioned if it was erected or placed before the date when section 69 of the Towns Improvement Clauses Act 1847 first applied in the area in which 1847 c. 34 the building in question is situated.

(8) If any such obstruction or projection was erected or placed before that date against or in front of a building in a street, a competent authority may, on the expiration of 30 days from the date of service on either the owner or the occupier of the building of a notice of their intention, remove or alter the obstruction or projection as they think fit, and, if the obstruction or projection was lawfully erected or placed, the authority shall pay

PART IX   reasonable compensation to every person who suffers damage by reason of its removal or alteration.

(9) For the purposes of this section—

(*a*) the competent authorities are the local authority in whose area the street is situated and also, where the street is a highway, the highway authority for it;

(*b*) a projection which is erected or placed against or in front of a building, and which by reason of its being insecurely fixed or of defective construction or otherwise is a source of danger to persons lawfully using a street, is to be deemed to be an obstruction to safe or convenient passage along the street.

Doors etc. in streets not to open outwards.

153.—(1) A door, gate or bar which is put up on any premises and opens on a street shall be so put up as not to open outwards unless, in the case of a door, gate or bar put up on a public building, the local authority for the area in which the building is situated and also, if the street is a highway, the highway authority consent to its being otherwise put up.

(2) Where a door, gate or bar is put up on any premises in contravention of subsection (1) above the local authority for the area in which the premises are situated or alternatively, if the street concerned is a highway, the highway authority may, by notice to the occupier, require him to alter, so as not to open outwards, the door, gate or bar.

(3) A notice under subsection (2) above may, at the option of the highway authority or local authority, be served on the owner of the premises instead of on the occupier or may be served on both the owner and the occupier of the premises.

(4) A person aggrieved by the refusal of a consent under subsection (1) above or by a requirement under subsection (2) above may appeal to a magistrates' court.

(5) Subject to any order made on appeal, if a person on whom a notice under subsection (2) above is served fails to comply, within 8 days from the date of service of the notice on him, with a requirement of the notice, he is guilty of an offence and liable to a fine not exceeding £25.

(6) Where a highway authority or local authority serve a notice under subsection (2) above on any person and he is guilty of an offence by reason of his failure to comply with a requirement of the notice within the time specified in subsection (5) above, then, whether or not proceedings are taken against him in respect of the offence, the authority may do the work required by the notice and recover the expenses reasonably incurred by them in

so doing from the owner or occupier of the premises if, in either
case, he is a person on whom the notice was served.

(7) Where a requirement under subsection (2) above is made
in connection with a door, gate or bar not put up by the occupier
of the premises Schedule 13 to this Act applies in relation to
any sum paid by the occupier in complying with a requirement
under subsection (2) above or, where the requirement is not
complied with, in reimbursing the authority for expenses reasonably incurred by them under subsection (6) above.

154.—(1) Where a hedge, tree or shrub overhangs a highway   Cutting or
or any other road or footpath to which the public has access so   felling etc.
as to endanger or obstruct the passage of vehicles or pedestrians,   trees etc. that
or obstructs or interferes with the view of drivers of vehicles or   overhang or
the light from a public lamp, a competent authority may, by   are a danger
notice either to the owner of the hedge, tree or shrub or to the   footpaths.
occupier of the land on which it is growing, require him within
14 days from the date of service of the notice so to lop or cut
it as to remove the cause of the danger, obstruction or interference.

For the purposes of this section the following are competent
authorities—

(a) in relation to a highway for which the Minister is the
highway authority and which is in a district or London
borough, the Minister and also the council of the
district or, as the case may be, borough ;

(b) in relation to a highway for which a local highway
authority are the highway authority, that authority and
also (outside Greater London) the council of the district in which the highway is situated ;

(c) in relation to a road or footpath that is not a highway,
the local authority in whose area the road or footpath
is situated ;

and "hedge, tree or shrub" includes vegetation of any
description.

(2) Where it appears to a competent authority for any highway, or for any other road or footpath to which the public has
access—

(a) that any hedge, tree or shrub is dead, diseased, damaged
or insecurely rooted, and

(b) that by reason of its condition it, or part of it, is likely
to cause danger by falling on the highway, road or
footpath,

PART IX   the authority may, by notice either to the owner of the hedge, tree or shrub or to the occupier of the land on which it is situated, require him within 14 days from the date of service of the notice so to cut or fell it as to remove the likelihood of danger.

(3) A person aggrieved by a requirement under subsection (1) or (2) above may appeal to a magistrates' court.

(4) Subject to any order made on appeal, if a person on whom a notice is served under subsection (1) or (2) above fails to comply with it within the period specified in those subsections, the authority who served the notice may carry out the work required by the notice and recover the expenses reasonably incurred by them in so doing from the person in default.

Penalties in connection with straying animals.

155.—(1) If any horses, cattle, sheep, goats or swine are at any time found straying or lying on or at the side of a highway their keeper is guilty of an offence ; but this subsection does not apply in relation to a part of a highway passing over any common, waste or unenclosed ground.

In this section " keeper ", in relation to any animals, means a person in whose possession they are.

(2) A person guilty of an offence under this section is liable to a fine not exceeding £20 for a first offence and £50 for a second or subsequent offence.

(3) A person guilty of an offence under this section is also liable to pay the reasonable expenses of removing any animal so found straying or lying to the premises of their keeper, or to the common pound, or to such other place as may have been provided for the purpose, and any person who incurs such expenses is entitled to recover them summarily as a civil debt.

For the purposes of this subsection " expenses ", in a case where an animal has been removed to the common pound, includes the usual fees and charges of the authorised keeper of the pound.

(4) If a person, without lawful authority or excuse, releases any animal seized for the purpose of being impounded under this section from the pound or other place where it is impounded, or on the way to or from any such place, or damages any such place, he is guilty of an offence and liable to a fine not exceeding £50.

(5) Nothing in this section prejudices or affects any right of pasture on the side of a highway.

156.—(1) Subject to the provisions of this section, a statutory power of undertakers to break up or open a highway maintainable at the public expense which consists of or comprises a carriageway, being a power conferred for any purpose other than road purposes or purposes of a railway undertaking or a tramway undertaking, is not exercisable in the highway during the 12 months following either—

(a) the end of any period during which the use by vehicles of the carriageway has been prohibited, or the width of the carriageway available for vehicular traffic has been reduced to less than two-thirds of its width, for the purposes of the execution of works for road purposes or of such works and other works, or

(b) the completion of a re-surfacing extending to one-third or more of the width of the carriageway,

if the conditions specified in subsection (2) below are satisfied.

(2) The conditions referred to in subsection (1) above are—

(a) that a competent authority had given to the undertakers, more than 3 months before the date on which the works for road purposes, or the re-surfacing works, as the case may be, were substantially begun, a notice stating that works for road purposes, or re-surfacing works, relevant for the purposes of this section were in prospect and specifying a date intended for beginning them, and

(b) that the works for road purposes, or the re-surfacing works, as the case may be, were substantially begun on, or within one month from, the date so specified or, if any undertakers' works were in progress in, under, over, across, along or upon the highway on that date, within one month from the completion of those undertakers' works, or in either case within some extended period agreed between a competent authority and the undertakers for the purposes of the operation of this subsection in relation to the works for road purposes, or the re-surfacing works, as the case may be.

For the purposes of this subsection the following are competent authorities:—

(i) in the case of a highway which is for the time being maintained by a district council by virtue of section 42 or 50 above, that council and also the highway authority, and

(ii) in the case of any other highway, the highway authority.

(3) Subsection (1) above does not apply to breaking up or opening for the purposes of emergency works.

(4) Subsection (1) above does not apply to breaking up or opening a part of the highway other than a carriageway for the purposes of—

    (a) works relating only to a service pipe or service line or an overhead telegraphic line or an overhead electric line, or

    (b) works required for satisfaction by the undertakers of an obligation of theirs created by an enactment, or created by an agreement made before the giving of the notice referred to in subsection (1) above, which it is not reasonably practicable for them to satisfy without the breaking up or opening in question;

but the exception in paragraph (a) above applies, in the case of a placing of a service pipe or service line, only if it is for affording a supply or service to premises to which it is not already afforded.

(5) Subsection (1) above does not apply to breaking up or opening done with the consent of the highway authority, and a consent for this purpose shall not be unreasonably withheld.

Any question whether the withholding of such a consent is unreasonable shall be determined by the Minister and the Minister of the Crown in charge of the department concerned with the purposes for which the power to break up or open is conferred acting jointly (any question which is the department so concerned being determined by the Treasury), and such a determination of the said Ministers shall not be impugned on the ground that either of them is himself the highway authority or the authority by whom the power is exercisable.

(6) Subsection (1) above does not apply to breaking up or opening a highway to which section 157 below applies.

(7) If undertakers break up or open a highway in any case in which it is unlawful by virtue of subsection (1) above for them to do so—

    (a) they shall pay to the highway authority an amount equal to any cost reasonably incurred by the authority of reinstating and making good the highway; and

    (b) without prejudice to their liability under paragraph (a) above, they are guilty of an offence and liable to a fine not exceeding £50.

If any question arises in relation to a claim made for a payment under paragraph (a) above the question shall be determined by a single arbitrator appointed, in default of agreement between the parties concerned, by the President of the Institution of Civil Engineers.

(8) Proceedings for the enforcement of the obligation imposed by subsection (1) above shall not, without the written consent of the Attorney-General, be taken by any person other than a person having an interest in the performance of the obligation.

(9) In so far as any failure of undertakers to satisfy an obligation to which they are subject by virtue of any enactment is attributable to the prohibition by this section of breaking up or opening for which the undertakers have duly sought the consent of the highway authority and for which consent has been withheld and (where the withholding has been questioned) has been determined to have been reasonably withheld, the failure shall not be treated as a contravention of that enactment.

(10) In this section—

(a) the reference to a power conferred for the purposes of a railway undertaking or a tramway undertaking includes a reference to a power conferred primarily for those purposes but for other purposes also;

(b) " emergency works ", " railway ", " reinstatement and making good ", " road purposes ", " service line ", " service pipe ", " telegraphic line ", " tramway ", " undertakers " and " undertakers' works " have the same meaning respectively as in the Public Utilities Street Works Act 1950.

1950 c. 39.

157.—(1) With a view to securing that the times for the execution of works of road maintenance and improvement by various highway authorities within Greater London may be so arranged as to mitigate as far as possible the congestion of traffic due to the closing of highways for the purposes of the execution of such works, every highway authority for highways within Greater London have the duty imposed by subsection (2) below.

Half-yearly programmes to be prepared of repair and improvement works in Greater London.

(2) The duty referred to in subsection (1) above is a duty to prepare and, except in the case of the Greater London Council, to submit to that Council in accordance with subsections (3) and (4) below statements of works of road maintenance and road improvement.

(3) The statements required by subsection (2) above of highway authorities, other than the Greater London Council, shall be submitted to the Council, and the statements required by the Council shall be prepared by them, on or before such half-yearly dates in each year as the Council may by order fix and

shall be in such form and shall contain such particulars as the Council may require, or in the case of a statement prepared by them, think fit, of the works specified in subsection (4) below.

(4) The works referred to in subsection (3) above are all works of road maintenance and improvement proposed to be begun or continued by the authority during the period of 6 months commencing at the expiration of such interval, not being less than 2 months, from the half-yearly dates referred to in subsection (3) above as the Council may by order fix, being works of such a nature as will involve the closing to vehicular traffic of any part of any highway to which this section applies either absolutely or to the extent of one-third or more of the width of the carriageway.

(5) The Council shall consider in relation to one another the proposals contained in the statements submitted to, or prepared by, them under this section and after consultation with the appropriate commissioner of police and the London Transport Executive shall draw up schemes prescribing the times during which the several works are to be begun and the order in which they are to be executed, or prohibiting or restricting the execution of any of the works.

(6) The Council shall send copies of each such scheme drawn up by them to all highway authorities and undertakers affected by it, and—

(a) if, within 14 days from the date on which copies of any scheme have been so sent, no objection in writing to the scheme has been received by the Council from any highway authority or undertakers affected by it, or every objection so made has been withdrawn, the Council may by order confirm the scheme ;

(b) if any objection so made to a scheme has been received by the Council within that time and has not been withdrawn, the Council may, after considering the objection, either by order confirm the scheme, with or without amendments, or revoke the scheme ;

and upon the confirmation of a scheme drawn up by the Council under this section it shall, subject to subsection (7) below, become final and binding on all the highway authorities affected, other than the Minister of Transport, and shall not be subject to appeal to any court.

(7) Nothing in this section—

(a) prevents a highway authority from carrying out works in a highway in the case of emergency, or (*b*) empowers the Council to impose any obligation on a highway authority to incur any expenditure on or in connection with the construction or improvement of a highway without the consent of that authority.

(8) The highways to which this section applies are such highways, or highways of such classes, being in either case highways maintainable at the public expense within Greater London and consisting of or comprising a carriageway, as may be prescribed by an order made by the Council.

(9) In this section and sections 158 to 160 below " undertakers " means the Post Office and persons having powers to break up or open highways in Greater London for the purposes of any sewerage system, or any water, gas, electricity, tramway or other undertaking.

158.—(1) Where, with a view to facilitating the movement of traffic, it is proposed to execute in Greater London works of road improvement of such a nature as will involve the closing to vehicular traffic as mentioned in subsection (4) of section 157 above of a part of a highway to which that section applies, the Greater London Council may, in accordance with subsection (2) below, if on grounds of urgency they consider it expedient, authorise those works— *Relaxation of section 157 in certain cases.*

(*a*) to be begun without being included in the scheme in force under that section, or

(*b*) (if they are so included) to be begun otherwise than in accordance with the scheme.

(2) An authorisation under subsection (1) above may be granted by the Council—

(*a*) in the case of any highway for which they are the highway authority, or

(*b*) on the application of the council of a London borough or the Common Council, in the case of any highway for which the borough council or Common Council, as the case may be, are the highway authority.

(3) Where the Council give authority under subsection (1) above for the execution of any works of road improvement, or receive notice from the Minister of Transport that such works of road improvement as are mentioned in that subsection are to be executed in the case of a highway for which he is the highway authority, they may by order modify in such manner as appears to them to be expedient the scheme under section 157 above.

(4) The Council shall send copies of any such order to all undertakers whose powers extend to highways to which the order relates and if the highway authority one month or more

PART IX   before they begin the works give to any such undertakers a notice containing the like particulars of the proposed works as would be required in a statement under section 157 above, section 159(2) to (4) below shall apply as if the undertakers had been sent copies of the proposals under section 159(1).

(5) In this section " undertakers " has the meaning provided by section 157(9) above.

Restrictions on breaking up by undertakers of highways in Greater London recently closed for repair.

159.—(1) With a view to securing that, so far as possible, all works involving breaking up or opening of highways to which section 157 above applies by undertakers are carried out at the same time as or in connection with works of road maintenance and improvement, the Greater London Council shall send to all undertakers copies of—

(a) the proposals of other highway authorities when submitted to them under section 157 above, and

(b) the proposals prepared by them under that section,

so far as the proposals relate to highways to which the powers of the undertakers extend and shall consider any representations made to them by those undertakers.

(2) Where works of road maintenance and improvement involving the closing to vehicular traffic of any part of a highway either absolutely or to the extent of one-third or more of the width of the carriageway have been executed in accordance with a scheme confirmed under section 157 above, it shall not be lawful for any undertakers during the 12 months following the completion of those works to break up or open the highway so closed without the previous consent of the Greater London Council and unless they prove to the satisfaction of the Council—

(a) that there were reasonable grounds for their failure or omission to execute, while the highway or part of it was closed, the works for the execution of which they require to break up or open the highway ; and

(b) that it is essential that the works should be executed or begun during the said 12 months.

(3) The Council may, if they think fit, make it a condition of giving their consent under subsection (2) above to breaking up or opening a highway that all works in connection with it are carried out at night by beginning them after 8 p.m. and completing them by 8 a.m., and if not then completed by carrying on the work continuously by day and night.

(4) The consent of the Council for the purposes of subsection (2) above shall not be unreasonably withheld and any

question whether the withholding of such consent is unreasonable shall be determined in like manner as any similar question arising under section 156(5) above; and section 156(7) and (8) have effect as if the references therein to section 156(1) included references to subsection (2) above.

(5) Nothing in this section prevents any undertakers from carrying out works in a highway in a case of emergency or from making, altering, repairing or disconnecting service connections.

(6) In this section " undertakers " has the meaning provided by section 157(9) above.

160.—(1) If, in the case of any highway in Greater London other than a metropolitan road, it appears to an officer of police authorised for the purpose that any of the following persons, namely—

(*a*) any undertakers acting in the exercise of a statutory power to break up or open that highway, or

(*b*) any person acting in the exercise of the power conferred by section 15(1) of the Pipelines Act 1962, or

(*c*) any person acting in the exercise of the power conferred by section 34(2) of the Public Health Act 1936,

has caused an unnecessary obstruction for the purposes of this section, he shall report the matter to the highway authority for the highway and that authority shall cause an inspection to be made.

If on the inspection it appears to the highway authority that the allegation is well founded they may proceed as provided by subsection (4) below.

(2) If, in the case of any highway in Greater London other than one for which the Minister of Transport is the highway authority, it appears to the Greater London Council that any of the following persons, namely—

(*a*) any person mentioned in paragraph (*a*), (*b*) or (*c*) of subsection (1) above, or

(*b*) where the highway is not a metropolitan road, the highway authority acting in the exercise of a statutory power to break up or open the highway,

has caused an unnecessary obstruction for the purposes of this section, the Council may proceed as provided by subsection (4) below.

(3) For the purposes of this section a person causes an unnecessary obstruction where by the deposit of excavated matter or other material, or by means of the erection of barriers, or otherwise, he creates an obstruction in a highway to a greater extent or for a longer period than is reasonably necessary.

Powers as respects certain unnecessary obstructions of highways in Greater London.

1962 c. 58.

1936 c. 49.

F 3

PART IX

(4) In the circumstances mentioned in subsection (1) or (2) above the highway authority or, as the case may be, the Greater London Council may by notice require the person causing the obstruction to take such steps as may appear to the highway authority or, as the case may be, the Council to be necessary, and as are specified in the notice, to mitigate or discontinue the obstruction.

(5) Subject to subsection (6) below, if the person causing the obstruction ("the defaulter") fails to comply with such requirement within 24 hours of the receipt of the notice the enforcing authority (that is to say, the highway authority or, as the case may be, the Greater London Council) may take the necessary steps and may recover any expenses reasonably incurred by them in connection therewith from the defaulter.

(6) If within 24 hours of receiving such a notice the defaulter, in a case where the obstructed highway is not one for which the Minister of Transport is the highway authority, makes representations to that Minister that the obstruction is not greater, or has not been continued for a longer period, than is reasonably necessary, and sends to the enforcing authority a copy of the representations so made, the enforcing authority shall not take any such steps as are authorised by subsection (5) above without the consent of that Minister.

(7) A highway authority may, if they think fit, delegate to an officer of the authority their powers under this section of causing inspection to be made and of making requirements, and the Greater London Council may, if they think fit, delegate to an officer of the Council their powers under this section of making requirements.

(8) In this section "undertakers" has the meaning provided by section 157(9) above.

Danger or annoyance to users of highways and streets

Penalties for causing certian kinds of danger or annoyance.

161.—(1) If a person, without lawful authority or excuse, deposits any thing whatsoever on a highway in consequence of which a user of the highway is injured or endangered, that person is guilty of an offence and liable to a fine not exceeding £100.

(2) If a person, without lawful authority or excuse, lights any fire, or discharges any firearm or firework, within 50 feet of the centre of a highway which consists of or comprises a carriageway, and in consequence a user of the highway is injured, interrupted or endangered, that person is guilty of an offence and liable to a fine not exceeding £20 for a first offence and £50 for a second or subsequent offence.

(3) If a person plays at football or any other game on a highway to the annoyance of a user of the highway he is guilty of an offence and liable to a fine not exceeding £10.

(4) If a person, without lawful authority or excuse, allows any filth, dirt, lime or other offensive matter or thing to run or flow on to a highway from any adjoining premises, he is guilty of an offence and liable to a fine not exceeding £10.

162. A person who for any purpose places any rope, wire or other apparatus across a highway in such a manner as to be likely to cause danger to persons using the highway is, unless he proves that he had taken all necessary means to give adequate warning of the danger, guilty of an offence and liable to a fine not exceeding £50.

Penalty for placing rope, etc. across highway.

163.—(1) A competent authority may, by notice to the occupier of premises adjoining a highway, require him within 28 days from the date of service of the notice to construct or erect and thereafter to maintain such channels, gutters or downpipes as may be necessary to prevent—

Prevention of water falling on or flowing on to highway.

    (*a*) water from the roof or any other part of the premises falling upon persons using the highway, or

    (*b*) so far as is reasonably practicable, surface water from the premises flowing on to, or over, the footway of the highway.

For the purposes of this section the competent authorities, in relation to any highway, are the highway authority and also (where they are not the highway authority) the local authority for the area in which the highway is situated.

(2) A notice under subsection (1) above may, at the option of the authority, be served on the owner of the premises in question instead of on the occupier or may be served on both the owner and the occupier of the premises.

(3) A person aggrieved by a requirement under this section may appeal to a magistrates' court.

(4) Subject to any order made on appeal, if a person on whom a notice is served under this section fails to comply with the requirement of the notice within the period specified in subsection (1) above he is guilty of an offence and liable to a fine not exceeding £20 ; and if the offence is continued after conviction he is guilty of a further offence and liable to a fine not exceeding £2 for each day on which the offence is so continued.

F 4

164.—(1) Where on land adjoining a highway there is a fence made with barbed wire, or having barbed wire in or on it, and the wire is a nuisance to the highway, a competent authority may by notice served on the occupier of the land require him to abate the nuisance within such time, not being less than one month nor more than 6 months from the date of service of the notice, as may be specified in it.

For the purposes of this section—

(*a*) the competent authorities, in relation to any highway, are the highway authority and also (where they are not the highway authority) the local authority for the area in which the highway is situated ;

(*b*) " barbed wire " means wire with spikes or jagged projections, and barbed wire is to be deemed to be a nuisance to a highway if it is likely to be injurious to persons or animals lawfully using the highway.

(2) If at the expiration of the time specified in the notice the occupier has failed to comply with the notice, a magistrates' court, if satisfied on complaint made by the authority that the wire is a nuisance to the highway, may order the occupier to abate the nuisance and, if he fails to comply with the order within a reasonable time, the authority may do whatever may be necessary in execution of the order and recover from him the expenses reasonably incurred by them in so doing.

(3) If the local authority who are a competent authority in relation to the highway concerned are the occupiers of the land in question proceedings under this section may be taken against them by any ratepayer within the area of that local authority and the foregoing provisions apply accordingly in relation to him and to the authority as they apply in relation to an authority and to an occupier of land.

165.—(1) If, in or on any land adjoining a street, there is an unfenced or inadequately fenced source of danger to persons using the street, the local authority in whose area the street is situated may, by notice to the owner or occupier of that land, require him within such time as may be specified in the notice to execute such works of repair, protection, removal or enclosure as will obviate the danger.

(2) A person aggrieved by a requirement under subsection (1) above may appeal to a magistrates' court.

(3) Subject to any order made on appeal, if a person on whom a notice is served under this section fails to comply with the notice within the time specified in it, the authority by whom the notice was served may execute such works as are

necessary to comply with the notice and may recover the expenses reasonably incurred by them in so doing from that person.

(4) Where the power conferred by subsection (1) above is exercisable in relation to land adjoining a street and has not been exercised by the local authority empowered to exercise it, then, if that authority are not the highway authority for the street, the highway authority for the street may request the local authority to exercise the power.

(5) If the local authority refuse to comply with a request made under subsection (4) above or fail within a reasonable time after the request is made to them to do so, the highway authority may exercise the power (and where they do so subsections (2) and (3) above apply accordingly).

166.—(1) If it appears to a competent authority that the forecourt of premises abutting on a street, or any steps or projection or goods (whether for sale or not) placed in such a forecourt, is or are a source of danger, obstruction or inconvenience to the public, the authority may by notice require the owner or occupier of the forecourt to fence the forecourt from the street or, at his election, to take such other steps as may be specified in the notice to obviate the danger, obstruction or inconvenience to the public.

Forecourt abutting on streets.

For the purposes of this section the following are competent authorities—

(a) in the case of a street outside Greater London which is a highway, a local authority and also the highway authority;

(b) in the case of any other street, a local authority.

(2) If it appears to a competent authority that a stall or other erection on a forecourt of premises abutting on a street is by reason of its character injurious to the amenities of the street, the authority may by notice require the owner or occupier of the forecourt to make such alterations in the stall or other erection as may be necessary to prevent its being injurious to the amenities of the street or, at his election, to remove it.

This subsection does not apply to any erection which has been in position in the forecourt of any premises at all times since 10th November 1960.

(3) A competent authority does not have power under subsection (1) or (2) above to give a notice applying to any advertisement as defined in section 290(1) of the Town and Country Planning Act 1971, or under subsection (2) above to

1971 c. 78.

PART IX give a notice applying to anything erected in conformity with planning permission granted on an application under Part III of that Act.

1936 c. 49. (4) The provisions of Part XII of the Public Health Act 1936 with respect to appeals against, and the enforcement of, notices requiring the execution of works apply in relation to any notice under this section as if this section were contained in that Act (and as if the references to the local authority included references to the highway authority) ; and section 290(6) of that Act shall authorise the authority at their election to take either of the courses which were open to the person on whom the notice was served in order to comply with it.

(5) In this section, " local authority " means any of the following, namely, the council of a district or London borough, the Common Council, the sub-treasurer of the Inner Temple, the under-treasurer of the Middle Temple, and the Council of the Isles of Scilly.

Powers relating to retaining walls near streets. **167.**—(1) This section applies to any length of a retaining wall, being a length—

   (*a*) any cross-section of which is wholly or partly within 4 yards of a street ; and

   (*b*) which is at any point of a greater height than 4 feet 6 inches above the level of the ground at the boundary of the street nearest that point ;

but does not apply to any length of a retaining wall erected on land belonging to any transport undertakers so long as that land is used by them primarily for the purpose of their undertaking or to any length of a retaining wall for the maintenance of which a highway authority are responsible.

(2) No length of retaining wall, being a length which when erected will be a length of retaining wall to which this section applies, shall be erected otherwise than in accordance with plans, sections and specifications approved by the local authority in whose area the street is situated ; and before giving such approval that authority, if they are not the highway authority for the street, shall consult the highway authority.

(3) Any person aggrieved by the refusal of a local authority to approve any plans, sections and specifications submitted to them under this section may appeal to a magistrates' court.

(4) If a person erects a length of retaining wall in contravention of this section, he is guilty of an offence and liable to a fine not exceeding £100.

(5) If a length of retaining wall to which this section applies is in such condition (whether for want of repair or some other reason) as to be liable to endanger persons using the street, the local authority in whose area the street is situated may, by notice served on the owner or occupier of the land on which that length of wall is, require him to execute such works as will obviate the danger.

(6) Where the power conferred by subsection (5) above is exercisable in relation to a length of wall and has not been exercised by the local authority empowered to exercise it, then, if that authority are not the highway authority for the street in question, the highway authority may request the local authority to exercise the power; and if the local authority refuse to comply with the request or fail within a reasonable time after the request is made to them to do so, the highway authority may exercise the power.

(7) Subsections (2) to (7) of section 290 of the Public Health 1936 c. 49. Act 1936 (appeals against and the enforcement of, certain notices under that Act) apply to any notice served under subsection (5) above as they apply to such notices as are mentioned in subsection (1) of that section, but subject to the following modifications:—

(a) references to the local authority are to be construed as including references to the highway authority;

(b) for paragraph (f) of subsection (3) there is substituted the following paragraph—

" (f) that some other person ought to contribute towards the expense of executing any works required by the notice ".

(8) Sections 300 to 302 of the Public Health Act 1936 (supplementary provisions relating to appeals under the said section 290) apply, with the necessary modifications, to appeals brought by virtue of subsection (7) above.

(9) In this section " retaining wall " means a wall, not forming part of a permanent building, which serves, or is intended to serve, as a support for earth or other material on one side only.

Precautions to be taken in doing certain works in or near streets or highways

168.—(1) If in the course of the carrying out of any building operation in or near a street there occurs an accident which— Building operations affecting public safety.

(a) gives rise to the risk of serious bodily injury to a person in the street, whether or not the death or disablement of any person is caused thereby; or (*b*) would have given rise to such risk but for the fact that a local authority or highway authority had in the exercise of their powers under section 25 of the Public Health Act 1961 (emergency measures to deal with dangerous buildings) or any other enactment taken steps to ensure that if an accident occurred it would not give rise to such risk,

then, subject to the provisions of this section, the owner of the land or building on which the building operation is being carried out is, without prejudice to any liability to which he or any other person may be subject apart from this section, guilty of an offence and liable to a fine not exceeding £500.

(2) Where the commission by any person of an offence under this section is due to the act or default of some other person, that other person is guilty of the offence, and a person may be charged with and convicted of the offence by virtue of this subsection whether or not proceedings are taken against the first-mentioned person.

(3) In any proceedings for an offence under this section it is a defence, subject to subsection (4) below, for the person charged to prove—

(*a*) that he took all reasonable precautions to secure that the building operation was so carried out as to avoid causing danger to persons in a street; or

(*b*) that the commission of the offence was due to the act or default of another person and that he took all reasonable precautions and exercised all due diligence to avoid the commission of such an offence by himself or any person under his control.

(4) A person charged with an offence under this section is not, without leave of the court, entitled to rely on the defence provided by subsection (3)(*b*) above unless, within a period ending 7 clear days before the hearing, he has served on the prosecutor a notice in writing giving such information identifying or assisting in the identification of that other person as was then in his possession.

(5) In this section " building operation " means the construction, structural alteration, repair or maintenance of a building (including re-pointing, external re-decoration and external cleaning), the demolition of a building, the preparation for, and laying the foundations of, an intended building and the erection or dismantling of cranes or scaffolding.

Control of scaffolding on highways.   **169.**—(1) Subject to subsection (6) below no person shall, in connection with any building or demolition work or the alteration, repair, maintenance or cleaning of any building, erect or retain on or over a highway any scaffolding or other structure which obstructs the highway (hereafter in this section referred to as a " relevant structure ") unless he is authorised to do so by a licence in writing issued for the purposes of this section by the highway authority (hereafter in this section referred to as " a licence ") and complies with the terms of the licence ; and a licence may contain such terms as the authority issuing it thinks fit.

(2) If a person applies to a highway authority for a licence in respect of any relevant structure and furnishes the authority with such particulars in connection with the structure as the authority reasonably demand, it is the duty of the authority to issue a licence to him in respect of the structure unless the authority consider—

(a) that the structure would cause unreasonable obstruction of a highway ; or

(b) that a relevant structure erected otherwise than as proposed by the applicant would cause less obstruction of a highway than the structure proposed by him and could conveniently be used for the work in question.

(3) If on an application for a licence in connection with a highway the highway authority refuse to issue a licence or issue a licence containing terms to which the applicant objects, the applicant may appeal to a magistrates' court against the refusal or terms ; and on such an appeal the court may—

(a) in the case of an appeal against a refusal, direct the highway authority to issue a licence in pursuance of the application ;

(b) in the case of an appeal against the terms of the licence, alter the terms.

(4) Subject to subsection (6) below, it is the duty of a person to whom a licence is issued by a highway authority in respect of a relevant structure—

(a) to ensure that the structure is adequately lit at all times between half an hour after sunset and half an hour before sunrise ;

(b) to comply with any directions given to him in writing by the authority with respect to the erection and maintenance of traffic signs in connection with the structure ; and

(c) to do such things in connection with the structure as any statutory undertakers reasonably request him to do for the purpose of protecting or giving access to any apparatus belonging to or used or maintained by the undertakers.

In this subsection and in section 171(2) below "statutory undertakers" means any of the following, namely, any body who are statutory undertakers within the meaning provided by section 329(1) below, the Post Office, any public authority exercising functions by virtue of any provision of sections 14 and 15 of the Water Act 1973 (which relate to sewerage) and any person entitled to the benefit of a licence in respect of the highway in question under section 181 below.

(5) A person who contravenes the provisions of subsection (1) above otherwise than by failing to comply with the terms of a licence or who fails without reasonable excuse to comply with the terms of a licence or to perform a duty imposed on him by subsection (4) above, is guilty of an offence and liable to a fine not exceeding £400.

(6) Nothing in the preceding provisions of this section applies to a relevant structure erected before 14th February 1977 or erected or retained by the British Railways Board, the British Waterways Board or the London Transport Executive in the exercise of powers conferred on the body in question by any enactment; and nothing in paragraph (a) or (b) of subsection (4) above applies to a relevant structure if no part of it is less than 18 inches in a horizontal direction from a carriageway of the relevant highway and no part of it over a footway of the relevant highway is less than 8 feet in a vertical direction above the footway.

(7) No civil or criminal proceedings lie in respect of any obstruction of a highway which is caused by a relevant structure if the structure is on or over the highway in accordance with a licence and the person to whom the licence is issued performs the duties imposed on him in respect of the structure by subsection (4) above; and a highway authority by whom a licence is issued do not incur any liability by reason of the issue of the licence.

Control of mixing of mortar etc. on highways.
170.—(1) Subject to subsection (2) below, a person who mixes or deposits on a highway any mortar or cement or any other substance which is likely to stick to the surface of the highway or which, if it enters drains or sewers connected with the highway, is likely to solidify in the drains or sewers is guilty of an offence and liable to a fine not exceeding £200.

(2) Nothing in subsection (1) above applies to any mixing or deposit—

   (a) in a receptacle or on a plate which prevents the substance in question from coming into contact with the highway and from entering any drains and sewers connected with the highway;

(*b*) by the highway authority or a local authority in connection with the maintenance or alteration of the highway or a bridge over which or a tunnel through which the highway passes ;

(*c*) by a body having a duty under an enactment to maintain—

(i) a bridge over which or a tunnel through which the highway passes, or

(ii) works or materials supporting or protecting the highway where it forms part of the approaches to such a bridge or tunnel,

if the mixing or deposit is in connection with the maintenance or alteration of the bridge, tunnel, works or materials ;

(*d*) by statutory undertakers in connection with apparatus in or the placing of apparatus in the highway ;

(*e*) by a person entitled to the benefit of a licence in respect of the highway under section 181 below if the mixing or deposit cannot reasonably be done elsewhere than on the highway.

(3) In subsection (2) above—

" local authority " means any of the following, namely, the council of a county, district or London borough, the Greater London Council, the Common Council and the Council of the Isles of Scilly ; and

" statutory undertakers " means any of the following, namely, any body who are statutory undertakers within the meaning provided by section 329(1) below, the Post Office and any public authority exercising functions by virtue of any provision of sections 14 and 15 of the Water Act 1973 (which relate to sewerage). 1973 c. 37.

171.—(1) A person may, with the consent of the highway authority for a street that is a highway maintainable at the public expense, temporarily deposit building materials, rubbish or other things in the street or make a temporary excavation in it.

Control of deposit of building materials and making of excavations in streets.

(2) A highway authority may give their consent under subsection (1) above subject to such conditions as they think fit including in particular, without prejudice to the generality of the foregoing, conditions for preventing damage or ensuring access to apparatus of statutory undertakers.

In this subsection " statutory undertakers " has the meaning provided by section 169(4) above.

(3) A person aggrieved by the refusal of consent under subsection (1) above, and a person to whom such a consent is given subject to conditions, may appeal to a magistrates' court against the refusal or, as the case may be, the conditions.

(4) It is the duty of a person who makes such a deposit or excavation as is mentioned in subsection (1) above to comply with any directions given to him in writing by the highway authority with respect to the erection and maintenance of traffic signs in connection with the deposit or excavation.

(5) Where a person places any building materials, rubbish or other thing in, or makes an excavation in, a street he shall—

(a) cause the obstruction or excavation to be properly fenced and during the hours of darkness to be properly lighted, and

(b) if required so to do by the highway authority for the street or, in the case of a street that is not a highway, by the local authority in whose area the street is situated, remove the obstruction or, as the case may be, fill in the excavation;

and in any case he shall not allow the obstruction or excavation to remain in the street longer than is necessary.

(6) A person who—

(a) without reasonable excuse contravenes any condition subject to which a consent is given to him under subsection (1) above, or

(b) without reasonable excuse fails to perform the duty imposed on him by subsection (4) above, or

(c) fails to perform a duty imposed on him by subsection (5) above,

is guilty of an offence and liable to a fine not exceeding £10 in respect of each day on which the contravention or failure occurs.

The liability of any person to a fine under this subsection by virtue of paragraph (b) or (c) above is without prejudice to any other liability to which he may be subject apart from this subsection.

(7) Where an offence under this section by virtue of subsection (6)(c) above is committed in a street, the highway authority for the street or, in the case of a street that is not a highway, the local authority in whose area the street is situated, may remove the obstruction or, as the case may be, fill in the excavation and recover the expenses reasonably incurred by them in so doing from the person convicted of the offence.

172.—(1) Subject to subsection (2) below, a person proposing to erect or take down a building in a street or court, or to alter or repair the outside of a building in a street or court, shall, before beginning the work, erect a close boarded hoarding or fence to the satisfaction of the appropriate authority so as to separate the building from the street or court.

For the purposes of this section the appropriate authority, in relation to any street or court, is the council of the county or London borough in which it is situated or, if it is situated in the City, the Common Council.

(2) The obligation to erect a hoarding or fence imposed by subsection (1) above may be dispensed with if the appropriate authority so consent.

(3) Where a person has erected a hoarding or fence in compliance with subsection (1) above, he shall—

(a) if the appropriate authority so require, make a convenient covered platform and handrail to serve as a footway for pedestrians outside the hoarding or fence ;

(b) maintain the hoarding or fence and any such platform and handrail in good condition to the satisfaction of the authority during such time as the authority may require ;

(c) if the authority so require, sufficiently light the hoarding or fence and any such platform and handrail during the hours of darkness ; and

(d) remove the hoarding or fence and any such platform and handrail when required by the authority.

(4) A person aggrieved by the refusal of a consent under subsection (2) above or by a requirement under subsection (3) above may appeal to a magistrates' court.

(5) Subject to any order made on appeal, if a person contravenes this section he is guilty of an offence and liable to a fine not exceeding £100 ; and if the offence is continued after conviction he is guilty of a further offence and liable to a fine not exceeding £2 for each day on which the offence is so continued.

173.—(1) No person shall use for any purpose a hoarding or similar structure that is in, or adjoins, any street unless it is securely fixed to the satisfaction of the council who, in relation to that street, are the appropriate authority for the purposes of section 172 above.

(2) If a person contravenes this section he is guilty of an offence and liable to a fine not exceeding £25 ; and if the offence is continued after conviction he is guilty of a further offence and liable to a fine not exceeding £1 for each day on which the offence is so continued.

PART IX
Precautions
to be taken
by persons
executing
works in
streets.
1950 c. 39.

174.—(1) Without prejudice to section 8 of the Public Utilities Street Works Act 1950 (requirements as to safety, obstruction and other matters to be observed during and in connection with the execution of certain works in streets and in controlled land within the meaning of that Act), where in the exercise of a power conferred by or under any enactment or otherwise any person is executing works in any street he—

(a) shall erect such barriers and traffic signs for preventing danger to traffic, for regulating traffic, and for warning traffic of danger, as may be necessary and remove them as soon as they cease to be needed for any of those purposes ;

(b) shall cause the works to be properly guarded and lighted during the hours of darkness ; and

(c) where the nature of the works so requires, shall cause any building adjoining the street to be shored up or otherwise protected.

(2) Subject to subsection (3) below, if any person fails to satisfy an obligation to which he is subject by virtue of subsection (1) above he is guilty of an offence and, without prejudice to any other liability to which he may be subject apart from this subsection, is liable to a fine not exceeding £10 in respect of each day of such failure.

(3) Where a person is subject to the same obligation by virtue of subsection (1) above and by virtue of some other enactment, then, without prejudice to section 18 of the Interpretation Act 1978 (offences under two or more laws), if a failure by him to satisfy that obligation is an offence under an enactment other than subsection (2) above, subsection (2) above does not apply in relation to a failure by him to satisfy that obligation.

(4) If a person, without lawful authority or excuse,—

(a) takes down, alters or removes any barrier, traffic sign, support or light erected or placed in pursuance of subsection (1) above or any fence, barrier, traffic sign or light erected or placed on or near a street in pursuance of any other enactment for the purpose of warning users of the street of any obstruction, whether caused by the execution of works in or near the street or otherwise, or of protecting them from danger arising out of such an obstruction, or

(b) extinguishes any light so placed,

he is guilty of an offence and liable to a fine not exceeding £100.

(5) For the purposes of section 312 below in its application to an offence under this section statutory undertakers and the Post Office are each to be deemed to be a person aggrieved.

175. If—

(*a*) any officer or servant of the highway authority for a highway, or

(*b*) any officer or servant of a district council maintaining a highway by virtue of section 42 or 50 above, or

(*c*) a person liable to maintain a highway by reason of tenure, enclosure or prescription,

causes any heap of materials or any other object to be laid on the highway, he is, if he allows it to remain there at night to the danger of traffic without taking all reasonable precautions for the prevention of accidents, guilty of an offence and liable to a fine not exceeding £25.

Miscellaneous

176.—(1) The highway authority for a highway may grant to the owner or occupier of any premises adjoining the highway a licence to construct a bridge over the highway on such terms and conditions, and to use it for such period and on such terms and conditions, as the authority think fit.

(2) No fine, rent or other sum of money, except a reasonable sum in respect of legal or other expenses, is payable in respect of a licence under this section.

(3) A licence under this section shall not authorise any interference with the convenience of persons using the highway, or affect the rights of owners of premises adjoining the highway, or the rights of tramway, railway, dock, harbour or electricity undertakers.

(4) It shall be a condition of every licence under this section that the person to whom it is granted is, at his own expense, to remove the bridge or alter it in such manner as the authority may require, if at any time they consider the removal or alteration necessary or desirable in connection with the carrying out of improvements to the highway.

The decision of the authority that the removal or alteration is necessary or desirable in that connection shall be final, and the condition shall be enforceable by the authority against the owner for the time being of the premises.

(5) Subject to subsection (6) below, a person aggrieved by the refusal of an authority to grant a licence under this section or by the period for which the licence is granted or by a term or condition of the licence (other than the condition mentioned in subsection (4) above) may appeal to the Crown Court.

(6) No appeal lies under subsection (5) above against any term or condition of a licence granted by the Minister under

PART IX   this section if he declares the term or condition to be necessary for the purpose of securing the safety of persons using the highway or of preventing interference with traffic on it.

(7) If a person, except in the exercise of statutory powers—

(a) constructs a bridge over a highway without a licence under this section, or

(b) constructs or uses a bridge otherwise than in accordance with the terms and conditions of such a licence, or

(c) fails to remove or alter a bridge when required to do so in accordance with any condition of the licence or within one month from the date of the expiration of the licence,

he is guilty of an offence and is liable to a fine not exceeding £50, and if the offence is continued after conviction he is guilty of a further offence and is liable to a fine not exceeding £5 for each day on which the offence is so continued.

(8) In this section " bridge " means a structure the sole purpose of which is to provide a way over a highway.

Restriction on construction of buildings over highways.

177.—(1) No person shall—

(a) except in the exercise of statutory powers, construct a building over any part of a highway maintainable at the public expense (whether it is intended to span the highway or not), or alter a building so constructed, without a licence granted under this section by the highway authority for that highway or otherwise than in accordance with the terms and conditions of a licence so granted ;

(b) use a building so constructed or altered in pursuance of a licence so granted otherwise than in accordance with the terms and conditions thereof:

and any person who contravenes any provision of this subsection is guilty of an offence and liable to a fine not exceeding £400 ; and if the offence is continued after conviction, he is guilty of a further offence and liable to a fine not exceeding £50 for each day on which the offence is so continued.

(2) Subject to subsections (3) and (4) below, a licence under this section may contain such terms and conditions, including terms and conditions with respect to the construction (including the headway over the highway), maintenance, lighting and use of the building, as the highway authority think fit ; and, any such term or condition is binding on the successor in title to every owner, and every lessee and occupier, of the building.

(3) No fine, rent or other sum of money is payable in respect of a licence granted under this section except—

> (*a*) a reasonable sum in respect of legal or other expenses incurred in connection with the grant of the licence ; and
>
> (*b*) an annual charge of a reasonable amount for administering the licence ;

and any sum payable by virtue of paragraph (*a*) above is recoverable from the applicant for the licence and any sum payable by virtue of paragraph (*b*) above is recoverable from the owner of the building.

(4) No such licence shall authorise any interference with the convenience of persons using the highway, or affect the rights of the owners of premises adjoining the highway, or the rights of statutory undertakers or of the Post Office.

(5) Where a licence under this section makes provision for the execution of any works or the provision of any facilities which in the opinion of the highway authority require to be executed or provided by them in connection with the building or its construction or alteration, the authority may execute those works or, as the case may be, provide those facilities and may recover the expenses reasonably incurred by them in so doing from the licensee or from the owner of the building.

(6) A person aggrieved by the refusal of a highway authority to grant a licence under this section or by a term or condition of the licence may appeal to the Crown Court, except that no such appeal lies—

> (*a*) if the land on which the highway in question is situated is owned by the highway authority, or
>
> (*b*) against any term or condition which the highway authority declare to be necessary for the purpose of securing the safety of persons using the highway or of preventing interference with traffic thereon.

(7) Where a person has constructed or altered a building for the construction, or, as the case may be, alteration, of which a licence is required by this section without such a licence or otherwise than in accordance with the terms and conditions of the licence, the highway authority may by notice served on the licensee or the owner of the building require him to demolish the building within such time as may be specified in the notice or, as the case may be, to make such alterations therein and within such time as may be so specified.

(8) Where there has been a failure to comply with any terms or conditions of a licence under this section with respect to the maintenance or use of a building, the highway authority may by

notice served on the licensee or the owner of the building require him to execute such works or take such steps as are necessary to secure compliance with those terms or conditions within such time as may be specified in the notice.

(9) If a person on whom a notice is served under subsection (7) or (8) above fails to comply with the notice within the time specified in it, the highway authority may demolish the building or, as the case may be, execute such works or take such steps as are necessary to comply with the notice and may recover the expenses reasonably incurred by them in so doing from that person.

(10) Where by virtue of subsection (9) above a highway authority demolish a building, they may dispose of the materials resulting from the demolition.

(11) In relation to any prohibition or restriction on the use of a building imposed by the Minister by virtue of any term or condition contained in a licence granted by him under 1975 c. 76. this section, section 1(1)(c) of the Local Land Charges Act 1975 has effect as if the references to the date of the commencement of that Act were references to 1st November 1971.

(12) Any work authorised or required by a licence under this section to be executed by the licensee is for the purpose of 1878 c. 76. section 7 of the Telegraph Act 1878 (alteration of the telegraphic lines of the Post Office) to be deemed to be work done in the execution of an undertaking authorised by an Act of Parliament and the person executing the work is to be deemed to be the undertakers.

(13) This section does not apply to a building which constitutes a bridge within the meaning of section 176 above, but subject to that in this section " building " includes any structure and any part of a building.

(14) Where the land on which a highway is situated is owned by the highway authority, nothing in subsection (3) above is to be taken as affecting the rights of that authority as the owner of that land to sell or lease the air-space above the surface of that land or grant any rights in relation to it.

Restriction on placing rails, beams etc. over highways. **178.**—(1) No person shall fix or place any overhead beam, rail, pipe, cable, wire or other similar apparatus over, along or across a highway without the consent of the highway authority for the highway, and the highway authority may attach to their consent such reasonable terms and conditions as they think fit.

(2) Subject to subsection (3) below, a person aggrieved by the refusal of a consent under subsection (1) above, or by any terms or conditions attached to such a consent, may appeal to a magistrates' court.

(3) No appeal lies under subsection (2) above against any term or condition attached by the Minister to a consent given by him under this section if he declares the term or condition to be necessary for the purpose of securing the safety of persons using the highway to which the consent relates or of preventing interference with traffic on it.

(4) If a person contravenes subsection (1) above, or the terms or conditions of any consent given under that subsection, he is guilty of an offence and liable to a fine not exceeding £25; and if the offence is continued after conviction he is guilty of a further offence and liable to a fine not exceeding £1 for each day on which the offence is so continued.

(5) This section does not apply to any works or apparatus belonging to any statutory undertakers, and for this purpose the Civil Aviation Authority and the Post Office are to be deemed to be statutory undertakers.

179.—(1) No person shall construct a vault, arch or cellar under—

Control of construction of cellars etc. under street.

(*a*) any street in Greater London, or

(*b*) the carriageway of any street outside Greater London, without the consent of the appropriate authority, and the authority may by notice served on a person who has constructed a vault, arch or cellar in contravention of this section require him to remove it, or to alter or deal with it in such manner as may be specified in the notice.

For the purposes of this section the appropriate authority is—

(i) in relation to a street outside Greater London which is a highway, the highway authority for the street; and

(ii) in relation to any other street, the local authority in whose area the street is situated.

(2) A person aggrieved by the refusal of a consent, or by a requirement of a notice, under subsection (1) above may appeal to a magistrates' court.

(3) A person who constructs a vault, arch or cellar in contravention of this section is guilty of an offence and is liable to a fine not exceeding £25; and, subject to any order made on appeal, if he fails to comply with a requirement of a notice served on him under subsection (1) above he is guilty of a further offence and is liable to a fine not exceeding £2 for each day during which the failure continues.

(4) The appropriate authority may also cause a vault, arch or cellar constructed in contravention of this section to be removed, altered or otherwise dealt with as they think fit, and may recover the expenses reasonably incurred by them in so doing from the offender.

(5) As soon as may be after an authority consent to the construction of a vault, arch or cellar under a street they shall give notice thereof to any public utility undertakers having any apparatus under the street.

Control of
openings into
cellars etc.
under streets,
and pavement
lights and
ventilators.
180.—(1) No person shall make an opening in the footway of a street as an entrance to a cellar or vault thereunder without the consent of the appropriate authority, and where an authority give consent under this subsection they shall require the person to whom the consent is given to provide a door or covering constructed in such manner and of such materials as they direct.

For the purposes of this section the appropriate authority is the same as for the purposes of section 179 above.

(2) No person shall carry out any works in a street to provide means for the admission of air or light to premises situated under, or abutting on, the street without the consent of the local authority, and the local authority in giving any consent under this subsection may impose any requirement as to the construction of the works.

(3) A person aggrieved by the refusal of a consent, or by a requirement, under subsection (1) above may appeal to a magistrates' court and a person who applies for consent under subsection (2) above may appeal to such a court against a refusal of consent, or a requirement, under subsection (2).

(4) Subject to any order made on appeal—

   (*a*) a person who—

      (i) makes an opening in the footway of a street in contravention of subsection (1) above, or

      (ii) fails to comply with a requirement made to him under that subsection,

   is guilty of an offence and, without prejudice to any other liability to which he may be subject, liable to a fine not exceeding £25 ;

   (*b*) a person who—

      (i) carries out any works in contravention of subsection (2) above, or

      (ii) fails to comply with a requirement made to him under that subsection,

   is guilty of an offence and, without prejudice to any other liability to which he may be subject, liable to a fine not exceeding £5.

(5) As soon as may be after an authority give consent under either subsection (1) or subsection (2) above they shall give notice thereof to any public utility undertakers having any apparatus under the street.

(6) The following, namely—

(a) every vault, arch and cellar under a street,

(b) every opening in the surface of any street into any such vault, arch or cellar,

(c) every door or covering to any such opening,

(d) every cellar-head, grating, light and coal hole in the surface of a street, and

(e) all landings, flags or stones of the street by which any of the above are supported,

shall be kept in good condition and repair by the owner or occupier of the vault, arch or cellar, or of the premises to which it belongs.

(7) If default is made in complying with subsection (6) above, the appropriate authority may, after the expiration of 24 hours from the service of a notice of their intention to do so on any person in default, cause any thing as respects which there has been such a default to be repaired or put into good condition, and may recover the expenses reasonably incurred by them in so doing from the owner or occupier thereof or of the premises to which it belongs.

181.—(1) If a person, without lawful authority or excuse, places any apparatus in or under a highway or breaks open a highway for the purpose of placing, maintaining, repairing or reinstating any apparatus in or under it, he is guilty of an offence and liable to a fine not exceeding £20 or, in the case of a second or subsequent offence, to a fine not exceeding £50. *Provisions relating to placing, etc. of certain apparatus in or under a highway.*

(2) The highway authority for a highway may by a licence granted under this section permit any person to place and leave, or to retain, and thereafter (in either case) to maintain, repair and reinstate, apparatus in or under the highway and to break open and to have access to the highway for those purposes.

(3) The highway authority may, as they think fit—

(a) grant a licence under this section to any person and insert in the licence a provision prohibiting assignment of the licence ; or

(b) grant a licence to any person and insert in the licence a provision permitting assignment of the licence ; or

(c) grant such a licence to the owner of any premises adjoining the highway and his successors in title, the licence, unless and until withdrawn or surrendered, to be annexed to those premises ;

and references in this section and section 182 below to the licensee are references to the person who is for the time being entitled by virtue of such a licence to do anything permitted by it to be done.

(4) No fine, rent or other sum of money is payable in respect of such a licence except—

    (*a*) a reasonable sum in respect of legal or other expenses incurred in connection with the grant of the licence ; and

    (*b*) an annual charge of a reasonable amount for administering the licence ;

and any such sum is recoverable from the licensee.

(5) Before granting a licence under this section a highway authority shall give not less than 14 days' notice of their intention so to do to any statutory undertakers or sewerage authority whose apparatus or plans for the installation of apparatus are likely to be affected by the works to be authorised by the licence.

1899 c. 19.

(6) The licensee is not for the purposes of section 17 of the Schedule to the Electric Lighting (Clauses) Act 1899 (power to alter apparatus under streets, etc.) a person in whom powers in relation to a street or place are vested nor are any works carried out by the licensee in pursuance of a licence under this section undertakers' works within the meaning of section 1 of the Public Utilities Street Works Act 1950.

1950 c. 39.

(7) A licence under this section shall not authorise any interference with the apparatus or works of any statutory undertakers or sewerage authority without the consent of those undertakers or that authority, as the case may be, nor shall such a licence authorise the installation of any apparatus for the installation or use of which the licence of the Secretary of State or the Post Office, or of both the Secretary of State and the Post Office, is required by virtue of any enactment unless and until that licence has been granted.

(8) This section does not apply to the apparatus of statutory undertakers or sewerage authorities.

(9) In this section and section 182 below references to statutory undertakers include references to the Post Office.

(10) Where the land on which a highway is situated is owned by the highway authority for the highway, nothing in subsection (4) above is to be taken as affecting the rights of that authority as the owner of that land to grant any person, for such consideration as they think fit, the right to place any thing in or under that land.

Supplementary provisions as to licences under section 181.

182.—(1) A highway authority may attach to any licence granted under section 181 above such conditions as they consider necessary to protect the apparatus of statutory undertakers and sewerage authorities, to ensure the safety and convenience of passengers in the highway and to prevent traffic therein being delayed, and it shall be a condition of every such licence that—

(a) before executing any works for the purpose of placing apparatus in or under the highway or for the purpose of the maintenance, repair or reinstatement thereof (except works for the purpose of carrying out emergency repairs), the licensee is to give not less than 7 days' notice in writing, stating the nature and place of the works proposed, to the highway authority and to any statutory undertakers or sewerage authority whose apparatus is likely to be affected, and is to satisfy their requirements as to the method of executing the works and as to the supervision thereof by them ;

(b) as soon as reasonably practicable after executing works for the purpose of carrying out emergency repairs to any apparatus placed and left in or under the highway the licensee is to inform any statutory undertakers or sewerage authority whose apparatus may have been affected ;

(c) any apparatus is, wherever practicable, to be laid by thrust boring ;

(d) while executing any works in or under the highway the licensee is to cause the works to be properly fenced and guarded and to be properly lighted during the hours of darkness ;

(e) as soon as reasonably practicable after executing any such works as are mentioned in paragraph (a) or (b) above, the licensee is to make good any damage to the highway occasioned by those works ;

(f) the licensee is to give the authority not less than 6 weeks' notice of his intention to cease using or abandon the apparatus or, if the licence is one the assignment of which is prohibited, of his intention to part with his interest in the apparatus.

(2) A highway authority may attach to a licence granted by them by virtue of section 181(3)(b) above a condition that before assigning the licence to any other person the licensee is to obtain the consent of the authority to the assignment; and it shall be a condition of every licence granted by virtue of section 181(3)(c) above that within one month after any change in the ownership of the premises in question takes place the licensee is to inform the highway authority of it.

(3) A highway authority may by notice served on the licensee withdraw a licence granted by them under section 181 above—

(a) on the expiration of such period as may be specified in the notice, being a period of not less than 7 days beginning with the date of service of the notice on the licensee, if any condition of the licence is contravened by the licensee, or if the highway authority become aware of the fact that the licensee intends to cease using or abandon the apparatus or (if the licence is one the assignment of which is prohibited) that the licensee intends to part with his interest in the apparatus ;

(b) on the expiration of such period as may be so specified, being a period of not less than 3 months beginning with the said date, if the authority consider the withdrawal of the licence is necessary for the purpose of the exercise of their functions as a highway authority.

(4) Where a licence under sectoin 181 above expires or is withdrawn or surrendered, the highway authority by whom it was granted—

(a) may remove the apparatus to which the licence relates or alter it in such manner as they think fit and reinstate the highway and may recover the expenses reasonably incurred by them in so doing from the last licensee ; or

(b) if satisfied that the last licensee can, within such reasonable time as they may specify, remove such apparatus or alter it in such manner as they may require and reinstate the highway, may authorise him to do so at his own expense.

In this subsection and subsection (5) below " the last licensee " means the person who immediately before the expiration, withdrawal or surrender of the licence in question was the licensee or, if that person has died, his personal representatives.

(5) Before executing any works under subsection (4) above a highway authority or the last licensee, as the case may be, shall give not less than 7 days' notice to any statutory undertakers or sewerage authority whose apparatus is likely to be affected and shall satisfy their requirements as to the method of executing the works and as to the supervision thereof by them.

(6) The licensee and the person who immediately before the expiration, withdrawal or surrender of a licence under this section was the licensee or, if that person has died, his personal representatives shall indemnify the highway authority against any claim in respect of injury, damage or loss arising out of—

(a) the placing or presence in or under a highway of apparatus to which the licence relates, or

(b) the execution by any person of any works authorised by the licence or by the highway authority under subsection (4) above, or

(c) the execution by or on behalf of the highway authority of any works under that subsection ;

but the foregoing provision is not to be taken as requiring any person to indemnify the highway authority against any claim in respect of injury, damage or loss which is attributable to the negligence of that authority.

183.—(1) Where the apparatus in respect of which an application for a licence under section 181 above is made to a local highway authority is to be placed or retained along a line crossing a highway, other than a special road, and not along the line of that highway, any person aggrieved—

> (*a*) by the refusal of that authority to grant him the licence, or
>
> (*b*) by their refusal to grant him a licence on the application other than a licence containing such a provision as is mentioned in section 181(3(*a*) above, or
>
> (*c*) where the application is granted, by any term or condition of the licence granted to him, other than a compulsory condition,

may appeal to the Minister.

(2) Before determining an appeal under this section the Minister may consult any person whose interests are in the opinion of the Minister liable to be affected by anything done in pursuance of the licence to which the appeal relates and shall consider any representations made by the local highway authority.

(3) Where on an appeal under this section the Minister reverses or varies any decision of a local highway authority, it shall be the duty of that authority to give effect to the decision of the Minister.

(4) In this section " compulsory condition " means a condition specified in any paragraph of section 182(1) above and, in the case of a licence granted by virtue of section 181(3)(*c*) above, the condition which section 182(2) above provides shall be a condition of every such licence.

184.—(1) Where the occupier of any premises adjoining or having access to a highway maintainable at the public expense habitually takes or permits to be taken a mechanically propelled vehicle across a kerbed footway or a verge in the highway to or from those premises, the highway authority for the highway may, subject to subsection (2) below, serve a notice on the owner and the occupier of the premises—

> (*a*) stating that they propose to execute such works for the construction of a vehicle crossing over the footway or verge as may be specified in the notice ; or
>
> (*b*) imposing such reasonable conditions on the use of the footway or verge as a crossing as may be so specified.

(2) A highway authority is not entitled by virtue of subsection (1) above to construct a vehicle crossing on, or on any part of, the site of a made-up vehicle crossing which has been constructed either under this section or under section 40 of the Highways Act 1971 (which this section replaces) or before the commencement of the said section 40, or to impose conditions on the use of such a crossing.

(3) Where any land is being, or is to be, developed in accordance with a planning permission granted, or deemed to have been granted, under the Town and Country Planning Act 1971, and it appears to the highway authority for a highway maintainable at the public expense that the development makes it necessary—

(a) to construct a crossing over a kerbed footway or a verge in the highway so as to provide an access for mechanically propelled vehicles to or from the carriageway of the highway from or to premises adjoining or having access to the highway ; or

(b) to improve or otherwise alter a made-up vehicle crossing that provides such an access as is mentioned in paragraph (a) above (whenever constructed),

that authority may serve on the owner and the occupier of the premises a notice stating that they propose to execute such works for the construction or, as the case may be, alteration of the crossing as may be specified in the notice.

(4) Unless the development giving rise to a notice under subsection (3) above consists solely of the provision of a new means of access to or from a highway from or to premises, there may be specified in a notice under that subsection works for the construction as part of the vehicle crossing proposed to be constructed or altered, as the case may be, of acceleration and deceleration lanes.

(5) In determining whether to exercise their powers under subsection (1) or (3) above, a highway authority shall have regard to the need to prevent damage to a footway or verge, and in determining the works to be specified in a notice under subsection (1)(a) or (3) an authority shall have regard to that and the following other matters, namely—

(a) the need to ensure, so far as practicable, safe access to and egress from premises ; and

(b) the need to facilitate, so far as practicable, the passage of vehicular traffic in highways.

(6) Schedule 14 to this Act has effect with respect to the making of objections to a notice under subsection (1) or (3) above and to the date on which such a notice becomes effective.

(7) Where a notice under subsection (1)(*a*) or (3) above has become effective, the highway authority by whom the notice was served may execute such works as are specified in the notice, subject to such modifications (if any) as may have been made by the Minister, and may recover the expenses reasonably incurred by them in so doing from the owner or occupier of the premises in question.

(8) A notice under subsection (1) or (3) above shall inform the person on whom it is served of his right to object to the notice and (except in the case of a notice under subsection (1)(*b*)) shall state the effect of subsection (7) above.

(9) Where a person who is carrying out, or proposes to carry out, such a development as is referred to in subsection (3) above offers to execute the works specified in a notice under that subsection, the highway authority by whom the notice was served may authorise him to execute those works in accordance with plans approved by them.

In relation to works executed under this subsection, Part II of the Public Utilities Street Works Act 1950 (code which has 1950 c. 39. effect where undertakers' apparatus is affected by certain works) applies as if the works were executed for road purposes and were mentioned in section 21(1)(*a*) of that Act and as if the person executing them were the promoting authority within the meaning of the said Part II.

(10) If a person authorised under subsection (9) above to execute any works fails to execute them to the satisfaction of the highway authority before the development is completed, the authority may execute the works or alter the works executed by that person and recover the expenses reasonably incurred by them in so doing from him.

(11) Any person may request the highway authority for a highway maintainable at the public expense to execute such works as are specified in the request for constructing a vehicle crossing over a footway or verge in the highway, and the authority may approve the request with or without modification, or may propose alternative works or reject the request; and in determining how to exercise their powers under this subsection an authority shall have regard to the matters mentioned in subsection (5) above.

(12) An authority to whom a request under subsection (11) above is made shall notify the person making the request of their decision and if they approve, with or without modification, the works proposed in the request or propose alternative works, they shall supply him with a quotation of the cost of the works as approved or proposed by them, and he may, on depositing with them the amount quoted, require them to execute those works.

PART IX

(13) As soon as practicable after such a deposit has been made with an authority the authority shall execute the works as approved or proposed by them.

1950 c. 39.

(14) If apart from this subsection Part II of the Public Utilities Street Works Act 1950 would not apply in relation to works executed by a highway authority under any provision of this section, the said Part II shall apply as if the works were executed for road purposes and were mentioned in section 21(1)(a) of that Act.

(15) The expenses recoverable under subsection (7) or (10) above and the cost of the works for the purposes of subsection (12) above include the cost of any works which are required by the said Act of 1950 to be executed in consequence of the construction of the crossing.

(16) Nothing in this section imposes on any person other than a highway authority any obligation to maintain a vehicle crossing.

(17) If a person knowingly uses a footway or verge as a crossing in contravention of any condition imposed under subsection (1)(b) above, or knowingly permits it to be so used, he is guilty of an offence and liable to a fine not exceeding £20 or, in the case of a second or subsequent offence, to a fine not exceeding £50.

Power to install refuse or storage bins in streets.

185.—(1) Subject to the provisions of this section, a competent authority may provide and maintain in or under a street orderly bins or other receptacles, of such dimensions and in such positions as the authority may determine, for the collection and temporary deposit of street refuse and waste paper, or the storage of sand, grit or other materials.

For the purposes of this section the following are competent authorities—

   (a) in relation to a street that is a highway, the highway authority for the highway and also the local authority in whose area it is situated acting with the consent of the highway authority;

   (b) in relation to any other street, the local authority in whose area the street is situated.

(2) An authority does not have power by virtue of this section to place a bin or other receptacle on a bridge over a railway, or under a bridge carrying a railway over a street, or within 10 feet of the abutments of a bridge carrying a railway over a street, except with the consent of the railway undertakers concerned.

(3) An authority shall not exercise the power conferred by this section so as to obstruct or render less convenient the access to or exit from—

   (a) a station or goods yard belonging to railway undertakers ; or

   (b) premises belonging to canal, inland navigation, dock, harbour, tramway, electricity, gas or water undertakers, or to persons authorised by any enactment to carry on any other public undertaking, and used by those undertakers or persons for the purposes of their undertaking.

(4) Nothing in this section is to be taken as empowering an authority to hinder the reasonable use of a street by the public or any person entitled to use it or as empowering an authority to create a nuisance to the owner or occupier of premises adjacent to a street.

PART X

NEW STREETS

New street byelaws

186.—(1) The council of every county and of every London borough and the Common Council may, and if required by the Secretary of State shall, make byelaws for regulating all or any of the following matters : —

   (a) the level, width and construction of new streets in their area, and

   (b) the provision for the sewerage of such streets ;

and the power to make byelaws under this subsection extends to the making of byelaws requiring any person constructing a new street to provide separate sewers for foul water drainage and surface water drainage respectively.

(2) No byelaw under this section shall regulate the level, width or construction of a new street in so far as it is to be carried by a bridge or is to form the approaches to a bridge.

(3) If a council, when required by the Secretary of State to make byelaws under subsection (1) above, do not within 3 months from the date on which the requirement is made to them make in accordance with the requirement byelaws satisfactory to him, the Secretary of State may himself make the byelaws.

(4) Byelaws for regulating matters that may be regulated under this section are hereafter in this Part of this Act referred to as " new street byelaws ".

Power of county councils and London boroughs and the Common Council to make new street byelaws.

G

(5) New street byelaws may include provision as to—

(a) the giving of notices and the deposit of plans ;

(b) the inspection of work, the testing of sewers, and the taking by the county council or London borough council, or the Common Council, of samples of the materials to be used in the execution of works.

(6) New street byelaws may require that plans to be deposited in pursuance of the byelaws shall be deposited in duplicate.

(7) The Secretary of State is the confirming authority as respects new street byelaws and any byelaws made by the Secretary of State under this section have effect as if they had been made by the county council or London borough council, or the Common Council, and confirmed by the Secretary of State.

1959 c. 25.

(8) A new street byelaw made under this section (or under section 157 of the Highways Act 1959, which this section replaces) shall cease to have effect on the expiration of 10 years from the date on which it was made or on the expiration of such longer period as the Secretary of State may by order allow.

Continuation of existing street to be a new street.

187. A continuation of an existing street may be deemed to be a new street for the purpose of the application to it of new street byelaws.

Power to declare existing highway to be a new street.

188.—(1) Where it appears to the council of a county or London borough, or the Common Council, that an existing highway in their area will be converted into a new street as a consequence of building operations which have been, or are likely to be, undertaken in the vicinity, the council may by order prescribe the centre line of the new street and outer lines defining the minimum width of the new street, which shall be the minimum width required by the relevant byelaw provisions.

In this subsection " the relevant byelaw provisions " means the provisions of new street byelaws in force in the area of the council regulating the width of a new street intended to be the principal means of access to any building and of a length equal to the length of the highway to which the order relates.

(2) Not less than one month before making an order under this section, the council shall cause notice of the intended order to be displayed at each end of, or in some conspicuous position in, the highway to which the order relates.

(3) Every such notice shall contain a statement that the intended order may be made by the council on or at any time after a day named in the notice, and shall state the right of appeal conferred by subsection (4) below.

(4) A person aggrieved by an order under this section may appeal to the Crown Court.

(5) Where an order under this section has effect, no person shall erect a new building on the land situated between the outer lines prescribed by the order (" the prescribed land ").

(6) If, where an order under this section has effect, work for the erection of a new building is commenced on land adjoining the prescribed land, then, on the commencement of that work—

    (*a*) the appropriate portion of the prescribed land shall become part of the existing highway, and

    (*b*) the owner of that portion shall remove any boundary fence or other obstruction situated on it and bring the level of it into conformity with that of the existing highway.

For the purposes of this subsection the appropriate portion of the prescribed land is the portion situated between the centre line prescribed by the order and the land on which the building is to be erected or which is to be occupied with it, other than land so situated which forms part of the existing highway.

(7) Land which becomes part of the existing highway in accordance with subsection (6) above does not become a highway maintainable at the public expense, even if the existing highway is so maintainable.

(8) Nothing in this section extends to a building (other than a dwelling-house) erected, in pursuance of their statutory powers, by any of the following undertakers and used or occupied, or intended to be used or occupied, by them for the following purposes respectively: —

    (*a*) railway undertakers for purposes of a railway comprised in the railway undertaking;

    (*b*) canal undertakers for purposes of a canal comprised in the canal undertaking;

    (*c*) inland navigation undertakers for purposes of a navigation comprised in the inland navigation undertaking;

    (*d*) dock undertakers for purposes of a dock comprised in the dock undertaking; or

    (*e*) harbour undertakers for purposes of a harbour comprised in the harbour undertaking.

(9) In this section " building " includes a wall.

G 2

PART X
Revocation
and
amendment of
orders under
section 188.

189.—(1) A county council, a London borough council or the Common Council may by an order in writing—

(*a*) revoke an order made by them under section 188 above ;

(*b*) amend any such order relating to 2 or more streets so as to reduce the number of streets to which the order relates ;

(*c*) amend any such order so as to exclude from it a part of a street but not so as to make the order relate to parts of the same street which are not continuous.

(2) A council who propose to make an order under subsection (1) above shall cause notice of the proposal to be displayed, at least one month before they make the order, in a conspicuous position in each street to which the proposal relates and shall include in the notice a statement indicating that the order may be made on or at any time after a date specified in the notice.

1975 c. 76.

(3) Where a county council make an order under subsection (1) above they shall send a copy of the order as soon as practicable to each registering authority for the purposes of the Local Land Charges Act 1975 within whose area any street or part of a street to which the order relates is situated.

Power to
relax byelaw
requirements.

190.—(1) Where the council of a county or London borough, or the Common Council, consider that the operation of a new street byelaw in force in their area would be unreasonable in relation to a particular case they may, with the consent of the Secretary of State, relax the requirements of the byelaw or dispense with compliance with it.

(2) The council shall give notice on any such proposed relaxation or dispensation in such manner and to such persons, if any, as the Secretary of State may direct, and the Secretary of State shall not give his consent before the expiration of one month from the date of the giving of the notice.

(3) Before giving his consent the Secretary of State shall take into consideration any objection which may have been received by him.

Passing of plans deposited under byelaws

Passing or
rejection of
plans etc.

191.—(1) Where plans of any proposed work are, in accordance with new street byelaws, deposited with the council of a county or London borough or the Common Council then, subject to section 190 above and section 193 below, the council—

(*a*) shall pass the plans unless they either are defective or show that the proposed work would contravene any of those byelaws ;

(b) if the plans are defective or show that the proposed work would contravene any of those byelaws, shall reject the plans.

(2) The council shall within the appropriate period from the deposit of the plans give notice to the person by whom or on whose behalf they were deposited whether or not they are passed, and—

  (a) a notice of rejection shall specify the defects on account of which, or the byelaw for non-conformity with which, plans have been rejected, and

  (b) a notice that plans have been passed shall state that the passing of the plans operates as an approval of them only for the purposes of the requirements of the byelaws.

(3) Any question arising under this section between the council of a county or London borough or the Common Council and the person by whom or on whose behalf plans are deposited whether the plans are defective, or whether the proposed work would contravene any of the byelaws, may on the application of that person be determined by a magistrates' court; but no such application shall be entertained unless it is made before the proposed work has been substantially begun.

192.—(1) Where plans of any proposed work have, in accordance with new street byelaws, been deposited with the council of a county or London borough or the Common Council and— *Deposit of plans to be of no effect after certain interval.*

  (a) either the plans have been passed by the council or notice of rejection of the plans has not been given within the appropriate period from the deposit of them, but

  (b) the work to which the plans relate has not been begun within 3 years from the date of the deposit of the plans,

the council may, at any time before the work is begun, by notice to the person by whom or on whose behalf the plans were deposited, or other the owner for the time being of the land to which the plans relate, declare that the deposit of the plans shall be of no effect.

(2) When such a notice is given this Part of this Act and the byelaws made under it have effect as respects the proposed work as if no plans had been deposited.

(3) The council of a county or London borough or, as the case may be, the Common Council shall attach a notice of the provisions of subsections (1) and (2) above to every notice of the passing of plans of proposed work deposited in accordance with new street byelaws.

Imposition of
requirements
as to width
of new streets
in certain
cases.

Requirements and prohibitions as to new streets

193.—(1) Where, in pursuance of a new street byelaw requiring plans to be deposited with them, application is made to the council of a county or London borough or the Common Council to pass plans of a new street and that street will, in the opinion of the council, form—

(*a*) a main thoroughfare or a continuation of a main thoroughfare, or means of communication between main thoroughfares, in their area, or

(*b*) a continuation of a main approach, or means of communication between main approaches, to their area,

the council—

(i) may, as a condition of passing the plans, require that the new street be formed of such width as they may determine, and

(ii) if they make a requirement under paragraph (i) above, shall, as such a condition, determine how much of the width of the street is to be laid out as a carriageway and how much as a footway or footways.

(2) If the council of a county or London borough or the Common Council under subsection (1) above require a new street to be formed of a width that exceeds the normal maximum width by an amount greater than 20 feet, they shall pay compensation for any loss or injury which may be sustained by reason of the requirement.

In this subsection and subsection (3) below, " the normal maximum width " means the maximum width of which, apart from this section, the street could have been required to be formed under any byelaw or enactment with respect to the width of new streets which is in force in the county or London borough in question or, as the case may be, in the City.

(3) Nothing in this section empowers a council to require any person to defray any greater expenses in the execution of any street works than would have been payable if the street had been of no greater width than the normal maximum width ; and any additional expense incurred in the execution of the street works by reason of the street being of such greater width shall be certified by the proper officer of the council, or in the case of dispute shall be determined by a magistrates' court, and shall be borne by the council.

(4) A person aggrieved by a condition imposed under this section may appeal to the Crown Court.

Power to vary
position or
direction, and
to fix beginning
and end, of
new street.

194.—(1) The council of a county or London borough or the Common Council may on the deposit with them of plans of a new street in pursuance of a new street byelaw, by order vary

the intended position, direction, termination or level of the new
street so far as is necessary for the purpose of securing—

> (a) more direct, easier or more convenient means of communication with any other street or intended street; or
>
> (b) an adequate opening at one or each of the ends of the new street; or
>
> (c) compliance with any byelaw in force within their area for the regulation of streets or buildings.

(2) The council of a county or London borough or the Common Council may by an order made under subsection (1) above fix the points at which the new street is to be deemed to begin or end, and the limits of the new street as determined by the points so fixed shall be treated as the limits of it for the purposes of this Part of this Act and of any byelaws made under this Part.

(3) A person aggrieved by an order under this section may appeal to the Crown Court.

(4) If a person lays out or constructs a new street in contravention of an order under this section he is guilty of an offence and is liable to a fine not exceeding £25; and if the offence is continued after conviction he is guilty of a further offence and liable to a fine not exceeding £2 for each day on which the offence is so continued.

(5) A council shall pay compensation to any person for any loss or injury sustained by him by reason of the exercise by the council of their powers under this section.

(6) A council shall not make an order under this section in a case in which it is shown to their satisfaction that compliance with the order would entail the purchase of additional land by the owner of the land on which the new street is intended to be laid out, or the execution of works elsewhere than on the last-mentioned land or land held with it on which building operations associated with the new street are intended to be undertaken.

195.—(1) No person shall, except in the exercise of statutory Construction powers, construct a bridge to carry a new street unless the bridge of bridge and the approaches to it are of such width and gradients as are carrying new approved— street.

> (a) in the case of a new street which is, or is to be, situated in a London borough or the City, by the council of the London borough or the Common Council, as the case may be, and
>
> (b) in any other case, by the council of the county in which the new street is, or is to be, situated,

and are constructed in accordance with plans so approved.

(2) A person aggrieved by the refusal of an approval under subsection (1) above may appeal to the Crown Court.

(3) If a person contravenes this section he is guilty of an offence and liable to a fine not exceeding £50; and the council of the county or London borough, or the Common Council, as the case may be, may remove, alter or pull down any work done in contravention of the section and may recover from him the expenses reasonably incurred by the council in so doing.

Power to allow widening of existing street on one side only to less than prescribed width.

196.—(1) Where—

(a) an owner of land adjoining one side of an existing highway proposes to lay out on that land a new street along the line of the highway, and

(b) buildings have been or are intended to be erected on that side only, and

(c) the case is one in which the appropriate authority are empowered, by a byelaw with respect to the width of new streets, to require the owner to widen the existing highway to the width prescribed for a new street,

the appropriate authority may, instead of requiring the owner to widen the existing highway as provided by paragraph (c) above, make an order under this section.

(2) An order under this section is an order permitting the owner to widen the highway on the side referred to in subsection (1)(a) and (b) above only, to such width as may be specified in the order, being a width—

(a) less than the width referred to in subsection (1)(c) above, but

(b) such that the distance between the centre line of the existing highway and the boundary, after the widening, of the highway on the said side is not less than one half of the width referred to in subsection (1)(c) above.

(3) Not less than 21 days before making an order under this section the appropriate authority shall send notice of the intended order to such owner as aforesaid and, unless he is the same person, to any owner of land adjoining the highway on the side of it opposite the land to which the order will relate.

(4) If, where an order under this section has effect, building is begun on the said land on that opposite side, the owner of that land shall widen the existing highway on the opposite side where it adjoins that land so that the distance between—

(*a*) the boundary, after widening, of the highway on that opposite side, and

(*b*) the boundary, after widening under the order, of the highway on the side to which the order relates,

is the width referred to in subsection (1)(*c*).

(5) Nothing in subsection (4) above imposes on any person an obligation to pull down a building erected before the date of an order under this section relating to the land in question.

(6) If a person fails to comply with subsection (4) above he is guilty of an offence and liable to a fine not exceeding £25 ; and if the offence is continued after conviction he is guilty of a further offence and liable to a fine not exceeding £2 for each day on which the offence is so continued.

(7) A person aggrieved by an order, or by the refusal to make an order, under this section may appeal to the Crown Court.

(8) For the purposes of this section the appropriate authority is—

(*a*) in relation to a highway outside Greater London, the county council ;

(*b*) in relation to a highway in Greater London, the local authority for the area in which the highway is situated.

Enforcement of byelaws and requirements of local authority

197.—(1) If any work to which new street byelaws are applicable contravenes any of those byelaws, the county council, the London borough council or, as the case may be, the Common Council, without prejudice to their right, if any, to take proceedings for a fine, may by notice require any person by whom, or on whose behalf, the work was executed either to remove the work or, if he so elects, to effect such alterations in it as may be necessary to make it comply with the byelaws.

(2) If, in any case in which new street byelaws require plans of a new street to be deposited with the council of a county or London borough, or the Common Council, the council concerned are of opinion that a new street in their area forms or will form such a way as is referred to in section 193(1)(*a*) or (*b*) above, and any work to which those byelaws are applicable is executed without plans having been passed, the council may, without prejudice to their right, if any, to take proceedings for a fine, by notice to any person by whom or on whose behalf the work was executed either—

(*a*) require him to remove the work, or

(b) require him either to remove the work or, if he so elects, to comply with any condition specified in the notice, being a condition which they could have imposed under section 193 above as a condition of the passing of plans deposited in accordance with the byelaws.

For the purposes of this subsection plans are to be deemed to have been passed if notice of their rejection was not given within the appropriate period from the deposit of them.

(3) If in a case falling within section 193 above any work to which new street byelaws are applicable is executed otherwise than in accordance with any condition imposed under that section, the council of the county or London borough or, as the case may be, the Common Council may, without prejudice to their right to take proceedings for a fine, by notice to any person by whom or on whose behalf the work was executed either—

(a) require him to remove the work, or

(b) require him either to remove the work, or if he so elects, to comply with any other condition specified in the notice, being a condition which they could have imposed under section 193 above as a condition of the passing of plans deposited in accordance with the byelaws.

(4) A person aggrieved by a requirement of a council under the foregoing provisions of this section may appeal to a magistrates' court.

(5) Subject to any order made on appeal, if a person to whom a notice has been given under the foregoing provisions of this section fails to comply with the notice before the expiration of 28 days from the date of the service of the notice on him, or such longer period as a magistrates' court may on his application allow, the council by whom the notice was given may remove the work in question, or effect such alterations in it as they deem necessary, and may recover from him the expenses reasonably incurred by the council in so doing.

(6) No notice under subsection (1) or subsection (2) or subsection (3) above shall be given after the expiration of 12 months from the date of the completion of the work in question, and it is not open to a council to give a notice under subsection (1) above in a case where plans have been deposited, if—

(a) either the plans were passed by the council, or notice of their rejection was not given within the appropriate period from the deposit of them, and

(b) the work has been executed in accordance with the plans and with any condition imposed under section 193(1) above.

(7) Nothing in this section affects the right of a council or of the Attorney-General, or of any other person, to apply for an injunction for the removal or alteration of any work on the ground that it contravenes any byelaws ; but if—

    (*a*) the work is one in respect of which plans were deposited and either the plans were passed by the council or notice of their rejection was not given within the appropriate period from the deposit of them, and

    (*b*) the work has been executed in accordance with the plans,

the court on granting an injunction may order the council to pay to the owner of the work such compensation as the court thinks just.

(8) Before making any order for compensation under subsection (7) above the court shall, in accordance with rules of court, cause the council, if not a party to the proceedings, to be joined as a party.

198. Where in a case falling within section 193 above the council of a county or London borough or the Common Council impose a condition on the passing of plans deposited in pursuance of new street byelaws, a person who executes work proposed in the plans otherwise than in accordance with that condition is liable to the like fine as if he had executed the work in contravention of a byelaw.

Fine for executing work otherwise than in accordance with conditions.

199. Where the council of a county or London borough or the Common Council pass plans for a new street subject to conditions imposed or authorised by new street byelaws in force in the area of that authority, then, those conditions may be enforced at any time by the council against the owner for the time being of the land to which the conditions relate.

Enforcement of conditions imposed by or under byelaws against owner.

In this section " owner " in relation to any land means a person, other than a mortgagee not in possession, who is for the time being entitled to dispose of the fee simple in the land, whether in possession or in reversion, and includes also a person holding or entitled to the rents and profits of the land under a lease the unexpired term of which exceeds 3 years.

Provisions as to regulation of new streets by enactment

200.—(1) Section 187 above applies for the purpose of the application to a continuation of an existing street of a provision in a local Act with respect to the width of a new street as it applies for the purpose of the application to such a continuation of new street byelaws.

Application of certain sections where new streets regulated by enactment.

PART X
(2) Section 193 above applies where application is made to the council of a county or London borough or the Common Council to pass plans of a new street in pursuance of an enactment requiring plans to be deposited with them as it applies where such an application is made in pursuance of a byelaw making such a requirement.

(3) The council of a county or London borough or the Common Council have the like power under section 194 above to vary the position, direction, termination or level of a new street for the purpose of securing compliance with an enactment in force in their area for the regulation of streets or buildings as they have to make such a variation for the purpose of securing compliance with a byelaw for such regulation, and subsections (2) to (6) of section 194 have effect accordingly.

(4) Section 196 above applies in a case where a council are empowered to require the widening of a highway to the width prescribed by an enactment with respect to the width of new streets as it applies where a council are empowered to require the widening of a highway to a width prescribed by a byelaw.

Supplemental provisions

Right of local authority to retain deposited plans.
201.—(1) Where new street byelaws require plans deposited in pursuance of the byelaws to be deposited in duplicate, the council concerned may retain one copy of any plans so deposited, whether the plans are passed or not.

(2) A council may retain any plans deposited with and passed by them in pursuance of any enactment regulating the construction of new streets for the time being in force in their area.

Interpretation of Part X.
202. For the purposes of this Part of this Act—

(a) "new street byelaws" has the meaning provided by section 186(4) above;

(b) "the appropriate period", in relation to the passing or rejection of plans, means one month, but new street byelaws for the area of a council whose meetings are normally held not more frequently than once a month may provide that, in the case of plans deposited less than 3 clear days before a meeting of the council, the appropriate period shall be 5 weeks;

(c) references to plans include references to sections, specifications and written particulars; and

(d) references to the passing of plans, in relation to any enactment or byelaw (not being an enactment contained in this Act or a byelaw made under it), include references to the approval of plans.

PART XI

MAKING UP OF PRIVATE STREETS

Introductory

203.—(1) In this Part of this Act (and elsewhere in this Act) Interpretation "the private street works code" means sections 205 to 218 of Part XI. below; and "the advance payments code" means sections 219 to 225 below.

(2) In this Part of this Act "private street" means a street that is not a highway maintainable at the public expense, and—

   (*a*) includes any land that is deemed to be a private street by virtue of a declaration made under section 232 below, and

   (*b*) for the purpose of the application of the advance payments code or section 229 below in relation to any building, includes—

      (i) any land shown as a proposed street on plans deposited with respect to that building either under building regulations or on an application for planning permission under the Town and Country Planning 1971 c. 78. Act 1971, and

      (ii) any land which, if work for the erection of that building had been commenced, would have become part of an existing highway by virtue of section 188(6) above;

but the fact that a part of a street is a highway maintainable at the public expense does not prevent any other part of it from being a part of a private street for the purposes of this Part of this Act.

(3) In this Part of this Act—

   "contributory place" has the same meaning as in section 343 of the Public Health Act 1936;   1936 c. 49.

   "fronting" includes adjoining, and "front" is to be construed accordingly;

   "industrial premises" means premises used or designed or suitable for use for the carrying on of any such process or research as is specified in section 66(1) of the Town and Country Planning Act 1971, and includes premises used for purposes ancillary to the carrying on of any such process or research;

   "local Act" includes a provisional order confirmed by Parliament and the confirming Act so far as it relates to that order;

" paving, metalling and flagging " includes all methods of making a carriageway or footway ;

" place of public religious worship " means a place of public religious worship which belongs to the Church of England or to the Church in Wales (within the meaning of the Welsh Church Act 1914), or which is for the time being certified as required by law as a place of religious worship ;

" street works " means any works for the sewering, levelling, paving, metalling, flagging, channelling and making good of a street, and includes the provision of proper means for lighting a street ;

" street works authority " means—

    (*a*) as respects a street outside Greater London, the council of the county in which the street is situated,

    (*b*) as respects a street in a London borough, the council of the borough, and

    (*c*) as respects a street in the City, the Common Council.

(4) For the purposes of the advance payments code and of section 229 below, the frontage of a building or proposed building on a street shall be deemed to be the frontage that the building itself and any land occupied or, as the case may be, proposed to be occupied, with the building and for the purposes of it has or will have on the street.

(5) In ascertaining a majority in number of owners for the purposes of any provision of this Part of this Act, joint owners are to be treated as one owner.

Purposes and
application
of private
street works
code and
advance
payments
code.

204.—(1) The private street works code has effect for securing the execution of street works in private streets anywhere in England or Wales.

(2) The advance payments code has effect for securing payment of the expenses of the execution of street works in private streets adjacent to new buildings, and applies—

    (*a*) in all outer London boroughs ;

    (*b*) in all areas in counties in which the advance payments code in the Highways Act 1959 (which is replaced by the advance payments code in this Act) was in force immediately before 1st April 1974 ; and

    (*c*) in any parish or community in which the advance payments code in the Highways Act 1959 was, after 1st April 1974, adopted in accordance with Schedule 14 to that Act, or in which the advance payments code is adopted in accordance with Schedule 15 to this Act.

The private street works code

205.—(1) Where a private street is not, to the satisfaction of the street works authority, sewered, levelled, paved, metalled, flagged, channelled, made good and lighted, the authority may from time to time resolve with respect to the street to execute street works and, subject to the private street works code, the expenses incurred by the authority in executing those works shall be apportioned between the premises fronting the street.

Street works in private streets.

(2) Where the authority resolve to execute street works with respect to a part only of the street (other than a part extending for the whole of the length of the street), the expenses incurred by them in executing the works shall be apportioned only between the premises fronting the length of the street which constitutes or comprises that part.

(3) Where an authority have passed a resolution under subsection (1) above, the proper officer of the council shall prepare—

    (*a*) a specification of the street works referred to in the resolution, with any necessary plans and sections,

    (*b*) an estimate of the probable expenses of the works, and

    (*c*) a provisional apportionment apportioning the estimated expenses between the premises liable to be charged with them under the private street works code ;

and the specification, plans, sections, estimate and provisional apportionment shall comprise the particulars specified in paragraphs 1 to 4 of Schedule 16 to this Act and shall be submitted to the authority, who may by a further resolution (hereafter in the private street works code referred to as " the resolution of approval ") approve them with or without modification or addition as they think fit.

(4) If, in the case of a street outside Greater London, the street works referred to in the resolution under subsection (1) above include the sewering of the street, the proper officer of the county council shall, when preparing the specification required by subsection (3) above, consult the council of the district in which the street works are to be carried out.

(5) After the resolution of approval has been passed, a notice containing the particulars specified in paragraph 5 of Schedule 16 to this Act shall—

    (*a*) be published once in each of 2 successive weeks in a local newspaper circulating in the area of the street works authority, and

    (*b*) be posted in a prominent position in or near to the street to which the resolution relates once at least in each of 3 successive weeks, and

PART XI

    (c) within 7 days from the date of the first publication under paragraph (a) above, be served on the owners of the premises shown in the provisional apportionment as liable to be charged ;

and during one month from the said date a copy of the resolution of approval, and the approved documents or copies of them certified by the proper officer of the council, shall be kept deposited and open to inspection free of charge at all reasonable hours at the offices of the street works authority and also, in the case of a street outside Greater London, at the offices of the council of the district in which the street concerned is situated.

(6) Where a notice is served on an owner of premises under subsection (5)(c) above it shall be accompanied by a statement of the sum apportioned on those premises by the provisional apportionment.

Incidental works.

206. A street works authority may include in street works to be executed under the private street works code with respect to a street any works which they think necessary for bringing the street, as regards sewerage, drainage, level, or other matters, into conformity with any other streets, whether maintainable at the public expense or not, including the provision of separate sewers for the reception of sewage and of surface water respectively.

Provisional apportionment of expenses.

207.—(1) In a provisional apportionment of expenses of street works under the private street works code, the apportionment of expenses between the premises liable to be charged with them shall, subject to the provisions of this section, be made according to the frontage of the respective premises.

(2) The street works authority may, if they think just, resolve that in settling the apportionment regard shall be had to the following considerations : —

    (a) the greater or less degree of benefit to be derived by any premises from the street works ;

    (b) the amount and value of any work already done by the owners or occupiers of any premises.

(3) The authority may—

    (a) if they think just, include in the apportionment any premises which do not front the street, but have access to it through a court, passage, or otherwise, and which will, in the opinion of the authority, be benefited by the works, and (*b*) fix, by reference to the degree of benefit to be derived by those premises, the amount to be apportioned on them.

208.—(1) Within one month from the date of the first publication of a notice under section 205(5)(*a*) above, an owner of premises shown in a provisional apportionment of expenses as liable to be charged with any part of the expenses of executing street works with respect to a private street or a part of a private street may, by notice to the street works authority, object to their proposals on any of the following grounds:—

Objections to proposed works.

(*a*) that the alleged private street is not a private street or, as the case may be, that the alleged part of a private street is not a part of a private street;

(*b*) that there has been some material informality, defect or error in, or in respect of, the resolution, notice, plans, sections or estimate;

(*c*) that the proposed works are insufficient or unreasonable;

(*d*) that the estimated expenses of the proposed works are excessive;

(*e*) that any premises ought to be excluded from or inserted in the provisional apportionment;

(*f*) that the provisional apportionment is incorrect in respect of some matter of fact to be specified in the objection or, where the provisional apportionment is made with regard to other considerations than frontage, in respect of the degree of benefit to be derived by any premises, or of the amount or value of any work already done by the owner or occupier of premises.

(2) Where premises are owned jointly by 2 or more persons, a notice under subsection (1) above may be given on behalf of those persons by one of their number, if he is authorised in writing by a majority of them to do so.

209.—(1) If an objection is made under section 208 above within the period there specified, and is not withdrawn, the street works authority may, after the expiration of that period, apply to a magistrates' court to appoint a time for hearing and determining all objections so made within that period, and shall serve on the objectors notice of the time and place so appointed.

Hearing and determination of objections.

(2) At the hearing the court shall hear and determine the objections in the same manner as nearly as may be as if the authority were proceeding summarily against the objectors to enforce payment of a sum of money summarily recoverable.

The court may quash in whole or in part or may amend the resolution of approval, specification, plans, sections, estimate

PART XI and provisional apportionment, or any of them, on the application either of an objector or of the authority, and may also, if it
thinks fit, adjourn the hearing and direct further notices to be
given.

(3) The costs of any proceedings before a magistrates' court
in relation to objections under the private street works code are
in the discretion of the court, and the court may, if it thinks fit,
direct that the whole or a part of any costs ordered to be paid
by an objector or objectors are to be paid in the first instance
by the authority, and charged as part of the expenses of the
works on the premises of the objector, or, as the case may be,
on the premises of the objectors in such proportions as may
appear just.

Power to
amend
specification,
apportion-
ment, etc.

210.—(1) Subject to the provisions of this section, the street
works authority may from time to time amend the specification,
plans, sections, estimate and provisional apportionment for any
street works proposed under section 205 above.

(2) If the street works authority propose to amend the estimate
so as to increase the amount of it, then, before the amendment
is made, a notice containing the particulars specified in paragraph 6 of Schedule 16 to this Act shall—

(a) be published once in each of 2 successive weeks in a
local newspaper circulating in the area of the street
works authority, and

(b) be posted in a prominent position in or near to the
street to which the resolution of approval relates once
at least in each of 3 successive weeks, and

(c) within 7 days from the date of the first publication
under paragraph (a) above, be served on the owners
of the premises shown in the provisional apportionment
as liable to be charged ;

and, during one month from the said date, a document certified
by the proper officer of the council giving details of the amendment of the estimate and of the consequential amendment of the
provisional apportionment shall be kept deposited and open to
inspection free of charge at all reasonable hours at the offices
of the street works authority and also, in the case of a street
outside Greater London, at the offices of the council of the
district in which the street concerned is situated.

(3) Where a notice is served on an owner of premises under
subsection (2)(c) above it shall be accompanied by a statement
of the sum apportioned on those premises by the provisional
apportionment as proposed to be amended.

(4) Within one month from the date of the first publication
of a notice under subsection (2)(a) above, objections may be

made and, if made, shall be heard and determined in like manner, and subject to the like provisions with respect to the persons entitled to be heard and otherwise, as objections under section 208 above.

211.—(1) When any street works to be executed under the private street works code have been completed, and the expenses of them ascertained, the proper officer of the council shall make a final apportionment by dividing the expenses in the same proportions as those in which the estimated expenses were divided in the original or amended provisional apportionment, as the case may be, and notice of the final apportionment shall be served on the owners of the premises affected by it.

Final apportionment and objections to it.

(2) Within one month from the date on which notice of the final apportionment is served on him, the owner of any premises shown in the apportionment as liable to be charged may, by notice to the authority, object to the apportionment on the following grounds, or any of them:—

(*a*) that there has been an unreasonable departure from the specification, plans and sections ;

(*b*) that the actual expenses have without sufficient reason exceeded the estimated expenses by more than 15 per cent. ;

(*c*) that the apportionment has not been made in accordance with this section

Objections under this section shall be determined in the like manner, and subject to the like provisions with respect to the persons entitled to be heard and otherwise, as objections to the provisional apportionment.

(3) The final apportionment, subject to any amendment made to it by a court on the hearing of objections to it under this section, is conclusive for all purposes.

212.—(1) A street works authority may from time to time recover from the owner for the time being of any premises in respect of which any sum is due for expenses of street works the whole or any portion of that sum together with interest at such reasonable rates as the authority may determine from the date of the final apportionment.

Recovery of expenses and charge thereof on premises.

(2) The sum apportioned on any premises by the final apportionment or, as the case may be, by that apportionment as amended by a court, together with interest from the date of the final apportionment is, until recovered, a charge on the premises and on all estates and interests therein.

(3) A street works authority, for the purpose of enforcing a charge under subsection (2) above before it is registered under the Local Land Charges Act 1975, have the same powers and

1975 c. 76.

PART XI
1925 c. 20.

remedies under the Law of Property Act 1925 and otherwise as if they were mortgagees by deed having powers of sale and lease and of appointing a receiver.

(4) A street works authority may by order declare the expenses apportioned on any premises by a final apportionment made by the proper officer of the council or, as the case may be, by that apportionment as amended by a court, to be payable by annual instalments within a period not exceeding 30 years, together with interest from the date of the final apportionment; and any such instalment and interest, or any part thereof, may be recovered from the owner or occupier for the time being of the premises.

Schedule 13 to this Act applies in relation to any sum paid by an occupier of premises under this subsection.

Power for limited owners to borrow for expenses.
1965 c. 56.

213. The owners of any premises, if they are persons who under the Compulsory Purchase Act 1965 are empowered to sell and convey or release lands, may charge those premises with—

(a) such sum as may be necessary to defray the whole or a part of any expenses which the owners of, or any other person in respect of, those premises for the time being are liable to defray under the private street works code, and

(b) the expenses of making such a charge;

and, for securing the repayment of that sum with interest, may mortgage the premises to any person advancing that sum so, however, that the principal due on any such mortgage shall be repaid by equal yearly or half-yearly payments within 20 years.

Financial provisions.

214.—(1) A street works authority shall keep separate accounts of all money expended and recovered by them in the execution of the private street works code.

(2) A street works authority may from time to time borrow money for the purpose of providing temporarily for expenses of street works in private streets.

(3) If the whole or a part of a loan raised in respect of expenses of street works is outstanding at the date when any sum is recovered in respect of the expenses of those street works

under section 212 above, the sum so recovered shall be applied   PART XI
in repayment of the loan.

215.—(1) The incumbent or minister, or trustee, of a place Exemption
of public religious worship is not liable to expenses of for place
street works under the private street works code as the owner of public
of that place, or of a churchyard or burial ground attached to worship.
it, and the proportion of expenses in respect of which an
exemption is allowed under this section shall be borne by the
street works authority.

(2) No such expenses as aforesaid are to be deemed—

    (*a*) to be a charge on such a place, or churchyard or burial
        ground, or

    (*b*) to subject such a place, or churchyard or burial ground,
        to distress, execution or other legal process.

216.—(1) No railway undertakers or canal undertakers shall Certain
be deemed to be owners or occupiers for the purposes of the railways and
private street works code of land upon which a street wholly canals not to
or partly fronts if the land has no direct communication with be chargeable
the street and at the time of the laying out of the street was used with expenses.
solely as part of their line of railway, canal, or siding, station,
towing path, or works—

    (*a*) by the undertakers, or

    (*b*) in a case where the rights of other railway or canal
        undertakers in respect of the land under section 22
        of the Private Street Works Act 1892, are vested in the 1892 c. 57.
        undertakers, by those other railway undertakers or
        canal undertakers.

(2) The amount of any expenses incurred by a street works
authority under the private street works code which, but for
subsection (1) above, the undertakers would be liable to pay
shall be paid to the authority by the owners of the other premises
included in the final apportionment in such proportion as may
be settled by the proper officer of the council.

(3) If the undertakers subsequently make a communication
with the street, they shall pay to the authority the amount of the
expenses which, but for subsection (1) above, the undertakers
or such other undertakers as aforesaid would in the first instance
have been liable to pay, and the authority shall divide among
the owners for the time being of the other premises included
in the final apportionment the amount so paid by the undertakers, less the costs and expenses attendant upon the division,
in such proportion as may be settled by the proper officer of the
council.

(4) This section does not apply to a street existing at the date when the Private Street Works Act 1892 or the code of 1892 under the Highways Act 1959, as the case may be, first became applicable in the area in which the street is situated.

Objections
only to be
made as
provided by
private street
works code.

217. No objection which could be made under any provision of the private street works code shall be made in any proceeding or manner otherwise than as provided by that code.

Saving for
Thames Water
Authority and
Port of
London
Authority.

218. Nothing in the private street works code affects property or works of the Thames Water Authority on the shores of the river Thames, or of the Port of London Authority on those shores, or renders either of those authorities liable to charges in respect of any such property or works.

The advance payments code

Payments to
be made by
owners of new
buildings in
respect of
street works.

219.—(1) Subject to the provisions of this section, where—

(a) it is proposed to erect a building for which plans are required to be deposited with the local authority in accordance with building regulations, and

(b) the building will have a frontage on a private street in which the street works authority have power under the private street works code to require works to be executed or to execute works,

no work shall be done in or for the purpose of erecting the building unless the owner of the land on which it is to be erected or a previous owner thereof has paid to the street works authority, or secured to the satisfaction of that authority the payment to them of, such sum as may be required under section 220 below in respect of the cost of street works in that street.

(2) If work is done in contravention of subsection (1) above, the owner of the land on which the building is to be erected and, if he is a different person, the person undertaking the erection of the building is guilty of an offence and liable to a fine not exceeding £100, and any further contravention in respect of the same building constitutes a new offence and may be punished accordingly.

Proceedings under this subsection shall not be taken by any person other than the street works authority.

(3) Where the person undertaking the erection of the building is not the owner of the land on which it is to be erected and is charged with an offence under subsection (2) above, it shall be a defence for him to prove that he had reasonable grounds for believing that the sum required under section 220 below had

been paid or secured by the owner of the land in accordance with subsection (1) above.

(4) This section does not apply—

(a) where the owner of the land on which the building is to be erected will be exempt, by virtue of a provision in the private street works code, from liability to expenses incurred in respect of street works in the private street in question;

(b) where the building proposed to be erected will be situated in the curtilage of, and be appurtenant to, an existing building;

(c) where the building is proposed to be erected in a parish or community and plans for the building were deposited with the district council or, according to the date of deposit, the rural district council before the date on which the New Streets Act 1951, or the advance payments code (either in this Act or in the Highways Act 1959) was applied in the parish or community or, as the case may require, in the part of the parish or community in which the building is to be erected; 1951 c. 40.
1959 c. 25.

(d) where an agreement has been made by any person with the street works authority under section 38 above providing for the carrying out at the expense of that person of street works in the whole of the street or a part of the street comprising the whole of the part on which the frontage of the building will be, and for securing that the street or the part thereof, on completion of the works, will become a highway maintainable at the public expense;

(e) where the street works authority, being satisfied that the whole of the street or such a part thereof as aforesaid is not, and is not likely within a reasonable time to be, substantially built-up or in so unsatisfactory a condition as to justify the use of powers under the private street works code for securing the carrying out of street works in the street or part thereof, by notice exempt the building from this section;

(f) where the street works authority, being satisfied that the street is not, and is not likely within a reasonable time to become, joined to a highway maintainable at the public expense, by notice exempt the building from this section;

(g) where the whole street, being less than 100 yards in length, or a part of the street not less than 100 yards in length and comprising the whole of the part on which the frontage of the building will be, was on the material date built-up to such an extent that the aggregate length of the frontages of the buildings on both sides of the street or part constituted at least one half of the aggregate length of all the frontages on both sides of the street or part ;

(h) where (in a case not falling within paragraph (g) above) the street works authority, being satisfied that the whole of the street was on the material date substantially built-up, by notice exempt the building from this section ;

(i) where the building is proposed to be erected on land belonging to, or in the possession of—

   (i) the British Railways Board, the British Transport Docks Board, the British Waterways Board, the London Transport Executive, the National Freight Corporation (as far as included in this paragraph by paragraph 15(a) of Schedule 23 to this

Act) or any wholly-owned subsidiary (within the meaning of the Transport Act 1968) or joint subsidiary (within the meaning of section 51(5) of that Act) of any of those bodies ;

   (ii) the council of a county, district or London borough, the Greater London Council or the Common Council ;

   (iii) the Commission for the New Towns or a new town development corporation ;

(j) where the building is to be erected by a company the objects of which include the provision of industrial premises for use by persons other than the company, being a company the constitution of which prohibits the distribution of the profits of the company to its members, and the cost of the building is to be defrayed wholly or mainly by a government department ;

(k) where the street works authority, being satisfied—

   (i) that more than three-quarters of the aggregate length of all the frontages on both sides of the street, or of a part of the street not less than 100 yards in length and comprising the whole of the part on which the frontage of the building will be, consists, or is at some future time likely to consist, of the frontages of industrial premises, and

   (ii) that their powers under the private street works code are not likely to be exercised in relation to the street, or to that part of it, as the case may be, within a reasonable time,

by resolution exempt the street, or that part of it, from this section.

(5) Where a sum has been paid or secured under this section by the owner of the land in relation to a building proposed to be erected on it, and thereafter a notice is served under subsection (4) above exempting the building from this section, or a resolution is passed under paragraph (*k*) of that subsection exempting the street or part of a street on which the building will have a frontage from this section, the street works authority shall refund that sum to the person who is for the time being owner of the land or shall release the security, as the case may be.

Where the said sum was paid, and after the payment but before the service of the said notice or the passing of the said resolution, as the case may be, the land in respect of which it was paid was divided into 2 or more parts each having a frontage on the private street in question, the sum is to be treated for the purposes of this subsection as apportioned between the owners of the land according to their respective frontages.

(6) For the purposes of this section " the material date " is—

(*a*) in relation to a building proposed to be erected in an area which before 1st April 1974 was a rural district or a contributory place within a rural district, the date on which the New Streets Act 1951 or the advance payments code (either in this Act or in the Highways Act 1959) was applied in that area ;

1951 c. 40.
1959 c. 25.

(*b*) in relation to a building proposed to be erected anywhere else, 1st October 1951.

220.—(1) In a case to which section 219 above applies the street works authority shall, within 6 weeks from the passing of any required plans relating to the erection of a building deposited with them or, in a case to which subsection (2) below applies, with the district council, serve a notice on the person by or on whose behalf the plans were deposited requiring the payment or the securing under section 219 above of a sum specified in the notice.

Determination of liability for, and amount of, payments.

In this subsection and subsection (2) below " required plans " means plans required to be deposited with the local authority in accordance with building regulations.

(2) Where (outside Greater London) the advance payments code is in force in the whole or any part of a district, the district council, in any case to which section 219 above may be applicable, shall within one week from the date of the passing of any required plans deposited with them relating to the erection of a building in an area in which that code is in force inform the street works authority that the plans have been passed.

(3) Subject to the provisions of this section, the sum to be specified in a notice under subsection (1) above is such

PART XI sum as, in the opinion of the street works authority, would be recoverable under the private street works code in respect of the frontage of the proposed building on the private street if the authority were then to carry out such street works in the street as they would require under that code before declaring the street to be a highway which for the purposes of this Act is a highway maintainable at the public expense.

In this subsection a reference to a street does not include a reference to a part of a street, except to a part which the street works authority think fit to treat as constituting a separate street for the purposes of this subsection and which comprises the whole of the part on which the frontage of the building will be.

(4) If, at any time after the service of a notice under subsection (1) above, the street works authority—

(a) are of opinion that the sum specified in the notice exceeds such sum as in their opinion would be recoverable as mentioned in subsection (3) above if they were then to carry out such street works as are so mentioned, or

(b) are of opinion that no sum would be so recoverable,

they may, by a further notice, served on the person who is for the time being owner of the land on which the building is to be, or has been, erected, substitute a smaller sum for the sum specified in the notice served under subsection (1) above or, as the case may be, intimate that no sum falls to be paid or secured.

This subsection does not apply where a sum has been paid or secured in compliance with a notice served under subsection (1) above and the case is one in which the authority have power to make a refund or release under section 221(1) below.

(5) Where, under a local Act, the erection of buildings on land having a frontage on a new street is prohibited until works for the construction or sewering of the street have been carried out in accordance with byelaws, the amount of the sum to be specified in a notice served under this section shall be calculated as if those works had been carried out.

(6) Where a notice is served on any person under this section (other than a notice intimating that no sum falls to be paid or secured) that person or, if he is a different person, the owner of the land on which the building is to be, or has been, erected, may, not later than one month from the date of the service of the notice, appeal to the Minister and the Minister may substitute a smaller sum for the sum specified by the street works authority.

On an appeal under this subsection, the Minister shall give the appellant an opportunity of being heard before a person appointed by the Minister.

(7) Where a sum has been paid or secured in compliance with a notice served under subsection (1) above and a notice is subsequently served under subsection (4) above substituting a smaller sum for the sum specified in the first-mentioned notice or intimating that no sum falls to be paid or secured, the street works authority—

(a) if the sum was paid, shall refund the amount of the excess or, as the case may be, the whole sum to the person who is for the time being owner of the land on which the building is to be, or has been, erected;

(b) if the sum was secured and the person whose property is security for the payment of it is for the time being owner of that land, shall release the security to the extent of the excess or, as the case may be, the whole security;

(c) if the sum was secured and the person whose property is security for the payment of it is not for the time being owner of that land, shall pay to that owner an amount equal to the excess or, as the case may be, the whole sum, and are entitled to realise the security for the purpose of recovering the amount so paid.

(8) Where land in respect of which a sum has been paid or secured in compliance with a notice under subsection (1) above is subsequently divided into 2 or more parts so that 2 or more owners would, if street works were carried out, incur liability in respect of it, the sum is to be treated as apportioned between those owners according to their respective frontages and, if the sum was secured and the security is the property of one only of those owners, the street works authority—

(a) are required under subsection (7)(b) above to release the security only to the extent of the amount apportioned to that owner, and

(b) are entitled to realise the security for the purpose of recovering the amount or amounts paid to the other owner or owners under subsection (7)(c) above.

(9) Where a security is realised for the purpose of recovering an amount paid by a street works authority under subsection (7)(c) above, and the sum produced by realising the security exceeds the amount so paid, the amount of the excess shall be held by the authority and dealt with under the advance payments code as if it had been an amount paid under section 219 above on the date on which the security was realised.

PART XI
Refunds etc.
where work
done otherwise
than at
expense of
street works
authority.

221.—(1) Where—

    (*a*) a sum has been paid or secured under section 219 above by the owner of land in respect of the cost of street works to be carried out in the private street on which that land has a frontage, and

    (*b*) any street works are subsequently carried out in the private street in respect of that frontage to the satis-faction of but otherwise than at the expense of the street works authority,

the authority may refund to the person at whose expense the works are carried out the whole or such proportion of that sum or, as the case may be, release the whole or such part of the security, as in their opinion represents the amount by which the liability of the owner of that land in respect of street works has been reduced as a result of the carrying out of the street works in question.

Where the person at whose expense the works are carried out is not the person who is for the time being owner of that land no refund or release shall be made under this subsection unless the owner has been notified of the proposal to make the refund or release and has been afforded an opportunity of making representations to the street works authority in relation to it.

(2) Where any land which has a frontage on a private street, and in respect of which a sum has been paid or secured under section 219 above, is subsequently divided into 2 or more parts each having a frontage on that private street, the sum is to be treated as apportioned between the owners thereof according to their respective frontages, and subsection (1) above has effect accordingly.

(3) Where—

    (*a*) a sum has been paid or secured under section 219 above by the owner of land in respect of the cost of street works to be carried out in the private street on which that land has a frontage, and

    (*b*) thereafter the street works authority enter into an agreement with any person under section 38 above providing for the carrying out at the expense of that person of street works in respect of that frontage,

that agreement may also provide for the refund of the said sum or a part of it either without interest or with interest at such rate as may be specified in the agreement, or for the release of the whole or a part of the security, as the case may be.

Sums paid or
secured to be
in discharge
of further
liability for
street works.

222.—(1) Where a sum has been paid or secured under section 219 above by the owner of land in respect of the cost of street works to be carried out in the private street on which that land has a frontage, the liability of that owner or any subsequent owner of that land in respect of the carrying out of street works in that street under the private street works code ("the street works liability") is, as respects that frontage, to be deemed to be discharged to the extent of the sum so paid or secured.

(2) If, when the street is declared to be a highway which for the purposes of this Act is a highway maintainable at the public expense, the said sum is found to exceed the total street works liability in respect of that frontage or there is no such liability because the street was not made up at the expense of the street works authority, the street works authority—

(*a*) if the sum was paid, shall refund the amount of the excess or, as the case may be, the whole sum to the person who is for the time being owner of the land;

(*b*) if the sum was secured and the person whose property is security for the payment of it is for the time being owner of the land, shall release the security to the extent of the excess or, as the case may be, the whole security;

(*c*) if the sum was secured and the person whose property is security for the payment of it is not for the time being owner of the land, shall pay to that owner an amount equal to the excess or, as the case may be, the whole sum, and are entitled to realise the security for the purpose of recovering the amount so paid.

(3) Where land in respect of which a sum has been paid or secured under section 219 above is subsequently divided into 2 or more parts so that 2 or more owners incur or would incur the street works liability, the sum is to be treated as apportioned between those owners according to their respective frontages, and if the sum was secured and the security is the property of one only of those owners the street works authority—

(*a*) are required under subsection (2)(*b*) above to release the security only to the extent to which the amount apportioned to that owner exceeds his street works liability or, as the case may be, to the extent of the whole of that amount, and

(*b*) are entitled to realise the security for the purpose of recovering the amount or amounts paid to the other owner or owners under subsection (2)(*c*) above.

(4) Where any refund, release or payment has been made under section 220(7) above, or under section 221 above, the foregoing provisions of this section have effect as if for references therein to a sum paid or secured there were substituted references to any sum remaining paid or secured.

PART XI
Determination
to cease to
have effect
when plans
not proceeded
with.
1936 c. 49.

223.—(1) Where, on the occasion of the deposit of plans for the erection of a building, the amount to be paid or secured under section 219 above has been determined under section 220 above, and subsequently—

(a) the local authority, under section 66 of the Public Health Act 1936, declare the deposit of the plans to be of no effect, or

(b) before any work has been done in or for the purpose of erecting the building the owner gives notice to the local authority of his intention not to proceed with the building,

the said determination and any payment made or security given in accordance with it are, unless there have already been carried out or commenced in the street under the private street works code street works in respect of which the owner of the land on which the building was to be erected is liable, of no effect for the purposes of this Part of this Act.

(2) Where by virtue of subsection (1) above a determination is of no effect and a sum has been paid or security given in accordance with it, the street works authority—

(a) if the sum was paid, shall refund it to the person who is for the time being owner of the land ;

(b) if the sum was secured and the person whose property is security for the payment of it is for the time being owner of the land, shall release the security ;

(c) if the sum was secured and the person whose property is security for the payment of it is not for the time being owner of the land, shall pay to that owner an amount equal to the said sum, and are entitled to realise the security for the purpose of recovering the amount so paid.

(3) Where land in respect of which a sum has been paid or secured as mentioned in subsection (2) above is subsequently divided into 2 or more parts so that 2 or more owners would, if street works were carried out, incur liability in respect thereof, the sum is to be treated as apportioned between those owners according to their respective frontages and, if the sum was secured and the security is the property of one only of those owners, the street works authority—

(a) are required under subsection (2)(b) above to release the security only to the extent of the amount apportioned to that owner, and

(b) are entitled to realise the security for the purpose of recovering the amount or amounts paid to the other owner or owners under subsection (2)(c) above.

(4) Where any refund, release or payment has been made under section 220(7) above, or under section 221 above, subsections (2) and (3) above have effect as if for references in those subsections to a sum paid and security given there were substituted references to, respectively, any sum remaining paid and any remaining security.

(5) Where—

    (a) a person notifies the local authority in accordance with subsection (1)(b) above of his intention not to proceed with the building and by reason thereof a determination is of no effect, and

    (b) subsequently notice is given to the local authority by the owner of the land that he intends to proceed with the building in accordance with the plans as originally deposited,

the notice to be served under subsection (1) of section 220 above by the street works authority shall, in lieu of being served as required by that subsection, be served on him within one month from the date of the service of the notice of his intention to proceed with the building, and section 220 has effect accordingly.

(6) Where the advance payments code is in force in the whole or any part of a district, the district council, in any case to which this section may be applicable, shall within one week inform the county council of the happening of any of the following events:—

    (a) the making of any declaration that the deposit of plans relating to the erection of a building is of no effect,

    (b) the giving of any notice by an owner of his intention not to proceed with a building, and

    (c) the giving of any notice by an owner of his intention to proceed with the building in accordance with the plans as originally deposited.

224.—(1) The matters specified in subsection (2) below are local land charges.

    Certain matters to be local land charges.

(2) The matters referred to in subsection (1) above are:—

    (a) notices served by a street works authority under section 220(1) or (4) above;

    (b) determinations by the Minister under section 220(6) above;

    (c) payments made and securities given under section 219 above;

    (d) notices served under subsection (4)(e), (f) or (h) of section 219 above exempting a building from that section;

(*e*) resolutions passed under subsection (4)(*k*) of section 219 above exempting a street or a part of a street from that section ; and

(*f*) refunds made and releases of securities granted under section 221, 222 or 223 above.

(3) As respects any matter that is a local land charge by virtue of this section, the street works authority for the street concerned are, notwithstanding anything in section 5(4) of the Local Land Charges Act 1975, to be treated as the originating authority for the purposes of that Act.

1975 c. 76.

Interest on sums paid under advance payments code.

225.—(1) Any sum paid by the owner of land to a street works authority under section 219 above, in so far as it continues to be held by the authority, carries simple interest at the appropriate rate from the date of payment until such time as the sum or a part of it remaining so held—

(*a*) falls to be set off under section 222 above against the liability of the owner of the land in respect of the carrying out of street works ; or

(*b*) falls to be refunded in full under the provisions of the advance payments code ;

and the interest shall be held by the authority until that time and dealt with under those provisions as if it formed part of the said sum.

This subsection does not apply to any sum in so far as it is repaid under any such agreement as is referred to in section 221(3) above.

(2) For the purposes of the advance payments code interest on any sum held by a street works authority shall be calculated in respect of each financial year during which it accrues at the appropriate rate prevailing at the commencement of that financial year.

(3) In this section " the appropriate rate " means the rate at the material time determined by the Treasury in respect of local loans for periods of 10 years on the security of local rates (being a determination under section 6(2) of the National Loans Act 1968, and subject to any relevant direction under the said section 6(2)).

1968 c. 13.

General

Power to vary width of carriageway and footway on making up a private street.

226.—(1) A street works authority may include in street works done in relation to a street under the private street works code a variation of the relative widths of the carriageway and of the footway or footways of the street.

(2) No greater charge shall be imposed on a person by reason of any such variation than could have been imposed in respect of a carriageway or footway of the width prescribed for a new street of the same class by a byelaw or enactment with respect to the width of new streets which applied to the street when it was laid out; and any sum in excess of that charge shall be borne by the authority.

227. Where, in the course of the execution of street works under the private street works code in a private street which consists of or comprises a highway, the street works authority widen the highway under Part V of this Act, the widening does not relieve any person of liability for expenses of the street works, and the amount of that liability is not greater or less than it would have been if the highway had not been widened.

Widening of highway comprised in private street.

228.—(1) When any street works have been executed in a private street, the street works authority may, by notice displayed in a prominent position in the street, declare the street to be a highway which for the purposes of this Act is a highway maintainable at the public expense, and on the expiration of one month from the day on which the notice was first so displayed the street shall, subject to subsections (2) to (4) below, become such a highway.

Adoption of private street after execution of street works.

(2) A street shall not become a highway maintainable at the public expense by virtue of subsection (1) above if, within the period there mentioned, the owner of the street or, if more than one, the majority in number of the owners of the street, by notice to the authority object; but within 2 months from the expiration of that period the street works authority may apply to a magistrates' court for an order overruling the objection.

(3) If an order overruling an objection under subsection (2) above is made pursuant to an application under that subsection and no appeal against the order is brought within the time limited for such an appeal, the street or part in question shall become a highway maintainable at the public expense on the expiration of that time.

(4) Where such an order is made or refused and an appeal, or an appeal arising out of that appeal, is brought against or arises out of the order or refusal, then—

(a) if the final determination of the matter is in favour of the authority, or

(b) the appeal is abandoned by the objectors,

the street shall become a highway maintainable at the public expense on that final determination or, as the case may be, on the abandonment of the appeal.

H

(5) Notwithstanding anything in any other enactment or provision, for the purposes of this section the time for bringing or seeking leave for any appeal (including an application for certiorari) is 2 months from the date of the decision or of the conclusion of the proceedings appealed against, unless apart from this subsection the time is less than that period ; and no power, however worded, to enlarge any such time is exercisable for the purposes of this section.

(6) Where street works have been executed in a part only of a street (other than a part extending for the whole of the length of the street), subsections (1) to (4) above have effect as if for references in those subsections to the street there were substituted references to the length of the street which constitutes or comprises that part.

(7) If all street works (whether or not including lighting) have been executed in a private street to the satisfaction of the street works authority, then, on the application of the majority in rateable value of the owners of premises in the street, the street works authority shall, within the period of 3 months from the date of the application, by notice displayed in a prominent position in the street, declare the street to be a highway which for the purposes of this Act is a highway maintainable at the public expense and thereupon the street shall become such a highway.

In this subsection a reference to a street does not include a reference to a part of a street.

Power of majority of frontagers to require adoption where advance payment made.   **229.**—(1) Where a majority in number of the owners of land having a frontage on a built-up private street, or as many of those owners as have between them more than half the aggregate length of all the frontages on both sides of the street, by notice request the street works authority to exercise their powers under the private street works code so as—

(a) to secure the carrying out of such street works in that street as the street works authority require under that code before declaring the street to be a highway which for the purposes of this Act is a highway maintainable at the public expense, and

(b) to declare the street to be such a highway,

the street works authority shall proceed to exercise their powers accordingly.

(2) Subsection (1) above does not apply unless, in at least one case, a payment has been made or security has been given under section 219 above by the owner of land having a frontage on the street and the payment has not been refunded, or the

security released or realised, under subsection (5) of that section, or under section 223 above.

(3) For the purposes of this section a street is to be deemed to be built-up if the aggregate length of the frontages of the buildings on both sides of the street constitutes at least one half of the aggregate length of all the frontages on both sides of the street.

(4) This section does not apply in relation to a part of a street unless it is a part not less than 100 yards in length which the owners of land having a frontage on that part of the street elect to treat as constituting a street for the purposes of this section.

230.—(1) Where repairs are needed to obviate danger to traffic in a private street the street works authority may by notice require the owners of the premises fronting the street to execute, within such time as may be specified in the notice, such repairs as may be so specified.

(2) Where such repairs as are mentioned in subsection (1) above are needed in a part only of the street (other than a part extending for the whole of the length of the street), a requirement under that subsection shall be made only of the owners of the premises fronting the length of the street which constitutes or comprises that part.

(3) A person aggrieved by a requirement of a street works authority under this section may appeal to a magistrates' court.

(4) Subject to any order made on appeal and to subsection (5) below, if, within the time specified in a notice served under subsection (1) above, the repairs required thereby have not been executed, the authority may execute the repairs, and may recover the expenses reasonably incurred by them in so doing from the owners in default, the expenses being apportioned between those owners according to the extent to which their respective premises front the street.

(5) If, within the time so specified, the majority in number or rateable value of owners of premises in the street by notice require the street works authority to proceed in relation to the street under the private street works code, the street works authority shall so proceed, and on the completion of the necessary works shall forthwith declare the street to be a highway which for the purposes of this Act is a highway maintainable at the public expense; and thereupon the street shall become such a highway.

H 2

(6) Where a requirement under subsection (1) above has been made in respect of a part only of a street (other than a part extending for the whole of the length of the street), subsection (5) above has effect as if for references therein to the street there were substituted references to the length of the street which constitutes or comprises that part.

(7) Without prejudice to the foregoing provisions of this section or to any other enactment for the time being in force relating to private street works, the street works authority and also, in the cases mentioned below, the district council may, in any street that is not a highway maintainable at the public expense, execute such repairs as are in their opinion urgently required to prevent or remove danger to persons or vehicles in the street.

The cases in which the district council may act under this subsection are those in which the street concerned is a footpath, bridleway or any such road as is mentioned in section 42(2)(c) above (urban roads).

(8) The power of a district council under subsection (7) above is subject to Part I of Schedule 7 to this Act.

Compensation for damage caused by execution of street works.

231. A street works authority shall pay compensation to any person who sustains damage by reason of the execution of street works by the authority under the private street works code.

Power to treat as a private street land designated for purposes of this section by development plan.

232.—(1) The provisions of this section apply in relation to land defined by a development plan—

(a) as the site of a proposed road, or

(b) as land required for the widening of an existing road which is of less than byelaw width,

and designated by the plan as land to which this section applies.

(2) Where any land is so defined and designated as aforesaid, the prospective street works authority, subject to subsection (3) below, may at any time by order declare the land (together with any land forming part of any such existing road as aforesaid) to be a private street, and thereupon the land is to be deemed to have been dedicated to the use of the public as a highway and to be a private street for the purposes of this Part of this Act.

The reference in this subsection to the prospective street works authority is a reference to the council who will be the street works authority as respects the private street constituted by the council's declaration.

(3) No order shall be made by the authority under subsection (2) above in relation to land which has not been acquired by them at the date of the order (other than land forming part of any such existing road as aforesaid) except with the consent of all persons interested in the land.

(4) In relation to land which is deemed to be a private street by virtue of a declaration under subsection (2) above the provisions of the private street works code apply subject to such exceptions, adaptations and modifications as may be prescribed by regulations made by the Minister of Transport.

(5) Regulations made for the purposes of subsection (4) above shall make provision for securing—

(a) that the amount of the expenses incurred in the execution of street works charged under the private street works code on the owners of adjoining land does not exceed the amount which would, at the date of the commencement of the works, have been the cost of the execution of street works in the course of the construction, widening or improvement if it had been carried out—

(i) so as to comply with the provisions of any byelaws, regulations or other enactments in force in the area, and

(ii) as respects matters for which no such provision is made, so as to comply with such requirements as would have been imposed by the street works authority at the date of the commencement of the works as a condition of declaring the street to be a highway which for the purposes of this Act is a highway maintainable at the public expense;

(b) that as soon as the street has been made up or widened by or to the satisfaction of the street works authority it becomes a highway maintainable at the public expense;

(c) that no expenses incurred in the execution of street works are recoverable against agricultural land or buildings until the land or buildings cease to be agricultural land or buildings; and

(d) that no expenses incurred in the execution of street works for the purpose of making a new street are recoverable in respect of any land (whether the site of a building or not) unless and until access is provided for and used by persons or vehicles from that land to the new street.

H 3

PART XI

(6) Regulations made for the purposes of subsection (4) above may provide—

(a) for the inclusion in the expenses recoverable as aforesaid in respect of street works carried out by the street works authority of any expenses incurred by a local authority after the date on which the land is defined and designated as mentioned in subsection (1) above, and before it is declared to be a private street under subsection (2) above, in the construction of sewers in or under the land ; and

(b) for authorising the street works authority to enter on any land adjoining the street for the purpose of executing street works on land comprised in the street.

(7) A highway constructed by a local highway authority on land deemed to be a private street by virtue of a declaration under subsection (2) above is not by virtue only of section 36(2)(a) above for the purposes of this Act a highway maintainable at the public expense.

(8) The provisions of this section, and any restrictions or powers imposed or conferred by it in relation to land, apply and may be exercised in relation to any land notwithstanding that provision is made for authorising or regulating any development of the land by any enactment in force on 6th August 1947 or by any local Act passed at any time during the Session of Parliament held during the regnal years 10 and 11 Geo. 6 (that date and that Session being, respectively, the date of passing of the Town and Country Planning Act 1947 and the Session during which that Act was passed, and that Act, now superseded by the Town and Country Planning Act 1971, being the Act that first made provision for development plans).

1947 c. 51.

1971 c. 78.

(9) In this section—

" byelaw width ", in relation to a road, means the width required by any byelaws, regulations or other enactments relating to the construction of streets in the area in which the road is situated ;

" construction " and " improvement ", in relation to a street, include the planting, laying out, maintenance and protection of trees, shrubs and grass verges in and beside the street ;

" development plan " has the meaning provided by section 20 of the Town and Country Planning Act 1971 and " local authority " has the same meaning as in that Act.

233.—(1) Subject to section 217 above, a person aggrieved by a decision of a street works authority in a case where the authority are empowered by section 212 above to recover any expenses incurred by them may appeal to the Minister, who may make such decision as to him seems equitable ; and the decision shall be final and binding on all parties.

PART XI

Appeal to Minister under private street works code.

(2) The time within which an appeal may be brought under subsection (1) above is 21 days from the date on which a demand for the payment of the expenses, or any part of them, was first served on the person wishing to appeal.

(3) A person appealing under subsection (1) above shall in his appeal state the grounds thereof, and shall serve a copy of his appeal on the street works authority ; and any proceedings commenced for the recovery of any such expenses as aforesaid by the street works authority shall, on the service on them of the copy of the appeal, be stayed.

(4) The Minister may, if he thinks fit, by his decision direct the authority to pay to the person so proceeded against such sum as he may consider to be a just compensation for the loss or damage sustained by that person by reason of the proceedings.

234.—(1) In a case where a part only of a private street is within the area of a street works authority, the authority may, with the consent of the street works authority in whose area any other part of the street is situated, and subject to subsection (3) below, resolve to treat that other part for the purposes of this Part of this Act as if it were within their own area.

Provisions as to private street in area of more than one street works authority.

(2) Where the authority so resolve, then, without prejudice to the operation of any enactment not contained in this Part of this Act, this Part of this Act applies in relation to that other part of the street as if it, together with the premises fronting it, were within the area of the authority passing the resolution.

(3) A street works authority shall not resolve under subsection (1) above to treat a part of a street as if it were within their own area if that part comprises a length of the street wholly outside that area.

(4) In a case where a private street is within the area of a street works authority but premises fronting the street are wholly or partly outside that area, then, without prejudice to the operation of any enactment not contained in this Part of this Act, this Part of this Act applies in relation to that street as if those premises were wholly within the area of tha authority.

In this subsection a reference to a street includes a reference to a length of the street but does not include a reference to any other part of it.

(5) A resolution passed by a street works authority under subsection (1) above shall be published by advertisement in one or more local newspapers circulating within the area in which the street .is situated and otherwise in such manner as the authority think sufficient for giving notice to all persons interested.

Evasion of private street works expenses by owners.

235.—(1) Where a street works authority are empowered by section 212 above to recover any sum from the owner of any premises, and the authority are unable by the exercise of their powers (other than powers conferred by this section) to recover that sum, then if—

(a) the said premises were previously transferred by a person (" the transferor ") who at the time of the transfer was the owner of other premises adjoining those premises, and

(b) a magistrates' court is satisfied that the transfer was intended for the purpose of evading the payment of expenses of street works,

the court may make an order under this section.

(2) An order under this section shall provide that, to such extent as the court making the order may determine, the street works authority may recover the said sum, and, where that sum is payable under an order made under section 212(4) above or section 305(2) below, any further sums which may fall due under that order, from the transferor.

(3) In this section " transfer " includes any disposal of land whether by way of sale, lease, exchange, gift or otherwise.

Contribution by street works authority to expenses of street works.

236.—(1) A street works authority may at any time resolve to bear the whole or a portion of the expenses of any street works in their area under the private street works code and where an authority so resolve the liabilities of the owners of premises in respect of those expenses are to be treated as discharged or as proportionately reduced, accordingly.

(2) Without prejudice to their powers under subsection (1) above, a street works authority may at any time resolve to bear the whole or a portion of the expenses of any street works in their area under the private street works code which would otherwise be apportioned on, or to the owner of, any premises of which the rear or a flank fronts the street; and where an

authority so resolve the liability of the owner of those premises in respect of those expenses is to be treated as discharged or reduced accordingly.

237.—(1) Where a person has paid, or advanced money for, expenses which by section 212 above a street works authority are empowered to recover, that person may apply to the authority for a charging order, and the authority, on being satisfied as to the amount of the expenditure on private street works, and, in the case of an advance, as to the sum advanced, may make an order accordingly charging on the premises in respect of which the expenses are recoverable, and on all estates and interests therein, an annuity to repay the sum expended or advanced.

Power of street works authority to grant charging order.

(2) The annuity charged shall be such sum as the street works authority may determine in respect of every £100 of the amount of the expenditure and so in proportion in respect of any fraction of that amount, and shall commence from the date of the order and be payable by equal half-yearly payments for a term of 30 years to the person named in the order, his executors, administrators or assigns.

(3) A person aggrieved by an order of a street works authority under subsection (1) above, or by the refusal of the authority to make an order under that subsection, may appeal to a magistrates' court.

(4) Schedule 13 to this Act applies in relation to any sum paid by an occupier of premises in respect of an annuity charged on those premises under this section.

PART XII

ACQUISITION, VESTING AND TRANSFER OF LAND ETC.

Introductory

238.—(1) Any power under sections 239 to 246 below to acquire land, except the power under section 246(2), is exercisable compulsorily or by agreement.

Interpretation etc. of Part XII.

(2) In this Part of this Act " common ", " fuel or field garden allotment " and " open space " have the same meaning respectively as in the Act of 1946.

Acquisition of land generally

Acquisition
of land for
construction,
improvement
etc. of
highway:
general
powers.

239.—(1) Subject to section 249 below, the Minister may acquire land required for the construction of a trunk road, and any highway authority may acquire land required for the construction of a highway which is to be a highway maintainable at the public expense, other than a trunk road.

(2) Subject to section 249 below, the Minister may acquire land which in his opinion is required—

(*a*) for the carrying out of any works authorised by an order relating to a trunk road under section 14 above, or

(*b*) for the provision of buildings or facilities to be used in connection with the construction or maintenance of a trunk road other than a special road.

(3) Subject to section 249 below, a highway authority may acquire land required for the improvement of a highway, being an improvement which they are authorised by this Act to carry out in relation to the highway.

(4) Subject to section 249 below, a special road authority may acquire land which in the opinion of the authority is required—

(*a*) for the improvement of a highway which is included in the route of the special road but has not been transferred to the authority by means of an order under section 18 above,

(*b*) for the purposes of any order made in relation to the special road under section 18 above, or

(*c*) for the provision of service stations or other buildings or facilities to be used in connection with the construction of the special road or with the use or maintenance of it.

(5) Where a highway authority have acquired, or propose to acquire, in exercise of any of the powers conferred by subsections (1) to (4) above, land forming part of a common, open space, or fuel or field garden allotment, and other land is required for the purpose of being given in exchange for the first-mentioned land, the authority may acquire that other land under the subsection in question as if it were land required for the construction or improvement of a highway, and nothing in section 249 below applies to an acquisition by virtue of this subsection.

(6) A highway authority may acquire land required for the improvement or development of frontages to a highway for which they are the highway authority or of the land adjoining or adjacent to that highway.

240.—(1) Subject to section 249 below, a highway authority may acquire land which is required for, or for use by them in connection with, the carrying out of works authorised by section 129 above, or by an order relating to a classified road under section 14 above.

(2) Without prejudice to any other powers conferred by this Act—

    (*a*) a highway authority may acquire land which is required for use by them in connection with the construction or improvement of a highway, or with the carrying out of works authorised by an order relating to a trunk road under section 14 above or an order under section 18 or section 108(1) above ; and

    (*b*) any power of a highway authority under subsection (1) above or under any provision of this Part of this Act not contained in this section to acquire land for a purpose whose achievement involves the diversion of a navigable watercourse or the carrying out of works under section 110 above includes power to acquire land which is required for carrying out the diversion or, as the case may be, the works.

(3) Subject to section 249 below, the Minister may acquire land which is required for the purpose of—

    (*a*) providing a trunk road picnic area ; or

    (*b*) providing public sanitary conveniences in the exercise of his powers under section 112(5) above.

(4) A local highway authority may acquire land which is required for the purpose of providing public sanitary conveniences in the exercise of their powers under section 114 above.

(5) Subject to section 249 below, a highway authority may acquire land which is required for the purpose of providing a lorry area in the exercise of their powers under section 115 above.

(6) Where, in exercise of any of the powers conferred by subsections (1) to (5) above, a highway authority have acquired, or propose to acquire, for any purpose land forming part of a common, open space or fuel or field garden allotment and other land is required for the purpose of being given in exchange for the first-mentioned land, the authority may acquire that other land.

241.—(1) Where a highway authority have prescribed an improvement line in relation to any street under section 73 above they may acquire any land, not occupied by buildings, lying between the improvement line and the boundary of the street.

PART XII

Acquisition of land in connection with construction, improvement etc. of highway: further general powers.

Acquisition of land between improvement line and boundary of street.

PART XII

(2) Any land acquired under this section shall, at such time or times as the highway authority may determine, be added to and made good as part of the street by the authority, and until it is so added the occupier of the land from which it is severed, and other persons with his permission, are entitled to reasonable access across the land so acquired to and from the street, and have the same rights in regard to the laying, altering, maintaining and removal of drains, mains, pipes or electric lines in that land as if it were already part of the street.

(3) Subsection (11) of section 73 above has effect in relation to this section as it has effect in relation to that section.

Acquisition of land for execution of works in connection with certain bridges.

242.—(1) A highway authority may, subject to subsection (3) below, acquire land which they require to enable them to comply with a requirement or direction contained in an order made under section 93 above.

(2) The Minister may, subject to subsection (3) below, authorise the owners of a bridge to acquire land which they require to enable them to comply with a requirement or direction contained in an order made under section 93 above.

(3) Nothing in this section authorises the compulsory acquisition of land which is the property of a council, or which has been acquired by transport undertakers for the purposes of their undertaking, but—

(a) a highway authority may acquire compulsorily a right upon, under or over such land for the purpose of executing any works which they are required or authorised by an order made under section 93 to execute or construct; and

(b) the Minister may authorise the owners of a bridge to acquire compulsorily a right upon, under or over such land for that purpose.

Acquisition of land for cattle-grids etc.

243. A highway authority may acquire land which they require for the purpose of providing, altering or improving a cattle-grid or by-pass in the exercise of powers conferred on them by this Act.

Acquisition of land for road-ferries.

244. A highway authority may acquire land which they require for the purpose of providing or improving a road-ferry in the exercise of powers conferred on them by this Act.

Acquisition of land for buildings etc. needed for discharge of functions of highway authority.

245. Without prejudice to section 239(4) above, a local highway authority may acquire land, whether situated within or without their area, which in their opinion is required for the provision of any buildings or facilities needed for the purposes of their functions as a highway authority.

246.—(1) Subject to subsection (3) below, a highway autho- PART XII
rity may acquire land for the purpose of mitigating any adverse Acquisition
effect which the existence or use of a highway constructed or of land for
improved by them, or proposed to be constructed or improved mitigating
by them, has or will have on the surroundings of the highway. adverse effects of constructing

(2) Subject to subsection (3) below, a highway authority may or improving
acquire by agreement (but not compulsorily)— highway.

    (*a*) land the enjoyment of which is seriously affected by
        the carrying out of works by the authority for the
        construction or improvement of a highway;

    (*b*) land the enjoyment of which is seriously affected by
        the use of a highway which the authority have con-
        structed or improved,

if the interest of the vendor is one which falls within section
192(3) to (5) of the Town and Country Planning Act 1971 1971 c. 78.
(interests qualifying for protection under blight provisions)
taking references to the date of service of a notice under section
193 of that Act as references to the date on which the purchase
agreement is made.

(3) The powers conferred by subsection (1) above to acquire
land compulsorily and the powers conferred by subsection (2)(*a*)
above shall not be exercisable unless the acquisition is begun
before the date on which the highway or, as the case may be,
the improved highway is first opened to public traffic (" the opening date "); and the powers conferred by subsection (1) above
to acquire land by agreement and the powers conferred by
subsection (2)(*b*) above shall not be exercisable unless the
acquisition is begun before the end of one year after the opening
date.

(4) For the purposes of subsection (3) above the acquisition
of any land is begun—

    (*a*) if it is compulsory, on the date on which the notice
        required by paragraph 3(1)(*a*) of Schedule 1 to the
        Act of 1946 is first published;

    (*b*) if it is by agreement, on the date on which the agree-
        ment is made;

and where the compulsory acquisition of any land under subsection (1) above is begun within the time limited by subsection (3) above but is not proceeded with, any subsequent
compulsory acquisition of that land under subsection (1) is to
be treated for the purposes of this section as begun within that
time.

PART XII

(5) Where under the powers of this section a highway authority have acquired, or propose to acquire, land forming part of a common, open space or fuel or field garden allotment and other land is required for the purpose of being given in exchange for the first-mentioned land, the authority may acquire that other land.

(6) For the purpose of assessing the compensation payable on the compulsory acquisition of land under this section the land is to be treated as if it were being acquired for the construction of the highway or, as the case may be, the improvement in question.

(7) In this section references to the construction or improvement of a highway include references to the construction or improvement of a highway by virtue of an order under section 14 or 18 above.

General
provision as
to acquisition
procedure
etc.

247.—(1) Any power to acquire land compulsorily conferred by any of the foregoing provisions of this Part of this Act on a local highway authority is exercisable in any particular case on their being authorised to do so by the Minister.

(2) In relation to the compulsory acquisition of land under any of the said provisions by a local highway authority the Act of 1946 has effect as if this Act had been in force immediately before the commencement of that Act.

(3) In relation to the compulsory acquisition of land under any of the said provisions by the Minister, the Act of 1946 has effect as if this Act had been in force immediately before the commencement of that Act and as if the said provisions were included among the enactments specified in section 1(1)(b) of that Act.

(4) In relation to the acquisition of land under section 242 above by the owners of a bridge, the Act of 1946, subject to subsection (5) below, has effect as if this Act had been in force immediately before the commencement of that Act, and as if references to a local authority in section 1(1)(a) and section 5 of that Act, and in Part I of Schedule 1 to that Act, and to an authority and an acquiring authority in section 3 of that Act, included references to the owners of a bridge.

(5) Notwithstanding anything in section 1(2) of the Act of 1946 or in Part III of Schedule 1 to that Act an order authorising the owners of a bridge to acquire a right compulsorily pursuant to section 242(3) above is not subject to special parliamentary procedure by reason only of its authorising the acquisition of

any such right, nor does anything in the said Part III prevent the acquisition of any right pursuant to section 242(3) above (whether by the owners of a bridge or by a highway authority).

(6) Where under this Part of this Act a highway authority are authorised to acquire land by agreement, the provisions of Part 1 of the Act of 1965 (so far as applicable) other than sections 4 to 8, section 10 and section 31, apply, and in the said Part 1 as so applied the word " land " has the meaning provided by section 329 below.

248.—(1) Any power of the Minister under any of the foregoing provisions of this Part of this Act, other than sections 240 and 246 to acquire by agreement land required for a purpose mentioned in the provision in question is exercisable in respect of any land which, in the opinion of the Minister, may be required for that purpose, notwithstanding that the land is not immediately required for that purpose.

Acquisition in advance of requirements.

(2) Subject to the following provisions of this section, where under any provision of this Act specified in column 1 of Schedule 17 to this Act a highway authority have power to acquire, or have acquired, land (" the initial stage area ") for a purpose specified in column 2 of that Schedule, then any power of the authority under this Act to acquire land compulsorily for a purpose specified in column 3 is, in the case of other land adjacent to the initial stage area (" the subsequent stage area "), exercisable by them notwithstanding that the other land is not immediately required for the purpose specified in column 3.

(3) A highway authority shall not acquire land compulsorily by virtue of subsection (2) above unless one or more of the following conditions are satisfied, namely—

(a) the authority intend, when they have acquired the subsequent stage area, forthwith to incorporate it within the boundaries of the highway or proposed highway or, as the case may be, of the service area, maintenance compound, trunk road picnic area or lorry area, for the purposes of which the initial stage area is to be, or has been, acquired ;

(b) the authority's proposed use of the initial stage area involves the carrying out of works wholly or partly on, or under or over, the subsequent stage area ;

(c) plans for the use of the subsequent stage area (for the purpose for which the authority have power by virtue of this section to acquire it) have been made or approved by the Minister.

(4) A highway authority shall not by virtue of subsection (2) above acquire land compulsorily for any purpose where, apart from this section, they would not have power to acquire it compulsorily if it were required immediately for that purpose.

Distance limits from highway applicable to compulsory acquisition.

249.—(1) Subject to subsection (3) below, a highway authority shall not in the exercise of a power to acquire land under any of the provisions of this Act specified in column 1 of Part I of Schedule 18 to this Act acquire compulsorily land lying beyond the limit specified in relation to that power in column 2 of that Schedule.

(2) Part II of Schedule 18 has effect with respect to limits specified in Part I of that Schedule.

(3) Nothing in this section applies to land required for purposes connected with the drainage of a highway or proposed highway, or of a maintenance compound, service area, trunk road picnic area or lorry area, or required for the purpose—

(a) of the diversion of a navigable watercourse,

(b) of the carrying out of works authorised by section 110 above, or

(c) of providing protection for a highway or proposed highway against snow, flood, landslide or other hazards of nature.

Additional provisions with respect to acquisition of rights over land

Land acquisition powers to extend to creation as well as acquisition of rights.

250.—(1) A compulsory purchase order made in the exercise of highway land acquisition powers may provide for the acquisition of rights over land by creating them as well as for the acquisition of rights already in existence.

In this Act " highway land acquisition powers " means powers in respect of acquisition of land which are exercisable by a highway authority under any of the following provisions of this Act, namely, sections 239, 240, 242 to 246 and 250(2).

(2) Where rights over land are, or are to be, acquired by a highway authority by means of a compulsory purchase order made in the exercise of highway land acquisition powers, and the land forms part of a common, open space or fuel or field garden allotment and other land is required for the purpose of being given in exchange for those rights, the authority may acquire by agreement or compulsorily that other land ; and subsections (1) to (3) of section 247 above apply in relation to this subsection as they apply in relation to the provisions there mentioned.

(3) In section 247(1) to (4) above references to acquisition of land include references to compulsory acquisition of rights by virtue of this section.

(4) The Acts of 1946 and 1965 have effect with the modifications necessary to make them apply to the compulsory acquisition of a right by virtue of this section as they apply to the compulsory acquisition of land, so that, in appropriate contexts, references in those Acts to land are to be read as referring, or as including references, to the right acquired or to be acquired, or to land over which the right is, or is to be, exercisable, according to the requirements of the particular context.

(5) For the purpose of giving effect to this section, and without prejudice to the general adaptation of enactments under subsection (4) above—

(a) Part I of Schedule 19 to this Act has effect for the adaptation of Part III of Schedule 1 to the Act of 1946 (requirement of special parliamentary procedure in case of acquisition of certain descriptions of land) to cases of compulsory acquisition of rights ;

(b) Part II of that Schedule has effect for the adaptation of Part I of the Act of 1965 to such cases ; and

(c) as respects compensation in such cases, the enactments relating to compensation for the compulsory purchase of land apply, with the necessary modifications, as they apply to compensation on the compulsory purchase of land and interests in land.

(6) References in any enactment or instrument to the acquisition of land, in a context relating to compulsory acquisition under highway land acquisition powers, are to be construed (except in so far as the context otherwise requires) as including references to the compulsory acquisition of a right or rights by virtue of this section.

(7) The provisions of this section are without prejudice to section 242(3) above, sections 254 and 255 below and any other provision of this Act which, by virtue of the definition of " land " in section 329(1) below, authorises the acquisition of interests in or rights over land.

(8) References in this section and in sections 251 and 252 below to rights over land include references to the right to do, or to place and maintain, any thing in, on or under land, or in the air-space above its surface.

251.—(1) Where by a deed or other instrument in which—

(a) it is stated that it is made in pursuance of a compulsory acquisition of rights by virtue of section 250 above ; or

Rights acquired to be binding on successive owners of the land.

(b) it is certified by a highway authority that the instrument is made in connection with the performance of their functions under this Act,

any person having an interest in the land grants or agrees to grant to a highway authority any right over the land, the grant or agreement is binding upon his successors in title and persons deriving title under him or them (otherwise than by a disposition taking effect before the date of the grant) to the same extent as it is binding upon the grantor, notwithstanding that it would not have been binding upon such persons apart from this subsection.

(2) Where by a deed poll under any provision of the Act of 1965 a highway authority vest in themselves any right over land as against some person having an interest in the land, that right is binding upon that person's successors in title and persons deriving title under him or them (otherwise than by a disposition taking effect before the date of the deed poll) to the same extent as it is, or would have been, binding upon the first-mentioned person.

(3) The foregoing provisions of this section apply whether or not (apart from this section) the right in question is capable in law of binding interests in the land other than the interest of the grantor or, as the case may be, the person first-mentioned in subsection (2) above.

(4) Where under any provisions of this Act any right conferred by a deed or other instrument to which subsection (1) or (2) above applies is transferred from one highway authority to another, this section applies after the transfer in relation to the other highway authority as it applied before the transfer to the first-mentioned authority.

(5) As respects registered land, nothing in this section prejudices the provisions of the Land Registration Acts 1925 to 1971.

Power of landowner affected by rights acquisition to compel acquisition of whole interest.

252.—(1) The following provisions have effect where there has come into force a compulsory purchase order made by a highway authority in the exercise of highway land acquisition powers and providing for the acquisition of a right over land and notice to treat in respect of the right has been served on a person having an interest in the land.

(2) A person for the time being entitled to that interest (" the landowner ") may, at any time within 6 weeks of service of the notice to treat, or such longer period as may be agreed in writing by the highway authority, but so long only as the notice has not been withdrawn, serve on the highway authority a counter-notice requiring them, instead of acquiring the right in question,

to acquire instead his interest so far as it subsists in the land which is shown in the notice to treat as that over which the right is to be acquired.

(3) As from the date of service of the landowner's counter-notice—

    (*a*) the compulsory purchase order shall, as against the landowner, cease to have effect so far as it authorises the acquisition of the right in respect of which the counter-notice was served and shall have effect instead so as to authorise the authority to acquire compulsorily the landowner's interest in the land referred to in subsection (2) above ; and

    (*b*) the notice to treat referred to in subsection (1) above shall be deemed to have been served (on the date on which it was in fact served) in respect of the said interest, instead of in respect of the right (without prejudice to the authority's power under section 31 of the Land Compensation Act 1961 to withdraw the notice).

1961 c. 33.

(4) Nothing in this section prevents the highway authority from exercising any powers (and, in particular, any power of entry) which they have by virtue of having served notice to treat ; and the operation of subsection (3) above does not prejudice any such power of the authority either as respects a previous exercise of it or as respects its continuance by virtue of subsection (3)(*b*).

253.—(1) For the purpose of mitigating any adverse effect which the construction, improvement, existence or use of a highway has or will have on the surroundings of the highway, the highway authority may enter into an agreement with any person interested in land adjoining or in the vicinity of the highway for restricting or regulating the use of the land either permanently or during such period as may be specified in the agreement.

Agreements as to use of land near highways.

Any such agreement may, in particular, make provision for the planting and maintenance of trees, shrubs or plants of any other description on the land and for restricting the lopping or removal of trees, shrubs or other plants on the land.

(2) An agreement under this section may contain such incidental and consequential provisions (including provisions of a financial character) as appear to the highway authority to be necessary or expedient for the purposes of the agreement.

(3) The provisions of any agreement made under this section with any person interested in land are binding on persons deriving title from that person in respect of the land.

(4) An agreement under this section is a local land charge.

(5) This section is without prejudice to section 52 of the Town and Country Planning Act 1971 (agreements regulating development or use of land).

Compulsory
acquisition
for certain
purposes of
rights in land
belonging
to local
authorities
etc.

254.—(1) Subject to the provisions of this section, an order made, or made and confirmed, in the like manner and subject to the like conditions as an order authorising compulsory acquisition of land under section 239 above may authorise a highway authority to acquire compulsorily, subject to such conditions (including conditions as to the persons by whom any works are to be constructed or maintained) as may be imposed by the order, a right upon, under or over any land which is the property of a local authority or which has been acquired, for the purposes of their undertaking, by statutory undertakers, if the acquisition is—

(*a*) for the purposes of the construction of a bridge or of the approaches to a bridge (not including the reconstruction or alteration of the bridge or approaches in existence at the date of the order) upon, under or over such land;

(*b*) for the purposes of the execution of any works (other than the reconstruction of a bridge on a different site) for the maintenance, improvement or alteration of the bridge or of the approaches to a bridge transferred to the Minister by virtue of section 266 below or transferred to a special road authority other than the Minister by virtue of section 267 below; or

(*c*) for the purposes of any system of road drainage;

and, notwithstanding anything in section 1(2) of the Act of 1946, nothing in paragraph 10 of Schedule 1 to that Act prevents the acquisition of any such right.

(2) The power to acquire a right compulsorily conferred by subsection (1) above may be exercised—

(*a*) if the acquisition is for a purpose specified in that subsection in connection with a trunk road in a London borough, both by the council of that borough and by the Greater London Council as well as by the Minister, and

(*b*) if the acquisition is for a purpose so specified in connection with any other trunk road, by the council of the county in which the road is situated as well as by the Minister.

(3) An order authorising the compulsory acquisition of a right under this section shall be made subject to such conditions as the Minister, after consultation with the local authority or statutory undertakers from whom the right is to be acquired, considers necessary for securing—

(*a*) that the bridge or approaches to be constructed, reconstructed or altered, as the case may be, will be so designed, placed and constructed, or so reconstructed or altered, or

(*b*) that the drainage system to be provided will be so designed, placed and constructed,

as to avoid unreasonable interference with the functions and future development of the body concerned.

(4) An order authorising the compulsory acquisition under this section of a right for the purposes of a system of road drainage shall be made subject to such conditions as the Minister considers necessary for securing that no highway is drained—

(*a*) into any watercourse under the control of an internal drainage board or water authority without the consent of that board or authority, or

(*b*) into any reservoir, river, canal, dock, harbour, basin, culvert, syphon or other work which belongs to or is under the jurisdiction of a local authority or statutory undertakers without the consent of that authority or those undertakers.

(5) Nothing in this section authorises the compulsory acquisition of a right upon, under or over any land for the purposes of the construction of a bridge under or over the Manchester Ship Canal; but this subsection does not prevent the acquisition of such a right if the acquisition is—

(*a*) for the purposes of the construction of a bridge for which provision is made by any such order as is mentioned in section 106(1) above, or

(*b*) for the purposes of the execution of any works (other than the reconstruction of a bridge on a different site) for the maintenance, improvement or alteration of a bridge transferred to the Minister by virtue of section 266 below.

(6) For the purposes of this section and section 255 below—
" local authority " has the same meaning as in the Act of 1946, and
the Civil Aviation Authority and the Post Office are to be deemed to be statutory undertakers.

255.—(1) Subject to the provisions of this section, an order authorising the compulsory acquisition of a right by a highway authority under section 254 above for a purpose specified in section 254(1)(*a*) or (*b*) shall, except so far as may be otherwise agreed, provide that the bridge or approaches to which the order relates is to be constructed, reconstructed or altered, as the case may be, and maintained, at the expense of the highway authority. *Liability for certain expenses resulting from order under section 254.*

(2) Where an order is made authorising the compulsory acquisition of a right by a highway authority under section 254 above for the purpose of substituting a bridge for a level crossing over a railway, the expenses of the construction and maintenance of the bridge and of the approaches to the bridge shall, subject to subsection (3) below, be defrayed either—

(a) wholly by the highway authority, or

(b) partly by the highway authority and partly by the person from whom the right is acquired (hereafter in this section referred to as " the railway owners ") as, in default of agreement, may be determined by arbitration.

(3) Unless otherwise agreed—

(a) the railway owners' share of the expenses of such construction and maintenance, except so much of those expenses as is attributable to works executed at the instance of the railway owners for the improvement of their undertaking, shall be an amount equivalent to the saving to the railway owners estimated to result from the substitution of a bridge for the level crossing ; and

(b) any additional expense incurred by the railway owners by reason of any alteration of a railway due to the provisions of the order, other than provisions applied for by the railway owners for the improvement of their undertaking, shall be defrayed by the highway authority.

(4) Where by virtue of an agreement or award made under subsection (2) above the railway owners are required to contribute to the expenses of a highway authority the contribution shall, at the option of the railway owners, be paid—

(a) as a lump sum, or

(b) by annual payments of such amount, and continuing for such number of years, as may be agreed between the railway owners and the highway authority or, in default of agreement, as may be determined by arbitration, or

(c) by perpetual annual payments of such amount as may be so agreed or determined.

(5) Where by means of an order authorising a compulsory acquisition under section 254 above a highway authority acquire a right from a local authority or statutory undertakers any additional expense which, in consequence of—

(a) the construction, reconstruction or alteration of the bridge to which the order relates, or of the approaches to that bridge, or *(b)* the construction of the drainage system to which the order relates,

is thereafter incurred by the local authority or statutory undertakers in connection with the widening or alteration, on land which was vested in them before the making or confirmation of the order, of any railway, canal, inland navigation, dock, harbour, works or apparatus belonging to them, shall be defrayed by the highway authority.

(6) Any question whether any such additional expense as is mentioned in subsection (5) above has been incurred as there mentioned, or as to the amount of any such additional expense, shall, in default of agreement, be determined by arbitration.

(7) An order authorising the compulsory acquisition of a right by a highway authority under section 254 above for the purposes of a system of road drainage shall, except so far as may be otherwise agreed, provide that the system is to be constructed and maintained at the expense of the highway authority.

Exchange of land

256.—(1) Subject to the provisions of this section, the highway authority for any highway maintainable at the public expense may, for the purpose of straightening or otherwise adjusting the boundaries of the highway, enter into an agreement with the owner of any land which adjoins or lies near to the highway providing for the exchange of any such land for land on which the highway is situated, with or without the payment by either party of money for equality of exchange.

Power to exchange land to adjust boundaries of highways.

(2) A highway authority proposing to enter into an agreement under this section shall—

(a) publish once at least in each of 2 successive weeks, in one or more newspapers circulating in the area concerned, a notice giving particulars of the proposed agreement; and

(b) not later than the date on which the notice is first published in pursuance of paragraph (a) above (" the publication date "), serve a copy of the notice—

(i) on any statutory undertakers appearing to the authority to be affected by the proposal; and

(ii) on any other person appearing to the authority to have an interest in the land proposed to be conveyed by the authority; and

(c) not later than the publication date, cause a copy of the notice to be displayed in a prominent position on the part of the highway to which the proposal relates ;

PART XII and shall not enter into the proposed agreement before the expiration of the period of 2 months from the publication date and, where an appeal under subsection (3) below is brought against the proposed agreement, until the determination or abandonment of the appeal and of any appeal arising out of that appeal.

(3) Any person who objects to a proposed agreement under this section may, before the expiration of the period aforesaid, appeal to a magistrates' court against the proposed agreement ; and the court shall, after considering any representations made by or on behalf of any party to the appeal and the desirability in the public interest of the proposed agreement, either dismiss the appeal or order the highway authority not to enter into the proposed agreement (without prejudice to the power of the authority to make the same proposal on a subsequent occasion).

(4) Where any land on which a highway is situated falls to be conveyed by the highway authority in pursuance of an agreement under this section, then—

(a) if the land belongs to the highway authority, nothing in this section dispenses with any consent of a government department which, under any enactment, is required for the conveyance, but where such consent is given or is not required the conveyance of the land by the authority operates, by virtue of this paragraph, to extinguish the public right of way over the land ;

(b) if the land does not belong to the highway authority, the authority may convey the land in accordance with the agreement and the conveyance operates, by virtue of this paragraph, to vest the land in the transferee for an estate in fee simple freed and discharged (subject to subsections (6) and (7) below and section 334(2) below) from all other estates, interests, rights and charges, including the public right of way, which subsisted in, over or on the land immediately before the conveyance.

(5) Where by virtue of subsection (4)(b) above any person suffers damage by being deprived of such an estate, interest, right or charge as is there mentioned, other than the public right of way, the highway authority shall pay him compensation equal to the amount of the damage.

(6) Where immediately before the conveyance of any land by a highway authority in pursuance of this section there is under, in, upon, over, along or across the land any apparatus belonging to or used by statutory undertakers for the purposes of their undertaking Part II of Schedule 12 to this Act applies to the land.

(7) Nothing in this section affects any mines or minerals under PART XII a highway.

Further provisions with respect to acquisition procedure for exercise of highway land acquisition powers

257.—(1) Where a compulsory purchase order is made or Compulsory proposed to be made in the exercise of highway land acquisition acquisition powers— proceedings taken

    (*a*) for the purpose of enabling one or more of the orders concurrently and schemes to which Schedule 1 to this Act applies with other (" the related instruments ") to be implemented when related it or they become operative, or proceedings, etc.

    (*b*) for a purpose connected with a highway or proposed highway to which one or more of the related instruments relate,

the proceedings required by Schedule 1 to the Act of 1946 to be taken for the purpose of confirming or making the compulsory purchase order may be taken concurrently (so far as practicable) with the proceedings required by Schedule 1 to this Act to be taken for the purpose of confirming or making the related instrument or, as the case may be, with two or more of the proceedings thereby required to be taken for the purpose of confirming or making the related instruments.

(2) Where—

    (*a*) a compulsory purchase order is made or proposed to be made in the exercise of highway land acquisition powers for the purpose of the provision of a new means of access to any premises, and

    (*b*) an order under section 124 above authorising the stopping up of a means of access to those premises is made or proposed to be made in connection with the provision of the new means of access,

the proceedings required by Schedule 1 to the Act of 1946 to be taken for the purpose of confirming or making the compulsory purchase order may be taken concurrently (so far as practicable) with the proceedings required by section 124 to be taken for the purpose of confirming or making the order under that section.

(3) A compulsory purchase order made in the exercise of highway land acquisition powers for a purpose specified in column 1 of Schedule 20 to this Act may come into operation on the same day as any order or scheme specified in relation thereto in column 2 of that Schedule.

(4) The Minister of Transport may make regulations for securing that proceedings required by Schedule 1 to the Act of

1946 to be taken in respect of the compulsory acquisition of any land—

> (a) for the purpose of enabling a highway authority or the owners of a bridge to comply with a requirement or direction contained in an order made under section 93 above, or
>
> (b) for the purpose of providing or improving a cattle-grid or by-pass in the exercise of powers conferred by this Act,

may be taken concurrently (so far as practicable) with proceedings required to be taken for the purposes of the order under section 93 or, as the case may be, the purposes of the determination under Schedule 10 to this Act of a question relating to the provision of the cattle-grid or by-pass.

258.—(1) Where proceedings required by Schedule 1 to the Act of 1946 to be taken in respect of a compulsory purchase order made or proposed to be made in the exercise of highway land acquisition powers for a purpose specified in column 1 of Schedule 20 to this Act are taken after the confirmation or making by the Minister of an order or scheme specified in relation thereto in column 2 of that Schedule, then—

> (a) in the case of a compulsory purchase order proposed to be made by the Minister, the Minister and the Secretary of State acting jointly,
>
> (b) in any other case, the Minister,

may disregard for the purposes of the said Schedule 1 any objection to the compulsory purchase order or draft thereof, as the case may be, which in his or their opinion amounts in substance to an objection to that order or scheme.

(2) Where objections to a compulsory purchase order made or proposed to be made in the exercise of highway land acquisition powers for purposes connected with the construction, improvement, diversion or alteration of a highway are to be the subject of a local inquiry or considered by a person appointed by the Minister, or by the Minister and the Secretary of State acting jointly, the Minister or, as the case may be, those Ministers may, by notice served on the persons making such objections or by the notice announcing the holding of the inquiry or hearing, direct that any person who intends at the inquiry to submit—

> (a) that any highway or proposed highway to which the order relates should follow an alternative route, or
>
> (b) that, instead of improving, diverting or altering a highway to which the order relates, a new highway should be constructed on a particular route,

shall send to the Minister within such period as may be specified in the notice, being a period of not less than 14 days and ending not less than 14 days before the date fixed for the holding of the inquiry or hearing, sufficient information about the alternative route or the route of the new highway, as the case may be, to enable it to be identified.

(3) Where the Minister or the Minister and the Secretary of State acting jointly have given a direction under subsection (2) above in relation to an inquiry or hearing, the person holding the inquiry or hearing and the Minister or, as the case may be, those Ministers may disregard so much of any objection as consists of a submission to which the direction applies unless the person making the objection has complied with the direction.

259.—(1) Where in the exercise of highway land acquisition powers a compulsory purchase order authorising the acquisition of any land is submitted to the Minister in accordance with Part I of Schedule 1 to the Act of 1946 or is prepared in draft by him in accordance with Part II of that Schedule, then, if the Minister—

Power to confirm, etc., compulsory purchase order in part and postpone consideration of remainder.

(a) is satisfied that the order ought to be confirmed or made so far as it relates to a part of the land comprised therein, but

(b) has not for the time being determined whether it ought to be confirmed or made so far as it relates to the remaining part,

he may confirm or, as the case may be, make the order so far as it relates to the part of the land mentioned in paragraph (a) above, and give directions postponing consideration of the order, so far as it relates to the remaining part, until such time as may be specified by or under the directions ; and where the Minister confirms or makes part of any such order, that part and the remaining part are each to be deemed for the purposes of this section and the said Schedule 1 to be a separate order.

(2) Where the Minister gives directions under this section, the notices required by paragraph 6 of the said Schedule 1, or by that paragraph as applied by paragraph 7C of that Schedule, to be published and served shall include a statement of the effect of the directions.

260.—(1) There may be included in a compulsory purchase order made by a highway authority in the exercise of highway land acquisition powers land in which the authority have already acquired interests by agreement in the exercise of such powers.

Clearance of title to land acquired for statutory purposes.

232   c. 66   *Highways Act 1980*

PART XII   (2) Where land is included in a compulsory purchase order as mentioned above, it is to be treated as subject to compulsory purchase for the purposes of the Act of 1965, and that Act shall apply accordingly, except as respects—

(a) the conveyance to the acquiring authority of any interest which they have acquired by agreement before the date of the coming into force of the compulsory purchase order ; and

(b) compensation, so far as already paid or the subject of agreement.

(3) Where—

(a) in the exercise of powers conferred by section 239(4)(c) above, a special road authority have acquired land for the provision of a service area, or

(b) in the exercise of powers conferred by section 240(3)(a) above, the Minister has acquired land for the provision of a trunk road picnic area, or

(c) in exercise of powers conferred by section 240(5) above, a highway authority have acquired land for the provision of a lorry area,

subsection (4) below has effect with respect to any activities carried on on the land in the course of its use for the purposes of a service area, trunk road picnic area or lorry area, as the case may be.

(4) Any such activities are, as against a person who apart from the acquisition would have had a right to restrain such activities, or a right the exercise of which would be calculated to interfere with them, to be treated as activities of the authority in question (that is to say, the special road authority, the Minister or the highway authority, as the case may be) carried on under statutory powers, notwithstanding that they are carried on by other persons under contract to the authority or otherwise.

Special compensation provisions as respects certain compulsory acquisitions for highway purposes

Benefit to vendor to be taken into account in assessing compensation on certain compulsory acquisitions for highway purposes.

261.—(1) Subject to subsection (3) below, in assessing the compensation payable in respect of the compulsory acquisition of land by a highway authority under section 239 above (except subsection (6) thereof), section 240 above, section 246 above or section 250(2) above, the Lands Tribunal—

(a) shall have regard to the extent to which the remaining contiguous lands belonging to the same person may be benefited by the purpose for which the land is authorised to be acquired ;

(b) without prejudice to the generality of paragraph (a) above, shall in the case of land authorised to be acquired for widening a highway set off against the value of the land to be acquired any increase in the value of other land belonging to the same person which will accrue to him by reason of the creation of a frontage to the highway as widened ; and

(c) shall take into account, and embody in its award, any undertaking given by the highway authority as to the use to which the land, or any part of it, will be put.

(2) Without prejudice to subsection (1) above, in assessing the compensation payable on a compulsory acquisition by virtue of section 252(3)(a) above the Lands Tribunal shall take into account, and embody in its award, any undertaking given by the acquiring authority as to rights of user or occupation, or other rights, which they are willing to accord to the landowner (or to him and his successors) as respects the land referred to in section 252(2) above.

(3) Where a highway authority, by virtue of section 250(1) above, compulsorily acquire rights under section 239 above (except subsection (6) thereof), section 240 above or section 246 above, then in assessing the compensation payable in respect of the acquisition the Lands Tribunal—

(a) shall have regard to the extent to which the land over which the right in question is, or is to be, acquired, or any contiguous land belonging to the same person, may be benefited by the purpose for which the right may be authorised to be acquired ;

(b) shall, in the case of a right acquired, or to be acquired, in connection with the widening of a highway, take into account as abatement of compensation any increase in the value of the land, or of other land belonging to the same person, which will accrue by reason of the creation of a frontage to the highway as widened ; and

(c) shall take into account, and embody in its award, any undertaking given by the highway authority as to the manner in which the right will be exercised.

(4) Where by a compulsory purchase order made in the exercise of a relevant power a highway authority acquire two or more rights over land belonging to the same person, or acquire not only rights (one or more) but also adjoining or adjacent land so belonging, then in applying subsection (1) or subsection (3) above the Lands Tribunal shall consider together the compensation payable in respect of both or all of the rights or, as the case may be, in respect of the right or rights and also the adjoining or adjacent land.

PART XII   In this subsection " relevant power " means a power under any provision of this Act to which subsection (1) or (3) above relates.

(5) In assessing the compensation payable in respect of the compulsory acquisition by a highway authority under section 241 above of land lying between an improvement line and the boundary of a street, the Lands Tribunal shall take into account any benefit accruing to the vendor by reason of the improvement of the street except in so far as it may have been previously taken into account in the assessment of compensation payable under section 73(9) above.

1961 c. 33.   (6) Section 5 of the Land Compensation Act 1961 shall, in its application to compulsory acquisition by a highway authority under a provision to which subsection (1), (3) or (5) above relates, have effect subject to subsection (1), (3) or (5) as the case may be.

Assumptions to be made in assessing compensation on certain compulsory acquisitions of land for service stations etc. and lorry areas for special roads. 1971 c. 78.

262.—(1) Where land is compulsorily acquired—

(a) under section 239(4)(c) above in a case where the acquisition is authorised by a compulsory purchase order which does not also authorise the acquisition of land required for the provision of the adjacent length of special road, or

(b) in pursuance of a notice under section 180, 188 or 189 of the Town and Country Planning Act 1971 (protection of owners of land affected by certain planning decisions) in a case where the Lands Tribunal is satisfied that there are proposals for using the whole or part of the relevant land for such purposes in connection with the special road as are mentioned in section 239(4)(c) above and that the amount of compensation would apart from this section be affected by the provision or proposed provision of the special road, or

1973 c. 26.   (c) in pursuance of a notice under section 193 of that Act or section 78 of the Land Compensation Act 1973 (protection of owner-occupiers in respect of planning blight) in a case where the appropriate enactment for the purposes of section 196 of the said Act of 1971 is or includes section 239(4)(c) above,

then subsection (3) below applies for the purpose of assessing compensation in respect of the compulsory acquisition.

(2) Where there are proposals for the provision of a lorry area on land adjoining, or in the vicinity of, a special road or

proposed special road then, if that land, or any land of which that land forms part, is compulsorily acquired—

    (*a*) under section 240(5) above in a case where the acquisition is authorised by a compulsory purchase order which does not also authorise the acquisition of land required for the provision of the adjacent length of special road, or

    (*b*) in pursuance of a notice under section 180, 188 or 189 of the Town and Country Planning Act 1971, in a case where the Lands Tribunal is satisfied that there are proposals for using the whole or part of the relevant land for the purpose of providing a lorry area, in connection with the special road, and that the amount of the compensation would apart from this section be affected by the provision or proposed provision of the special road, or

    (*c*) in pursuance of a notice under section 193 of that Act or section 78 of the Land Compensation Act 1973 in a case where the appropriate enactment for the purposes of section 196 of the said Act of 1971 is or includes section 240(5) above,

1971 c. 78.

1973 c. 26.

subsection (3) below applies for the purpose of assessing compensation in respect of the compulsory acquisition.

(3) In any such case as is mentioned in subsection (1) or (2) above the value of the relevant interest shall be ascertained—

    (*a*) so far as it is attributable to any relevant planning permission, on the assumption that traffic carried by the special road will not have direct or indirect access to the relevant land ; and

    (*b*) so far as it is not attributable to any such planning permission, on the assumption that traffic carried by the special road will not have direct access to the relevant land.

(4) In this section—

    " direct access " means access otherwise than by means of a highway which is not a special road and " indirect access " means access by means of a highway which is not a special road ;

    " lorry area development " means development for the purpose of providing a lorry area for use in connection with a special road or proposed special road ;

    " relevant planning permission " means any planning permission for service area development or, as the case may be, lorry area development, which is in force on the date of service of the notice to treat, or as to the grant of which any assumption is required to be

made by virtue of section 15 or 16 of the Land Compensation Act 1961, or the possibility of the grant of
which is taken into account in assessing the
compensation ;

" service area development " means development of the
relevant land, or of any part of it, for the purpose
of providing such service stations or other buildings
or facilities as are mentioned in section 239(4)(c) above
or of providing any other buildings or facilities designed
to cater to a significant extent for traffic carried or to
be carried by the special road ;

and any expression which is also used in the Land Compensation Act 1961 has the same meaning as in that Act.

Vesting of highways etc.

263.—(1) Subject to the provisions of this section, every
highway maintainable at the public expense, together with the
materials and scrapings of it, vests in the authority who are for
the time being the highway authority for the highway.

(2) Subsection (1) above does not apply—

(a) to a highway with respect to the vesting of which, on
its becoming or ceasing to be a trunk road, provision is
made by section 265 below, or

(b) to a part of a trunk road with respect to the vesting
of which provision is made by section 266 below, or

(c) to a part of a special road with respect to the vesting
of which provision is made by section 267 below.

(3) Where a scheme submitted to the Minister jointly by two
or more local highway authorities under section 16 above determines which of those authorities are to be the special road
authority for the special road or any part of it (" the designated
authority ") and the designated authority are not the highway
authority for the road or that part of it, the road or that part
of it vests in the designated authority.

(4) Where—

(a) the responsibility for the maintenance of a bridge or
other part of a highway is transferred to a highway
authority by means of an order under section 93 above,
but the property in it is not so transferred, or

(b) the responsibility for the maintenance of a part of a
highway is transferred to a highway authority in pursuance of an agreement made under section 94 above,
but the property in that part is not so transferred,

the part of the highway in question does not by virtue of
subsection (1) above vest in that highway authority.

(5) Notwithstanding anything in subsection (1) above, any such material as is referred to in that subsection which is removed from a highway by a district council in exercise of their powers under section 42, 50 or 230(7) above vests in the district council and not in the highway authority.

264.—(1) The drains belonging to a road for which the council of a county are the highway authority vest in the council of the county in which the road is situated and where any other drain or any sewer was at the material date used for any purpose in connection with the drainage of such a road, that council continue to have the right of using the drain or sewer for that purpose.

Vesting of drains etc. of certain roads.

For the purposes of this subsection the material date is—

    (*a*) in the case of any highway which first became maintainable at the public expense before the commencement of this Act, the date on which it first became so maintainable or 1st April 1974, whichever date was later ; and

    (*b*) in the case of any highway which first becomes maintainable at the public expense after the commencement of this Act, the date on which it first becomes so maintainable.

(2) The drains belonging to a highway which is for the time being a metropolitan road vest in the Greater London Council and where any other drain or sewer was, at the date when the highway became a metropolitan road, used for any purpose in connection with the drainage of that highway, that Council continue to have the right of using the drain or sewer for that purpose.

(3) Any difference arising under this section—

    (*a*) between a county council and a district council—

        (i) as to the council in whom a drain is vested, or

        (ii) as to the use of a drain or sewer ;

    (*b*) between the Greater London Council and a London borough council or the Common Council—

        (i) as to the council in whom a drain is vested, or

        (ii) as to the use of a drain or sewer ; or

    (*c*) between a county council or the Greater London Council, on the one hand, and a water authority, on the other, as to the use of a sewer ;

shall, if either party to the dispute so elect, be referred to and determined by the Secretary of State.

I

*Transfer of property and liabilities on change of status of
highway etc.*

Transfer of
property and
liabilities upon
a highway
becoming or
ceasing to be
a trunk road.

265.—(1) Where a highway becomes a trunk road, then,
subject to the provisions of this section, as from the date on
which the highway becomes a trunk road (" the operative date "),
there are transferred to the Minister by virtue of this section—

(a) the highway, in so far as, immediately before the operative date, it was vested in the former highway authority,

(b) the property mentioned in subsection (3) below, in so
far as, immediately before the operative date, it was
vested—

(i) in the former highway authority for the purposes of their functions in relation to the highway, or

(ii) in a council for the purposes of functions
in relation to the highway under any enactment to
which this section applies, and

(c) all liabilities incurred by any such authority or council
for the purposes of their functions in relation to the
highway and not discharged before the operative date,
other than loans and loan charges,

and the highway and other property so transferred vest, by virtue
of this section, in the Minister.

(2) There is not transferred to the Minister by virtue of this
section any right or liability in respect of—

(a) work done, services rendered, goods delivered, or money
due for payment, before the operative date, or

(b) damages or compensation for any act or omission before
that date, or

(c) the price of, or compensation for, any land purchased,
or for which a contract to purchase has been concluded,
before that date.

(3) The property referred to in subsection (1)(b) above is—

(a) land, other than land—

(i) vested in the former highway authority for the
purpose of being used for the storage of materials
required wholly or mainly for the maintenance and
improvement of other highways, or

(ii) acquired for the improvement or development
of frontages to the highway, or of land adjoining or
adjacent to the highway, and

(b) all other property (including the unexpended balances of any grants paid by the Minister to the former highway authority, or to any council for the purposes of their functions in relation to the highway), other than—

    (i) materials to be used for the maintenance or improvement of the highway, and

    (ii) the unexpended balances of any loans raised by the former highway authority, or by any council for the purposes of their functions in relation to the highway.

(4) Any property vested in the Minister by virtue of this section shall be held by him subject to all covenants, conditions and restrictions subject to which the property was held by the authority or council from whom it was transferred and to all liabilities affecting the property, except liabilities referred to in subsection (2) above.

(5) The Minister and the former highway authority may agree, on such terms as they think fit—

(a) that any property or liabilities (except loans and loan charges) acquired or incurred by the former highway authority for the purposes of their functions in relation to a highway which has become a trunk road, other than property or liabilities transferred to the Minister by virtue of this section, shall be transferred to him, or

(b) that any property or liabilities transferred to the Minister by virtue of this section shall be re-transferred to the authority.

(6) Any dispute between the Minister and any person as to the property or liabilities transferred by virtue of this section shall be determined by arbitration.

(7) The foregoing provisions of this section apply in a case where a trunk road ceases to be a trunk road (otherwise than by virtue of section 10(8) above) in like manner as they apply where a highway becomes a trunk road, with the substitution—

(a) for the references to the former highway authority and to a council, of references to the Minister, and

(b) for references to the Minister, of references to the council who become the highway authority for the road or, so far as relates to property and liabilities vested in or incurred by the Minister for the purposes of any functions under any enactment to which this section applies, to the council who are to exercise those functions in relation to the road.

(8) The former highway authority shall produce to the Minister such documents relating to their functions, property and liabilities in respect of a highway which has become a trunk road, and furnish to him such other information relating to those matters, as he may require.

(9) Schedule 21 to this Act has effect for the purpose of providing for transitional matters arising where a highway becomes a trunk road or a trunk road ceases to be a trunk road.

(10) The enactments to which this section applies are sections 42, 50, 230(7) and 271 of this Act and sections 1, 21 and 75 of the Road Traffic Regulation Act 1967.

1967 c. 76.

(11) For the purposes of this section—

" former highway authority " means, in relation to a highway which has become a trunk road, the council in whom the highway was vested immediately before it became a trunk road ; and

" property " includes property, rights and powers of every description.

Transfer to Minister of privately maintainable bridges carrying trunk roads.

266.—(1) Where a highway comprising a bridge to which this section applies becomes a trunk road, the bridge by which that highway is carried is, subject to subsection (2) below, transferred to the Minister by virtue of this section on the date on which the highway becomes a trunk road (" the transfer date ").

(2) If on the transfer date a part of the highway carried by the bridge is not a trunk road, the bridge is not transferred to the Minister by virtue of this section unless and until that part becomes a trunk road.

(3) Where a bridge is transferred to the Minister by virtue of this section, then, subject to subsection (4) below—

(a) the bridge, including any building or structure comprised in it and the highway carried by it, vests by virtue of this section in the Minister for all the estate or interest of the owners therein, and

(b) any statutory provision in force, in relation to the bridge, for the protection or benefit of statutory undertakers has effect, subject to any necessary modifications, as if for any reference therein to the owners of the bridge there were substituted a reference to the Minister.

(4) The Minister and the owners may, by agreement in writing made either before or after the transfer date, agree that the provisions of subsection (3) above with respect to the transfer

of property shall not apply or, as the case may be, shall be deemed not to have applied, to such property comprised in the bridge as may be specified in the agreement.

(5) In respect of any bridge which is transferred to the Minister by virtue of this section, the Minister shall pay to the owners such sum as may be agreed between the Minister and the owners, or in default of agreement such sum as may be determined by arbitration to represent the value to the owners of the bridge as an asset productive of revenue.

For the purposes of this subsection a bridge is not to be treated as an asset productive of revenue unless at the time when the bridge is transferred by virtue of this section—

(a) a contract is in force under which payments have been made or will accrue to the owners in respect of the use of the bridge ; or

(b) the bridge includes a building constructed or adapted for use by the owners for the purposes of their undertaking or for letting to some other person.

(6) Where a bridge transferred to the Minister by virtue of this section carries the highway over a railway, canal, way or other works used for the purposes of an undertaking carried on by the owners, then, so long as those works are so used—

(a) the Minister shall, before entering on any land of the owners for the purpose of executing works for the maintenance, improvement or alteration of the bridge, give notice to the owners specifying the general nature of the works proposed to be executed ;

(b) except with the consent of the owners, the Minister shall not reduce the headway or any span of the bridge ; and

(c) if the headway of the bridge is reduced in consequence of subsidence due to mining operations, or of works carried out by the owners for the purpose of raising the railway, canal, way or other works to a level not higher than their level before the subsidence occurred, the Minister shall, if so required by the owners, raise the bridge so far as may be necessary to give the same headway as before the subsidence occurred.

(7) A consent required for the execution of works by the Minister under subsection (6) above shall not be unreasonably withheld, and any question whether the withholding of such a consent is unreasonable shall be determined by arbitration.

(8) Any dispute between the Minister and any person as to the property or liabilities transferred by virtue of this section, or as to

PART XII   the liability imposed on the Minister by subsection (6)(c) above to carry out works, shall be determined by arbitration.

(9) This section applies to all bridges (not being highways maintainable at the public expense) which carry the highway over a railway or highway or over a canal, river, watercourse, marsh or other place where water flows or is collected or over a ravine or other depression, other than—

   (a) swing bridges,

   (b) bridges which carry a railway as well as a highway, and

   (c) bridges to which a right to levy tolls is attached ;

but this section does not apply to Rochester Bridge.

(10) In this section—

   " bridge " includes so much of the approaches thereto as supports or protects the surface of the trunk road ;

   " owners ", in relation to a bridge, means the persons who immediately before the transfer of the bridge to the Minister were responsible for the maintenance of it, and includes any persons who, in pursuance of any agreement with the persons so responsible, were then discharging that responsibility on their behalf.

Transfer to local highway authorities of privately maintainable bridges carrying special roads.

267.—(1) Where the route prescribed by a scheme under section 16 above authorising the provision of a special road by a local highway authority includes a highway carried by a bridge which, if the special road were a trunk road, would be transferred to the Minister by virtue of section 266 above, any order under section 18 above by which the highway is appropriated by or transferred to the special road authority may provide for the transfer of the bridge to that authority.

(2) Where a bridge is so transferred to a special road authority, subsections (3) to (8) of section 266 above apply as they apply in relation to a bridge transferred by virtue of that section and accordingly have effect as if, for references therein to the Minister and to the trunk road there were substituted references to the special road authority and to the special road ; and no order shall be made by virtue of section 268 below in respect of liabilities of the owners of the bridge.

(3) In this section " bridge " and " owners " are to be construed in accordance with section 266(10) above, but with the substitution, in the definition of " owners ", of a reference to the special road authority for the reference to the Minister.

268.—(1) Where provision is made by an order under section 14 or 18 above—

    (*a*) for transferring a highway from one highway authority to another,

    (*b*) for enabling a highway authority to alter a highway vested in another, or

    (*c*) in the case of an order under section 18 above, for authorising or requiring any functions of a local authority (within the meaning of that section) to be exercised by a highway authority,

the order may, subject to section 267(2) above, transfer to the highway authority to whom the highway is transferred, or in whom it is vested, or by whom those functions are to be exercised, any property, rights or liabilities (other than loans or loan charges) vested in or incurred by the other authority in connection with the highway or the alteration, or for the purposes of those functions, as the case may be.

(2) An order transferring property, rights or liabilities under subsection (1) above may for that purpose (whether or not the highway in question is a trunk road) apply any of the provisions of section 265 above, subject to such modifications as may be specified in the order.

(3) No order relating to a trunk road under section 14 above shall provide for transferring to any authority (except by agreement with that authority) any bridge over or tunnel under the trunk road, as distinct from the highway carried by the bridge or through the tunnel, and from any approaches to the bridge or tunnel.

(4) No order relating to a classified road under section 14 above and no order under section 18 above shall provide for transferring to any authority (except by agreement with that authority) any bridge over or tunnel under a classified road or, as the case may be, a special road, as distinct from the highway carried by the bridge or through the tunnel, and from any approaches to the bridge or tunnel.

269. Where a highway in a London borough or the City becomes or ceases to be a metropolitan road, the council of the borough or the Common Council, as the case may be, and the Greater London Council may agree for the transfer to the new highway authority for the highway from the former highway authority of such property and liabilities relating to the highway, on such terms and conditions, as may be specified in the agreement.

270.—(1) In this section—

"footway lighting system" means a system of lighting, provided for a highway, which satisfies the following conditions, namely, that either—

(a) no lamp is mounted more than 13 feet above ground level, or

(b) no lamp is mounted more than 20 feet above ground level and there is at least one interval of more than 50 yards between adjacent lamps in the system,

or such other conditions as may be prescribed by order of the Minister in substitution for the above-mentioned conditions;

"road lighting system" means a lighting system that is not a footway lighting system;

and references in this section, as respects a transfer from a lighting authority to a highway authority, to "the agreed date" are references to such date as may be determined by agreement between the two authorities or, in default of such agreement, as the Minister may direct.

(2) Subsections (3) to (6) below have effect where a road lighting system is at any time provided by a lighting authority for the purposes of a highway for which they are not the highway authority, and this includes cases where a footway lighting system maintained by a lighting authority other than the highway authority becomes a road lighting system—

(a) in consequence of any order made by the Minister under subsection (1) above (as respects the conditions referred to in the definition of "footway lighting system"), or

(b) in consequence of any alterations effected by the lighting authority.

(3) On the agreed date there are transferred to the highway authority—

(a) all lamps, lamp-posts and other apparatus which, immediately before the agreed date, were vested in the lighting authority as part of the road lighting system; and

(b) except as provided by subsection (4) below, all other property or rights which, immediately before the agreed date, were vested in the lighting authority for the purposes of that system, and all liabilities incurred by that authority for those purposes and not discharged before that date;

PART XII

and any property or rights so transferred vest, by virtue of this section, in the highway authority.

(4) There is not transferred to a highway authority by virtue of this section any right or liability of a lighting authority in respect of work done, services rendered, goods (including gas and electricity) supplied or money due for payment before the agreed date, and there is not transferred to the Minister by virtue of this section any liability of a lighting authority in respect of loans or loan charges.

(5) A highway authority and a lighting authority, or any two or more highway authorities, may make agreements with respect to the transfer of property, rights and liabilities under this section, including agreements—

(a) for defining the property, rights and liabilities thereby transferred to the highway authority or any of those authorities, and

(b) for the transfer or retention of property, rights or liabilities held or incurred for the purposes of two or more road lighting systems, or partly for the purposes of such a lighting system and partly for other purposes.

(6) Any dispute between the authorities concerned as to the property, rights or liabilities transferred by this section shall be determined—

(a) where the Minister is one of those authorities, by arbitration ;

(b) in any other case, by the Minister.

(7) If in the case of a road or part of a road in which a footway lighting system is maintained by a lighting authority other than a highway authority the highway authority propose to provide a road lighting system (either as a separate system or by means of alterations of the footway lighting system), they may give notice to that effect to the lighting authority ; and where such notice is given subsections (2) to (6) above apply in relation to the footway lighting system as if for the references in subsections (3) and (4) to the agreed date there were substituted references to such date as may be specified for the purpose in the notice.

271.—(1) Where a person has by virtue of a charter or special Act the right to charge tolls in respect of the use of a highway, then, an appropriate authority—

(a) may agree with that person that he shall, on such terms as may be agreed, or

(b) subject to the provisions of this section, may by a notice to treat require that person to,

Provisions with respect to transfer of toll highways to highway authorities.

PART XII

transfer that right to the appropriate authority, together with the property in the highway and all his other property, rights and obligations under the charter or special Act (being property, rights and obligations connected with the highway), or such of them as may be specified in the agreement or, as the case may be, the notice to treat.

For the purposes of this section the following are appropriate authorities:—

(i) in the case of a trunk road, the Minister;

(ii) in the case of any other highway, except a highway in a London borough or the City, the council of the county in which the highway is situated;

(iii) in the case of a highway in a London borough or the City, other than a trunk road, the council of the borough or the Common Council, as the case may be, and also the Greater London Council.

(2) Upon the making of the transfer under subsection (1) above the right to charge tolls and any other property, rights or obligations transferred vest in and are exercisable by and imposed upon the appropriate authority.

(3) The consideration to be paid to any person for a compulsory transfer under this section shall, in default of agreement, be determined by the Lands Tribunal, and the rules in 1961 c. 33. section 5 of the Land Compensation Act 1961 apply to the calculation of any such consideration.

(4) Subject to any agreement with respect to the date of transfer, the person on whom a notice to treat is served under this section shall, on payment to him of the consideration determined as provided by subsection (3) above, transfer to the appropriate authority all such property, rights and obligations vested in or imposed upon him as are required by the notice to treat to be so transferred.

(5) A council in whose area part only of the highway is situated have in relation to that highway the same powers as they would have under subsection (1) above if the highway were wholly situated within their area, but shall not exercise those powers except in pursuance of an agreement made under subsection (6) below.

(6) Any two or more councils having under either subsection (1) or subsection (5) above powers in relation to a highway may enter into agreements with respect to the exercise of those powers by one council on behalf of the other or others of them and with respect to the making of contributions by any of them towards the expenses of any action so taken; and where those

powers are exercised in pursuance of any such agreement the transfer of the highway and any other property, rights and obligations to be transferred shall be made to such council or councils as may be provided by the agreement.

(7) The provisions of this section with respect to compulsory transfers shall not apply in relation to—

    (a) a highway vested in dock undertakers as such,

    (b) a highway vested in harbour undertakers as such, or

    (c) the property in a bridge vested in railway undertakers.

PART XIII

FINANCIAL PROVISIONS

272.—(1) Subject to subsection (4) below, the Minister may, Advances for with the approval of the Treasury, make advances to a highway highway authority for any of the purposes mentioned in paragraphs (a) purposes. to (k) below, or in respect of the expenses mentioned in paragraph (l) or (m) below:—

    (a) the construction of a highway which is to be a highway maintainable at the public expense ;

    (b) the maintenance of a highway ;

    (c) the improvement of a highway ;

    (d) the provision, maintenance and improvement of a road-ferry ;

    (e) the acquisition of highway land ;

    (f) the provision of a lorry area or the exercise of any other power under section 115 above ;

    (g) the provision of public sanitary conveniences on or under land forming part of, or adjoining, or in the vicinity of, a highway or proposed highway ;

    (h) the provision of a new means of access to a highway in pursuance of any such order as is mentioned in paragraph (i) below or under section 129 above ;

    (i) the stopping up of a private means of access in pursuance of an order made under section 14, 18 or 124 above, or an order made under section 211 of the Town 1971 c. 78. and Country Planning Act 1971, or in pursuance of an agreement made under section 127 above ;

    (j) the exercise of any powers conferred by section 246 or 253 above or section 282 below ;

(*k*) the discharge or exercise of any duty or power imposed or conferred on the authority under section 20 of the Land Compensation Act 1973 ;

(*l*) any amount by which the annual expenditure incurred by the authority in maintaining highway land during the period between its acquisition and the construction or improvement of the highway in question, and in the payment of loan charges accruing due during that period in respect of any debt incurred by the authority for the purpose of acquiring the land, exceeds the annual income accruing to the authority from the land during that period ;

(*m*) any loan charges accruing due after the end of the period mentioned in paragraph (*l*) above in respect of any money borrowed by the authority for the purpose of acquiring highway land ;

or may, with the like approval, and in conjunction with a local highway authority, make advances to some other person for any of the said purposes.

In paragraph (*e*) above " highway land " means land which the Minister is satisfied that the authority have acquired or are to acquire with a view to the construction of a new highway or the improvement of an existing highway, and in paragraphs (*l*) and (*m*) above it means land which the Minister is satisfied that the authority have acquired with a view as aforesaid ; and in paragraphs (*l*) and (*m*) above " loan charges ", in relation to any borrowed money, means the sums required for the payment of interest on that money and for the repayment of it either by instalments or by means of a sinking fund.

(2) The purposes for which advances may be made by the Minister under paragraphs (*a*) to (*k*) of subsection (1) above include the carrying out of surveys with a view to ascertaining the need for the construction or improvement of highways (whether or not any such construction or improvement is carried out) and other purposes incidental or conducive to the purposes described in those paragraphs.

(3) The power of the Minister to make advances to himself in his capacity of highway authority for any purpose specified in subsection (1) above is a power conferred on him to expend money for that purpose.

(4) The power of the Minister to make advances to a local highway authority under subsection (1) above is exercisable only in cases where it appears to him that, notwithstanding the grants for which provision is made in Part I of the Local Government Act 1974, the whole or any part of any expenditure in respect of which any advances could be made under subsection (1) above should not fall on that authority.

(5) The Minister may, with the approval of the Treasury, make advances to a district council in respect of any work done by them in a highway in exercise of their powers under section 96 above.

PART XIII

(6) The Minister may make advances under this section either by way of grant or by way of loan, or partly in one way and partly in the other, and on such terms and subject to such conditions as he thinks fit.

(7) In deciding whether to make an advance under this section in respect of a work the execution of which will require the employment of labour on a considerable scale, the Minister shall have regard to the general state and prospects of employment.

273. The council of a county may contribute towards the expenses incurred by the council of any district in the county in exercise of their powers under section 96 above.

Contributions by county councils to expenses of district councils under section 96.

274. A council may contribute towards any expenses incurred or to be incurred by a highway authority if, in the opinion of the council, the expenditure is or will be of benefit to the council's area.

Contributions by councils towards expenses of highway authorities.

275. A council or a local planning authority may defray or contribute towards, or undertake to defray or contribute towards, the expenses incurred or to be incurred by any other council or local planning authority for the purposes of—

Contributions by councils and local planning authorities towards expenses incurred in connection with footpaths and bridleways.

(a) the provisions of Part III of this Act relating to the creation of footpaths and bridleways by means of public path creation agreements or public path creation orders, to the making up of footpaths and bridleways and to the payment of compensation for loss caused by a public path creation order;

(b) the provisions of Part VIII of this Act relating to the making of public path extinguishment orders and public path diversion orders, to the making up of footpaths and bridleways and to the payment of compensation for loss caused by any such order.

PART XIII

Contributions to land drainage works which will benefit trunk roads.

276. Where it appears to the Minister that the execution or maintenance by a water authority or internal drainage board of any drainage works is desirable for the protection or enjoyment of a trunk road, he may make such contributions as he thinks fit towards any expenses incurred by the authority or board in the execution or maintenance of those works.

Contribution towards maintenance of bridge where road ceases to be a trunk road.

277. Where a trunk road carried by a bridge vested in the Minister by virtue of section 266 above ceases to be a trunk road, the Minister may contribute towards the expenses to be incurred in the maintenance of the bridge by the council who become the highway authority for the road.

In this section " bridge " includes the highway carried by the bridge and so much of the approaches thereto as supports or protects the surface of the trunk road.

Contributions towards highway works by persons deriving special benefit from them.

278.—(1) Subject to subsection (4) below, a highway authority proposing to execute any works which they are authorised by or under any enactment to execute may enter into an agreement under this section with any other person who would derive a special benefit if those works incorporated particular modifications, additions or features or were executed at a particular time or in a particular manner.

(2) An agreement under this section is an agreement whereby the other party to the agreement agrees that if one or more (as the agreement may provide) of the following conditions, that is to say—

(a) a condition that the works to be executed by the highway authority will incorporate such modifications, additions or features as may be specified in the agreement;

(b) a condition that the execution of the said works will be begun, or (as the agreement may provide) completed, before such date as may be so specified;

(c) a condition that the said works will be executed in such manner as may be so specified,

is or are fulfilled, he will make towards the expenses incurred by the authority in executing the said works a contribution (whether by a single payment or by periodical payments) of such amount as may be so specified.

(3) An agreement under this section may provide for the making to the highway authority by the other party to the agreement of payments in respect of the maintenance of the works to which the agreement relates and may contain such incidental and consequential provisions as appear to the highway authority to be necessary or expedient for the purposes of the agreement.

(4) A highway authority shall not enter into an agreement under this section unless they are satisfied that it will be of benefit to the public.

(5) Where for the purpose of executing any works to which an agreement under this section relates a highway authority have power to acquire land either by agreement or compulsorily and they would not need to exercise that power for that purpose had they not entered into an agreement under this section they shall not exercise their power to acquire land compulsorily for that purpose.

279. A council may borrow for the purposes of this Act.

Borrowing power of councils.

280.—(1) Any sum paid to, or recovered by, a local highway authority under any of the provisions of this Act mentioned in subsection (2) below, being a sum which for the purpose of any such provision is a lump sum, and so much of any other sum paid to, or recovered by, any such authority under any of those provisions as represents capital, shall be applied by the authority for purposes for which capital money is applicable by them.

Application of certain sums payable to local highway authorities.

(2) The provisions of this Act referred to in subsection (1) above are sections 53(3) and (4), 54(1) and (2), 55(2) to (4) and 255(4), and paragraph 19 of Schedule 11.

281. If the Minister certifies that any stamp duty which, but for this section, would be payable on any instrument made by, to or with him in relation to a highway or proposed highway which is, or is to become, a trunk road would be payable as an expense incurred by him under this Act, that stamp duty is not payable.

Exemption from stamp duty.

PART XIV

MISCELLANEOUS AND SUPPLEMENTARY PROVISIONS

Miscellaneous powers etc. of highway authorities and local authorities

Power of
highway
authority
to execute
works for
mitigating
adverse
effect of
constructing or
improving
etc. highway.

282.—(1) A highway authority may carry out—

(a) on land acquired by them under section 246 above ;

(b) on any other land belonging to them ;

(c) on any highway for which they are the highway
authority ;

(d) on any highway which they have been authorised to
improve or construct by virtue of an order under
section 14 or 18 above,

works for mitigating any adverse effect which the construction,
improvement, existence or use of a highway has or will have
on the surroundings of the highway.

(2) Without prejudice to the generality of subsection (1)
above, the works that may be carried out under that subsection
include the planting of trees, shrubs or plants of any other
description and the laying out of any area as grassland.

(3) A highway authority may develop or redevelop any land
acquired by them under section 246 above, or any other land
belonging to them, for the purpose of improving the surroundings of a highway in any manner which they think desirable
by reason of its construction, improvement, existence or use.

Power of
Minister
to conduct
experiments.

283.—(1) The Minister may, either by himself or through an
authority or other organisation approved by him, conduct experiments or trials for the purpose of—

(a) improving the construction of highways, road-ferries
or subways, or

(b) testing the effect of various classes of vehicles on various
types of highways.

(2) The Minister may construct such highways and works,
erect such plant, and provide such accommodation, as may be
necessary for the purpose of conducting an experiment or trial
under this section.

(3) An experiment or trial under this section shall not be
conducted on any highway except with the consent of the
highway authority or other person responsible for the maintenance of the highway.

(4) If damage is caused to the property of any person by anything done in exercise of the powers conferred by this section, that person is entitled to recover from the Minister compensation in respect of the damage.

A person is not entitled to compensation under this subsection if the damage was caused by his own negligence; and if his own negligence contributed to the damage the compensation shall be reduced accordingly.

284. Where a trunk road comprises a highway which a person is liable to maintain under a charter or special enactment or by reason of tenure, enclosure or prescription, the Minister is entitled to exercise in relation to that highway any power which he would be entitled to exercise in relation thereto if that highway were a highway maintainable at the public expense.

PART XIV

Powers of Minister in relation to privately maintainable parts of trunk roads.

285.—(1) Subject to subsection (3) below, where either the Minister of Transport or the Greater London Council ("the Council"), after consultation with the highway authority, are of the opinion that, with a view to facilitating the movement of traffic it is expedient for works to be executed for the improvement of a highway in Greater London to which this section applies, being works which the highway authority could execute and which do not involve the widening of the highway, then—

Power of Minister and Greater London Council to execute in Greater London road improvements not involving widening.

   (a) the highway authority shall, within 3 months of being notified of that fact, inform the Minister or, as the case may be, the Council whether they are prepared to undertake those works and, if so, within what time; and

   (b) if the Minister or, as the case may be, the Council at the expiration of the said 3 months are not satisfied that the highway authority will with reasonable dispatch undertake those works (or within the said 3 months are satisfied that they will not), the Minister or, as the case may be, the Council may execute those works or other works appearing to him or them to secure the same or an equivalent improvement of the highway.

For the purposes of this subsection it is not to be treated as widening a highway to take into the highway land not forming part of it but situated within its outer limits.

(2) The highways to which subsection (1) above applies are highways for which a London borough council or the Common Council are the highway authority and also, where the power

under that subsection is exercised by the Minister, metropolitan roads.

(3) The Minister shall exercise his powers under subsection (1) above only if he considers it necessary in connection with any order made or proposed to be made by him under section 6 or section 9 of the Road Traffic Regulation Act 1967 by virtue of section 84A(2) or (4) of that Act.

1967 c. 76.

(4) Where the Minister or the Council execute or propose to execute works under this section for the improvement of a highway, then for the purpose of or in connection with the execution of those works—

> (a) he or they shall (subject to the following provisions of this section) have all the powers and rights, and be subject to all the obligations and liabilities, of the highway authority ; and

> (b) he or they may exercise of his or their own motion any powers which, if the works were executed by the highway authority, he or they could exercise on the application of that authority ; and

> (c) he or they may do or require the highway authority to do anything which that authority has power to do in some capacity other than that of highway authority.

(5) Where the Minister or the Council execute works under this section for the improvement of a highway the amount of his or their expenses in connection therewith, as certified by him or them, shall (except, where the expenses are the Minister's, in so far as they may be met by any grant made by the Minister) be paid to him or, as the case may be, them on demand by the highway authority ; and that authority have the like power of raising money required to make such payment, and the like right to recover the whole or any part of any sum paid, as if the expenses of the Minister or the Council had been incurred in executing the works as their agent.

(6) Subsection (4) above does not transfer to the Minister or the Council in connection with the execution of any works any powers, rights, obligations or liabilities of a highway authority under any enactment to which this subsection applies ; but where the Minister or the Council proceed under this section to execute works in a highway, any such enactment applies in relation to those works as if the Minister or the Council were acting as agent of the highway authority, but so that the highway authority are to comply with any directions of the Minister or, as the case may be, the Council as to the exercise of their powers and rights.

This subsection applies to the Public Utilities Street Works Act Part XIV 1950 and, in the case of any works, to such other enactments as 1950 c. 39. the Minister or the Council may specify for this purpose in a notice given by him or them to the highway authority.

(7) Without prejudice to the generality of the foregoing provisions of this section, the powers exercisable under this section by the Minister or the Council in place of a highway authority include any power of that authority to acquire land, or an interest or right in, over or under land ; and any land, or any interest or right in, over or under land, acquired by the Minister or the Council by virtue of this section shall be acquired in the name and on behalf of the highway authority, and shall vest in that authority accordingly.

(8) A highway authority shall produce to the Minister or, as the case may be, the Council such documents relating to matters affecting the exercise of the Minister's or the Council's powers under this section, and furnish him or them with such other information relating to those matters, as he or they may require in connection with the exercise of those powers or any proposal to exercise them.

286.—(1) A local authority or, if there is a local highway authority for either of the two streets in question, that highway authority, may require the corner of a building intended to be erected at the corner of two streets in the area of the local authority to be rounded or splayed off to the height of the first storey or to the full height of the building, and to such extent otherwise as they may determine.

Power to require angles of new buildings at corners of streets to be rounded off.

(2) A person aggrieved by a requirement of a local authority or local highway authority under this section may appeal to a magistrates' court.

(3) A local authority or local highway authority shall pay compensation for any loss which may be sustained through the exercise by them of their powers under this section.

(4) This section does not apply to a building, other than a dwelling-house, belonging to any of the following undertakers and used by them for the following purposes respectively:—

    (a) railway undertakers, for purposes of a railway comprised in the railway undertaking ;

    (b) canal undertakers, for purposes of a canal comprised in the canal undertaking ;

    (c) inland navigation undertakers, for purposes of a navigation comprised in the inland navigation undertaking ;

    (d) dock undertakers, for purposes of a dock comprised in the dock undertaking ;

PART XIV

(e) harbour undertakers, for purposes of a harbour comprised in the harbour undertaking;

(f) pier undertakers for purposes of a pier comprised in the pier undertaking.

Power to erect barriers in streets in cases of emergency etc.

287.—(1) Subject to the provisions of this section, for the purpose of securing public order or public safety or preventing congestion of traffic a competent authority may, in any case of emergency or on any occasion on which it is likely by reason of some special attraction that any street will be thronged or obstructed, cause barriers to be erected in any street and kept in position for so long as may be necessary for that purpose.

For the purposes of this section the following are competent authorities—

(a) in the case of a street outside Greater London which is a highway, a local authority and also the highway authority;

(b) in the case of any other street, a local authority.

(2) For the purpose of erecting barriers in a street under this section a competent authority may provide and maintain sockets or slots in or under the surface of the street.

(3) A competent authority shall not exercise the powers conferred by this section in such a way as to deprive pedestrians of reasonable access to any premises.

(4) Schedule 8 to this Act applies to the powers conferred on competent authorities by this section.

(5) If a person wilfully removes a barrier, socket or slot erected or provided under this section, he is guilty of an offence and liable to a fine not exceeding £5.

(6) In this section " local authority " means any of the following, namely, the council of a district or London borough, the Greater London Council, the Common Council and the Council of the Isles of Scilly.

Power to require gas and water pipes to be moved.
1875 c. 55.
1950 c. 39.

288.—(1) Section 153 of the Public Health Act 1875 (power to require gas and water pipes to be moved) applies for the purposes of any provisions of this Act to which this section applies as it applies for the purposes of that Act; but the said section 153 does not apply in any case in which the code in Part II of the Public Utilities Street Works Act 1950 (relations between an authority carrying out road alterations and undertakers whose apparatus is affected thereby) has effect.

(2) A local authority shall pay compensation to any person who sustains damage by reason of the execution by them of works under this section.

(3) This section applies to section 294 below and to the other provisions of this Act which are specified in Schedule 22 to this Act.

289.—(1) A person duly authorised in writing by a highway authority may at any reasonable time enter on any land for the purpose of surveying that or any other land in connection with the exercise by that authority, in their capacity as a highway authority, of any of their functions.

(2) The power conferred by this section to enter on land includes power to place and leave on or in the land any apparatus for use in connection with any survey of that or any other land (whether from the air or on the ground) and to remove such apparatus.

(3) The power conferred by this section to survey land includes power to search and bore for the purpose of ascertaining—

    (*a*) the nature of the subsoil or the presence of minerals in it ;

    (*b*) whether any damage to a highway maintainable at the public expense for which the authority are the highway authority is being caused or is likely to be caused by mining operations or other activities taking place under the highway or in or under land adjoining, or in the vicinity of the highway.

290.—(1) A person authorised under section 289 above to enter on any land shall, if so required, produce evidence of his authority before or after entering on that land.

(2) A person so authorised may take with him on to the land in question such other persons, and such vehicles and equipment, as he may consider necessary.

(3) Subject to subsection (6) below, a person shall not under section 289 above demand admission as of right to any land which is occupied unless at least 7 days' notice of the intended entry has been given to the occupier.

(4) Subject to subsection (6) below, a person shall not, in the exercise of a power conferred by section 289 above, place or leave any apparatus on or in any land or remove any apparatus therefrom unless notice of his intention to do so has been included in the notice required by subsection (3) above and a like notice has been given to the owner of the land.

(5) A person shall not execute any works authorised by section 289(3) above unless notice of his intention to do so was included in the notices required by subsections (3) and (4) above and, where the interests of the National Coal Board, or of any water authority or statutory undertakers are liable to be affected by the proposed works, a like notice has been given to that Board or, as the case may be, to the water authority or statutory undertakers concerned.

PART XIV

(6) Where a highway authority intend to place and leave apparatus on or in a highway or to remove apparatus therefrom, or to execute in relation thereto such works as are authorised by section 289(3) above, no notice need be given to the occupier or owner of the land over which the highway subsists; but if the highway authority are not the highway authority for the highway, they shall give to that authority such notice as is required by subsections (4) and (5) above to be given to the owner.

(7) If the National Coal Board, or any water authority or statutory undertakers to whom notice is given under subsection (5) above object to the proposed works on the ground that the execution thereof would be seriously detrimental to the carrying on of their undertaking or, in the case of a water authority, would obstruct or impede the performance of their functions under any enactment, the works shall not be executed except with the authority of the appropriate Minister.

(8) Where in the exercise of a power conferred by section 289 above works authorised by subsection (3) of that section are to be executed in a street or controlled land within the meaning of the Public Utilities Street Works Act 1950, section 26 of that Act (obligations on undertakers executing works which are likely to affect other undertakers' apparatus) applies in relation to those works as if they were works to which that section applies and as if the highway authority by whom they are to be executed were operating undertakers within the meaning of that section.

1950 c. 39.

(9) The Post Office and the Civil Aviation Authority are to be deemed to be statutory undertakers and their respective undertakings statutory undertakings for the purposes of the foregoing provisions of this section.

(10) In this section " the appropriate Minister " means—

(a) in relation to a water authority, other than a water authority in their capacity as a sewerage authority, the Secretary of State and the Minister of Agriculture, Fisheries and Food acting jointly;

(b) in relation to statutory undertakers carrying on any railway, tramway, road transport, dock, harbour or pier undertaking, the Minister of Transport; and

(c) in all other cases, the Secretary of State.

Powers of entry of highway authority for purpose of maintaining, etc. certain structures and works.

291.—(1) Where a highway authority have power or a right to maintain, alter or remove any structure or work which is situated on, over or under any land, and that land neither belongs to the highway authority nor forms part of a highway for which they are the highway authority, then, if for the purpose of exercising that power or that right it is necessary for a person to enter on that land or any other land, a person duly authorised in writing by that authority may at any reasonable time enter on that land or any other land for that purpose.

(2) Subsections (1), (2) and (3) of section 290 above have effect in relation to a person authorised under this section to enter on any land as they have effect in relation to a person authorised under section 289 above to enter on any land.

(3) In relation to a bridge to which section 118 of the Transport Act 1968 (duty of highway authorities, etc. as respects bridges over railways or inland waterways) applies, and which belongs to a highway authority, subsections (1) and (2) above have effect subject to the provisions of that section.

1968 c. 73.

(4) In this section—

" structure " includes a bridge, fence, barrier or post ;

" work " includes a tunnel, ditch, gutter, watercourse, culvert, drain, soak-away or pipe.

(5) Nothing in this section affects the powers of a highway authority under section 100 above.

(6) Nothing in this section affects any agreement for the time being in force between a highway authority having power or a right to maintain, alter or remove a structure or work and any person having an interest in the land on, over or under which it is situated, being an agreement relating to the maintenance of or other dealing with the structure or work.

292.—(1) Where, in the exercise of a power conferred by section 289 or 291 above to enter, or to do anything, on any land, any damage is caused to that land or to any chattels on it, any person interested in that land or those chattels may, subject to subsection (2) below, recover compensation in respect of that damage from the highway authority by whom or on whose behalf the power was exercised ; and where in consequence of the exercise of such a power any person interested in the land or in any chattels on it is disturbed in his enjoyment thereof, he may recover from that authority compensation in respect of the disturbance.

Compensation for damage resulting from, and offences connected with, exercise of powers of entry etc. under section 289 or 291.

(2) Where any person is entitled under section 26 of the Public Utilities Street Works Act 1950, as applied by section 290(8) above, to compensation in respect of any matter, he is not entitled to recover compensation under subsection (1) above in respect of the same matter.

1950 c. 39.

(3) A person who wilfully obstructs a person acting in the exercise of a power conferred by section 289 or 291 above, or who removes or otherwise interferes with any apparatus

PART XIV placed or left on or in any land in exercise of a power conferred by section 289 above, is guilty of an offence and liable to a fine not exceeding £50.

(4) If a person who, in compliance with the provisions of section 289 or 291 above, is admitted into a factory, workshop or workplace discloses to any person any information obtained by him therein as to any manufacturing process or trade secret, then, unless the disclosure is made in the course of performing his duty in connection with the purposes for which he was authorised to enter the land, he is guilty of an offence and liable—

1980 c. 43.

(a) on summary conviction to a fine not exceeding the prescribed sum within the meaning of section 32(9) of the Magistrates' Courts Act 1980 (£1,000 or such other sum as may be fixed by order under section 143(1) of that Act); or

(b) on conviction on indictment to imprisonment for a term not exceeding 2 years or to a fine, or both.

Powers of entry for purposes connected with certain orders relating to footpaths and bridleways.

293.—(1) A person duly authorised in writing by the Secretary of State or other authority having power under this Act to make a public path creation order, a public path extinguishment order or a public path diversion order may enter upon any land for the purpose of surveying it in connection with the making of the order.

(2) For the purpose of surveying land, or of estimating its value, in connection with a claim for compensation payable by an authority in respect of that or any other land under section 28 above, or under that section as applied by section 121(2) above, a person who is an officer of the Valuation Office or who has been duly authorised in writing by the authority from whom the compensation is claimed may enter upon the land.

(3) A person authorised under this section to enter upon any land shall, if so required, produce evidence of his authority before entering; and a person shall not under this section demand admission as of right to any land which is occupied unless at least 7 days' notice in writing of the intended entry has been given to the occupier.

(4) A person who wilfully obstructs a person acting in the exercise of his powers under this section is guilty of an offence and liable to a fine not exceeding £50.

Entry, etc., of premises by highway authority or council for certain purposes.

294.—(1) If, in the discharge of functions conferred or imposed on an authority, being a highway authority or council, by a provision of this Act to which this section applies, it becomes necessary for an authorised officer of the authority to enter, examine or lay open any premises for the purpose of—

(a) surveying,

(b) making plans,

(c) executing, maintaining or examining works,

(d) ascertaining the course of sewers or drains,

(e) ascertaining or fixing boundaries, or

(f) ascertaining whether any hedge, tree or shrub is dead, diseased, damaged or insecurely rooted,

and the owner or occupier of the premises refuses to permit the premises to be entered, examined or laid open for any such purpose, the authority, after giving notice to the owner or occupier of their intention to do so, may make a complaint to a magistrates' court for an order authorising the authority by any authorised officer to enter, examine and lay open the premises for any such purpose.

(2) If on the hearing of the complaint no sufficient cause is shown against the making of the order for which the complaint is made, the court may make the order, and thereupon any authorised officer of the complainant authority may, subject to subsection (3) below, at all reasonable times between the hours of 9 a.m. and 6 p.m., enter, examine or lay open the premises described in the order for such of the purposes mentioned in subsection (1) above as are specified in the order.

(3) Except in a case of emergency, no entry shall be made on any premises, and no works shall be begun therein, under subsection (2) above unless at least 7 days' notice of the intended entry, and of the object thereof, has been given to the occupier of the premises.

(4) Where, in the course of an entry on or examination or laying open of premises authorised by an order under this section, damage is caused to land or to chattels, any person interested in the land or chattels may recover compensation in respect of that damage from the authority on whose complaint the order was made; and where by reason of any such entry, examination or laying open any person is disturbed in his enjoyment of land or chattels, he may recover from that authority compensation in respect of the disturbance.

(5) This section applies to sections 101 and 154(2) above and to the other provisions of this Act specified in Schedule 22 to this Act.

295.—(1) The council of a county or a council who are a local authority may remove, appropriate, or use, sell or otherwise dispose of all old materials existing in any street other than a highway maintainable at the public expense at the time of the execution by the council of any works in the street, unless those materials are removed by the owners of premises in the street within 3 days from the date of service of a notice from the

PART XIV   proper officer of the council requiring the owners of those premises to remove the materials.

(2) Where a council remove, appropriate, or use, sell or otherwise dispose of any materials in a street under subsection (1) above, they shall, on demand, pay or allow to the owner of any premises in the street such proportion of the reasonable value of the material as is attributable to those premises, and the amount thereof shall be settled, in case of dispute, by arbitration, or, if the amount claimed does not exceed £50 and either party so requires, by a magistrates' court.

Power of highway authority or council to execute certain works on behalf of other person.

296. A highway authority or a council may by agreement with any person execute at his expense any work which they have under this Act (except under Part XI) required him to execute, or any work in connection with a highway which he is otherwise under an obligation or is entitled to execute, and for that purpose they have all such rights as he would have.

Power of highway authority or council to require information as to ownership of land.

297.—(1) A highway authority or a council may, for the purpose of enabling them to discharge or exercise any of their functions under this Act, require the occupier of any premises and any person who, either directly or indirectly, receives rent in respect of any premises, to state in writing the nature of his own interest therein and the name and address of any other person known to him as having an interest therein, whether as freeholder, mortgagee, lessee or otherwise.

(2) Any person who, having been required in pursuance of this section to give any information, fails to give that information is guilty of an offence and liable to a fine not exceeding £100.

(3) Any person who, having been so required to give any information, knowingly makes any mis-statement in respect thereof is guilty of an offence and liable—

(a) on summary conviction to a fine not exceeding the prescribed sum within the meaning of section 32(9) of

1980 c. 43   the Magistrates' Courts Act 1980 (£1,000 or such other sum as may be fixed by order under section 143(1) of that Act) ; or

(b) on conviction on indictment to imprisonment for a term not exceeding 2 years or to a fine, or both.

Duty of local authorities to furnish information to county councils and the Greater London Council.

298.—(1) Every district council shall furnish, and shall instruct their officers to furnish, any information in their power which may reasonably be required by any county council for the purpose of enabling that council to discharge their functions under this Act.

(2) Every London borough council and the Common Council shall furnish, and shall instruct their officers to furnish, any

information in their power which may reasonably be required by the Greater London Council for the purpose of enabling that Council to discharge their functions under this Act.

299.—(1) Where there has been constructed or laid in land, Right to or in the exercise of rights, acquired by a highway authority discharge in the exercise of highway land acquisition powers, any drain water. or other work for the purpose of draining surface water from a highway, proposed highway, maintenance compound, trunk road picnic area, lorry area or service area, the water may be discharged into or through that drain or other work and into any inland waters, whether natural or artificial, or any tidal waters.

(2) A highway authority shall pay compensation to the owner or occupier of any land who suffers damage by reason of the exercise by the authority of any right under subsection (1) above.

(3) This section is without prejudice to any enactment the purpose of which is to protect water against pollution.

300.—(1) No statutory provision prohibiting or restricting the Right of local use of footpaths, footways or bridleways shall affect the use by a authorities to competent authority of appliances or vehicles, whether mechan- use vehicles ically operated or propelled or not, for cleansing, maintaining and appliances or improving footpaths, footways or bridleways or their verges, and or for maintaining or altering structures or other works situated bridleways. therein.

For the purposes of this section—

> (a) the following are competent authorities, namely, the council of any county, district or London borough, the Common Council, the Council of the Isles of Scilly, any parish or community council, or parish meeting, the Sub-Treasurer of the Inner Temple and the Under-Treasurer of the Middle Temple ; and
>
> (b) " statutory provision " means a provision contained in, or having effect under, any enactment.

(2) The Minister of Transport and the Secretary of State acting jointly may make regulations prescribing the conditions under which the rights conferred by this section may be exercised, and such regulations may in particular make provision as to—

> (a) the construction of any appliances or vehicles used under this section,
>
> (b) the maximum weight of any such appliances or vehicles, or the maximum weight borne by any wheel or axle,
>
> (c) the maximum speed of any such appliances or vehicles,
>
> (d) the hours during which the appliances or vehicles may be used, and

(*e*) the giving by the Minister of Transport or the Secretary of State of directions dispensing with or relaxing any requirement of the regulations as it applies to a particular authority or in any particular case.

Restriction on exercise of powers of lighting authorities.

301.—(1) Subject to subsection (2) below, the powers of a lighting authority shall not be exercised for purposes of the lighting of any highway for which they are not the highway authority except with the consent of the highway authority (which may be given either generally or in respect of any particular highway or length of highway, and either without conditions or subject to such conditions as the highway authority think fit).

1966 c. 42.

(2) Subsection (1) above does not apply to the exercise of powers for the purpose only of the operation or maintenance of a lighting system not transferred to the highway authority under Part III of the Local Government Act 1966 or under section 270 above.

1875 c. 55.
1957 c. 42.

(3) References in this section to the powers of a lighting authority are references to their powers under section 161 of the Public Health Act 1875 or section 3 of the Parish Councils Act 1957 or any corresponding local enactment.

Inquiries

Provisions as to inquiries.

1972 c. 70.

302.—(1) Subject to subsection (2) below, the Minister and the Secretary of State may each cause such inquiries to be held as he may consider necessary or desirable for the purposes of his functions under this Act, and subsections (2) to (5) of section 250 of the Local Government Act 1972 (giving of evidence at, and defraying of costs, of inquiries) apply, subject to subsection (2) below, in relation to any inquiry which either of the said Ministers may cause to be held under this section, or in compliance with any requirement of this Act, with the substitution in the case of an inquiry held by the Secretary of State, for references to a Minister, of references to the Secretary of State.

(2) Subsection (4) of the said section 250 (costs of the Minister holding the inquiry to be defrayed by the parties) does not apply in relation to—

(*a*) an inquiry caused to be held by the Minister for the purposes of his functions under section 93 above, or

(*b*) an inquiry held in compliance with paragraph 3 of Schedule 10 to this Act, or with paragraph 9 of Schedule 11 to this Act, in so far as the Minister is of opinion, having regard to the object and result of the inquiry, that the Minister's costs should be defrayed by him.

Obstruction of persons executing Act

303. A person who wilfully obstructs any person acting in the execution of this Act or any byelaw or order made under it is, in any case for which no other provision is made by this Act, guilty of an offence and liable to a fine not exceeding £25 ; and if the offence is continued after conviction, he is guilty of a further offence and liable to a fine not exceeding £5 for each day on which the offence is so continued.

Penalty for obstructing execution of Act.

304. If on a complaint made by the owner of any premises, it appears to a magistrates' court that the occupier of the premises prevents the owner from executing any work which he is by this Act required to execute, the court may order the occupier to permit the execution of the work.

Power to require occupier to permit works to be executed by owner.

Recovery of expenses

305.—(1) Where a council or a highway authority have incurred expenses for the repayment of which the owner of the premises in respect of which the expenses were incurred is liable—

Recovery of expenses by councils and highway authorities.

(*a*) under any of the provisions of this Act to which this section applies, or

(*b*) by agreement with the council or highway authority,

those expenses, together with interest at such reasonable rate as the council may determine from the date of service of a demand for the expenses, may be recovered by the council or the highway authority from the owner for the time being of the premises ; and as from the date of the completion of the works the expenses and interest accrued due thereon are, until recovered, a charge on the premises and on all estates and interests therein.

(2) A council or highway authority may by order declare any expenses and interest recoverable by them under this section to be payable by annual instalments within a period not exceeding 30 years, together with interest on them at such reasonable rate as the authority may determine ; and any such instalment

PART XIV

and interest, or any part thereof, may be recovered from the owner or occupier for the time being of the premises in respect of which the expenses were incurred.

(3) A person aggrieved by an order of a council or highway authority under subsection (2) above, or by the refusal of a council or highway authority to make such an order, may, except in a case where an appeal lies to the Minister under section 233 above, appeal to a magistrates' court.

(4) Schedule 13 to this Act applies in relation to any sum paid by an occupier of premises under the foregoing provisions of this section.

(5) Any sum which a council or highway authority are entitled to recover under this section or any other provision of this Act, and with respect to the mode of recovery of which provision is not made by any other section of this Act, may be recovered either summarily as a civil debt or in any court of competent jurisdiction.

1975 c. 76.

(6) Any charge acquired by the Minister by virtue of subsection (1) above is (without prejudice to the operation of section 1 of the Local Land Charges Act 1975 as regards any charge acquired by a council by virtue of that subsection) a local land charge.

(7) This section applies to the following provisions of this Act, namely, sections 152, 153, 165, 167, 177, 180, 184 and 230, except 230(7).

Time-limit for summary proceedings for recovery of expenses.

306. The time within which summary proceedings may be taken for the recovery of any sum which a highway authority or council are entitled to recover under this Act shall be reckoned—

(a) in all cases except the one mentioned in paragraph (b) below, from the date of the service of a demand for the sum; and

(b) in a case in which an appeal has been made to the Minister under section 233 above, from the date on which the decision on the appeal is notified to the appellant or the appeal is withdrawn, as the case may be.

Determination of disputes as to compensation   PART XIV

307.—(1) Any dispute arising on a claim for compensation under any provision of this Act to which this section applies shall be determined by the Lands Tribunal.

The provisions of this Act to which this section applies are sections 21, 22, 28, 73, 74, 109, 110, 121(2), 126, 193, 200(2) and 292.

(2) For the purposes of any reference to the Lands Tribunal under this section, section 4 of the Land Compensation Act 1961 (costs) has effect with the substitution, for references to the acquiring authority, of references to the authority from whom the compensation in question is claimed.

(3) Rules 2 to 4 of the Rules in section 5 of the said Act of 1961 (rules for valuation on a compulsory acquisition) apply to the calculation of compensation under any provision of this Act to which this section applies, in so far as it is calculated by reference to the depreciation of the value of an interest in land.

(4) In determining the amount of compensation payable under section 109, 110 or 126 above the Lands Tribunal shall have regard to any new means of access to the premises of the claimant or, as the case may be, any new right of access to a watercourse from the premises of the claimant, provided by the highway authority from whom the compensation is claimed.

(5) In determining the amount of compensation payable under section 73 above in respect of injurious affection, the Lands Tribunal—

   (*a*) shall take into account any benefit accruing to the claimant by reason of the improvement of the street in relation to which an improvement line has been prescribed under that section, and

   (*b*) may take into account and embody in their award any undertaking with regard to the exercise of the powers of a highway authority under that section in relation to the property affected which the authority have offered to give to the claimant;

and the terms of any undertaking so embodied in the award are binding on and enforceable against the authority.

(6) In determining the amount of compensation payable under section 74 above, the Lands Tribunal shall take into account any benefit accruing to the claimant by reason of any improvement made or about to be made to the highway in relation to which a building line has been prescribed under that section.

Disputes as to compensation which are to be determined by Lands Tribunal and related provisions.

1961 c. 33.

PART XIV   (7) In determining the amount of compensation payable under section 193 or section 200(2) above, the Lands Tribunal shall take into account any benefit accruing to the claimant by reason of the widening of a street under the said section 193 or the said section 200(2), as the case may be.

Disputes as to compensation which are to be determined by arbitration or county court.   **308.**—(1) Any dispute arising on a claim for compensation under this Act, being a dispute for the determination of which provision is not made by or under any section of this Act other than this section, shall be determined, if the parties so agree, by arbitration or, in default of agreement, by a county court.

(2) A county court shall have jurisdiction to deal with any dispute which by virtue of subsection (1) above is to be determined by such a court notwithstanding that, by reason of the amount of the claim or otherwise, the case would not, but for this provision, be within the jurisdiction of a county court.

Compensation in respect of depreciation in value of interest in land subject to mortgage.   **309.** Where an interest in land is subject to a mortgage—

(a) any compensation payable under this Act in respect of the depreciation in value of that interest shall be calculated as if the interest were not subject to the mortgage ;

(b) a claim for the payment of any such compensation may be made by any mortgagee of the interest under a mortgage made before the happening of the event giving rise to the compensation, but without prejudice to the making of a claim by any other person ;

(c) a mortgagee is not entitled to claim any such compensation in respect of his interest as such ; and

(d) any such compensation payable in respect of the interest subject to the mortgage shall be paid to the mortgagee or, where there is more than one mortgagee, to the first mortgagee, and shall in either case be applied by him as if it were proceeds of sale.

Prosecutions, appeals, etc.

Summary proceedings for offences.   **310.** All offences under this Act or under byelaws made under it are, except as provided by sections 292(4) and 297(3) above, punishable on summary conviction.

Continuing offences.   **311.**—(1) Where by virtue of any provision of this Act, or of byelaws made under it, a person convicted of an offence is, if the offence in respect of which he was convicted is continued after conviction, guilty of a further offence and liable to a fine for each day on which the offence is so continued, the court before whom the person is convicted of the original offence may fix a reasonable period from the date of conviction for compliance by the defendant with any directions given by the court. PART XIV

(2) Where a court fixes such a period the defendant is not liable to a fine in respect of the further offence for any day before the expiration of that period.

312.—(1) Proceedings for an offence under any provision of this Act to which this section applies or under byelaws made under any such provision shall not, without the written consent of the Attorney General, be taken by any person other than the person aggrieved, or a highway authority or council having an interest in the enforcement of the provision or byelaws in question. Restriction on institution of proceedings.

(2) This section applies to sections 167 and 177 above and to the provisions of this Act specified in Schedule 22 to this Act.

313. Where two or more sums are claimed from any person as being due under this Act, a complaint, summons or warrant issued for the purposes of this Act, or of any byelaws made under it, in respect of that person may contain in the body thereof or in a schedule thereto a statement of all or any of the sums so claimed. Inclusion of several sums in one complaint, etc.

314.—(1) Where an offence under any provision of this Act to which this section applies is committed by a body corporate and it is proved to have been committed with the consent or connivance of, or to be attributable to any neglect on the part of, any director, manager, secretary or other similar officer of the body corporate or any person who was purporting to act in any such capacity, he as well as the body corporate is guilty of that offence and liable to be proceeded against and punished accordingly. Offences by body corporate.

(2) Where the affairs of a body corporate are managed by its members, subsection (1) above applies in relation to the acts and defaults of a member in connection with his functions of management as if he were a director of the body corporate.

(3) This section applies to sections 139, 140, 167, 168, 177 and 181 above.

315. Where an appeal lies under this Act to the Crown Court or a magistrates' court against a requirement, order, refusal or other decision of a highway authority or a council, the notice given by the authority or council to the person concerned of the making of the requirement or order or of the refusal or other Notice to be given of right of appeal.

K

PART XIV   decision against which such an appeal lies shall state the right of appeal to the Crown Court or a magistrates' court, as the case may be, and the time within which such an appeal may be brought.

Appeals and applications to magistrates' courts.

316.—(1) Where any provision of this Act provides—

(a) for an appeal to a magistrates' court against a requirement, order, refusal or other decision of a highway authority or a council, or

(b) for any other matter to be determined by, or an application in respect of any matter to be made to, a magistrates' court,

the procedure shall be by way of complaint for an order.

(2) The time within which an appeal such as is mentioned in subsection (1)(a) above may be brought is 21 days from the date on which notice of the decision of the highway authority or council is served on the person wishing to appeal, and for the purpose of this subsection the making of the complaint is to be deemed to be the bringing of the appeal.

Appeals to the Crown Court from decisions of magistrates' courts.

317.—(1) Where a person aggrieved by an order, determination or other decision of a magistrates' court under this Act is not by any other enactment authorised to appeal to the Crown Court he may appeal to that court.

(2) The applicant for an order under section 116 above or any person who was entitled under subsection (7) of that section to be, and was, or claimed to be, heard on the application may appeal to the Crown Court against the decision made by the magistrates' court on the application.

Effect of decision of court upon an appeal.

318. Where on an appeal under this Act a court varies or reverses a decision of a highway authority or of a council it shall be the duty of the authority or the council to give effect to the order of the court and, in particular, to grant or issue any necessary consent, certificate or other document, and to make any necessary entry in any register.

Judges and justices not to be disqualified by liability to rates.

319. The judge of any court or a justice of the peace is not disqualified for acting in cases arising under this Act by reason only of his being as one of several ratepayers, or as one of any other class of persons, liable in common with the others to con-

tribute to, or to be benefited by, any rate or fund out of which   PART XIV
any expenses of a council are to be defrayed.

Notices, etc.

320. All notices, consents, approvals, orders, demands, Form of
licences, certificates and other documents authorised or required notices etc.
by or under this Act to be given, made or issued by, or on
behalf of, a highway authority or a council, and all notices,
consents, requests and applications authorised or required by or
under this Act to be given or made to a highway authority or
a council, shall be in writing.

321.—(1) Any notice, consent, approval, order, demand, Authentication
licence, certificate or other document which a council (whether of documents
as a highway authority or in any other capacity) are authorised etc.
or required by or under this Act to give, make or issue may be
signed on behalf of the council—

    (*a*) by the proper officer of the council, or

    (*b*) by any officer of the council authorised by them in
           writing to sign documents of a particular kind or, as
           the case may be, the particular document.

(2) Any document purporting to bear the signature of the
proper officer of the council, or of an officer expressed to be duly
authorised by the council to sign such a document or the
particular document, shall for the purposes of this Act, and of
any byelaws, regulations and orders made under it, be deemed,
until the contrary is proved, to have been duly given, made or
issued by the council.

In this subsection " signature " includes a facsimile of a
signature by whatever process reproduced.

322.—(1) Any notice, consent, approval, order, demand, Service of
licence, certificate or other document required or authorised notices etc
by or under this Act to be given or served on a corporation is
duly given or served if it is given to or served on the secretary
or clerk of the corporation.

(2) Subject to the provisions of this section, any notice, consent, approval, order, demand, licence, certificate or other
document required or authorised by or under this Act to be
given or served on any person may be given or served either—

    (*a*) by delivering it to that person, or

(*b*) by leaving it at his proper address, or

(*c*) by post ;

so, however, that where any such document is sent by post otherwise than in a registered letter, or by the recorded delivery service, it shall be deemed not to have been given or served if it is proved that it was not received by the person to whom it was addressed.

(3) For the purposes of this section, and of section 7 of the Interpretation Act 1978 in its application to this section, the proper address of any person to or on whom any such document is to be given or served—

1978 c. 30.

(*a*) where the person has furnished an address for service in accordance with arrangements agreed to in that behalf, is the address furnished ;

(*b*) where the person has not furnished an address as provided by paragraph (*a*) above, is

(i) in the case of the secretary or clerk of a corporation, that of the registered or principal office of the corporation, and

(ii) in any other case, the person's usual or last known place of abode.

(4) If the name or the address of any owner, lessee or occupier of premises to or on whom any such document is to be given or served cannot after reasonable inquiry be ascertained by the person seeking to give or serve the document, the document may be given or served by—

(*a*) addressing it to the person to whom it is to be given or on whom it is to be served by the description of " owner ", " lessee ", or " occupier " of the premises (describing them) to which the document relates, and

(*b*) delivering it to some responsible person resident or appearing to be resident on the premises or if there is no such person to whom it can be delivered, affixing it or a copy of it to some conspicuous part of the premises.

(5) The foregoing provisions of this section do not apply to the service of—

(*a*) a notice required or authorised to be served under Schedule 1 to the Act of 1946 as applied by this Act, or

(*b*) a summons.

323.—(1) For the purposes of this Act—

   (*a*) in reckoning any period which is therein expressed to be a period from or before a given date, that date is to be excluded; and

   (*b*) in reckoning any period therein mentioned of 8 days or less which apart from this provision would include a Sunday, Christmas Day, Good Friday or a bank holiday, that day is to be excluded.

PART XIV

Reckoning
of periods.

(2) In this section "bank holiday" means a day which is a bank holiday under the Banking and Financial Dealings Act 1971.

1971 c. 80.

Regulations, schemes, orders, etc.

324.—(1) Subject to Schedule 1 to this Act, the Minister of Transport may make regulations for prescribing the procedure to be followed in connection with the making and confirmation of schemes under section 16 above and orders under sections 17 and 18 above.

(2) The Minister shall make regulations for securing that the centre line of—

   (*a*) a special road authorised by a scheme under section 16 above,

   (*b*) a proposed highway directed by an order under section 10 above to become a trunk road, or

   (*c*) a new highway to be constructed in pursuance of an order under section 14 or 18 above,

Regulations
for procedure
in connection
with, and
centre line
of roads
authorised
etc. by, certain
schemes and
orders.

is indicated on a map on such scale as may be prescribed by the regulations and for securing that any limits of deviation which apply in relation to the centre line of that road or highway or any part thereof by virtue of subsection (3) below are indicated or stated in such manner as may be prescribed by the regulations.

(3) Where any such scheme or order as is referred to in subsection (2) above so provides in relation to a road or highway to which it relates or any part thereof, being such a road or highway as is referred to in that subsection, the centre line of that road or highway or that part thereof, as the case may be, may deviate from the centre line as indicated on the map referred to in that subsection within such limits of deviation, not exceeding 55 yards on either side of the centre of that line, as may be specified in the scheme or order.

325.—(1) The following powers conferred by this Act on a Minister of the Crown are exercisable by statutory instrument:—

   (*a*) all powers to make regulations,

Provisions as
to regulations,
schemes and
orders.

(b) the power to make or confirm schemes under section 16 above, and the power to confirm schemes under section 106(3) above,

(c) the power to make byelaws under section 186 above, and

(d) all powers to make or confirm orders, except those conferred by any of the following provisions of this Act, namely, sections 14, 18, 20, 26, 27, 108(1), 118, 119, 120 and 124 and paragraph 2 of Schedule 21.

(2) A statutory instrument containing—

(a) regulations made under this Act, other than a statutory instrument containing only regulations made under section 257(4) above, or

(b) an order made under section 344(4) below,

is subject to annulment in pursuance of a resolution of either House of Parliament.

(3) A statutory instrument containing an order made under section 17 above is of no effect unless it is approved by resolution of each House of Parliament.

Revocation and variation of schemes and orders.
1978 c. 30.

326.—(1) Section 14(b) of the Interpretation Act 1978 (implied power to revoke or amend orders made by statutory instrument) does not apply to an order made under section 74, 93 or 186 of this Act.

(2) An order made or confirmed by the Minister, or the Secretary of State, under section 14, 18, 20, 27, 108(1), 120, or 124 of, or paragraph 2 of Schedule 21 to, this Act (which confer power to make orders otherwise than by statutory instrument) may be revoked or varied by a subsequent order made or confirmed in the like manner and subject to the like provisions.

(3) Subject to the provisions of subsection (4) below, an order made by the Greater London Council under this Act may be revoked or varied by a subsequent order made in the like manner and subject to the like provisions.

(4) Subsection (3) above does not apply to—

(a) an order made under subsection (6) of section 157 confirming a scheme made under that subsection but the Greater London Council may subsequently by order modify such a scheme, in so far as it imposes a prohibition or restriction on the execution of any works, in such manner as they may consider expedient,

(b) an order made under section 158.

(5) Without prejudice to subsection (2) above, an order to which this subsection applies confirmed by the Minister, or the Secretary of State, or confirmed as an unopposed order by the authority making it, may be revoked or varied by a subsequent order made or confirmed in the like manner and subject to the like provisions, except that an order confirmed in either way may be revoked or varied by an order confirmed in the other way.

This subsection applies to a public path creation order, a public path extinguishment order, a public path diversion order and an order under section 124 above.

(6) Subject to the following provisions of this section, a scheme revoking or varying a scheme made or confirmed under section 16 or section 106(3) above, and an order varying or revoking an order made or confirmed under section 14, 17, 18, 108(1) or 124 above may contain such consequential provisions as appear to the Minister to be expedient.

(7) Where a scheme under section 16 above is revoked by a subsequent scheme, any part of the special road authorised to be provided by the scheme which has been constructed before the date on which the revoking scheme comes into operation and any highway appropriated by or transferred to the special road authority before that date shall cease on that date to be a special road within the meaning of this Act, but shall, where the special road is a trunk road, continue to be a trunk road.

(8) Where a scheme under section 16 above is varied by a subsequent scheme, subsection (7) above applies in relation to any part of the special road which ceases to form part of a route of that road in consequence of the variation.

(9) Subject to the foregoing provisions of this section, the revocation or variation of a scheme under section 16 or section 106(3) above does not affect the validity of anything done in pursuance of the scheme before the date on which the revoking or varying scheme comes into force, or the validity of any order made under section 18 above before that date in connection with the special road to be provided under the scheme.

Crown application

327.—(1) The provisions of this section apply in relation to any land belonging to Her Majesty in right of the Crown or of the Duchy of Lancaster, or belonging to the Duchy of Cornwall, or belonging to a government department, or held in trust for Her Majesty for the purposes of a government department.

Application of Act to Crown land.

K 4

(2) The appropriate authority in relation to any land and a highway authority may agree that any provisions of this Act specified in the agreement shall apply to that land and, while the agreement is in force, those provisions shall apply to that land accordingly, subject however to the terms of the agreement.

(3) Any such agreement as is mentioned in subsection (2) above may contain such consequential and incidental provisions, including provisions of a financial character, as appear to the appropriate authority to be necessary or equitable, but provisions of a financial character shall not be included in an agreement made by a government department without the approval of the Treasury.

(4) In this section " the appropriate authority " means—

(a) in the case of land belonging to Her Majesty in right of the Crown, the Crown Estate Commissioners or other government department having the management of the land in question ;

(b) in the case of land belonging to Her Majesty in right of the Duchy of Lancaster, the Chancellor of that Duchy ;

(c) in the case of land belonging to the Duchy of Cornwall, such person as the Duke of Cornwall, or the possessor for the time being of the Duchy of Cornwall, appoints ;

(d) in the case of land belonging to a government department or held in trust for Her Majesty for the purposes of a government department, that department ;

and, if any question arises as to what authority is the appropriate authority in relation to any land, that question shall be referred to the Treasury, whose decision shall be final.

Interpretation

Meaning of
" highway ".
328.—(1) In this Act, except where the context otherwise requires, " highway " means the whole or a part of a highway other than a ferry or waterway.

(2) Where a highway passes over a bridge or through a tunnel, that bridge or tunnel is to be taken for the purposes of this Act to be a part of the highway.

(3) In this Act, " highway maintainable at the public expense " and any other expression defined by reference to a highway is to be construed in accordance with the foregoing provisions of this section.

329.—(1) In this Act, except where the context otherwise requires—

PART XIV
Further
provision as to
interpretation.
1946 c. 49.
1965 c. 56.

" Act of 1946 " means the Acquisition of Land (Authorisation Procedure) Act 1946 ;

" Act of 1965 " means the Compulsory Purchase Act 1965 ;

" adjoining " includes abutting on, and " adjoins " is to be construed accordingly ;

" advance payments code " has the meaning provided by section 203(1) above ;

" agriculture " includes horticulture, fruit growing, seed growing, dairy farming, the breeding and keeping of livestock (including any creature kept for the production of food, wool, skins or fur, or for the purpose of its use in the farming of land), the use of land as grazing land, meadow land, osier land, market gardens and nursery grounds, and the use of land for woodlands where that use is ancillary to the farming of land for other agricultural purposes, and " agricultural " is to be construed accordingly ;

" apparatus " includes any structure constructed for the lodging therein of apparatus ;

" approach ", in relation to a bridge or tunnel, means the highway giving access thereto, that is to say, the surface of that highway together with any embankment, retaining wall or other work or substance supporting or protecting the surface ;

" bridge " does not include a culvert, but, save as aforesaid, means a bridge or viaduct which is part of a highway, and includes the abutments and any other part of a bridge but not the highway carried thereby ;

" bridleway " means a highway over which the public have the following, but no other, rights of way, that is to say, a right of way on foot and a right of way on horseback or leading a horse, with or without a right to drive animals of any description along the highway ;

" by-pass " has the meaning provided by section 82(6) above ;

" canal undertakers " means persons authorised by any enactment to carry on a canal undertaking ;

" carriageway " means a way constituting or comprised in a highway, being a way (other than a cycle track) over which the public have a right of way for the passage of vehicles ;

" cattle-grid " has the meaning provided by section 82(6) above ;

" City " means the City of London ;

" classified road " means a highway or proposed highway which is a classified road in accordance with section 12 above ;

" Common Council " means the Common Council of the City of London ;

" contravention " in relation to a condition, restriction or requirement, includes failure to comply with that condition, restriction or requirement, and " contravene " is to be construed accordingly ;

" council " means a county council, the Greater London Council or a local authority ;

" cycle track " means a way constituting or comprised in a highway, being a way over which the public have the following, but no other, rights of way, that is to say, a right of way on pedal cycles with or without a right of way on foot ;

" dock undertakers " means persons authorised by any enactment to carry on a dock undertaking ;

" drainage authority " means a water authority or an internal drainage board ;

" electricity undertakers " means persons authorised by any enactment to carry on an undertaking for the supply of electricity ;

" enactment " includes an enactment in a local or private Act of Parliament and a provision of an order, scheme, regulations or other instrument made under or confirmed by a public general, local or private Act of Parliament ;

" financial year " means a year ending on 31st March ;

" footpath " means a highway over which the public have a right of way on foot only, not being a footway ;

" footway " means a way comprised in a highway which also comprises a carriageway, being a way over which the public have a right of way on foot only ;

" functions " includes powers and duties ;

" gas undertakers " means persons authorised by any enactment to carry on an undertaking for the supply of gas ;

" harbour undertakers " means persons authorised by any enactment to carry on a harbour undertaking ;

" highway land acquisition powers " has the meaning provided by section 250(1) above ;

" highway maintainable at the public expense " means a highway which by virtue of section 36 above or of any other enactment (whether contained in this Act or not) is a highway which for the purposes of this Act is a PART XIV highway maintainable at the public expense ;

" horse " includes pony, ass and mule, and " horseback " is to be construed accordingly ;

" hours of darkness " means the time between half an hour after sunset and half an hour before sunrise ;

" improvement " means the doing of any act under powers conferred by Part V of this Act and includes the erection, maintenance, alteration and removal of traffic signs, and the freeing of a highway or road-ferry from tolls ;

" inland navigation undertakers " means persons authorised by any enactment to carry on an inland navigation undertaking ;

" land " includes land covered by water and any interest or right in, over or under land ;

" lease " includes an underlease and an agreement for a lease or underlease, but does not include an option to take a lease or mortgage, and " lessee " is to be construed accordingly ;

" lighting authority " means a council or other body autho- rised to provide lighting under section 161 of the Public 1875 c. 55. Health Act 1875 or under section 3 of the Parish 1957 c. 42. Councils Act 1957 or any corresponding local enact- ment ;

" local authority " means the council of a district or London borough or the Common Council ;

" local highway authority " means a highway authority other than the Minister ;

" local planning authority " has the same meaning as in the Town and Country Planning Act 1971 ; 1971 c. 78.

" lorry area " means an area provided under section 115 above ;

" made-up carriageway " means a carriageway, or a part thereof, which has been metalled or in any other way provided with a surface suitable for the passage of vehicles ;

" maintenance " includes repair, and " maintain " and " maintainable " are to be construed accordingly ;

" maintenance compound " means an area of land (with or without buildings) used or to be used in connection with the maintenance of highways, or a particular high- way ;

" metropolitan road " means a highway, or a proposed high- way, which is a metropolitan road in accordance with section 15 above ;

   " the Minister ", subject to subsection (5) below, means as respects England, the Minister of Transport and as respects Wales, the Secretary of State ; and in section 258 of, and paragraphs 7, 8(1) and (3), 14, 15(1) and (3), 18(2), 19 and 21 of Schedule 1 to, this Act, references to the Minister and the Secretary of State acting jointly are to be construed, as respects Wales, as references to the Secretary of State acting alone ;

" navigation authority " means persons authorised by any enactment to work, maintain, conserve, improve or control any canal or other inland navigation, navigable river, estuary, harbour or dock ;

" owner ", in relation to any premises, means a person, other than a mortgagee not in possession, who, whether in his own right or as trustee or agent for any other person, is entitled to receive the rack rent of the premises or, where the premises are not let at a rack rent, would be so entitled if the premises were so let ;

   " petty sessions area " has the same meaning as in the Magistrates' Courts Act 1980 ;

" pier undertakers " means persons authorised by any enactment to carry on a pier undertaking ;

" premises " includes land and buildings ;

" private street works code " has the meaning provided by section 203(1) above ;

" proposed highway " means land on which, in accordance with plans made by a highway authority, that authority are for the time being constructing or intending to construct a highway shown in the plans ;

" public general enactment " means an enactment in an Act treated as a public general Act under the system of division of Acts adopted in the regnal year 38 George 3, other than an Act for confirming a provisional order ;

" public path creation agreement " means an agreement under section 25 above ;

" public path creation order " means an order under section 26 above ;

" public path diversion order " means an order under section 119 above ;

" public path extinguishment order " means an order under section 118 above ;

" public utility undertakers " means persons authorised by any enactment to carry on any of the following undertakings, that is to say, an undertaking for the supply of electricity, gas, water or hydraulic power ;

"rack rent", in relation to any premises, means a rent which is not less than two-thirds of the rent at which the premises might reasonably be expected to let from year to year, free from all usual tenant's rates and taxes and tithe rentcharge (if any), and deducting therefrom the probable average annual cost of the repairs, insurance and other expenses (if any) necessary to maintain the same in a state to command such rent ;

"railway" includes a light railway ;

"railway undertakers" means persons authorised by any enactment to carry on a railway undertaking ;

"reconstruction", in relation to a bridge, includes the construction of a new bridge and approaches thereto in substitution for the existing bridge and the approaches thereto ;

"road-ferry" means a ferry connecting the termination of a highway which is, or is to become, a highway maintainable at the public expense with the termination of another highway which is, or is to become, such a highway ;

"service area" means an area of land adjoining, or in the vicinity of, a special road, being an area in which there are, or are to be, provided service stations or other buildings or facilities to be used in connection with the use of the special road ;

"sewerage authority" means a water authority in their capacity as an authority exercising functions under or by virtue of section 14 of the Water Act 1973 ;

"special enactment" means any enactment other than a public general enactment ;

"special road" means a highway, or a proposed highway, which is a special road in accordance with section 16 above ;

"special road authority" has the meaning provided by section 16(4) above ;

"statutory undertakers" means persons authorised by any enactment to carry on any of the following undertakings: —

(a) a railway, tramway, road transport, water transport, canal, inland navigation, dock, harbour, pier or lighthouse undertaking, or

(b) an undertaking for the supply of electricity, gas, water or hydraulic power,

and "statutory undertaking" is to be construed accordingly ;

"street" includes any highway and any road, lane, footpath, square, court, alley or passage, whether a thoroughfare or not, and includes any part of a street;

"swing bridge" includes any opening bridge operated by mechanical means;

"traffic" includes pedestrians and animals;

"traffic sign" has the same meaning as in section 54 of the Road Traffic Regulation Act 1967;

"tramway undertakers" means persons authorised by any enactment to carry on a tramway undertaking;

"transport undertakers" means persons authorised by any enactment to carry on any of the following undertakings, that is to say, a railway, canal, inland navigation, dock, harbour or pier undertaking, and "transport undertaking" is to be construed accordingly;

"trunk road" means a highway, or a proposed highway, which is a trunk road by virtue of section 10(1) or section 19 above or by virtue of an order or direction under section 10 above or under any other enactment;

"trunk road picnic area" has the meaning provided by section 112(1) above;

"water undertakers" means persons authorised by any enactment to carry on an undertaking for the supply of water.

(2) A highway at the side of a river, canal or other inland navigation is not excluded from the definition in subsection (1) above of either "bridleway" or "footpath", by reason only that the public have a right to use the highway for purposes of navigation, if the highway would fall within that definition if the public had no such right thereover.

(3) In a case where two or more parishes are grouped under a common parish council, references in this Act to a parish are to be construed as references to those parishes.

(4) Any reference in this Act to property of railway undertakers, canal undertakers, inland navigation undertakers, dock undertakers, harbour undertakers or pier undertakers is, where the undertakers are a body to which this subsection applies, to be taken as a reference to property of that body held or used by them wholly or mainly for the purposes of so much of their undertaking as consists of the carrying on of a railway undertaking or, as the case may be, of a canal undertaking, an inland navigation undertaking, a dock undertaking, a harbour undertaking or a pier undertaking.

This subsection applies to the following bodies, namely, the British Railways Board, the British Transport Docks Board, the British Waterways Board, the London Transport Executive, the National Freight Corporation (as far as included in this subsection by paragraph 15(*b*) of Schedule 23 to this Act) or any wholly-owned subsidiary (within the meaning of the Transport Act 1968) or joint subsidiary (within the meaning of section 51(5) of that Act) of any of those bodies.

1968 c. 73.

(5) In relation to that part of the road constructed by the Minister of Transport along the line described in Schedule 1 to the North of Almondsbury—South of Haysgate Trunk Road Order 1947 and referred to in that Order as " the new road " which lies to the east of the most easterly point before reaching the River Wye at which eastbound traffic of Classes I and II (as specified in Schedule 4 to this Act) can leave that road by another special road, the functions of the Minister under this Act shall be exercisable by the Minister of Transport and not by the Secretary of State.

S. R. & O. 1947/1562.

330.—(1) Where by any enactment empowering statutory undertakers to execute works under, in, upon, over, along or across a highway the undertakers are thereby required—

Construction of certain enactments relating to execution of works by statutory undertakers.

(*a*) to give notice to, or obtain the consent or approval of, a council,

(*b*) to carry out the works under the superintendence of a council,

(*c*) to reinstate the highway to the satisfaction of a council, or

(*d*) to do anything in relation to a road for which a county council are the highway authority (whether so described or described as a " county road "),

any such requirement, and any provision of the enactment empowering the council to act in default of the undertakers. or otherwise to enforce any such requirement, has effect, in relation to a trunk road, with the substitution, for references to the council, of references to the Minister and, for references to a road for which a county council are the highway authority (or a county road), of references to a trunk road.

(2) Notwithstanding the provisions of any enactment as to the determination of disputes arising between statutory undertakers and a council in connection with the execution of any such works, any such dispute arising in the case of a trunk road between statutory undertakers and the Minister shall be determined by a single arbitrator appointed, in default of agreement between the parties concerned, by the President of the Institution of Civil Engineers.

(3) Nothing in this section affects Part I of the Public Utilities Street Works Act 1950.

1950 c. 39.

PART XIV

References to functions of council as respects any highway.

331. Except where this Act otherwise requires, any enactment or document relating to the functions of a council as respects any highway is, in relation to functions not exercisable in the case of a trunk road by the Minister, to be construed as if references therein to highways included references to trunk roads.

Widening of carriageway not to cease to be improvement by reason of diminution etc. of footway.

332. For the purposes of this Act and of any other enactment relating to highways, the widening of the carriageway of a highway is not to be treated as being otherwise than an improvement by reason only of the fact that it involves diminution or removal of a footway thereon.

Savings etc.

Saving for rights and liabilities as to interference with highways.

333. No provision of this Act relating to obstruction of or other interference with highways is to be taken to affect any right of a highway authority or other person under any enactment not contained in this Act, or under any rule of law, to remove an obstruction from a highway or otherwise abate a nuisance or other interference with the highway, or to affect the liability of any person under such an enactment or rule to proceedings (whether civil or criminal) in respect of any such obstruction or other interference.

Savings for Post Office.

334.—(1) Subject to the provisions of this section, nothing in this Act or in any scheme or order made under it affects any powers or duties of the Post Office under the provisions of the Telegraph Acts or applies to any telegraphic lines placed or maintained by virtue of any of those provisions ; but this subsection does not affect the operation of section 20 above as it has effect in relation to powers of the Post Office by virtue of subsection (9) of that section, or the operation of sections 156 to 159 above.

(2) Where—

(a) land is conveyed by a highway authority in pursuance of section 256 above, or

(b) a highway is stopped up or diverted in pursuance of an order to which this paragraph applies,

and immediately before the conveyance or, as the case may be, the date on which the order comes into force there is under, in, upon, over, along or across the land conveyed or, as the case may be, the highway stopped up or diverted any telegraphic line belonging to or used by the Post Office, then the provisions of subsection (3) below have effect.

Paragraph (b) above applies to the following orders, namely, an order made or confirmed by the Minister under section 14

or 18 above, a public path extinguishment order and a public
path diversion order.

(3) In the circumstances mentioned in subsection (2) above,
the Post Office have the same powers in respect of the telegraphic
line as if the conveyance had not been made or, as the case may
be, the order had not come into force; but if the transferee of
the land, or, as the case may be, any person entitled to land over
which the stopped up or diverted highway subsisted requires the
telegraphic line to be altered, paragraphs (1) to (8) of section 7 of
the Telegraph Act 1878 apply to the alteration and accordingly 1878 c. 76.
have effect, subject to the necessary modifications, as if references
therein to undertakers included references to the person so
requiring the line to be altered.

(4) Where in pursuance of an order made by a magistrates'
court under section 116 above a highway is stopped up or
diverted, the following provisions of this subsection have effect
in relation to so much of any telegraphic line belonging to or
used by the Post Office as is under, in, upon, over, along or
across land which by reason of the stopping up or diversion
ceases to be a highway ("the affected line"):—

    (a) the power of the Post Office to remove the affected line
is exercisable notwithstanding the making of the order,
so however that the said power is not exercisable, as
respects the whole or any part of the affected line, after
the expiration of a period of 3 months from the date
of the sending of the notice referred to in subsection (5)
below unless before the expiration of that period the
Post Office have given notice to the authority on whose
application the order was made of their intention to
remove the affected line or that part of it, as the case
may be;

    (b) the Post Office may by notice in that behalf to the said
authority abandon the affected line or any part of it,
and are to be deemed, as respects the affected line or
any part of it, to have abandoned it at the expiration
of the said period of 3 months unless before the expiration of that period they have removed it or given
notice of their intention to remove it;

    (c) the Post Office are entitled to recover from the said
authority the expense of providing, in substitution for
the affected line and any telegraphic line connected
with it which is rendered useless in consequence of the
removal or abandonment of the affected line, a telegraphic line in such other place as they may require;

    (d) where under paragraph (b) above the Post Office have
abandoned the whole or any part of the affected line,
it vests in the authority there referred to and the provisions of the Telegraph Acts do not apply in relation to

it as respects anything done or omitted after the abandonment.

(5) As soon as practicable after the making of an order under section 116 above the authority on whose application the order was made shall by notice to the Post Office inform them of the making of the order.

(6) Where an order under section 14 or 18 above provides for the alteration of a highway and, immediately before the date on which the order comes into force, there is under, in, upon, over, along or across the highway any telegraphic line belonging to or used by the Post Office, then, if the highway authority for the highway require that line to be altered, paragraphs (1) to 1878 c. 76. (8) of section 7 of the Telegraph Act 1878 apply in relation to the alteration and accordingly have effect, subject to any necessary modifications, as if references therein to undertakers included references to the highway authority.

This subsection does not have effect so far as it relates to the alteration of any telegraphic line for the purposes of authority's 1950 c. 39. works as defined in Part II of the Public Utilities Street Works Act 1950.

(7) Where in pursuance of an order under section 14 or 18 above a highway is stopped up or diverted, or an order under either of those sections provides for the alteration of a highway, and, immediately before the date on which the order comes into force, there is under, in, upon, over, along or across the highway any telegraphic line belonging to or used by the Post Office, then, without prejudice to subsections (2), (3) and (6) above, the provisions of subsection (8) below have effect.

(8) In the circumstances mentioned in subsection (7) above, if for purposes connected with the construction or improvement of the trunk road, special road or classified road, as the case may be, to which the order relates or with the execution of any works authorised by the order the Minister or other highway authority by whom the order in question was made requires the telegraphic line to be altered, paragraphs (1) to (8) of section 7 of the Telegraph Act 1878 apply in relation to the alteration and accordingly have effect, subject to any necessary modifications, as if references therein to undertakers included references to the Minister or that other authority.

(9) Without prejudice to the code in Part II of the Public Utilities Street Works Act 1950 (relations between an authority carrying out road alterations and undertakers whose apparatus is thereby affected)—

   (a) any work authorised or required by an order under section 93 above to be done by a highway authority or the owners of a bridge, (*b*) any work proposed to be done by a highway authority in exercise of powers conferred on them by section 96 above, and

(*c*) any work authorised or required by a licence under section 176 above to be done by the person to whom the licence is granted,

is, for the purposes of section 7 of the Telegraph Act 1878, 1878 c. 76. to be deemed to be work proposed to be done in the execution of an undertaking authorised by an Act of Parliament, and the authority or person carrying out the work are to be deemed to be the undertakers.

(10) Where, in pursuance of any order or scheme made or confirmed under this Act, a navigable watercourse is diverted and, immediately before the date on which the order or scheme comes into force, there is under, in, upon, over, along or across the watercourse, or any towing path or other way adjacent to it, any telegraphic line belonging to or used by the Post Office, the Post Office have the same powers in respect of that line as if the order or scheme had not come into force; but if—

(*a*) the highway authority by whom the order or scheme was made, or

(*b*) any person entitled to land on which so much of the watercourse, towing path or way as is diverted in pursuance of the order or scheme was previously situated,

requires the line to be altered, paragraphs (1) to (8) of section 7 of the Telegraph Act 1878 apply in relation to the alteration and accordingly have effect, subject to any necessary modifications, as if references therein to undertakers included references to the highway authority or to the person so requiring the line to be altered, as the case may be.

(11) For the purposes of the placing or maintenance of overground telegraphic lines under the powers conferred by the Telegraph Acts a bridge constructed or used in accordance with a licence under section 176 above is to be deemed to be part of any highway which it crosses.

(12) The fact that the Telegraph Acts are not expressed to be binding on the Crown does not prevent those Acts having effect in relation to a street or public road, as defined for the purposes of those Acts, which is a trunk road or other highway for which the Minister is the highway authority, as they have effect in relation to any other street or public road as so defined, but this provision is without prejudice to section 20(9) above.

(13) No provision of section 7 of the Telegraph Act 1878 creating a liability to a fine for breach of any obligation applies to an obligation in so far as, by virtue of a provision of this section, it falls to be performed by the Minister.

PART XIV
1863 c. 112.
1892 c. 59.
1908 c. 33.
1909 c. 20.
1911 c. 39.
1916 c. 40.

(14) In this section " alter " and " telegraphic line " have the same meanings respectively as in the Telegraph Act 1878, and " the Telegraph Acts " means the Telegraph Act 1863, the Telegraph Act 1878, the Telegraph Act 1892, the Telegraph (Construction) Act 1908, the Telegraph (Arbitration) Act 1909, the Telegraph (Construction) Act 1911 and the Telegraph (Construction) Act 1916.

Saving for minerals etc.

335.—(1) Notwithstanding anything in Part XII of this Act all mines and minerals of any description whatsoever under any highway vested in a highway authority by virtue of any provision contained in the said Part XII belong to the person who would be entitled thereto if the highway were not vested in the authority, and the person entitled to any such mine or minerals has the same powers of working and of getting the same as if the highway were not vested in a highway authority.

(2) Nothing in this section affects any liability (whether civil or criminal) of the person entitled to any such mine or minerals in respect of damage to the highway resulting from the exercise of the said powers.

Saving for Coast Protection Act 1949.
1949 c. 74.

336. Nothing in this Act authorises the excavation or removal of any materials the excavation or removal of which is prohibited by section 18 of the Coast Protection Act 1949 (which makes it unlawful except as therein mentioned to excavate or remove certain materials on, under or forming part of any portion of the seashore to which the provisions of that section are applied), or the carrying out of any operation in contravention of section 34 of that Act (which restricts the carrying out of certain operations detrimental to navigation).

Saving for obligation to obtain planning permission.
1971 c. 78.

337. Nothing in this Act authorises the carrying out of any development of land for which permission is required by virtue of section 23 of the Town and Country Planning Act 1971 and which is not authorised by permission granted or deemed to be granted under or for the purposes of Part III of that Act.

Saving for works, etc., of dock, harbour and canal undertakers.

338.—(1) Subject to the provisions of this section, nothing in any of the provisions of this Act to which this section applies authorises a highway authority or council, without the consent of the dock, harbour or canal undertakers concerned—

(*a*) to execute any works in, across, or under any dock, harbour, basin, wharf, quay or lock ; or

(*b*) to execute any works which will interfere with the improvement of, or the access to, any river, canal, dock, harbour, basin, lock, reservoir or towing path, or with any works appurtenant thereto or any land necessary for the enjoyment or improvement thereof.

(2) A consent required for the purposes of subsection (1) above shall not be unreasonably withheld, and if any question arises whether the withholding of a consent is unreasonable either party may require it to be referred to an arbitrator to be appointed, in default of agreement, by the President of the Institution of Civil Engineers.

(3) On an arbitration under this section, the arbitrator shall determine—

    (*a*) whether any works which the highway authority or council propose to execute are such works as under subsection (1) above they are not entitled to execute without the consent of the undertakers concerned; and

    (*b*) if they are such works, whether the injury, if any, to the undertakers will be of such a nature as to admit of being fully compensated by money; and

    (*c*) if the works are of such a nature, the conditions subject to which the authority or council may execute the works, including the amount of the compensation, if any, to be paid by them to the undertakers.

If the arbitrator determines that the proposed works are such works as the highway authority or council are not entitled to execute without the consent of the undertakers and that the works would cause injury to the undertakers of such a nature as not to admit of being fully compensated by money, the authority or council shall not proceed to execute the works; but in any other case they may execute the works subject to compliance with such conditions, including the payment of such compensation, as the arbitrator determines.

(4) For the purposes of this section, dock, harbour and canal undertakers are to be deemed to be concerned with any river, canal, dock, harbour, basin, lock, reservoir, towing path, wharf, quay or land if it belongs to them and forms part of their undertaking, or if they have statutory rights of navigating on or using it, or of demanding tolls or dues in respect of navigation thereon or the use thereof.

(5) This section applies to section 230(7) and section 294 above and to the provisions specified in Schedule 22 to this Act, but subsections (2) and (3) above do not apply as respect a consent required in relation to section 230(7).

(6) In this section " canal " includes inland navigation.

339.—(1) Subject to the provisions of this section, nothing in any of the provisions of this Act to which this section applies authorises a highway authority or any other person to use or interfere with any watercourse (including the banks thereof), or

PART XIV

1976 c. 70.

any drainage or other works, vested in or under the control of a water authority or other drainage body within the meaning of the Land Drainage Act 1976 without the consent of that authority or body.

(2) A consent required for the purposes of subsection (1) above shall not be unreasonably withheld, and if any question arises whether the withholding of a consent is unreasonable either party may require it to be referred to an arbitrator to be appointed, in default of agreement, by the President of the Institution of Civil Engineers.

(3) This section applies to sections 45, 100, 101, 110, 294 and 299 above and to the provisions specified in Schedule 22 to this Act.

(4) In its application to sections 100, 110, and 299 above this section applies in relation to a navigation authority as it applies in relation to a water authority or other drainage body within the meaning of the Land Drainage Act 1976.

Preservation of amendments.

1959 c. 25.
1957 c. 42.

340.—(1) Notwithstanding the repeal by this Act of the Highways Act 1959—

(a) subsection (10) of section 3 of the Parish Councils Act 1957 (which was inserted by section 310 of the Highways Act 1959 and defines " road " for the purposes of the said section 3) continues to have effect, but subject to the amendments made to that subsection, in consequence of this Act, by Schedule 24 to this Act ;

(b) the enactments mentioned in Schedule 22 to the said Act of 1959 continue to have effect with the amendments there made but subject, in the case of such of those enactments as are mentioned in Schedule 24 to this Act, to the amendments made, in consequence of this Act, by the said Schedule 24.

1971 c. 41.

1967 c. 76.

(2) Notwithstanding the repeal by this Act of the Highways Act 1971 (referred to below as " the 1971 Act ")—

(a) section 29A and section 31(1A) of the Road Traffic Regulation Act 1967 (which were inserted by section 9(1) and (3) of the 1971 Act and are concerned with provision of access to premises through off-street parking places) continue to have effect and section 30(1) and (3) and 32(5) of the said Act of 1967 (which were amended by section 9(2) and (4) of the 1971 Act in consequence of the insertion of section 29A and section 31 (1A)) continue to have effect with the amendments so made ;

1964 c. 83.

(b) section 3(6) of the New Forest Act 1964 (which provides for the fencing of a source of danger in the New

Forest) continues to have effect with the amendment PART XIV
made by section 34(2) of the 1971 Act;

(c) paragraph 11(1)(b) of Schedule I to the Act of 1946
(which applies special parliamentary procedure in the
case of compulsory purchase of land forming part
of a common, open space, etc.) continues to have effect
with the amendments made by section 56 of the 1971
Act;

(d) paragraph 8 of Part III of Schedule 3 to the Country- 1968 c. 41.
side Act 1968 (which relates to the re-classification of
roads used as public paths) continues to have effect
with the amendment made by section 75 of the 1971
Act; and

(e) the definition of " road purposes " in section 39 of the 1950 c. 39.
Public Utilities Street Works Act 1950 continues to have
effect with the amendment made by section 78(1) of
the 1971 Act, but subject to the amendment made to
that definition, in consequence of this Act, by
Schedule 24 to this Act.

341. In section 303 of the Public Health Act 1875 (power of Amendment of
Secretary of State to repeal and alter local Acts by means of section 303
provisional orders), the reference to any local Act which relates Health Act
to the same subject matters as that Act is to be construed as 1875.
including a reference to any local Act which relates to the same 1875 c. 55.
subject matters as the following provisions of this Act, namely,
sections 288, 294, 312, 338, 339 and the provisions specified in
Schedule 22 to this Act.

342. In section 41 of the Countryside Act 1968— Amendment
of section 41
(a) in subsection (1), at the end of paragraph (c) insert " or " of Countryside
and after that paragraph insert— Act 1968.

" (d) a trunk road picnic area as respects which 1968 c. 41.
functions of the Minister stand delegated to the local
authority under section 113(1) of the Highways Act
1980, or are functions of the local authority by virtue
of an agreement under section 113(3) of that Act,";

(b) after subsection (1) insert—

" (1A) The power of a local authority under subsection (1)(d) above is exercisable only in so far as
any conditions attached to the relevant delegation or,
as the case may be, included in the relevant agreement do not otherwise provide.".

PART XIV
Transitional
provisions,
amendments
and repeals.

343.—(1) Schedule 23 to this Act, which contains transitional provisions, has effect.

(2) The enactments specified in Schedule 24 to this Act are, in consequence of this Act, amended as there provided.

(3) The enactments specified in Schedule 25 to this Act are repealed to the extent specified in the third column of that Schedule.

Application
to Isles
of Scilly.

344.—(1) Subject to the provisions of this section, the provisions of this Act specified in subsection (2) below do not extend to the Isles of Scilly.

(2) The provisions referred to in subsection (1) above are—

   (a) sections 25 to 29, 118 to 121, 134, 135, 146, 147, 275 and 293 ; and

   (b) sections 219 to 225 and 229.

(3) The Secretary of State may, after consultation with the Council of the Isles of Scilly, by order provide that all or any of the provisions of this Act specified in subsection (2)(a) above are, subject to such modifications as may be specified in the order, to apply in the Isles of Scilly as if those Isles were a separate county.

(4) The Secretary of State may, on the application of the Council of the Isles of Scilly, by order provide that the provisions of this Act specified in subsection (2)(b) above are to apply in those Isles and, on the making of an order under this subsection, any reference in the said provisions to the street works authority is to be construed as a reference to the Council of those Isles.

(5) On the making of an order under subsection (4) above the Council of the Isles of Scilly shall take such steps for notifying the public of its having been made as the Secretary of State may direct.

(6) Section 232 above, in its application in the Isles of Scilly, has effect subject to the modification that any reference therein to the street works authority or the prospective street works authority is to be construed as a reference to the Council of those Isles, and any regulations made under that section are in their application to those Isles to be construed accordingly.

(7) Sections 9, 97, 98, 270 and 301 of this Act, in their application in relation to the Isles of Scilly, have effect subject to such modifications as the Secretary of State may by order direct.

345.—(1) This Act may be cited as the Highways Act 1980.

(2) This Act shall come into force on 1st January 1981.

(3) This Act (except paragraph 18(*c*) of Schedule 24) extends to England and Wales only.

SCHEDULES

SCHEDULE 1

PROCEDURES FOR MAKING OR CONFIRMING CERTAIN ORDERS
AND SCHEMES

PART I

ORDERS

1. Where the Minister proposes to make an order under any of the following provisions of this Act, that is to say, section 10, section 18, section 106 or section 108(1), or an order relating to a trunk road under section 14 of this Act, he shall prepare a draft of the order and shall publish in at least one local newspaper circulating in the area in which any highway, or any proposed highway, to which the order relates is situated, and in the London Gazette, a notice—

(a) stating the general effect of the proposed order ;

(b) naming a place in the said area where a copy of the draft order and of any map or plan referred to therein may be inspected by any person free of charge at all reasonable hours during a period specified in the notice, being a period of not less than 6 weeks from the date of the publication of the notice ; and

(c) stating that, within the said period, any person may by notice to the Minister object to the making of the order.

2. Where an order under section 18 or section 108(1) of this Act, or an order relating to a classified road under section 14 of this Act, is submitted to the Minister by a local highway authority, that authority shall publish, in the manner specified in paragraph 1 above, the notice there referred to, and that paragraph shall have effect in relation to a notice published by any such authority as if, for the references to the draft order and the making of the order, there were substituted references to the order as submitted to the Minister and the confirmation of the order respectively.

3. Not later than the day on which the said notice is published or, if it is published on 2 or more days, the day on which it is first published, the Minister or the local highway authority, as the case may be, shall serve on each person specified in such head or heads of the Table set out at the end of this paragraph as apply in the case of the order in question—

(a) a copy of the said notice ;

(b) a copy of the draft order or of the order, as the case may be ; and

(c) a copy of any map or plan referred to in the draft order or the order relating to a matter which, in the opinion of the Minister or of the local highway authority, as the case may be, is likely to affect the said person.

TABLE

*Persons to be served with copies of the documents
specified in paragraph 3 of this Schedule*

(i) In the case of every order proposed to be made under section 10 or section 106 of this Act, and every order relating to a trunk road proposed to be made under section 14 of this Act—

Every council in whose area any highway or proposed highway to which the proposed order relates is situated.

(ii) In the case of an order proposed to be made under section 10, 14, 18 or 108(1) of this Act which provides for the construction of a bridge over or tunnel under navigable waters or for the diversion of a navigable watercourse, and in the case of every order proposed to be made under section 106 of this Act—

Every navigation authority and water authority concerned with or having jurisdiction over the waters affected or the area comprising those waters or that watercourse and, if the waters or watercourse affected are or is within the London excluded area as defined in section 116(1) of the Land Drainage Act 1976, the Greater London Council.

1976 c. 70.

(iii) In the case of an order proposed to be made under section 18 of this Act or an order relating to a classified road, proposed to be made under section 14 of this Act, which (in either case) authorises the carrying out of any works—

Every council in whose area any works authorised by the proposed order are to be carried out.

(iv) In the case of an order under section 18 of this Act, or an order relating to a classified road under section 14 of this Act, which (in either case) provides for transferring any highway from one highway authority to another—

The highway authorities to and from whom the highway is to be transferred.

(v) In the case of an order proposed to be made under section 14 or 18 of this Act which authorises the stopping up of any private means of access to any premises—

The owner (within the meaning of section 21 of this Act) and the occupier of those premises.

(vi) In the case of an order proposed to be made under section 14 or 18 of this Act which authorises the stopping up or diversion of any highway—

The council or, in the case of a parish not having a separate council, the parish meeting, of every parish in which the highway is situated and the council of every community in which the highway is situated.

Any public utility undertakers having apparatus under, in, upon, over, along or across the highway.

4. Where the proposed order authorises the stopping up or diversion of a highway, the Minister or the local highway authority, as the case may be, shall, not later than the day on which the said

SCH. 1   notice is published or, if it is published on 2 or more days, the day on which it is first published, cause a copy of it to be displayed in a prominent position at the ends of so much of any highway as is proposed to be stopped up or diverted under the order.

5. At any time, whether before or after the expiration of the period specified in the notice in pursuance of paragraph 1(*b*) above, the Minister or the local highway authority, as the case may be, by whom the notice was published may, by a subsequent notice published in at least one local newspaper circulating in the area in which any highway, or any proposed highway, to which the proposed order relates is situated, and in the London Gazette, substitute for the period specified in the first notice such longer period as may be specified in the subsequent notice.

6. Where the period specified in a notice published by the Minister or a local highway authority under paragraph 1 above is extended by a notice published under paragraph 5 above, paragraph 3 above shall apply as if the notice under paragraph 5 were a notice under paragraph 1, but the foregoing provision shall not be taken as requiring a copy of the proposed order or of any map or plan referred to in that order to be served on a person on whom it was previously served.

7.—(1) If any objection to the proposed order is received by the Minister—

 (*a*) from any person on whom a copy of the notice is required to be served under paragraph 3 above within the period specified in the notice in pursuance of paragraph 1(*b*) above or, if that period has been extended by a subsequent notice under paragraph 5 above, within the period specified in the subsequent notice, or

 (*b*) from any other person appearing to him to be affected within the period specified in the notice or the subsequent notice, as the case may be,

and the objection is not withdrawn, then—

 (i) in the case of an order proposed to be made by the Minister, the Minister and the Secretary of State acting jointly, or

 (ii) in the case of an order made by a local highway authority and submitted to the Minister, the Minister,

shall, subject to sub-paragraph (2) below, cause a local inquiry to be held.

(2) Except where the objection is made by a person entitled to receive a copy of the notice relating to the order in question by virtue of paragraph 3 above and such one or more of the following heads of the Table set out at the end of that paragraph, that is to say, heads (i), (ii), (iii) and (iv), as apply in the case of that order, the Minister and the Secretary of State acting jointly or, as the case may be, the Minister may, if satisfied that in the circumstances of the case the holding of an inquiry under this paragraph is unnecessary, dispense with such an inquiry.

8.—(1) After any objections to the proposed order which are not withdrawn and, where a local inquiry is held, the report of the person who held the inquiry have been considered—

    (*a*) in the case of an order proposed to be made by the Minister, by the Minister and the Secretary of State acting jointly, or

    (*b*) in the case of an order made by a local highway authority and submitted to the Minister, by the Minister,

the Minister may make or confirm the order either without modification or subject to such modifications as he thinks fit.

(2) The power under this paragraph to make or confirm the order includes power to make or confirm it so far as relating to part of the proposals contained in it (either without modification or subject to such modifications as the Minister thinks fit) while deferring consideration of the remaining part ; and where the Minister makes or confirms part of the order, that part and the remaining part are each to be deemed for the purposes of this Act to be a separate order.

(3) Where the Minister proposes to exercise the power to make or confirm the order subject to modifications, and the modifications will in his opinion make a substantial change in the order—

    (*a*) he shall notify any person who appears to him to be likely to be affected by the proposed modifications ;

    (*b*) he shall give that person an opportunity of making representations to him with respect to the modifications within such reasonable period as he may specify ; and

    (*c*) before he exercises the power, the Minister or, in the case of an order proposed to be made by the Minister, the Minister and the Secretary of State acting jointly shall consider any representations made to the Minister with respect to the proposed modifications within that period.

9. In this Part of this Schedule references to a proposed order or an order proposed to be made include references to an order made by a local highway authority and submitted to the Minister.

Part II

Schemes Under Sections 16 and 106(3)

10. Where the Minister proposes to make a scheme under section 16 of this Act, or where a scheme under that section or section 106(3) of this Act is submitted to the Minister by a local highway authority, the Minister or that authority, as the case may be, shall publish in a least one local newspaper circulating in the area in which the special road, or, as the case may be, the site of the bridge or tunnel, to which the scheme relates is situated, and in the London Gazette, a notice—

    (*a*) stating the general effect of the proposed scheme ;

    (*b*) naming a place in the said area where a copy of a draft of the scheme or of the scheme as submitted to the Minister, as the case may be, and of any map or plan referred to in it may be inspected by any person free of charge at all reasonable hours during a period specified in the notice, being a period of not less than 6 weeks from the date of the publication of the notice ; and

(c) stating that, within the said period, any person may by notice to the Minister object to the making or confirmation of the scheme.

11. Not later than the day on which the said notice is published or, if it is published on 2 or more days, the day on which it is first published, the Minister or the local highway authority, as the case may be, shall serve a copy of it (together with a copy of the draft scheme or of the scheme, as the case may be, and of any map or plan referred to in it)—

(a) on every council in whose area any part of the route of the special road or, as the case may be, the site of the bridge or tunnel is situated ; and

(b) where the scheme provides for the construction of a bridge over or tunnel under any navigable waters, on every navigation authority and water authority concerned with or having jurisdiction over the waters affected or the area comprising those waters.

12. At any time, whether before or after the expiration of the period specified in the notice in pursuance of paragraph 10(b) above, the Minister or, as the case may be, the local highway authority by whom the notice was published may, by a subsequent notice published in at least one local newspaper circulating in the area in which the special road, or, as the case may be, the site of the bridge or tunnel, to which the proposed scheme relates is situated, and in the London Gazette, substitute for the period specified in the first notice such longer period as may be specified in the subsequent notice.

13. Where the period specified in a notice published by the Minister or a local highway authority under paragraph 10 above is extended by a notice published under paragraph 12 above, paragraph 11 above, with the omission of the reference to a copy of the draft scheme or of the scheme and of any map or plan referred to in it, shall apply as if the notice under paragraph 12 were a notice under paragraph 10.

14.—(1) If any objection to the proposed scheme is received by the Minister—

(a) from any council or authority on whom a copy of the notice is required to be served under paragraph 11 above within the period specified in the notice in pursuance of paragraph 10(b) above or, if that period has been extended by a subsequent notice under paragraph 12 above, within the period specified in the subsequent notice, or

(b) from any other person appearing to him to be affected within the period specified in the notice or the subsequent notice, as the case may be, and the objection is not withdrawn, then—

    (i) in the case of a scheme proposed to be made by the Minister, the Minister and the Secretary of State acting jointly, or

    (ii) in the case of a scheme made by a local highway authority and submitted to the Minister, the Minister,

shall, subject to sub-paragraph (2) below, cause a local inquiry to be held.

(2) Except where the objection is made by any such council or authority as aforesaid, the Minister and the Secretary of State acting jointly or, as the case may be, the Minister may, if satisfied that in the circumstances of the case the holding of an inquiry under this paragraph is unnecessary, dispense with such an inquiry.

15.—(1) After any objections to the proposed scheme which are not withdrawn and, where a local inquiry is held, the report of the person who held the inquiry have been considered—

    (a) in the case of a scheme proposed to be made by the Minister, by the Minister and the Secretary of State acting jointly, or

    (b) in the case of a scheme made by a local highway authority and submitted to the Minister, by the Minister,

the Minister may make or confirm the scheme either without modification or subject to such modifications as he thinks fit.

(2) The power under this paragraph to make or confirm the scheme includes power to make or confirm it so far as relating to part of the proposals contained in it (either without modification or subject to such modifications as the Minister thinks fit) while deferring consideration of the remaining part ; and where the Minister makes or confirms part of the scheme, that part and the remaining part are each to be deemed for the purposes of this Act to be a separate scheme.

(3) Where the Minister proposes to exercise the power to make or confirm the scheme subject to modifications, and the modifications will in his opinion make a substantial change in the scheme,—

    (a) he shall notify any person who appears to him to be likely to be affected by the proposed modifications ;

    (b) he shall give that person an opportunity of making representation to him with respect to the modifications within such reasonable period as he may specify ; and

    (c) before the Minister exercises the power, the Minister or, in the case of a scheme proposed to be made by the Minister, the Minister and the Secretary of State acting jointly shall consider any representations made to the Minister with respect to the proposed modifications within that period.

16. In this Part of this Schedule " proposed scheme " includes a scheme made by a local highway authority and submitted to the Minister.

Part III

General

17. If, on or after publishing a notice required by Part I or Part II of this Schedule to be published in connection with the making or confirmation of an order or scheme, it appears to the Minister or a local highway authority desirable to do so, he or they shall take such steps, in addition to those required by the said Part I or Part II to be taken, as will in his or their opinion secure that additional publicity is given in the area affected by the order or scheme to the proposals contained in it.

18.—(1) Any person who objects to the making or confirmation of an order or scheme pursuant to this Schedule shall include in the notice of objection a statement of the grounds of objection.

(2) If any notice of objection to the making or confirmation of an order or scheme pursuant to this Schedule does not state the grounds of objection the Minister or, in the case of an order or scheme proposed to be made by the Minister, the Minister and the Secretary of State acting jointly may disregard the objection.

19.—(1) Where objections to the making or confirmation of an order or scheme pursuant to this Schedule are to be the subject of a local inquiry, the Minister or, in the case of an order or scheme proposed to be made by the Minister, the Minister and the Secretary of State acting jointly may, by notice served on the persons making such objections or by the notice announcing the holding of the inquiry, direct that any person who intends at the inquiry to submit—

(a) that any highway or proposed highway to which the order or scheme in question relates should follow an alternative route, or

(b) that, instead of improving, diverting or altering a highway in accordance with the order in question, a new highway should be constructed on a particular route,

shall send to the Minister within such period as may be specified in the notice, being a period not less than 14 days and ending not less than 14 days before the date fixed for the holding of the inquiry, sufficient information about the alternative route or the route of the new highway, as the case may be, to enable it to be identified.

(2) Where the Minister or the Minister and the Secretary of State acting jointly have given a direction under sub-paragraph (1) above in relation to an inquiry, the person holding the inquiry and the Minister or, as the case may be, those Ministers may disregard so much of any objection as consists of a submission to which the direction applies unless the person making the objection has complied with the direction.

20. Proceedings required by this Schedule to be taken for the purposes of an order relating to a trunk road under section 14 of this Act or for the purposes of an order relating to a special road under section 18 of this Act may be taken concurrently (so far as

practicable) with proceedings required by this Schedule to be taken for the purposes of an order under section 10 of this Act or, as the case may be, for the purposes of a scheme under section 16 of this Act, relating to that road.

21. Where—

   (a) proceedings required to be taken for the purposes of an order relating to a trunk road under section 14 of this Act are taken after the making by the Minister of an order relating to that road under section 10 of this Act, or

   (b) proceedings required to be taken for the purposes of an order relating to a special road under section 18 of this Act are taken after the making or confirmation by the Minister of a scheme relating to that road under section 16 of this Act,

the Minister or, in the case of an order proposed to be made by the Minister, the Minister and the Secretary of State acting jointly may disregard any objection to the order under section 14 or 18 which in his or their opinion amounts in substance to an objection to the order under section 10 or, as the case may be, to the scheme under section 16.

SCHEDULE 2

VALIDITY AND DATE OF OPERATION OF CERTAIN SCHEMES AND ORDERS

1.—(1) Subject to sub-paragraph (2) below, as soon as may be after a scheme or order to which this Schedule applies has been made or confirmed by the Minister, he shall publish in the London Gazette, and in such other manner as he thinks best adapted for informing persons affected, a notice stating that the scheme or order has been made or confirmed, and naming a place where a copy of it may be inspected free of charge at all reasonable hours.

(2) There is no requirement under sub-paragraph (1) above to publish a notice in the London Gazette of the making or confirmation of an order under section 124 of this Act; and if an order under that section is one that has been confirmed by a local highway authority the notice relating to it required to be published under sub-paragraph (1) above (otherwise than in the London Gazette) shall be published by that authority.

2. If a person aggrieved by a scheme or order to which this Schedule applies desires to question the validity of it, or of any provision contained in it, on the ground that it is not within the powers of this Act or on the ground that any requirement of this Act or of regulations made under this Act has not been complied with in relation to the scheme or order, he may, within 6 weeks from the date on which the notice required by paragraph 1 above is first published, make an application for the purpose to the High Court.

3. On any such application, the Court—

    (*a*) may by interim order suspend the operation of the scheme or order, or of any provision contained in it, either generally or in so far as it affects any property of the applicant, until the final determination of the proceedings ; and

    (*b*) if satisfied that the scheme or order, or any provision contained in it, is not within the powers of this Act or that the interests of the applicant have been substantially prejudiced by a failure to comply with any such requirement as aforesaid, may quash the scheme or order or any provision contained in it, either generally or in so far as it affects any property of the applicant.

4. Subject to paragraph 3 above, a scheme or order to which this Schedule applies shall not, either before or after it has been made or confirmed, be questioned in any legal proceedings whatever, and shall become operative on the date on which the notice required by paragraph 1 above is first published, or on such later date, if any, as may be specified in the scheme or order.

5. In relation to any scheme or order to which this Schedule applies that is subject to special parliamentary procedure, the foregoing provisions of this Schedule have effect subject to the following modifications :—

    (*a*) if the scheme or order is confirmed by Act of Parliament under section 6 of the Statutory Orders (Special Procedure) Act 1945, paragraphs 2 to 4 do not apply ; and

    (*b*) in any other case, paragraph 2 has effect as if, for the reference in it to the date on which the notice required by paragraph 1 is first published, there were substituted a reference to the date on which the scheme or order becomes operative under the said Act of 1945, and paragraph 4 has effect as if the words from " and shall become operative " to the end of the paragraph were omitted.

1945 c. 18
(9 & 10 Geo. 6).

Section 11.

SCHEDULE 3

Provisions of this Act Referred to in Section 11

Part I

Provisions conferring functions exercisable in relation to trunk roads by the Minister exclusively

1. *Provisions contained in Part IV.* Section 38(1) and section 57(2).

2. *Provisions contained in Part V.* Section 73.

3. *Provisions contained in Part IX.* Section 133, section 171(1) and sections 176 and 178.

4. *Provisions contained in Part XII.* Sections 241 and 271.

PART II

Provisions conferring functions exercisable in relation to trunk roads by the Minister as well as by other authorities

5. *Provisions contained in Part IX.* Sections 151 and 152, section 154(1), 154(4) so far as relating to a notice under 154(1), and sections 163 and 164.

PART III

Provisions conferring functions exercisable in relation to trunk roads by the Minister and by other authorities with the consent of the Minister

6. *Provisions contained in Part V.* Section 66(2) and section 96(4).

7. *Provisions contained in Part IX.* Section 185.

SCHEDULE 4

Section 17.

CLASSES OF TRAFFIC FOR PURPOSES OF SPECIAL ROADS

CLASS I:

Heavy and light locomotives, motor tractors, heavy motor cars, motor cars and motor cycles whereof the cylinder capacity of the engine is not less than 50 cubic centimetres, and trailers drawn thereby, which comply with general regulations as to construction and use made, or having effect as if made, under section 40 of the Road Traffic Act 1972 and in the case of which the following conditions are satisfied :— 1972 c. 20.

(i) that the whole weight of the vehicle is transmitted to the road surface by means of wheels ;

(ii) that all wheels of the vehicle are equipped with pneumatic tyres ;

(iii) that the vehicle is not controlled by a pedestrian ;

(iv) that the vehicle is not a vehicle chargeable with duty under paragraph 2 of Part I of Schedule 3 to the Vehicles (Excise) Act 1971 ; and 1971 c. 10.

(v) in the case of a motor vehicle, that it is so constructed as to be capable of attaining a speed of 25 miles per hour on the level under its own power, when unladen and not drawing a trailer.

CLASS II:

Motor vehicles and trailers the use of which for or in connection with the conveyance of abnormal indivisible loads is authorised by order made, or having effect as if made, by the Minister under section 42(1) of the Road Traffic Act 1972.

Motor vehicles and trailers constructed for naval, military, air force or other defence purposes, the use of which is authorised by

L 2

SCH. 4

order made, or having effect as if made, by the Minister under section 42(1) of the Road Traffic Act 1972.

S.I. 1973/1101.

Motor vehicles and trailers, to which any of the following Articles of the Motor Vehicles (Authorisation of Special Types) General Order 1973 namely, Article 16 (which relates to vehicles for moving excavated material), Article 17 (which relates inter alia to vehicles constructed for use outside the United Kingdom) and Article 21 (which relates to engineering plant) relate and which are authorised to be used by any of those Articles of the said order or by any other order under section 42(1) of the Road Traffic Act 1972, the said motor vehicles being vehicles in respect of which the following condition is satisfied, that is to say, that the vehicle is so constructed as to be capable of attaining a speed of 25 miles per hour on the level under its own power, when unladen and not drawing a trailer.

CLASS III:

Motor vehicles controlled by pedestrians.

CLASS IV:

All motor vehicles (other than invalid carriages and motor cycles whereof the cylinder capacity of the engine is less than 50 cubic centimetres) not comprised in Class I, Class II or Class III.

CLASS V:

Vehicles drawn by animals.

CLASS VI:

Vehicles (other than pedal cycles, perambulators, push-chairs and other forms of baby carriages) drawn or propelled by pedestrains.

CLASS VII:

Pedal cycles.

CLASS VIII:

Animals ridden, led or driven.

CLASS IX:

Pedestrians, perambulators, push-chairs and other forms of baby carriages and dogs held on a lead.

CLASS X:

Motor cycles whereof the cylinder capacity of the engine is less than 50 cubic centimetres.

CLASS XI:

Invalid carriages.

1972 c. 20.

S.I. 1973/1101.

In this Schedule any expression defined for the purposes of the Road Traffic Act 1972 has the same meaning as in that Act and the expression "abnormal indivisible load" has the same meaning as in the Motor Vehicles (Authorisation of Special Types) General Order 1973.

SCHEDULE 5

MODIFICATIONS OF CERTAIN PROVISIONS OF THE TOWN AND COUNTRY
PLANNING ACT 1971 AS APPLIED BY SECTION 21

PART I

MODIFICATIONS IN RELATION TO LAND REFERRED TO IN
PARAGRAPH (*a*) OR (*b*) OF SECTION 21(2)

1. For references in sections 230, 231, 237(2) and (3), 238 and 240
of the Town and Country Planning Act 1971 (referred to in this 1971 c. 78.
Schedule as "the 1971 Act") to the acquiring or appropriating
authority substitute references to the special road authority.

2. In subsection (1) of the said section 230 omit the words from
" if satisfied " to " appropriated " and after that subsection insert the
following:—

> " (1A) A notice under this section shall not be served by the
> special road authority unless they are satisfied that the extinguish-
> ment of the statutory undertakers' right or, as the case may
> be, the removal of their apparatus, is necessary for the purpose
> of carrying out any works in pursuance of the scheme or order
> or, as the case may be, for the purpose of ensuring that the
> highway can be safely used as a special road.".

3. The references in subsection (4) of the said section 230 and in
subsection (2) of the said section 231 to a local authority or statutory
undertakers include references to the special road authority, when a
local highway authority.

4. In paragraph (*b*) of section 232(1) of the 1971 Act for the
words " development to be carried out on the land is " substitute
" the works to be executed by the special road authority or, as
the case may be, that the effect of the conversion of the highway
into a special road, will be ".

5. For subsection (2) of the said section 232 substitute the
following:—

> " (2) No notice under this section shall be served later than
> 21 days after the date of the commencement of the works or
> as the case may be, the date of the coming into operation of
> the order by means of which the highway is appropriated by or
> transferred to the special road authority.".

6. For references in subsections (3) and (6) of the said section
232 to the authority or the acquiring or appropriating authority
substitute references to the special road authority.

PART II

MODIFICATIONS IN RELATION TO LAND REFERRED TO IN
PARAGRAPH (*c*) OF SECTION 21(2)

1. For references in sections 230, 231, 237(2) and (3), 238 and 240
of the 1971 Act to the acquiring or appropriating authority substitute 1971 c. 78.

SCH. 5   references to the Minister, the special road authority or the local highway authority, as the case may be, by whom the order in question was made.

2. In subsection (1) of the said section 230 omit the words from " if satisfied " to " appropriated " and after that subsection insert the following: —

" (1A) A notice under this section shall not be served by the Minister, the special road authority or the local highway authority, as the case may be, unless he or they is or are satisfied that the extinguishment of the statutory undertakers' right, or as the case may be, the removal of their apparatus, is made necessary by the works in connection with which the stopping up or diversion of the highway is or was authorised.".

3. The references in subsection (4) of the said section 230 and in subsection (2) of the said section 231 to a local authority or statutory undertakers include references to a local highway authority.

4. For subsections (1) and (2) of section 232 of the 1971 Act substitute the following: —

" (1) Subject to the provisions of this section, where the stopping up or diversion of a highway is or was authorised by an order under section 14 or section 18 of the Highways Act 1980, and—

(*a*) there is on, under or over the land over which that highway subsists or subsisted any apparatus vested in or belonging to statutory undertakers ; and

(*b*) the undertakers claim that the works in connection with which the stopping up or diversion of the highway is or was authorised are such as to require, on technical or other grounds connected with the carrying on of their undertaking, the removal or re-siting of their apparatus,

the undertakers may serve on the Minister, the special road authority or the local highway authority, as the case may be, by whom the order was made a notice claiming the right to enter on the land and carry out such works for the removal or re-siting of the apparatus or any part of it as may be specified in the notice.

(2) No notice under this section shall be served later than twenty-one days after the later of the following dates, that is to say, the date of the coming into operation of the order in question and the date of the commencement of the works in connection with which the stopping up or diversion of the highway is or was authorised.".

5. For references in subsections (3) and (6) of the said section 232 to the authority or to the acquiring or appropriating authority substitute references to the Minister, the special road authority or the local highway authority as the case may be, by whom the order in question was made.

SCHEDULE 6

PROVISIONS AS TO MAKING, CONFIRMATION, VALIDITY AND DATE OF OPERATION OF CERTAIN ORDERS RELATING TO FOOTPATHS AND BRIDLEWAYS

PART I

PROCEDURE FOR MAKING AND CONFIRMING CERTAIN ORDERS RELATING TO FOOTPATHS AND BRIDLEWAYS

1.—(1) Before a public path creation order, a public path extinguishment order or a public path diversion order is submitted to the Secretary of State for confirmation or confirmed as an unopposed order, the authority by whom the order was made shall give notice in the prescribed form—

(*a*) stating the general effect of the order and that it has been made and is about to be submitted for confirmation or to be confirmed as an unopposed order,

(*b*) naming a place in the area in which the land to which the order relates is situated where a copy of the order and of the map referred to therein may be inspected free of charge at all reasonable hours, and

(*c*) specifying the time (which shall not be less than 28 days from the date of the first publication of the notice) within which, and the manner in which, representations or objections with respect to the order may be made.

(2) Before the Secretary of State makes a public path creation order, a public path extinguishment order or a public path diversion order, he shall prepare a draft of the order and shall give notice—

(*a*) stating that he proposes to make the order and the general effect of it,

(*b*) naming a place in the area in which the land to which the draft order relates is situated where a copy of the draft order and of the map referred to in it may be inspected free of charge at all reasonable hours, and

(*c*) specifying the time (which shall not be less than 28 days from the date of the first publication of the notice) within which, and the manner in which, representations or objections with respect to the draft order may be made.

(3) The notices to be given under sub-paragraph (1) or (2) above shall be given—

(*a*) in the case of a public path creation order, by publication in the London Gazette and in at least one local newspaper circulating in the area in which the land to which the order relates is situated, and by serving a like notice on every owner, occupier and lessee (except tenants for a month or any period less than a month and statutory tenants within the meaning of the Rent (Agriculture) Act 1976 and the Rent Act 1977) of any of that land, so however that— 1976 c. 80 1977 c. 42.

(i) except in the case of an owner, occupier or lessee being a local authority or statutory undertakers, the

L 4

Secretary of State may in any particular case direct that it shall not be necessary to serve notice as aforesaid, but

(ii) if the Secretary of State so directs in the case of any land, then in addition to publication the notice shall be addressed to " the owners and any occupiers " of the land (describing it) and a copy or copies of it shall be affixed to some conspicuous object or objects on the land ;

(b) in the case of a public path extinguishment order or a public path diversion order, by publication and the service of notices as mentioned in head (a) of this sub-paragraph and also—

(i) by serving such a notice as is therein mentioned on every council, the council of every parish or community, and the parish meeting of every parish not having a separate parish council, being a council, parish or community whose area includes any of the land to which the order relates, and

(ii) by causing a copy of the notice to be displayed in a prominent position at the ends of so much of any footpath or bridleway as is to be stopped up or diverted by virtue of the order.

(4) Where under this paragraph a notice is required to be served on an owner of land and the land belongs to an ecclesiastical benefice, a like notice shall be served on the Church Commissioners.

2.—(1) If no representations or objections are duly made, or if any so made are withdrawn, then—

(a) the Secretary of State may, if he thinks fit, confirm or make the order, as the case may be, with or without modifications ;

(b) the authority by whom the order was made (where not the Secretary of State) may, instead of submitting the order to the Secretary of State, themselves confirm the order (but without any modification).

(2). If any representation or objection duly made is not withdrawn, the Secretary of State shall, before confirming or making the order, as the case may be, if the objection is made by a local authority cause a local inquiry to be held, and in any other case either—

(a) cause a local inquiry to be held, or

(b) afford to any person by whom any representation or objection has been duly made and not withdrawn an opportunity of being heard by a person appointed by him for the purpose,

and, after considering the report of the person appointed to hold the inquiry or to hear representations or objections, may, subject as provided below, confirm or make the order, as the case may be, with or without modifications.

In the case of a public path creation order or a public path diversion order, if objection is made by statutory undertakers on the ground that the order provides for the creation of a public right of way over land covered by works used for the purposes of their undertaking or the curtilage of such land, and the objection is not withdrawn, the order is subject to special parliamentary procedure.

(3) Notwithstanding anything in the foregoing provisions of this paragraph, the Secretary of State shall not confirm or make an order so as to affect land not affected by the order as submitted to him or the draft order prepared by him, as the case may be, except after—

(a) giving such notice as appears to him requisite of his proposal so to modify the order, specifying the time (which shall not be less than 28 days from the date of the first publication of the notice) within which, and the manner in which, representations or objections with respect to the proposal may be made,

(b) holding a local inquiry or affording to any person by whom any representation or objection has been duly made and not withdrawn an opportunity of being heard by a person appointed by him for the purpose, and

(c) considering the report of the person appointed to hold the inquiry or to hear representations or objections, as the case may be,

and, in the case of a public path creation order or a public path diversion order, if objection is made by statutory undertakers on the ground that the order as modified would provide for the creation of a public right of way over land covered by works used for the purposes of their undertaking or the curtilage of such land, and the objection is not withdrawn, the order is subject to special parliamentary procedure.

3.—(1) The Secretary of State may, subject to the provisions of this Part of this Schedule, by regulations make such provision as to the procedure on the making, submission and confirmation of orders to which this Schedule applies as appears to him to be expedient.

(2) Provision may be made by regulations of the Secretary of State for enabling proceedings preliminary to the confirmation of a public path extinguishment order to be taken concurrently with proceedings preliminary to the confirmation of a public path creation order or a public path diversion order.

(3) In this Part of this Schedule—

(a) " local authority " means any council and any other authority who are a local authority within the meaning of the Local 1875 c. 83. Loans Act 1875 and includes any drainage authority and any joint board or joint committee if all the constituent authorities are such local authorities as aforesaid :

(b) " prescribed " means prescribed by regulations made by the Secretary of State ;

and for the purposes of this Schedule the Civil Aviation Authority and the Post Office are to be deemed to be statutory undertakers and their undertakings statutory undertakings.

PART II

VALIDITY AND DATE OF OPERATION OF CERTAIN ORDERS
RELATING TO FOOTPATHS AND BRIDLEWAYS

4. As soon as may be after an order to which this Schedule
applies has been confirmed or made by the Secretary of State or
confirmed as an unopposed order, the authority by whom the order
was made or, in the case of an order made by the Secretary of
State, the Secretary of State, shall publish, in the manner required
in relation to the class of order in question by paragraph 1(3) above,
a notice in the prescribed form describing the general effect of the
order, stating that it has been confirmed or made, and naming a
place where a copy of it as confirmed or made may be inspected
free of charge at all reasonable hours, and—

  (*a*) where under paragraph 1(3) above notice was required to be
       served, shall serve a like notice and a copy of the order
       as confirmed or made on any persons on whom notices
       were required to be served under the said paragraph 1(3)
       or under paragraph 1(4) above ; and

  (*b*) where under paragraph 1(3) above a notice was required
       to be displayed, shall cause a like notice to be displayed in
       the like manner as the notice required to be displayed under
       the said paragraph 1(3) ;

but no such notice or copy need be served on a person unless he
has sent to the authority or the Secretary of State (according as the
notice or copy would require to be served by an authority or by the
Secretary of State) a request in that behalf specifying an address
for service.

5. Schedule 2 to this Act (except paragraph 1 thereof) applies
in relation to an order to which this Schedule applies as it applies
in relation to a scheme or order to which that Schedule applies, but
with the following modifications : —

  (*a*) for references to a scheme or order to which that Schedule
       applies substitute references to an order to which this
       Schedule applies ;

  (*b*) for the references in paragraphs 2, 4 and 5 thereof to the
       date on which the notice required by paragraph 1 thereof
       is first published substitute references to the date on which
       the notice required by paragraph 4 above is first published ;
       and

  (*c*) paragraph 4 of that Schedule has effect as if the words " or
       on such later date, if any, as may be specified in the
       scheme or order " were omitted.

6. In this Part of this Schedule " prescribed " means prescribed
by regulations made by the Secretary of State.

SCHEDULE 7

MAINTENANCE OF CERTAIN HIGHWAYS BY DISTRICT COUNCILS

PART I

REGULATIONS GOVERNING EXERCISE OF POWERS

1. Before exercising the relevant powers in relation to any highway in respect of which those powers are exercisable, the council of a district shall give notice of their intention to do so to the county council who are the local highway authority, specifying the highway or highways concerned.

In this Schedule " the relevant powers " means the powers of a district council under sections 42, 50(2) and 230(7) of this Act.

2. If the county council are of the opinion that any highway specified in a notice under paragraph 1 above does not fall within the relevant powers, they may, at any time within the period of 6 weeks beginning with the date on which they receive the notice, serve a counter-notice on the district council disputing the right of the district council to exercise in relation to the highway concerned any of the relevant powers; and if the dispute is not resolved by the county council and the district council within 6 weeks after the receipt of the counter-notice by the district council the dispute shall be referred to the Minister for his decision.

3.—(1) The relevant powers with respect to a highway specified in a notice under paragraph 1 above become exercisable—

   (a) where no counter-notice is served in respect of the highway under paragraph 2 above, at the expiry of the period of 6 weeks first specified in that paragraph; and

   (b) where such a counter-notice is served, when the dispute is resolved in favour of the district council by the councils concerned or, as the case may be, when the Minister's decision on the dispute in favour of the district council is received by the district council;

but if a dispute resulting from the service of a counter-notice under paragraph 2 above is resolved or decided by the Minister against the district council, the relevant powers are not exercisable by the district council in respect of the highway concerned and no further notice under paragraph 1 above may be given by the district council in respect of that highway unless its status is changed or there is such a change in the character of the road as to give reasonable ground for believing that it has become an urban road.

(2) In the event that a highway in respect of which the relevant powers have become exercisable in accordance with sub-paragraph (1) above or paragraph 4(2) below becomes a trunk road or classified road, the relevant powers thereupon cease with respect to that highway.

4.—(1) Without prejudice to paragraph 3(2) above, the relevant powers cease to be exercisable with respect to any highway—

   (a) on such day as may be agreed between the district council and the county council who are the local highway authority for the highway; or (*b*) 6 months after the receipt by that county council of a notice from the district council stating the intention of the district council to cease to exercise those powers ;

and any such agreement or notice may relate either to such highway or highways as may be specified in the agreement or notice or to all the highways in respect of which the relevant powers are exercisable at the time the agreement is made, or as the case may be, the notice is served.

(2) Where the relevant powers have ceased to be exercisable with respect to a highway by virtue of an agreement or notice under sub-paragraph (1) above, those powers shall not, except with the consent of the county council who are the highway authority for that highway, again become exercisable with respect to that highway at any time within the period of 10 years beginning with the day on which the powers cease to be so exercisable ; but if, at any time after the expiry of that period or, with the consent of the county council, before the expiry, the district council intend again to exercise those powers with respect to that highway, paragraphs 2 and 3(1) above do not apply and those powers become exercisable at the expiry of the period of 6 weeks beginning with the date on which the county council who are the highway authority receive notice of the district council's intention under paragraph 1 above.

(3) If, by virtue of paragraph 3(2) or sub-paragraph (1) above, the relevant powers cease to be exercisable with respect to any highway, the cessation does not affect the continued existence, on and after the day on which the powers cease to be so exercisable, of any rights or liabilities of the district council in respect of the highway which are in existence immediately before that day.

5.—(1) Every district council shall prepare and keep up to date a list of the highways in respect of which the relevant powers are for the time being exercisable by them, and the council shall make the list available for public inspection free of charge at all reasonable hours at the offices of the council.

(2) A copy of any list of highways prepared by a district council under sub-paragraph (1) above and of all amendments for the time being made thereto shall be furnished by the district council to the county council who are the highway authority for the highways concerned.

(3) Except in so far as the relevant powers with respect to a highway cease to be exercisable by a district council in accordance with paragraph 3(2) or paragraph 4(1) above, an entry in the list kept under this paragraph is conclusive evidence that the highway specified in the entry is one in respect of which the relevant powers are exercisable by the district council.

6. A statement by or on behalf of the Minister that a highway is or is not a classified road is conclusive for the purposes of sections 42 and 230(7) of this Act and of this Schedule.

7. A district council shall indemnify a county council in respect of any claim made against the county council, as highway authority,—

    (*a*) in respect of a failure to maintain a highway at a time when the relevant powers were exercisable by the district council with respect to the highway, or

    (*b*) arising out of any works of maintenance on a highway carried out by the district council in exercise of those powers.

PART II

REIMBURSEMENT BY HIGHWAY AUTHORITIES OF CERTAIN EXPENSES OF DISTRICT COUNCILS

8. The provisions of this Part of this Schedule apply where a district council are exercising the power under section 42 of this Act in relation to any highways within their district, and references in the following provisions of this Part of this Schedule to a district council and to their maintenance power are to be construed accordingly.

9. On or before 15th December in each year the district council shall submit to the county council for their approval a detailed estimate of the cost for the ensuing financial year of the maintenance of every highway in respect of which their maintenance power is exercisable, and on any such estimate being approved by the county council, either with or without modifications, the amount to be paid by the county council under section 42(3) of this Act is, subject to paragraph 10 below, the amount of that estimate, or of that estimate as amended by any supplementary estimate submitted to and approved by the county council, or such less sum as may have been actually expended by the district council on the highways in question during that financial year.

10. The county council are not liable to make a payment towards the cost of the maintenance of any highway until they are satisfied, by a report of such one of their officers or such other person as they may appoint for the purpose, that the works of maintenance are being or have been properly executed.

11. The district council may at any time, and from time to time, submit to the county council for their approval a detailed supplementary estimate.

12. A county council shall not unreasonably withhold approval of an estimate submitted to them under this Part of this Schedule, and any question whether their approval has been unreasonably withheld, or whether any works of maintenance are being or have been properly executed, or as to the liability of a county council to make a payment under section 42(3) of this Act, shall be determined by the Minister.

SCHEDULE 8

CONSENTS REQUIRED FOR EXECUTION OF CERTAIN WORKS IN STREETS

1. In this Schedule " the authority " means the highway authority or local authority (within the meaning of section 67 or section 287 of this Act) having power to carry out the works to which this Schedule applies.

2. The authority shall not carry out any works to which this Schedule applies in any such situation or position as is described in the first column of the following Table except with the consent of the person described in relation thereto in the second column of that Table.

TABLE

In any street which is a highway for which there is a highway authority other than the authority carrying out the works.	The highway authority.
In any street belonging to and repairable by any railway, dock, harbour, canal, inland navigation or passenger road transport undertakers and forming the approach to any station, dock, wharf or depot of those undertakers.	The undertakers.
On any bridge not vested in the authority carrying out the works or on the approaches to any such bridge.	The authority or other person in whom the bridge is vested.
On any bridge carrying a street over any railway, canal or inland navigation, or on the approaches to any such bridge, or under any bridge carrying a railway, canal or inland navigation over a street.	The railway, canal or inland navigation undertakers concerned.
In the case of works under section 67 of this Act, in a position obstructing or interfering with any existing access to any land or premises abutting upon a street.	The owner and the occupier of the land or premises.

3. A consent required by this Schedule in respect of any works shall not unreasonably be withheld but may be given subject to any reasonable conditions, including a condition that the authority shall remove the works either at any time or at or after the expiration of a period if reasonably required so to do by the person giving the consent.

4. Where the consent of the Minister is required under this Schedule, any dispute between the Minister whose consent is required and the authority as to whether the Minister's consent is unreasonably withheld or is given subject to reasonable conditions,

or whether the removal of anything to the provision of which the consent relates in accordance with any condition of the consent is reasonably required shall be referred to and determined by an arbitrator to be appointed in default of agreement by the President of the Institution of Civil Engineers.

SCHEDULE 9

IMPROVEMENT LINES AND BUILDING LINES

1. Before a line is prescribed by the Minister he shall consult the councils of the county and district, or in Greater London the local authority, in whose area is situated the street or highway in relation to which the line is to be prescribed.

2. Before a line is prescribed by a county council, as highway authority, they shall consult the council of the district in which is situated the street or highway in relation to which the line is to be prescribed.

3. Before a line is prescribed by the Greater London Council, they shall consult the council of the London borough in which is situated the street or highway in relation to which the line is to be prescribed or, if that street or highway is in the City, they shall consult the Common Council.

4. A line which a highway authority propose to prescribe shall be shown on a plan to be signed, if the authority are a council, by the proper officer of the council.

5. The plan shall be deposited at the offices of the authority or, if the Minister is the authority, at such place as he may direct, and may be inspected by any person free of charge at all reasonable hours during a period of one month from the day on which it is so deposited.

6. As soon as the plan has been so deposited the authority shall give notice of the proposal to prescribe the line and of the times and place at which the plan may be inspected, and of the effect of section 73 of this Act or, as the case may require, section 74 of this Act and of paragraph 7 below to every owner, lessee and occupier of land affected.

7. The authority shall consider any objection to the proposed line made within 6 weeks from the date on which the notices aforesaid were given and may then prescribe the line.

8. Not later than 6 weeks after the date on which the authority prescribe the line they shall prepare a plan, duly sealed and authenticated, on which the line shall be shown and shall give notice of the prescribing of the line and of the time and place at which the said plan may be inspected to every owner, lessee and occupier of land affected.

9. If the authority revoke the line, they shall—

   (*a*) give notice of the revocation to every owner, lessee or occupier of land affected and to the council keeping the local land charges register for the area within which the land to which the line relates is situated ; and

(b) indicate on the plan prepared in accordance with paragraph 8 above the extent to which the line has been revoked.

10. Where a local highway authority prescribe a line or revoke a line or any part thereof they shall do so by resolution.

SCHEDULE 10

PROCEDURE FOR DETERMINATION BY HIGHWAY AUTHORITY OF CERTAIN QUESTIONS ARISING IN CONNECTION WITH PROVISION OF CATTLE-GRID OR BY-PASS

1.—(1) Before determining, under section 82 or 86 of this Act, the question—

(a) whether it is expedient to place any part of a cattle-grid in, or provide a by-pass on, any such land not forming part of a highway and not belonging to the highway authority therefor as is mentioned in section 82(4), or

(b) whether it is expedient to provide a by-pass along any part of a highway, or

(c) whether the purpose for which a right to install gates is exercisable will be adequately achieved by the provision of a cattle-grid,

a highway authority shall comply with the requirements specified in sub-paragraph (2) below.

(2) The requirements referred to in sub-paragraph (1) above are as follows, namely, that the authority shall—

(a) publish in 2 successive weeks in one or more local newspapers circulating in the area where the cattle-grid is to be, or has been, provided a notice—

(i) stating generally the question for determination,

(ii) naming a place within the said area where a copy may be inspected free of charge at all reasonable hours of such plans or other descriptive matter as appear to the highway authority to be requisite for enabling the nature of the question to be understood, and

(iii) specifying the time (which shall not be less than 28 days from the date of the first publication of the notice) within which and the manner in which representations may be made to the highway authority, and

(b) display a like notice in a prominent position at the place where the cattle-grid is to be or has been provided.

2. If no representation is duly made under paragraph 1 above, or if every representation so made is withdrawn, the highway authority may proceed to determine the question.

3.—(1) Where a representation is duly made as aforesaid and not withdrawn, the following provisions have effect.

(2) Where the highway authority is not the Minister, the authority shall forward the representation to the Minister, together with their observations thereon and their proposals, in the light of the representations, for determining the question.

(3) The Minister shall consider any representations received by him (and, where the highway authority is not the Minister, the authority's observations and proposals forwarded to him as aforesaid) and shall either cause a local inquiry to be held or afford to any person by whom a representation has been duly made and not withdrawn and, where the highway authority is not the Minister, to that authority, an opportunity of appearing before and being heard by a person appointed by the Minister for the purpose.

(4) After the Minister has considered the report of the person who held the inquiry under sub-paragraph (3) above, or the person appointed under that sub-paragraph, as the case may be,—

(a) the Minister may, where he is the highway authority, proceed to determine the question;

(b) where he is not the highway authority, the authority may determine the question in the affirmative if the Minister consents, but not otherwise, and subject to compliance with any conditions subject to which his consent is given.

(5) Notwithstanding anything in sub-paragraph (3) above, except where a representation is made by a highway authority other than the Minister, the Minister may, if satisfied that in the special circumstances of the case the holding of a local inquiry or the affording to the person making such representation as aforesaid of an opportunity to be heard by a person appointed by the Minister is unnecessary, proceed without compliance in this respect with the provisions of the said sub-paragraph (3).

(6) As soon as may be after the determination of the question, a notice of the determination shall be sent by the Minister to any person by whom a representation has been made under the foregoing provisions of this Schedule.

4. For the purpose of displaying a notice as required by paragraph 1 above, a highway authority may, on the highway or on adjoining land (whether or not belonging to the authority), erect and maintain posts or boards or affix a notice to any building or structure; but the powers conferred by this paragraph shall not be exercised on land off the highway which is occupied, except with the consent of the occupier.

5. In relation to the exercise by a council of functions of the Minister as highway authority delegated to the council under section 89 of this Act, the foregoing provisions of this Schedule apply as if the council, and not the Minister, were the highway authority.

SCHEDULE 11

PROVISIONS AS TO ORDERS UNDER SECTION 93 OF THIS ACT

Limitations on matters to be dealt with by orders

1. The Minister shall not by an order under section 93 of this Act (hereafter in this Schedule referred to as " an order ") direct that a

SCH. 11   swing bridge crossing a canal is to be operated otherwise than by the owners of the canal unless he is satisfied, after considering any representations made to him by the owners of the canal, that the facilities for traffic on the canal will not be prejudiced thereby.

2. The Minister shall not by an order with respect to a swing bridge modify any statutory provisions relating to precedence of traffic.

3. The Minister shall not by an order with respect to a bridge crossing a railway or a canal modify any statutory provisions relating to the headway of the bridge or the width of the canal without the consent of the owners of the railway or canal.

4. An order made with respect to—

(a) a bridge owned by railway undertakers which carries a highway over a railway of the undertakers, or carries both a highway and such a railway, or

(b) a bridge owned by dock undertakers or harbour undertakers, or

(c) a bridge, other than one falling within sub-paragraph (a) above, owned by the British Waterways Board and forming part of so much of the undertaking of that Board as corresponds to the undertaking of the Weaver Navigation Trustees prior to the vesting of that undertaking in the British Transport Commission (the predecessors of the British Waterways Board) under the Transport Act 1947,

1947 c. 49.

shall not, without the consent of the owners of the bridge, either—

(i) require works for the reconstruction or improvement of the bridge to be carried out otherwise than by the owners, or

(ii) direct the bridge to be maintained otherwise than by the owners, or

(iii) transfer the property in the bridge to a highway authority, or

(iv) in the case of a swing bridge, direct the bridge to be operated otherwise than by the owners.

5. Nothing in an order made with respect to—

(a) a bridge owned by railway undertakers and crossing a railway of the undertakers, or

(b) a bridge owned by canal undertakers and crossing a canal of the undertakers, or

(c) a bridge owned by dock undertakers, or by harbour undertakers, crossing a railway, lock, passage or other work of the undertakers,

shall, without the consent of the owners of the bridge, require the bridge to be altered or reconstructed in such a manner as to necessitate an alteration in the level, or reduction in the width, of the railway, canal, lock, passage or work, or to reduce the headway of the bridge as existing at the date of the order.

6. An order requiring the reconstruction of a bridge crossing a canal, or of the approaches to such a bridge, shall, unless the owners of the bridge agree to the contrary, direct the bridge, the highway carried by the bridge, and the approaches to the bridge to be maintained by a highway authority.

Procedure for making orders

7.—(1) An order to which this paragraph applies shall be prepared in draft and made by the Minister in accordance with this paragraph and paragraphs 8 to 10 below.

(2) The order shall describe by reference to a map the land on which the works to which the order relates are proposed to be executed or constructed.

(3) Subject as aforesaid, the form of the order shall be such as the Minister may determine.

(4) This paragraph applies to an order which requires or authorises the owners of a bridge or a highway authority to execute or construct any works.

8. Before making an order to which paragraph 7 above applies the Minister shall in 2 successive weeks publish in one or more local newspapers circulating in the area in which the proposed works are to be executed or constructed a notice—

(a) stating the general effect of the proposed order,

(b) naming a place in the said area where a copy of the draft order, the map referred to in it, and plans and sections of the proposed works, may be inspected free of charge at all reasonable hours, and

(c) specifying the time (which shall not be less than 21 days from the date of the first publication of the notice) within which and the manner in which objections to the draft order may be made,

and shall serve on all statutory undertakers appearing to him to be affected by the proposed works a notice stating the general effect of the order and that it is proposed to be made, and specifying the time (which shall not be less than 21 days from the date of service of the notice) within which and the manner in which objections to the draft order may be made.

9.—(1) If no objection is duly made by any person who will be affected by the proposed works, or if all objections so made are withdrawn, the Minister, on being satisfied that the proper notices have been published and served, may, if he thinks fit, make the order with or without modifications.

(2) If an objection duly made as aforesaid is not withdrawn, the Minister shall, before making the order, either cause a local inquiry to be held or afford to any person by whom any objection has been duly made as aforesaid and not withdrawn an opportunity of appearing before and being heard by a person appointed by the Minister for the purpose and, after considering the objection and

the report of the person who held the inquiry or the person appointed as aforesaid, may make the order either with or without modifications.

(3) If any person by whom an objection has been made avails himself of the opportunity of being heard, the Minister shall afford to the local highway authority, or to the owners of a bridge, by whom the proposed works are to be executed or constructed, and to any other person to whom it appears to him expedient to afford it, an opportunity of being heard on the same occasion.

(4) Notwithstanding anything in sub-paragraphs (2) and (3) above, the Minister may require any person who has made an objection to state in writing the grounds of it.

10. As soon as may be after the order has been made the Minister shall publish in one or more local newspapers circulating in the area in which the proposed works are to be executed or constructed a notice describing the proposed works, stating that the order has been made and naming the place where a copy of the order and of the map referred to therein, and a copy of plans and sections of the proposed works, may be inspected free of charge at all reasonable hours, and shall serve a like notice and a copy of the order on any statutory undertakers on whom a notice was required to be served under paragraph 8 above.

11. Subject to paragraphs 7 to 10 above, the Minister of Transport may make regulations for prescribing the procedure to be followed in connection with the making of orders.

Power to postpone commencement of orders

12. The Minister may postpone the date of the coming into operation of an order in a case where it appears to him that, owing to the number or nature of the orders and applications affecting the same highway authority or affecting bridges belonging to the same owners, the making of an order which would be immediately operative would work hardship to that authority or to those owners.

Provisions as to public utility undertakers

13.—(1) Before making an order for the reconstruction or improvement of a bridge, the Minister shall take into consideration the desirability of the provision of special facilities or accommodation for carrying across the bridge the mains, pipes, cables or wires of public utility undertakers; but in a case where the provision of facilities or accommodation greater than those available in the bridge before reconstruction or improvement would increase the cost of the reconstruction or improvement, he shall have regard to the amount of any contribution towards the cost of the reconstruction or improvement which any public utility undertakers may be willing to make.

(2) In this paragraph, and in paragraph 14 below, " public utility undertakers " includes persons authorised by any enactment to carry on an undertaking for the operation of a light railway, a tramway, or trolley vehicles (that is to say, mechanically propelled vehicles adapted for use upon highways without rails and moved by power transmitted thereto from some external source).

14.—(1) Where an order provides for the transfer to a highway authority—

(a) of the property in a bridge, or in the highway carried by a bridge, or in the approaches to a bridge, or

(b) of the responsibility for the maintenance of a bridge, or of any such highway or approaches, or

(c) of rights or obligations attaching to a bridge or to any such highway or approaches,

any statutory provisions in force in relation thereto for the protection or benefit of any public utility undertakers shall, except so far as may be otherwise expressly provided by the order for giving effect to an agreement made between the parties concerned, remain in force notwithstanding the transfer.

(2) In relation to property, responsibilities, rights or obligations transferred by an order which provides as aforesaid, any such statutory provisions shall apply to the highway authority, and to the exercise by them of any powers under the order, in like manner as they applied, before the transfer, to the owners of the bridge, highway or approaches, and to the exercise of powers by the owners thereof.

Apportionment of expenses

15.—(1) Subject to sub-paragraph (2) below, where an order has been made with respect to a bridge other than a trunk road bridge—

(a) requiring the reconstruction or improvement of the bridge, or of the highway carried by the bridge, or of the approaches to the bridge, or

(b) relating to the maintenance of the bridge, or of any such highway or approaches, or

(c) relating to the operation of the bridge, being a swing bridge,

the expense of such reconstruction, improvement, maintenance or operation shall be defrayed either by the owners of the bridge or by one or more of the highway authorities entitled to make application with respect thereto by virtue of section 95 of this Act, or partly by the owners of the bridge and partly by one or more of those highway authorities, as, in default of agreement, may be determined by arbitration.

(2) Sub-paragraph (1) above is subject to the following, namely that, unless otherwise agreed,—

(a) where the bridge is a bridge crossing a railway of railway undertakers, or a canal of canal undertakers, or a railway, lock, passage or other work of dock undertakers or of harbour undertakers, any additional expense incurred by the owners of that railway, canal, lock, passage or work by reason of any alteration thereof due to the provisions of the order (other than provisions applied for by the undertakers for the improvement of their undertaking) shall be defrayed by one or more of the highway authorities ;

(b) where the bridge is a swing bridge, any additional expense incurred by the owners in relation to the operation of the bridge due to the provisions of the order (other than provisions applied for by the owners for the improvement of their undertaking) shall be defrayed by one or more of the highway authorities ; and

(c) except so far as any additional expense is due to works executed at the instance of the owners of the bridge for the improvement of their undertaking, the owners' share of the expense of the reconstruction, improvement, maintenance or operation shall be an amount equivalent to what would have been the amount of the owners' liability if no such order had been made.

16. Where the reconstruction or improvement of a bridge crossing—

(a) a railway of railway undertakers, or

(b) a canal of canal undertakers, or

(c) a railway, lock, passage or other work of dock undertakers or of harbour undertakers,

effected in pursuance of an order made otherwise than upon the application of the owners of the bridge, has caused the width between the parapets of the bridge, or the width of the approaches to it, to be increased, any additional expense thereafter incurred in consequence of the increase by the owners of that railway, canal, lock, passage or work in connection with the widening or alteration thereof under the bridge or the approaches to it shall be defrayed by one or more of the highway authorities referred to in paragraph 15 above, and any question whether any such additional expense has been so incurred or as to the amount thereof shall, in default of agreement, be determined by arbitration.

17. Where an order providing for a matter referred to in any of sub-paragraphs (a), (b) and (c) of paragraph 15(1) above relates to a trunk road bridge the provisions of paragraphs 15 and 16 above have effect as if, for references to the highway authorities entitled to make application with respect to a bridge by virtue of section 95 of this Act, there were substituted references to the Minister.

18. Where it is determined by agreement or an award that the whole or part of the expenses of reconstruction, improvement, maintenance or operation is to be borne by two or more highway authorities, the expenses or part thereof shall be apportioned between them in such manner as, in default of agreement, may be determined by arbitration.

19. Where it is determined by agreement or an award that the owners of a bridge are to contribute to the expense of a highway authority, the contribution shall, at the option of the owners of the bridge, be paid—

    (*a*) as a lump sum, or

    (*b*) by annual payments of such amount, and continuing for such number of years, as may be agreed between the owners and the authority or, in default of agreement, as may be determined by arbitration, or

    (*c*) by perpetual annual payments of such amount as may be so agreed or determined.

Arbitration

20. Where a question is by any provision of this Schedule, or of an order, to be determined by arbitration, the arbitrator shall be a single arbitrator appointed, in default of agreement between the parties concerned, by the President of the Institution of Civil Engineers.

SCHEDULE 12

PROVISIONS AS TO ORDERS UNDER SECTION 116 AND CONVEYANCES UNDER SECTION 256

PART I

NOTICES TO BE GIVEN BY APPLICANT FOR ORDER UNDER SECTION 116

1. At least 28 days before the day on which an application for an order under section 116 of this Act is made in relation to a highway the applicant authority shall give notice of their intention to apply for the order, specifying the time and place at which the application is to be made and the terms of the order applied for (embodying a plan showing what will be the effect thereof)—

    (*a*) to the owners and occupiers of all lands adjoining the highway;

    (*b*) to any statutory undertakers having apparatus under, in, upon, over, along or across the highway;

    (*c*) if the highway is a classified road, to the Minister;

    (*d*) if the highway is a classified road, to the district council and, if the highway is in, or partly in, a parish or community which has a separate parish council or community council, to the parish or community council, as the case may require or, in the case of a parish which does not have a separate parish council, to the chairman of the parish meeting.

2. Not later than 28 days before the day on which the application is made the applicant authority shall cause a copy of the said notice to be displayed in a prominent position at the ends of the highway.

3. At least 28 days before the day on which the application is made the applicant authority shall publish in the London Gazette and in at least one local newspaper circulating in the area in which the highway is situated a notice containing the particulars specified in paragraph 1 above, except that there may be substituted for the plan a statement of a place in the said area where the plan may be inspected free of charge at all reasonable hours.

PART II

APPARATUS OF STATUTORY UNDERTAKERS

4. Where this Part of this Schedule applies in relation to a highway, the statutory undertakers whose apparatus is under, in, upon, over, along or across the highway have the same powers and rights in respect of that apparatus, subject to the provisions of this Schedule, as if the order authorising the highway to be stopped up or diverted had not been made or, as the case may be, as if the conveyance of land pursuant to section 256 of this Act had not been made.

5. Where a highway is stopped up or diverted in pursuance of an order under section 116 or land is conveyed pursuant to section 256, the statutory undertakers whose apparatus is under, in, upon over, along or across the highway may, and, if reasonably requested so to do by the authority on whose application the order was made, or who conveyed the land, as the case may be, shall—

(a) remove the apparatus and place it or other apparatus provided in substitution for it in such other position as they may reasonably determine and have power to place it ; or

(b) provide other apparatus in substitution for the existing apparatus and place it in such position as aforesaid.

Any works executed under this paragraph (including the provision of apparatus thereunder) are hereafter in this Part of this Schedule referred to as " undertakers' works ".

6. Subject to the following provisions of this Part of this Schedule, the authority on whose application an order under section 116 stopping up or diverting a highway was made or, as the case may be, the authority who conveyed the land pursuant to section 256, shall pay to any statutory undertakers an amount equal to the cost reasonably incurred by them in or in connection with—

(a) the execution of undertakers' works required in consequence of the stopping up or diversion of that highway or, as the case may be, the conveyance of the land, and

(b) the doing of any other work or thing rendered necessary by the execution of undertakers' works.

7. If in the course of the execution of undertakers' works under paragraph 5 above—

(a) apparatus of better type, of greater dimensions or of greater capacity is placed in substitution for existing apparatus

of worse type, of smaller dimensions or of smaller capacity,
or

(*b*) apparatus (whether existing apparatus or apparatus substituted for existing apparatus) is placed at a depth greater than the depth at which the existing apparatus was,

and the placing of apparatus of that type, dimensions or capacity or the placing of apparatus at that depth, as the case may be, is not agreed by the authority concerned, or, in default of agreement, is not determined by arbitration to be necessary, then, if it involves cost in the execution of the undertakers' works exceeding that which would have been involved if the apparatus placed had been of the existing type, dimensions or capacity, or at the existing depth, as the case may be, the amount which apart from this paragraph would be payable to the undertakers by virtue of paragraph 6 above shall be reduced by the amount of that excess.

8. For the purposes of paragraph 7 above—

(*a*) an extension of apparatus to a length greater than the length of existing apparatus shall not be treated as a placing of apparatus of greater dimensions than those of the existing apparatus ;

(*b*) where the provision of a joint in a cable is agreed, or is determined to be necessary, the consequential provision of a jointing chamber or of a manhole shall be treated as if it also had been agreed or had been so determined.

9. An amount which apart from this paragraph would be payable to undertakers in respect of works of theirs by virtue of paragraph 6 above (and having regard, where relevant, to paragraph 7 above) shall, if the works include the placing of apparatus provided in substitution for apparatus placed more than $7\frac{1}{2}$ years earlier so as to confer on the undertakers any financial benefit by deferment of the time for renewal of the apparatus in the ordinary course, be reduced by the amount which represents that benefit.

10. Any question arising under this Part of this Schedule shall, in default of agreement between the parties concerned, be determined by arbitration.

SCHEDULE 13

DEDUCTIONS FROM RENTS

1. An occupier of premises by whom any sum in relation to which this Schedule applies is paid under this Act shall be entitled to deduct from the rent payable by him in respect of the premises—

(*a*) if he holds the premises at a rent not less than the rack rent, an amount equal to three-quarters of the said sum, or

(*b*) if he holds the premises at a rent less than the rack rent, such proportion of an amount equal to three-quarters of the said sum as the rent at which he holds the premises bears to the rack rent.

SCH. 13

2. Where a deduction from rent payable to a landlord is made under this Schedule, and the landlord himself holds the premises under a lease for a term of which less than 20 years is unexpired, the landlord is entitled to deduct from any rent payable by him under the lease such proportion of the amount deducted from the rent payable to him as the rent so payable by him bears to the rent payable to him, and so on in succession with respect to every landlord holding the premises for a term of which less than 20 years remains unexpired and who is both receiving and liable to pay rent in respect thereof.

3. Nothing in paragraph 2 above entitles a person to deduct from the rent payable by him more than the whole amount deducted from the rent payable to him.

Section 184.

SCHEDULE 14

PROVISIONS WITH RESPECT TO NOTICES UNDER SECTION 184

1. A person on whom a notice under section 184(1) or (3) of this Act is served may within 28 days from the date of his being served therewith object to the notice on any of the following grounds which are appropriate in the circumstances of the particular case:—

(a) that the notice is not justified by the terms of section 184(1) or (3);

(b) that there has been some defect or error in, or in connection with, the notice;

(c) that the proposed works are unreasonable in character or extent, or are unnecessary;

(d) that the conditions imposed by the notice are unreasonable;

(e) that some other person having an interest in the premises also habitually takes or permits to be taken a mechanically propelled vehicle across the footway or verge and should be required to defray part of the expenses of executing the proposed works;

(f) that the authority are not entitled to serve the notice by reason of section 184(2);

(g) that a person carrying out or proposing to carry out such a development as is referred to in section 184(3) offers to execute the works himself.

2. An objection under paragraph 1 above shall be made by notice to the highway authority, and the notice shall state the grounds of objection.

3. Where objection is made to a notice given by a local highway authority under section 184(1) or (3), that authority shall send a copy of the notice and of the notice of objection to the Minister.

4. If objection is made to such a notice and the objection is not withdrawn the notice does not become effective until it has been confirmed by the Minister, and the Minister after considering the

objection may confirm the notice without modification or subject to   Sᴄʜ. 14
such modifications as he thinks fit.

5. Subject to paragraph 4 above, such a notice becomes effective
at the expiration of the period during which the person served
therewith may object to it.

SCHEDULE 15

APPLICATION OF ADVANCE PAYMENTS CODE

Section 204.

1. Where the advance payments code does not apply in a parish
or community or any part of a parish or community, the council
of the county in which the parish or community is situated may,
subject to the provisions of this Schedule, by resolution adopt that
code for the parish or community or, as the case may be, for that
part at a meeting of which not less than one month's notice has
been duly given to all the members of the council specifying the
intention to propose the resolution.

2. The resolution shall come into operation at such time, not
being less than one month from the date of the first publication of
an advertisement under paragraph 3(*a*) below, as the council may by
the resolution fix, and upon its coming into operation the advance
payments code shall apply in the parish or community, or part of
the parish or community specified in the resolution.

3. When it has been passed, the resolution shall be published—

    (*a*) by advertisement in at least one local newspaper circulating
in the parish or community concerned or, as the case may
be, the part of the parish or community concerned, and

    (*b*) by notice thereof fixed to the principal doors of every church
and chapel in the parish or community concerned or, as
the case may be, the part of the parish or community
concerned, in the place to which notices are usually fixed,
and

    (*c*) otherwise in such manner as the council think sufficient for
giving notice thereof to all persons interested,

and a copy of the resolution shall be sent to the Minister.

4. A copy of the advertisement of the resolution published under
paragraph 3(*a*) above is sufficient evidence of the passing of
the resolution unless the contrary is shown, and, on the expiration
of 3 months from the date of the first publication of that advertisement, an objection to the resolution on the ground—

    (*a*) that notice to propose it was not duly given, or

    (*b*) that the resolution was not sufficiently published,

is of no effect.

5. For the purposes of this Schedule a notice is to be deemed
to have been duly given to a member of a council if—

    (*a*) it is given in the mode in which notices to attend meetings of
the council are usually given, or

(b) where there is no such mode, it is signed by the proper officer of the council and delivered to the member or left at his usual or last known place of abode in England or Wales, or sent by post in a prepaid registered letter, or letter sent by the recorded delivery service, addressed to the member at his usual or last-known place of abode in England or Wales.

Sections 205, 210.

SCHEDULE 16

PARTICULARS TO BE STATED IN SPECIFICATIONS, NOTICES, ETC., UNDER THE PRIVATE STREET WORKS CODE

1. The specification shall describe generally the works and things to be done, and, in the case of structural works, shall specify so far as may be practicable the foundation, form, material and dimensions thereof.

2. The plans and sections shall show the constructional character of the works, the connections (if any) with existing streets, sewers or other works, and the lines and levels of the works, subject to such limits of deviation (if any) as may be indicated on the plans and sections respectively.

3. The estimate shall show the particulars of the probable cost of the whole works, including any additional charge in respect of surveys, superintendence and notices.

4. The provisional apportionment shall state the amounts charged on the respective premises and the names of the respective owners, or reputed owners, and shall also state whether the apportionment is made according to the frontage of the respective premises or not, and the measurements of the frontages, and the other considerations (if any) on which the apportionment is based.

5. The notice under section 205 of this Act shall contain the following particulars:—

   (a) a statement that the street works authority have resolved to execute street works in the private street in question;

   (b) the address of the offices of the authority at which a copy of the resolution of approval, and the approved documents or copies of them certified by the proper officer, may be inspected, and the times at which, and the period during which, they may be inspected; and

   (c) a statement that an owner of premises liable to be charged with any part of the expenses of executing the street works may object to the proposal to execute the works, giving the period during which such objection may be made.

6. The notice under section 210 of this Act shall contain the following particulars:—

   (a) a statement that the street works authority propose to amend the estimate so as to increase the amount of it, specifying the former amount and the amount to which it is to be increased;

(b) the address of the offices of the authority at which a document certified by the proper officer giving details of the proposed amendment and of the proposed consequential amendment of the provisional apportionment may be inspected, and the times at which, and the period during which, it may be inspected ; and

(c) a statement that an owner of premises liable to be charged with any part of the expenses of executing the street works may object to the proposed amendments, giving the period during which such objection may be made.

SCHEDULE 17

PURPOSES FOR WHICH ADDITIONAL LAND MAY BE TAKEN IN ADVANCE OF REQUIREMENTS

Provision authorising acquisition	Initial stage	Subsequent stage
Section 239(1) ...	The construction of a highway.	The improvement of that highway.
Section 239(2)(a)	The carrying out of works authorised by an order relating to a trunk road under section 14 of this Act.	The improvement or alteration of a highway or proposed highway to which the order relates.
Section 239(2)(b)	The provision of a maintenance compound for a trunk road.	The extension of the maintenance compound.
Section 239(3) ...	The improvement of a highway.	The further improvement of that highway.
Section 239(4)(a)	The improvement of a highway included in the route of a special road.	The further improvement of the highway.
Section 239(4)(b)	The purposes of an order made in relation to a special road under section 18 of this Act.	The improvement or alteration of a highway or proposed highway to which the order relates.
Section 239(4)(c)	The provision of a service area or maintenance compound for a special road.	The extension of the service area or maintenance compound.
Section 240(1) ...	The carrying out of works authorised by an order relating to a classified road under section 14 of this Act.	The improvement or alteration of a highway or proposed highway to which the order relates.
Section 240(3) ...	The provision of a trunk road picnic area.	The extension of the trunk road picnic area.
Section 240(5) ...	The provision of a lorry area.	The extension of the lorry area.

SCHEDULE 18

DISTANCE LIMITS FROM HIGHWAY APPLICABLE TO COMPULSORY ACQUISITION

PART I

Table of limits

Acquisition provision	Distance limit
1. Section 239(1) or 239(3)	220 yards from the middle of the highway or proposed highway.
2. Section 239(2)(*a*) or 239(4)(*a*) or (*b*)	220 yards from the middle of the trunk road or of the special road, as the case may be, or, where the land is required for the improvement, alteration or construction of any other highway, from the middle of that other highway or proposed highway.
3. Section 239(2)(*b*) or 239(4)(*c*)	880 yards from the middle of the trunk road or special road, as the case may be.
4. Section 240(1) so far as it relates to works authorised by an order relating to a classified road under section 14 of this Act.	220 yards from the middle of the classified road to which the order relates or, where the land is required for the improvement, alteration or construction of any other highway, from the middle of that other highway or proposed highway.
5. Section 240(1) so far as it relates to works authorised by section 129 of this Act.	880 yards from the middle of the highway or proposed highway from which new means of access to premises are to be provided.
6. Section 240(3)(*a*)	880 yards from the middle of the trunk road in connection with which a trunk road picnic area is to be provided.
7. Section 240(3)(*b*) or 240(4)	220 yards from the middle of the highway or proposed highway on land adjoining, or in the vicinity of which, public sanitary conveniences are to be provided.
8. Section 240(5)	880 yards from the middle of the highway or proposed highway on land adjoining, or in the vicinity of which, a lorry area is to be provided

PART II

Further provision with respect to the limits under Part I

1. In the entries numbered 2 and 4 in Part I of this Schedule the distance limit specified in column 2 shall, in relation to land required for the provision of new means of access to premises from a highway or proposed highway, have effect with the substitution for the distance there mentioned of a distance of 880 yards from the middle of that highway or proposed highway.

2. Where the boundaries of any highway will be altered in consequence of any improvement proposed to be made under this Act in relation to the highway, then, for the purposes of Part I of this Schedule the middle of that highway shall be the middle of it as proposed to be improved.

Section 250

SCHEDULE 19

COMPULSORY ACQUISITION OF RIGHTS: MODIFICATION OF 1946 AND 1965 ACTS

PART I

ADAPTATION OF 1946 ACT, SCHEDULE 1, PART III

1. In paragraphs 2 to 4 below, "the Schedule" means Schedule 1 to the Act of 1946; and in relation to compulsory acquisition of rights by virtue of section 250 of this Act that Schedule applies with the modifications made by those paragraphs.

2. In paragraph 9 of the Schedule (compulsory purchase order to be subject to special parliamentary procedure in certain cases) for references to compulsory purchase of land substitute references to compulsory acquisition of rights over land.

3. In paragraph 10 of the Schedule (land of statutory undertakers)—

   (*a*) for "land comprised in the order" substitute "land over which a right is to be acquired by virtue of the order";

   (*b*) for "purchase of" substitute "acquisition of a right over";

   (*c*) for "it can be purchased and not replaced" substitute "the right can be acquired"; and

   (*d*) for sub-paragraph (ii) substitute the following—
       "(ii) that any detriment to the carrying on of the undertaking, in consequence of the acquisition of the right, can be made good by the undertakers by the use of other land belonging to, or available for acquisition by, them".

4.—(1) In paragraph 11 of the Schedule (common land, open spaces, etc.) substitute the following for sub-paragraph (1)—

   "(1) In so far as a compulsory purchase order authorises the acquisition of a right over land forming part of a common, open space or fuel or field garden allotment, it shall be subject

SCH. 19   to special parliamentary procedure unless the Secretary of State is satisfied—

(*a*) that the land, when burdened with that right, will be no less advantageous to those persons in whom it is vested and to the persons, if any, entitled to rights of common or other rights, and to the public, than it was before ; or

(*b*) that there has been or will be given in exchange for the right additional land which will as respects the persons in whom there is vested the land over which the right is to be acquired, the persons, if any, entitled to rights of common or other rights over that land, and the public, be adequate to compensate them for the disadvantages which result from the acquisition of the right, and that the additional land has been or will be vested in the persons in whom there is vested the land over which the right is to be acquired, and subject to the like rights, trusts and incidents as attach to that land apart from the compulsory purchase order ; or

(*c*) that the land affected by the right to be acquired does not exceed 250 square yards in extent or the right is required in connection with the widening or drainage of an existing highway or in connection partly with the widening and partly with the drainage of such a highway, and that the giving of other land in exchange for the right is unnecessary, whether in the interests of the persons, if any, entitled to rights of common or other rights or in the interests of the public,

and certifies accordingly.".

(2) In the said paragraph 11, in sub-paragraph (3), substitute the following for the words from " and for discharging " to the end—

" and for discharging the land over which any right is to be acquired from all rights, trusts and incidents to which it has previously been subject so far as their continuance would be inconsistent with the exercise of that right ".

PART II

ADAPTATION OF 1965 ACT, PART I

5. In relation to a compulsory acquisition of a right by virtue of section 250 of this Act, the Act of 1965 applies with the modifications made by paragraphs 6 to 11 below.

6. For section 7 of the Act (measure of compensation) substitute the following:—

" 7. In assessing the compensation to be paid by the acquiring authority under this Act regard shall be had not only to the extent (if any) to which the value of the land over which the right is to be acquired is depreciated by the acquisition of the right but also to the damage (if any) to be sustained by the owner of the land by reason of its severance from other land of his, or injuriously affecting that other land by the exercise of the powers conferred by this or the special Act.".

7. For section 8(1) of the Act (protection for vendor against severance of house, garden, etc.) substitute the following—

" (1) No person shall be required to grant any right over part only—

(a) of any house, building or manufactory ; or

(b) of a park or garden belonging to a house,

if he is willing to sell the whole of the house, building, manufactory, park or garden, unless the Lands Tribunal determines that—

(i) in the case of a house, building or manufactory, the part over which the right is proposed to be acquired can be made subject to that right without material detriment to the house, building or manufactory ; or

(ii) in the case of a park or garden, the part over which the right is proposed to be acquired can be made subject to that right without seriously affecting the amenity or convenience of the house ;

and if the Lands Tribunal so determine, the Tribunal shall award compensation in respect of any loss due to the acquisition of the right, in addition to its value ; and thereupon the party interested shall be required to grant to the acquiring authority that right over that part of the house, building, manufactory, park or garden.

(1A) In considering the extent of any material detriment to a house, building or manufactory, or any extent to which the amenity or convenience of a house is affected, the Lands Tribunal shall have regard not only to the right which is to be acquired over the land, but also to any adjoining or adjacent land belonging to the same owner and subject to compulsory purchase.".

8. The following provisions of the Act (being provisions stating the effect of a deed poll executed in various circumstances where there is no conveyance by persons with interests in the land)—

section 9(4) (refusal by owners to convey) ;

Schedule 1, paragraph 10(3) (owners under incapacity) ;

Schedule 2, paragraph 2(3) (absent and untraced owners) ; and

Schedule 4, paragraphs 2(3) and 7(2) (common land),

are so modified as to secure that, as against persons with interests in the land which are expressed to be overridden by the deed, the right which is to be compulsorily acquired is vested absolutely in the acquiring authority.

9. Section 11 of the Act (powers of entry) is so modified as to secure that, as from the date on which the acquiring authority have served notice to treat in respect of any right, they have power,

M

SCH. 19   exercisable in the like circumstances and subject to the like conditions, to enter for the purpose of exercising that right (which shall be deemed for this purpose to have been created on the date of service of the notice); and sections 12 (penalty for unauthorised entry) and 13 (entry on sheriff's warrant in the event of obstruction) are modified correspondingly.

10. Section 20 of the Act (protection for interests of tenants at will, etc.) applies with the modifications necessary to secure that persons with such interests as are mentioned in that section are compensated in a manner corresponding to that in which they would be compensated on a compulsory acquisition of that land, but taking into account only the extent (if any) of such interference with such an interest as is actually caused, or likely to be caused, by the exercise of the right in question.

11. Section 22 of the Act (protection of acquiring authority's possession where by inadvertence an estate, right or interest has not been got in) is so modified as to enable the acquiring authority, in circumstances corresponding to those referred to in that section, to continue entitled to exercise the right acquired, subject to compliance with that section as respects compensation.

Sections 257,
258.

SCHEDULE 20

ACQUISITION OF LAND OR RIGHTS:
RELATED SCHEMES AND ORDERS

Purposes for which acquisition of land or rights is required	*Related schemes and orders*
Purposes connected with a trunk road, not being a special road.	An order under section 10 of this Act relating to the trunk road.
	An order under section 14 of this Act relating to the trunk road.
Purposes connected with a special road.	A scheme under section 16 of this Act relating to the special road.
	An order under section 18 of this Act relating to the special road.
The construction, in pursuance of an order under section 106(1) of this Act, as part of a trunk road of a bridge over or a tunnel under navigable waters.	The order under the said section 106(1).

Purposes for which aquisition of land or rights is required	*Related schemes and orders*
The construction, in pursuance of a scheme under section 106(3) of this Act, as part of a highway or proposed highway of a bridge over or a tunnel under navigable waters.	The scheme under the said section 106(3).
Purposes connected with a classified road, not being a special road.	An order under section 14 of this Act relating to the classified road.
The provision of a new means of access to any premises from a highway or proposed highway.	An order under section 124 of this Act stopping up a means of access to those premises from that or any other highway.
The diversion, in pursuance of an order under section 108(1) of this Act, of a navigable watercourse.	The order under the said section 108(1).

Sch. 20

Section 265.

SCHEDULE 21

TRANSITIONAL MATTERS ARISING WHERE A HIGHWAY BECOMES A TRUNK ROAD OR A TRUNK ROAD CEASES TO BE A TRUNK ROAD

1. All orders and regulations made, all directions, consents and notices given, and all building lines and improvement lines prescribed, with respect to a highway which becomes a trunk road, either by the former highway authority for the purposes of their functions with respect to that highway or by a council under any enactment to which section 265 of this Act applies, if they were in force immediately before the highway became a trunk road, have effect with respect thereto as if made, given or prescribed by the Minister; but nothing in this paragraph is to be taken as transferring to the Minister any liability not transferred to him by or under the said section 265.

2. Any order, byelaw, regulation or other instrument made by a council with respect to a highway which becomes a trunk road, which would, if it had been made after the highway became a trunk road, have required the consent or approval of the Minister, may be revoked or varied by an order made by the Minister in like manner and subject to the like conditions as the original instrument, so, however, that no appeal lies to the Crown Court or to a magistrates' court against any order made by the Minister under this paragraph.

3. All contracts, deeds, bonds or agreements entered into or made by the former highway authority for a highway which becomes a trunk road, or by a council for the purposes of functions in

M 2

SCH. 21

relation to the highway under any enactment to which section 265 of this Act applies, and subsisting on the day on which the highway became a trunk road, have effect, in so far as they relate to the property and liabilities transferred to the Minister in respect of that highway, with the substitution of the Minister for the authority or council and may be enforced by or against the Minister accordingly.

4. Where any such contract as aforesaid provides for the execution of works or the rendering of services by a person other than the authority or council in connection with the construction, maintenance or improvement of, or other dealing with, the highway, then—

(a) if the works or services have been completed before the day on which the highway becomes a trunk road but the price or payment, or any part thereof, has not accrued due before that day, the Minister may recover from the authority or council the price or payment, or part thereof, as the case may be ; and

(b) if the works or services have not been completed before the said day, the value of any works executed, or services rendered, before that day, shall be ascertained, regard being had to the terms of the contract, and the Minister may recover from the authority or council the amount of the said value less any sum paid by the authority or council in pursuance of the contract, and if the authority or council have paid in pursuance of the contract a sum greater than the amount of the said value, the Minister shall repay the excess to the authority or council.

5. Where, before the day on which a highway becomes a trunk road, the former highway authority or any council having functions in relation to the highway under any enactment to which section 265 of this Act applies have been themselves executing works in connection with the construction, maintenance or improvement of, or other dealing with, the highway, but have not completed the works before that day, the Minister shall, if required to do so by the authority or council, purchase all unused materials necessarily acquired by the authority or council for the purpose of the works and hire from the authority or council all plant so acquired which is still necessary for the purpose of the works.

6. In calculating—

(a) the amount of any sum to be recovered or paid by the Minister under paragraph 4 above, or

(b) the price of the materials to be purchased, or the hire of plant to be hired, by the Minister under paragraph 5 above, account shall be taken of any grant paid or payable by the Minister to the authority or council for the purpose of the works or services.

7. If any dispute arises under paragraph 4, 5 or 6 above as to the materials to be purchased, or the plant to be hired, by the Minister from any authority or council, or as to the sums to be paid by any authority or council to the Minister, or by the Minister to any authority or council, it shall be determined by arbitration.

8. All proceedings, legal or other, begun before the day on which a highway becomes a trunk road and relating to any property or liabilities transferred to the Minister in respect of that highway, may be carried on with the substitution of the Minister as party to the proceedings, in lieu of the authority or council from whom the property or liabilities was or were transferred, and any such proceedings may be amended in such manner as may be necessary for that purpose.

9. The provisions of this Schedule, except paragraph 2, apply in a case where a trunk road ceases to be a trunk road in like manner as they apply where a highway becomes a trunk road, with the substitution, for the references to the former highway authority and to a council, of references to the Minister, and, for references to the Minister, of references to the council who become the highway authority for the road or, as far as relates to functions under any enactment to which section 265 of this Act applies and to property and liabilities vested in or incurred by the Minister for the purposes of those functions, to the council who are to exercise those functions in relation to the road.

SCHEDULE 22

PROVISIONS OF THIS ACT TO WHICH SECTIONS 288, 294, 312, 338, 339 AND 341 OF THIS ACT APPLY

1. *Provisions contained in Part IV*

Section 36(6) and (7) and section 38.

2. *Provisions contained in Part V*

Section 66(2) to (8), sections 73 and 77 and section 96(4) and (5).

3. *Provisions contained in Part IX*

Sections 133, and 151 to 153, section 154(1), and 154(4) so far as relating to a notice under 154(1), sections 163 and 165, sections 171 to 174, 176, 178 and 179, section 180 other than subsection (2) and subsection (4) so far as relating to subsection (2), and section 185.

4. *Provisions contained in Part X*

Sections 186 to 188, 190 to 197, 200 and 201.

5. *Provisions contained in Part XI*

The private street works code, sections 226 and 228, section 230(1) to (6), and sections 231, 233, 236 and 237.

6. *Provisions contained in Part XII*

Section 239(6) and section 241.

7. *Provisions contained in Part XIV*

Sections 286, 295, 297, 303, 304, and 305.

Section 343(1).

SCHEDULE 23

TRANSITIONAL PROVISIONS

Delegation of functions

1. Section 6(1) and section 7(1) of this Act shall have effect in relation to land acquired by a Minister in connection with a trunk road or, as the case may be, acquired by the Greater London Council in connection with a metropolitan road, under subsection (5) or (6) of section 214 of the Highways Act 1959 (or, in the case of a Minister, under so much of section 13 of the Restriction of Ribbon Development Act 1935 as is re-enacted in those subsections) as they have in relation to land so acquired under section 246 of this Act (or, by virtue of paragraph 17 below, under section 22 of the Land Compensation Act 1973).

1959 c. 25.

1935 c. 47.

1973 c. 26.

Trunk roads and related roads

2. Section 11(1) of this Act applies to a highway which at the commencement of this Act is a trunk road as it applies to a highway which becomes a trunk road after the said commencement.

3.—(1) The provisions of this Act (except section 19) and of paragraph 5 of Schedule 5 to the Town and Country Planning Act 1971 apply in relation to the trunk roads described in sub-paragraph (2) below, which are trunk roads by virtue of orders made under section 1 of the Trunk Roads Act 1946, as if they were special roads provided by the Minister in pursuance of schemes made under section 16 of this Act for the use of traffic of the classes specified in the third column of the table in sub-paragraph (2) below.

1971 c. 78.

1946 c. 30.

(2) The trunk roads referred to in sub-paragraph (1) above are the trunk roads for which provision was made by the orders specified in the first column of the following table (referred to below as " the original orders "), as those roads are now constituted, having regard to any orders or schemes varying the original orders:

Original Order	Description of Road	Class of Traffic (as described in Schedule 4)
S.R. & O. 1947, No. 2248.	Stevenage By-Pass, part of A1(M) motorway.	Classes I and II.
S.R. & O. 1947, No. 1562.	Severn Bridge and adjoining sections of M4 motorway.	For main carriageways: Classes I and II. For cycle track on Severn Bridge: Classes VII, X and XI. For footway on Severn Bridge: Class IX.
S.I. 1948, No. 924.	Haysgate to Crick, part of M4 motorway.	Classes I and II.
S.I. 1948, No. 62.	Newport By-Pass, part of M4 motorway.	Classes I and II.
S.I. 1949, No. 2360.	Twyning to Lydiate Ash, part of M5 motorway.	Classes I and II.
S.I. 1949, No. 2459.	Port Talbot By-Pass, part of M4 motorway.	Classes I and II.

(3) Without prejudice to the generality of sub-paragraph (1) above,   Sch. 23
the power (under section 14 of the Interpretation Act 1978) to revoke   1978 c. 30.
or amend schemes under section 16 of this Act includes power to
revoke or amend any of the original orders and to amend the provisions of the third column of the table in sub-paragraph (2) above.

4.—(1) Any order under section 1(3) of the Trunk Roads Act   1936 c. 5
1936 (power to provide that a road superseding part of a trunk   (1 Edw. &
road should itself become a trunk road) continued in force by para-   1 Geo. 6).
graph 29 of Schedule 24 to the Highways Act 1959, and still in force   1959 c. 25.
(whether or not varied under that paragraph) immediately before the
commencement of this Act, continues in force and may be varied or
revoked by a subsequent order made in the like manner and subject
to the like provisions.

(2) Schedule 2 to this Act has effect as to the validity and date of
operation of an order made under this paragraph.

(3) If an order under the said section 1(3) continued in force by
sub-paragraph (1) above provides that on a date specified therein a
route described therein is to become a trunk road and the order is
revoked or varied by an order under this paragraph at any time
before the route is opened for the purposes of through traffic, the
revoking or varying order is not to be deemed for the purposes of
section 2 of this Act to be an order directing that a trunk road is to
cease to be a trunk road.

5.—(1) Any order under section 4 of the Trunk Roads Act 1946   1946 c. 30.
(certain powers relating to side roads connected with trunk roads)
continued in force by paragraph 30 of Schedule 24 to the Highways
Act 1959 and still in force (whether or not varied under that paragraph) immediately before the commencement of this Act, continues
in force and the provisions of subsections (1) to (3) of the said section
4 continue to apply to them as if that section had not been repealed.

(2) Subject to sub-paragraph (3) below, an order under the said
section 4 continued in force by sub-paragraph (1) above may be
varied or revoked by a subsequent order made in the like manner
and subject to the like provisions.

(3) Parts I and III of Schedule 1 to this Act have effect as to the
making of an order under this paragraph as they have effect as
to the making of an order in relation to a trunk road under section
14 of this Act ; and Schedule 2 to this Act has effect as to the validity
and date of operation of an order under this paragraph.

(4) Section 265 of this Act applies in relation to a highway for
which any council become the highway authority by virtue of an
order under the said section 4 or this paragraph as if it had previously
been a trunk road.

Special roads

6.—(1) In schemes under section 11 of the Highways Act 1959   1959 c. 25.
made before 30th June 1961 references to traffic in Class VII set
out in Schedule 4 to that Act are to be construed as including
references to traffic in Classes X and XI set out in Schedule 4 to
this Act.

(2) Sub-paragraph (1) above is without prejudice to the operation of sections 17(2)(*a*) and 23(3) of the Interpretation Act 1978 as respects the construction of references generally in such schemes as are referred to in that sub-paragraph, and without prejudice to the powers under section 14 of that Act and section 17(3) of this Act to amend such schemes and to amend Schedule 4 to this Act.

Vehicle crossings

7.—(1) If a person knowingly uses a grass verge or a footway as a crossing as mentioned in subsection (1) of section 155 of the Highways Act 1959 (carriage crossings across grass verges or kerbed footways) in contravention of any condition imposed under paragraph (*c*) of the said subsection (1) and in force immediately before the commencement of this Act, or knowingly permits it to be so used, he is (notwithstanding the repeal of the said section 155 by the Highways Act 1971) guilty of an offence and liable to a fine not exceeding £20.

(2) As respects any expenses recoverable by a council under subsection (3) of the said section 155 and outstanding at the commencement of this Act, section 305 of this Act has effect as though they were incurred under a provision of this Act to which that section applies.

Maintenance of highways

8. Any question of liability for non-repair of a highway in respect of damage resulting from an event which occurred before 3rd August 1964 shall be determined in accordance with the former rule of law (abrogated by section 1 of the Highways (Miscellaneous Provisions) Act 1961) which exempted the inhabitants at large and any other persons as their successors from liability for non-repair of highways ; and section 58 of this Act does not apply in relation to any such damage.

Cattle-grids etc.

9.—(1) Without prejudice to the application of this Act to any cattle-grid, works or by-pass provided, or deemed to have been provided, under the Highways Act 1959, sub-paragraphs (2) and (3) below have effect as respects—

(*a*) any cattle-grid provided for a highway which consists of or comprises a carriageway,

(*b*) any gate or other works on such a highway for use in connection with such a cattle-grid,

(*c*) any by-pass for use in connection with such a cattle-grid, and

(*d*) any gate or other works for the proper control of traffic passing over such a by-pass,

being a cattle-grid, works or by-pass provided before 28th July 1950, where application is made to the Minister for his approval thereof by the highway authority for the highway.

(2) If, where such an application is made—

    (*a*) the Minister approves the cattle-grid, works or by-pass unconditionally, or

    (*b*) he gives his approval subject to conditions as to the carrying out of works, the conclusion of an agreement under section 88 of this Act or any other matter, and those conditions have been complied with,

then, as from the giving of the Minister's approval unconditionally or, as the case may be, compliance with all conditions subject to which he gives his approval, the cattle-grid, works or by-pass are to be deemed to have been provided under this Act by the highway authority for whom the application for approval was made.

(3) Where the Minister gives his approval of the cattle-grid, works or by-pass subject to conditions, the highway authority by whom the application for approval was made may carry out any work, or do any other thing, which is requisite for complying with the conditions ; and in particular (but without prejudice to the foregoing provisions of this sub-paragraph) sections 85, 87 and 243 of this Act apply in relation to the exercise of the powers conferred by the foregoing provisions of this sub-paragraph as they apply in relation to the corresponding powers conferred by this Act.

New streets

10.—(1) Without prejudice to paragraphs 17 to 19 below section 189 of this Act applies, in relation to any council, as respects—

    (*a*) an order made by the council under section 159 of the Highways Act 1959, or   1959 c. 25.

    (*b*) an order, so far as it relates to the council's area, made by an earlier authority under that section,

as it applies to an order made by the council under section 188 of this Act (which replaces the said section 159).

(2) Any order under section 30 of the Public Health Act 1925 1925 c. 71. which had effect immediately before the commencement of this Act (by virtue of paragraph 22 of Schedule 24 to the Highways Act 1959) shall, subject to sub-paragraph (3) below, continue to have effect as if that section had not been repealed.

(3) Section 189 of this Act applies, in relation to any council, as respects an order having effect by virtue of sub-paragraph (2) above, so far as it relates to the council's area, as it applies to an order made by the council under section 188 of this Act.

(4) While any order under the said section 30 has effect in relation to a highway no order under section 188 of this Act shall be made in relation to that highway.

11. The repeal by this Act of the Highways Act 1959 does not affect the operation of any order under section 312(6) of that Act (orders extending period of operation of byelaws made under an enactment corresponding to section 157 of that Act) and any such order in force at the commencement of this Act may be varied or revoked by the Secretary of State.

Private Street Works Code

12.—(1) Sub-paragraph (2) below has effect where—

(a) before 1st January 1960 street works were executed under any of the relevant street works enactments with respect to part only of a private street, being a part consisting of the whole or part of a footway on one side only of the street, and those works were executed only by, or at the expense only of, the owners or occupiers of the premises fronting the footway or part of the footway, as the case may be ; and

(b) the street works authority resolve under section 205(1) of this Act to execute street works with respect to any part of the street constituting or comprising the whole or a part of the footway on the side of the street other than that in which street works were executed as mentioned in paragraph (a) above.

In this paragraph " the relevant street works enactments " means section 150 of the Public Health Act 1875, the Private Street Works Act 1892 and any local Act making provision corresponding to the provisions of that section or of the said Act of 1892.

(2) In the circumstances mentioned in sub-paragraph (1) above, the expenses incurred by the authority in executing the works mentioned in sub-paragraph (1)(b) above with respect to the footway or part of the footway there mentioned shall (notwithstanding anything in section 205(1) or (2) of this Act but subject to the other provisions of the private street works code) be apportioned only between the premises fronting that footway or part, as the case may be, and references in Part XI of this Act to the premises liable to be charged with the expenses of street works under the private street works code are to be construed in accordance with this subparagraph.

(3) References in this paragraph to a footway include references to any roadside waste, and to any channel by the side of a footway.

13.—(1) Subject to sub-paragraph (3) below, where a highway in existence on 16th December 1949 (the date of the coming into force of the National Parks and Access to the Countryside Act 1949, referred to below as " the 1949 Act ")—

(a) was immediately before 1st January 1960 a highway repairable by the inhabitants at large by virtue only of section 47(1) of the 1949 Act (which extended to all public paths the then rule of law whereby a highway was repairable by the inhabitants at large), and

    (*b*) would, if the said section 47 had not been enacted, be a   Sᴄʜ. 23
        private street for the purposes of the private street works
        code,

the fact that the highway is a highway maintainable at the public expense by virtue of section 36(1) of this Act shall not prevent its being treated for the purposes of the private street works code as a private street.

This sub-paragraph does not apply to a highway in Greater London other than the outer London boroughs.

(2) Subject to sub-paragraph (3) below, where a highway in existence on 3rd August 1968 (the date of the coming into force of the Countryside Act 1968) would, if paragraph 9(2)(*a*) of Schedule 3 1968 c. 41. to that Act (which provides that as from the date of publication of the definitive map and statement in a review carried out by an authority under Part III of that Schedule certain ways shown on the map are to be highways maintainable at the public expense) had not been enacted, be a private street, the fact that the highway is a highway so maintainable by virtue of the said paragraph 9(2) shall not prevent its being treated for the purposes of the private street works code as a private street.

(3) Where the street works authority exercise the powers exercisable by them by virtue of sub-paragraph (1) or (2) above in relation to a highway or part of it, the sub-paragraph in question shall not thereafter apply to that highway or to that part, as the case may be, so as to enable the authority to exercise those powers in relation to it on any subsequent occasion.

Likewise, where before the commencement of this Act the street works authority exercised the powers exercisable by them by virtue of—

    (*a*) paragraph 24 of Schedule 24 to the Highways Act 1959 1959 c. 25.
        (from which sub-paragraph (1) above is derived) or section
        50 of the 1949 Act (from which the said paragraph 24 was
        derived), or

    (*b*) section 76(1) of the Highways Act 1971 (from which sub- 1971 c. 41.
        paragraph (2) above is derived),

in relation to a highway or part of it, sub-paragraph (1) or, as the case may be, (2) above shall not apply to that highway or part, as the case may be, so as to enable the authority to exercise the powers exercisable by virtue of sub-paragraph (1) or (2) above in relation to it.

Acquisition of land

14.—(1) Notwithstanding anything in section 1(2) of the Act of 1946 or in paragraph 9 of Schedule 1 to that Act, neither—

    (*a*) an order authorising a highway authority to acquire a right
        compulsorily as mentioned in section 242(3) of this Act,
    nor

SCH. 23

(*b*) an order made as mentioned in section 254(1) of this Act, or so made and confirmed,

is, where notice of the making or preparation in draft of the order was first published before the 6th April 1976, subject to special parliamentary procedure by reason only of its authorising the acquisition of any such right as is mentioned in the said section 242(3) or, as the case may be, the said section 254(1).

1980 c. 65.
1975 c. 77.

(2) Sub-paragraph (1) above is without prejudice to the operation of section 120 of the Local Government, Planning and Land Act 1980 (which re-enacts with modifications section 41 of the Community Land Act 1975) in relation to any such order as is mentioned in that sub-paragraph where notice of the making or preparation in draft of the order was or is first published on or after 6th April 1976.

National Freight Corporation

1980 c. 34.

15. Until the appointed day within the meaning of Part II of the Transport Act 1980—

　(a) subsection (4) of section 219 of this Act has effect as if the National Freight Corporation were included amongst the bodies mentioned in paragraph (i) of that subsection,

　(*b*) subsection (4) of section 329 of this Act has effect as if the National Freight Corporation were included amongst the bodies mentioned in that subsection.

Continuing offences

16. Where an offence for the continuance of which a penalty was provided has been committed under any enactment repealed by this Act proceedings may be taken under this Act in respect of the continuance of the offence after the commencement of this Act in the like manner as if the offence had been committed under the corresponding provision of this Act.

General

17. Any reference in this Act (whether express or implied) to a thing done or required or authorised to be done, or omitted to be done, or to an event which has occurred, under or for the purposes of, or by reference to any provision of this Act includes, except where the context otherwise requires, a reference to the corresponding thing done or required or authorised to be done, or omitted, or to the corresponding event which occurred, as the case may be, under or for the purposes of or by reference to the corresponding enactment repealed by this Act.

18. Without prejudice to paragraph 17 above, any reference in this Act (whether express or implied) to a thing done by a highway authority or other authority under a provision of this Act includes, except where the context otherwise requires, a reference to the corresponding thing done, or having effect as if done, by a

predecessor authority under the corresponding enactment repealed   SCH. 23
by this Act.

In this paragraph " predecessor authority " means—

(a) in relation to the Secretary of State, the Minister of Transport or other Minister exercising the relevant function before the transfer of the function to the Secretary of State ;

(b) in relation to the Minister of Transport, the Secretary or State or other Minister exercising the relevant function before the transfer of the function to the Minister of Transport ;

(c) in relation to a council, the authority exercising the relevant function before the function vested in the council under the Local Government Act 1972 or, as the case may be, the London Government Act 1963.

1972 c. 70.
1963 c. 33.

19. Without prejudice to paragraph 17 or 18 above, any power which was exercisable by a highway authority or other authority immediately before the commencement of this Act, under an enactment repealed by this Act, by reference (whether express or implied) to anything done before the said commencement may be exercised by that authority under the corresponding provision of this Act.

20. Where a period of time specified in any enactment repealed by this Act is current at the commencement of this Act, this Act has effect as if the corresponding provision of this Act had been in force when that period began to run.

21. For the purposes of the operation in relation to this Act of section 32(1) of the Public Utilities Street Works Act 1950 (provision as to payments falling to be made under enactments passed before the passing of that Act and instruments made under or confirmed by such enactments), any provision of this Act derived from the Highways Act 1959 is to be deemed to have been passed on the date of its antecedent enactment.

1950 c. 39.

1959 c. 25.

In this paragraph " antecedent enactment " means the enactment from which the relevant provision of the said Act of 1959 was derived (whether or not modified by the 1959 Act).

22. Any enactment or other document of any kind referring to a highway repairable by the inhabitants at large or a highway maintainable by the inhabitants at large is to be construed as referring to a highway which for the purposes of this Act is a highway maintainable at the public expense.

23. Any enactment or other document of any kind referring to a surveyor of highways or a highway board is to be construed as referring to a highway authority.

References to Magistrates' Courts Act 1980

24. Until the day appointed for the coming into force of the Magistrates' Courts Act 1980—

(a) the references in sections 292(4) and 297(3) of this Act to sections 32(9) and 143(1) of the Magistrates' Courts Act 1980 shall be construed respectively as references to sections 28(7) and 61(1) of the Criminal Law Act 1977 ;

1980 c. 43.

1977 c. 45.

SCH. 23
1952 c. 55.

(b) the reference in section 329(1) of this Act in the definition of " petty sessions area " to the Magistrates' Courts Act 1980 shall be construed as a reference to the Magistrates' Courts Act 1952.

Section 343(2).

SCHEDULE 24
CONSEQUENTIAL AMENDMENTS

1892 c. 43.

Military Lands Act 1892

1. In the Military Lands Act 1892—

(a) in section 13, for " the Highways Act 1959 " substitute " the Highways Act 1980 ", for " section one hundred and eight " substitute (in both places) " section 116 " and for " section two hundred and seventy-five of the said Act of 1959 " substitute " section 317 of the said Act of 1980 " ;

(b) in section 16(2), for " the Highways Act 1959 " substitute " the Highways Act 1980 ".

1925 c. 18.

Settled Land Act 1925

2. In section 56(3) of the Settled Land Act 1925, for " the Highways Act 1959 " substitute (in paragraph (a) and paragraph (b)) " the Highways Act 1980 ".

1925 c. 24.

Universities and College Estates Act 1925

3. In section 16(3) of the Universities and College Estates Act 1925, for " the Highways Act 1959 " substitute (in paragraph (a) and paragraph (b)) " the Highways Act 1980 ".

1936 c. 49.

Public Health Act 1936

4. In the Public Health Act 1936—

(a) in section 20(1)(b), for " Part IX of the Highways Act 1959 " substitute " Part XI of the Highways Act 1980 " ;

(b) in section 21, for subsection (4) substitute—

" (4) Nothing in this section shall be construed as limiting the rights of a county council under section 264 of the Highways Act 1980.".

1950 c. 39.

Public Utilities Street Works Act 1950

5. In section 39(1) of the Public Utilities Street Works Act 1950—

(a) in the definition of " highway authority " and " local highway authority ", for " the Highways Act 1959 " substitute " the Highways Act 1980 " ;

(b) in the definition of " road purposes ", for " subsection (1) of section two hundred and ninety-five of the Highways Act 1959 as amended by the Highways Act 1971 " substitute " section 329(1) of the Highways Act 1980 ".

1955 c. 20
(4 & 5 Eliz. 2.)

Agriculture (Improvement of Roads) Act 1955

6. In section 5(1) of the Agriculture (Improvement of Roads) Act 1955, in the definition of " unclassified road ", for " under the Ministry of Transport Act 1919 " substitute " within the meaning of the Highways Act 1980 ".

Parish Councils Act 1957

7. In section 3(10) of the Parish Councils Act 1957—

(*a*) for " the Highways Act 1959 " substitute " the Highways Act 1980 " ;

(*b*) for " section eleven of the said Act of 1959 " substitute " section 16 of the said Act of 1980 ".

Land Compensation Act 1961

8. In section 8(7) of the Land Compensation Act 1961 for paragraph (*c*) substitute—

" (*c*) section 261(1) of the Highways Act 1980 (or its predecessor, section 222(6) of the Highways Act 1959) ; ".

Public Health Act 1961

9. In section 51(2), (4) and (11) of the Public Health Act 1961, for " section one hundred and fifty-six of the Highways Act 1959 " substitute " section 185 of the Highways Act 1980 ".

Pipelines Act 1962

10. In the Pipelines Act 1962—

(*a*) in section 15(10), in the definition of " special road ", after " Highways Act 1959 ", insert " or section 16 of the Highways Act 1980 ", for " section nineteen of " substitute " paragraph 3 of Schedule 23 to ", and for " section eleven thereof " substitute " section 16 thereof " ;

(*b*) in section 18(1) for " section one hundred and thirty-seven of the Highways Act 1959 " substitute " section 157 of the Highways Act 1980 (or its predecessor, section 137 of the Highways Act 1959) ", and for " section eighteen of the Road Traffic and Roads Improvement Act 1960 " substitute " section 158 of the Highways Act 1980 (or its predecessor section 18 of the Road Traffic and Roads Improvement Act 1960) " ;

(*c*) in section 66(1), in the definition of " carriageway " for " subsection (1) of section two hundred and ninety-five of the Highways Act 1959 " substitute " section 329(1) of the Highways Act 1980 ".

London Government Act 1963

11. In Schedule 9 to the London Government Act 1963, in Part II, in paragraph 5, omit the words from " and " to the end.

Licensing Act 1964

12. In section 9(4) of the Licensing Act 1964—

(*a*) in paragraph (*a*), for " the Highways Act 1959 " substitute " the Highways Act 1980 " and for " section 19 of that Act " substitute " paragraph 3 of Schedule 23 to that Act " ;

(*b*) in paragraph (*b*), for " section 12 " substitute " section 17 ".

New Forest Act 1964

13. In section 3 of the New Forest Act 1964—

   (*a*) in subsection (2), subsection (3) and subsection (4), for " the Highways Act 1959 " substitute " the Highways Act 1980 " ;

   (*b*) in subsection (6), for " section 144 of the Highways Act 1959 " substitute " section 165 of the Highways Act 1980 ".

1965 c. 24.

Severn Bridge Tolls Act 1965

14. In the Severn Bridge Tolls Act 1965—

   (*a*) in section 1(4), for " the Highways Act 1959 ", in the second place where it occurs, substitute " the Highways Act 1980 " ;

   (*b*) in section 2(4), for " the Highways Act 1959 " substitute " the Highways Act 1980 " ;

   (*c*) in section 15(3), for " the Highways Act 1959 " substitute " the Highways Act 1980 " ;.

   (*d*) in section 16(1), for " section 11 or section 13 of the Highways Act 1959 " substitute " section 16 or 18 of the Highways Act 1980 " ;

   (*e*) in section 16(2), for " the Highways Act 1959 (other than sections 11 and 13 thereof) " substitute " the Highways Act 1980 (other than sections 16 and 18 thereof) ", for " section 13 of that Act " substitute " section 18 of that Act " and for " section 215 " substitute " section 239(2) and (4) " ;

   (*f*) in section 22(1), in the definition of " carriageway " and in the definition of " verge ", for " the Highways Act 1959 " substitute " the Highways Act 1980 " ;

   (*g*) in section 22(2), for " the Highways Act 1959 " substitute " the Highways Act 1980 ", omit " (whether before or after the passing of this Act) " and for " section 12(3) " substitute " section 17(3) ".

1965 c. 59.

New Towns Act 1965

15. In the New Towns Act 1965—

   (*a*) in section 25, for " the Highways Act 1959 " substitute " the Highways Act 1980 " ;

   (*b*) in Schedule 3, in paragraph 7(2)(*b*), for " section 7 or 9 of the Highways Act 1959 " substitute " section 10 or, so far as it relates to trunk roads, section 14 of the Highways Act 1980 ", and for the words from " section 1(3) " onwards substitute " section 7 or 9 of the Highways Act 1959 (to which, respectively, the said section 10 and, so far as it relates to trunk roads, the said section 14 correspond) and the enactments to which the said sections 7 and 9 corresponded (namely, section 1(3) of the Trunk Roads Act 1936, sections 1 and 4 of the Trunk Roads Act 1946 and section 14(1) of the Special Roads Act 1949) ".

Road Traffic Regulation Act 1967

16. In the Road Traffic Regulation Act 1967—

 (*a*) in section 13(1), after "the Highways Act 1959" insert "or section 16 of the Highways Act 1980", for "section 19 thereof" substitute "paragraph 3 of Schedule 23 to that Act", and for "that section" substitute "that paragraph";

 (*b*) in section 13(2)(*a*), for "the said section 19" substitute "the said paragraph 3";

 (*c*) in section 14(1), for "section 7 of the Highways Act 1959" substitute "section 10 of the Highways Act 1980", and for "the said section 7" substitute "the said section 10";

 (*d*) in section 44(3)(*d*), for "the Highways Act 1959" substitute "the Highways Act 1980";

 (*e*) in section 50, in the definition of "road", for "section 11 of the Highways Act 1959" substitute "section 16 of the Highways Act 1980";

 (*f*) in section 72(6)(*a*) for the words from "classified" to "or as" substitute "by virtue of section 12 of the Highways Act 1980 (whether as falling within subsection (1) or as being so classified under subsection (3)) a principal road, or";

 (*g*) in section 84B(8) for paragraph (*a*) substitute—

 "(*a*) by virtue of section 12 of the Highways Act 1980 (whether as falling within subsection (1) or as being so classified under subsection (3)); or";

 (*h*) in section 104(1), in the definition of "special road", after "Highways Act 1959" insert "or section 16 of the Highways Act 1980", for "section 19 of" substitute "paragraph 3 of Schedule 23 to" and for "section 11 thereof" substitute "section 16 thereof";

 (*i*) in section 108(3) for "the Highways Act 1959" substitute "the Highways Act 1980";

 (*j*) in Schedule 5, in paragraph 24, for "section 249 of the Highways Act 1959" substitute "section 283 of the Highways Act 1980".

Countryside Act 1968

17. In the Countryside Act 1968—

 (*a*) in section 27(6), for the words from the beginning to "traffic sign)" substitute "Section 131(2) of the Highways Act 1980 (destruction or defacement of a traffic sign)";

 (*b*) in section 49(2), in the definition of "bridleway" and "footpath", for "section 295(1) of the Highways Act 1959" substitute "section 329(1) of the Highways Act 1980".

 (*c*) in Schedule 3, in Part I, in paragraph 2(*d*) of the entry relating to the Acquisition of Land (Authorisation Procedure) Act 1946, for "Schedule 7 to the Highways Act 1959, as amended below," substitute "Schedule 6 to the Highways Act 1980".

Transport Act 1968

18. In the Transport Act 1968—

(*a*) in section 119(1), for " section 229 of the Highways Act 1959 " substitute " section 266 of the Highways Act 1980 ", for " section 230 of the said Act of 1959 " substitute " section 267 of the said Act of 1980 ", for " section 58(2) of the said Act of 1959 " substitute " section 55(2) of the said Act of 1980 " and for " section 229(3) or 230(2) of the said Act of 1959 " substitute " section 266(5) or 267(2) of the said Act of 1980 " ;

(*b*) in section 121(6), for " the Highways Act 1959 " substitute " the Highways Act 1980 " and for " paragraph (iii) of the proviso to " substitute " sub-paragraph (2)(*c*) of " ;

(*c*) in section 121(7), for " the Highways Act 1959 " substitute " the Highways Act 1980 " and for " paragraph (iii) of the proviso to " substitute " sub-paragraph (2)(*c*) of " ;

(*d*) in section 159(1), in paragraph (*a*) of the definition of " highway authority ", for " the Highways Act 1959 " substitute " the Highways Act 1980 ".

Chronically Sick and Disabled Persons Act 1970

19. In section 20(2) of the Chronically Sick and Disabled Persons Act 1970, in the definition of " footway ", for " the Highways Act 1959 " substitute " the Highways Act 1980 ".

Town and Country Planning Act 1971

20. In the Town and Country Planning Act 1971—

(*a*) in section 16—

(i) for the words from " section 7 " onwards in paragraph (*a*) substitute " section 10, 14, 16, 18, 106(1), 106(3) or 108(1) of the Highways Act 1980 (trunk road orders, special road schemes, orders or schemes for bridges over or tunnels under navigable waters, orders for diversion of navigable waters, and supplementary orders relating to trunk roads, classified roads or special roads) " ;

(ii) for paragraph (*b*) substitute—

" (*b*) an order or scheme under any provision replaced by the provisions of the Highways Act 1980 mentioned in paragraph (*a*) above (namely, an order or scheme under section 7, 9, 11, 13 or 20 of the Highways Act 1959, section 3 of the Highways (Miscellaneous Provisions) Act 1961 or section 1 or 10 of the Highways Act 1971) ;" ;

(iii) omit paragraph (*c*).

(*b*) in section 20(1), for " the Highways Act 1959 " substitute " the Highways Act 1980 " ;

(*c*) in section 24(8)(*b*) for " the Highways Act 1959 " substitute " the Highways Act 1980 " and after " being an enactment " insert " (derived from the Highways Act 1959) " ;

(*d*) in section 192(1)(*d*) for the words from " the Highways Act 1959 " to " the said Act of 1971) " substitute " the Highways Act 1980 relating to trunk roads, special roads or classified roads (or under the corresponding provisions of Part II of the Highways Act 1959 or section 1 of the Highways Act 1971) being land in relation to which a power of compulsory acquisition conferred by any of the provisions of Part XII of the said Act of 1980 (including a power compulsorily to acquire any right by virtue of section 250) " ;

(*e*) in section 206(4)—

(i) in paragraph (*a*), before " under " insert " made, or having effect as if made ", and for " the Highways Act 1959 " substitute " the Highways Act 1980 " ;

(ii) in paragraph (*b*), before " under " insert " made or having effect as if made " ;

(iii) in paragraph (*c*), for the words from " under " onwards substitute " made, or having effect as if made, under section 106(3) of the said Act " ;

(iv) in paragraph (*d*), for the words from " under " onwards substitute " relating to a classified road made, or having effect as if made, under section 14 of the said Act " ;

(*f*) in section 209(2), for " the Highways Act 1959 " substitute (in paragraph (*a*) and paragraph (*c*)) " the Highways Act 1980 " ;

(*g*) in section 255(1), for the words from " section 238(1) and (3) " to " highways) " substitute " section 274 of the Highways Act 1980 (contributions by local authorities towards expenses of highway authorities) " ;

(*h*) in section 290(1), in the definitions of " bridleway ", " footpath " and " highway ", for " the Highways Act 1959 ", in each case, substitute " the Highways Act 1980 ", and in the definition of " improvement " for " the Highways Act 1959 as amended by the Highways Act 1971 " substitute " the Highways Act 1980 " ;

(*i*) in Schedule 5—

(i) in paragraph 5(1)(*a*) for " section 7 of the Highways Act 1959 " substitute " section 10 of the Highways Act 1980 (or has made an order under section 7 of the Highways Act 1959) " ;

(ii) for paragraph 5(1)(*b*) substitute—

" (*b*) makes an order relating to a trunk road under section 14 of the Highways Act 1980 (or has made an order under section 9 of the Highways Act 1959) or makes or confirms a scheme or order under section 16 or 18 of the Highways Act 1980 (or has made or confirmed a scheme or order under section 11 or 13 of the Highways Act 1959) " ;

SCH. 24   (*j*) in Schedule 7, in paragraph 2, for " the Highways Act 1959 " substitute " the Highways Act 1980 " ;

(*k*) in Schedule 22, for paragraph 2 substitute—

" 2. The following provisions of the Highways Act 1980 : —

section 73(1) to (3), (6) and (9) to (11).
section 74 except subsection (6).
sections 188, 193 and 196.
section 200(2) and (4).
section 241.
section 261(5) and, so far as it relates to (5), (6).
section 307(5) and (7).
Schedule 9." ;

(*l*) in Schedule 22, for paragraph 3 substitute—

" 3. The following further provisions of the Highways Act 1980 : —

(*a*) sections 187 and 200(1) so far as applicable for the purposes of section 188 of that Act ;

(*b*) section 247(6) so far as applicable for the purposes of section 241 of that Act ;

(*c*) in section 307—

(i) subsections (1) to (3) so far as applicable for the purposes of section 73 of that Act ;

(ii) subsections (1), (3) and (6) so far as applicable for the purposes of section 74 of that Act ;

(iii) subsections (1) and (3) so far as applicable for the purposes of sections 193 and 200(2) of that Act ;

(*d*) section 311 so far as applicable for the purposes of section 74 of that Act." ;

(*m*) in Schedule 22, for paragraph 4 substitute—

" 4. Section 279 of the Highways Act 1980 so far as the purposes in question are the purposes of the exercise—

(*a*) by a county council in relation to roads maintained by that council ; or

(*b*) by the Greater London Council in relation to any road that is for the time being a metropolitan road within the meaning of that Act,

of their powers under section 73(1) to (3), (6) and (9) to (11) or section 241 of that Act.".

Road Traffic Act 1972

1972 c. 20.

21. In the Road Traffic Act 1972, in section 36A(4) and in section 36B(8) for " the Highways Act 1959 " substitute " the Highways Act 1980 ".

22. In Schedule 16 to the Local Government Act 1972, in para- 1972 c. 70.
graph 17(*a*), after " under " insert " section 12(3) of the Highways
Act 1980 or ".

Land Compensation Act 1973   1973 c. 26.

23. In the Land Compensation Act 1973—

(*a*) in section 19(1), in the definition of " highway ", for " section 295(1) of the Highways Act 1959 " substitute " section 329(1) of the Highways Act 1980 " ;

(*b*) in section 44(2), for " paragraph 7 of Schedule 6 to the Highways Act 1971 " substitute " paragraph 6 of Schedule 19 to the Highways Act 1980 " ;

(*c*) in section 58(2)(*a*), for " paragraph 8 of Schedule 6 to the Highways Act 1971 " substitute " paragraph 7 of Schedule 19 to the Highways Act 1980 " ;

(*d*) in section 69, for subsection (1) substitute—

" (1) In section 192(1)(*d*) of the Act of 1971 (land on or adjacent to line of highway proposed to be constructed etc. as indicated in an order or scheme which has come into operation under the provisions of Part II of the Highways Act 1980 relating to trunk roads, special roads or classified roads, or under the corresponding provisions of Part II of the Highways Act 1959 or section 1 of the Highways Act 1971) the reference to an order or scheme which has come into operation as aforesaid shall include a reference to—

(*a*) an order or scheme which has been submitted for confirmation to, or prepared in draft by, the Minister of Transport or the Secretary of State under the provisions of Part II of the said Act of 1980 relating to trunk roads, special roads or classified roads and in respect of which a notice has been published under paragraph 1, 2 or 10 of Schedule 1 to that Act ;

(*b*) an order or scheme under Part II of the Highways Act 1959 or section 1 of the Highways Act 1971, being an order or scheme which corresponds to any such order or scheme as is mentioned in paragraph (*a*) above and which has been submitted for confirmation to, or been prepared in draft by, the Minister of Transport or the Secretary of State and in respect of which a notice has been published under paragraph 1, 2 or 7 of Schedule 1 to the said Act of 1959." ;

(*e*) in section 74(1) omit paragraph (*a*) and in paragraph (*b*) for " the said section 22(1) " substitute " section 246(1) of the Highways Act 1980 " ;

(*f*) in section 74(2), for " the said section 22(1) " substitute " the said section 246(1) " ;

(g) in section 76(1)(a)(i), for " section 159 of the Highways Act 1959 " substitute " section 188 of the Highways Act 1980 (or its predecessor, section 159 of the Highways Act 1959) " ;

(h) in section 76(3), for " section 214(8) of the said Act of 1959 " substitute " section 239(6) of the said Act of 1980 " ;

(i) in section 87, omit subsection (3).

Control of Pollution Act 1974

24. In the Control of Pollution Act 1974—

(a) in section 22(4), in the definitions of " highway ", " special road " and " trunk road " for " the Highways Act 1959 " substitute, in each case, " the Highways Act 1980 " ;

(b) in section 32(1)(c), for " section 103 of the Highways Act 1959 " substitute " section 100 of the Highways Act 1980 ".

Road Traffic Act 1974

25. In section 17 of the Road Traffic Act 1974—

(a) in subsection (1) for " the Highways Act 1959 " substitute " the Highways Act 1980 " ;

(b) in subsection (4) for " section 279 of the Highways Act 1959 " substitute " section 302 of the Highways Act 1980 ".

Local Land Charges Act 1975

26. In section 1(1)(a) of the Local Land Charges Act 1975 omit " the Highways Act 1959 " and for " the Highways Act 1971 " substitute " the Highways Act 1980 (or any Act repealed by that Act) ".

Local Government (Miscellaneous Provisions) Act 1976

27. In the Local Government (Miscellaneous Provisions) Act 1976—

(a) in section 13(4), for " section 47 of the Highways Act 1971 " substitute " section 250 of the Highways Act 1980 " ;

(b) in section 15(9), for " section 64(1) of the Highways Act 1971 " substitute " section 289(1) of the Highways Act 1980 " ;

(c) in section 44(1)—

(i) in the definition of " highway " for " the Highways Act 1959 " substitute " the Highways Act 1980 ",

(ii) in the definition of " statutory undertakers " for " the Highways Act 1959, the Post Office," substitute " the Highways Act 1980, the Post Office and " ; and omit the words from " and, except " to " highways) " ;

(d) in section 44(2), for " section 282 of the Highways Act 1959 " substitute " section 322 of the Highways Act 1980 " and for the words from " any provision of sections 1 to 7 " onwards substitute " section 7 of this Act as if that section were a provision of that Act ".

Development of Rural Wales Act 1976

28. In Schedule 3 to the Development of Rural Wales Act 1976—

(a) in paragraph 9(2)(b) after "purposes of" insert "section 10 or 14 of the Highways Act 1980 or of";

(b) in paragraph 40 for "the Highways Act 1959" substitute "the Highways Act 1980'.

Rent Act 1977

29. In both section 34(1)(a) and section 50(1)(a) of the Rent Act 1977, for the words from "(certain" onwards substitute "or section 205 of the Highways Act 1980 (execution of street works under private street works code), or".

Refuse Disposal (Amenity) Act 1978

30. In section 3(3) of the Refuse Disposal (Amenity) Act 1978 for "the Highways Act 1959" substitute "the Highways Act 1980".

SCHEDULE 25
REPEALS

Chapter	Short Title	Extent of Repeal
7 & 8 Eliz. 2. c. 25.	Highways Act 1959.	The whole Act.
7 & 8 Eliz. 2. c. 53.	Town and Country Planning Act 1959.	Sections 48 and 49.
8 & 9 Eliz. 2. c. 63.	Road Traffic and Roads Improvement Act 1960.	Sections 18 to 20. Section 23(1).
9 & 10 Eliz. 2. c. 24.	Private Street Works Act 1961.	The whole Act.
9 & 10 Eliz. 2. c. 63.	Highways (Miscellaneous Provisions) Act 1961.	The whole Act.
9 & 10 Eliz. 2. c. 64.	Public Health Act 1961.	Sections 43 and 44. Sections 46 to 50. In Schedule 1, in Part III, the entries relating to the Highways Act 1959.
10 & 11 Eliz. 2. c. 46.	Transport Act 1962.	In Schedule 2, in Part I, the entries relating to the Highways Act 1959.
10 & 11 Eliz. 2. c. 58.	Pipelines Act 1962.	Section 19.
1963 c. 33.	London Government Act 1963.	Section 14(1) to (4). Sections 16 to 18. In Schedule 5, in Part II, paragraphs 6 to 8. Schedule 6. In Schedule 9, in Part II, in paragraph 5, the words from " and " to the end. In Schedule 11, in Part I, paragraph 37.

Chapter	Short Title	Extent of Repeal
1965 c. 24.	Severn Bridge Tolls Act 1965.	In section 22(2) the words " (whether before or after the passing of this Act) ".
1965 c. 30.	Highways (Amendment) Act 1965.	The whole Act.
1965 c. 56.	Compulsory Purchase Act 1965.	In Schedule 6, the entry relating to the Highways Act 1959.
1965 c. 59.	New Towns Act 1965.	Section 48(3).
1966 c. 42.	Local Government Act 1966.	Part III.
1967 c. 76.	Road Traffic Regulation Act 1967.	In Schedule 6, the entry relating to section 14(2) of the London Government Act 1963.
1967 c. 80.	Criminal Justice Act 1967.	In Schedule 3, the entries relating to the Highways Act 1959.
1968 c. 13.	National Loans Act 1968.	In section 6(1), the words " section 198(2) of the Highways Act 1959 ".
1968 c. 41.	Countryside Act 1968.	Sections 28 and 29. Section 47(5). In Schedule 3, in Part I, the entries relating to the Highways Act 1959.
1968 c. 72.	Town and Country Planning Act 1968.	In Schedule 9, paragraph 9.
1968 c. 73.	Transport Act 1968.	Section 130(6)(e). In section 139(1), in paragraph (a), the words " section 215 (2)(c) of the Highways Act 1959 or ", in paragraph (b), the words " section 180, 188 or 189 of the Town and Country Planning Act 1971 or " and " 215(2)(c) or ", and in paragraph (c) the words " section 193 of the said Act of 1971 or " and " section 196 of the said Act of 1971 or, as the case may be," and " 215 (2)(c) or ". In section 139(2), in the definition of " relevant planning permission ", the words " section 15 or 16 of the Land Compensation Act 1961 or ", in the definition of " service area development " the words " the said section 215(2)(c) or ", and (in the concluding part of the subsection) the words " 1961 or " and " as respects England and Wales, as in the said Act of 1961 and,". Section 140. In Schedule 16, paragraph 7(2)(f).

Chapter	Short Title	Extent of Repeal
1969 c. 35.	Transport (London) Act 1969.	Sections 29 and 31. Section 34(1).
1969 c. 48.	Post Office Act 1969.	In Schedule 4, paragraphs 65 and 69 and paragraph 93(1) (xv).
1971 c. 23.	Courts Act 1971.	In Schedule 8, in Part II, paragraph 36. In Schedule 9, in Parts I and II, the entries relating to the Highways Act 1959.
1971 c. 41.	Highways Act 1971.	The whole Act.
1971 c. 75.	Civil Aviation Act 1971.	In Schedule 5, paragraph 5(*m*) and (*ee*).
1971 c. 78.	Town and Country Planning Act 1971.	In section 16, paragraph (*c*). In Schedule 23, in Part II, the entries relating to the Highways Act 1959, the Highways Act 1971 and section 139(1) of the Transport Act 1968.
1972 c. 60.	Gas Act 1972.	In Schedule 4, in paragraph 1(6) the words " section 15 of the Highways Act 1959 and ".
1972 c. 70.	Local Government Act 1972.	Section 187(1)(2)(3)(*b*) and (4) to (8). Section 188. Schedule 20. In Schedule 21, Part I and, in Part II, paragraphs 99 and 100.
1973 c. 26.	Land Compensation Act 1973.	Section 20(10). Sections 22 to 25. Section 74(1)(*a*). Section 78(5). Section 87(3).
1973 c. 37.	Water Act 1973.	In Schedule 8, paragraphs 70 and 71.
1974 c. 7.	Local Government Act 1974.	In section 6(8) the words " the Highways Act 1959 and ". Section 40. In Schedule 1, in Part II, in paragraph 6, paragraph (*a*) and the words " paragraph (*a*),". In Schedule 6, entry number 12. In Schedule 7, paragraph 2.
1975 c. 76.	Local Land Charges Act 1975.	In Schedule 1, the entries relating to the Highways Act 1959 and the Highways Act 1971.

Chapter	Short title	Extent of Repeal
1976 c. 57.	Local Government (Miscellaneous Provisions) Act 1976.	Sections 1 to 6. In section 44(1) in the definition of " statutory undertakers " the words from " and except " to " highways) ". In Schedule 2, the entries relating to the Highways Act 1959 and the Highways (Miscellaneous Provisions) Act 1961.
1976 c. 70.	Land Drainage Act 1976.	In Schedule 7, paragraphs 2 and 7.
1977 c. 45.	Criminal Law Act 1977.	In Schedule 6, the entry relating to the Highways Act 1959.
1980 c. 43.	Magistrates' Courts Act 1980.	In Schedule 7, paragraph 29.
1980 c. 65.	Local Government, Planning and Land Act 1980.	In Schedule 7, paragraphs 1(2), 2(1), (2)(*b*), (3) and (4), 3(1), (3) and 5.

Printed in the United Kingdom for the Stationery Office Limited
Dd 5065222 8/97 1731 56219 ON 341616

Printed in the UK by The Stationery Office Limited
under the authority and superintendence of Peter Macdonald,
Controller of Her Majesty's Stationery Office and Queen's Printer of
Acts of Parliament.

1st Impression December 1980
8th Impression August 1997